ALSO BY JOSEPH LELYVELD

Omaha Blues: A Memory Loop

Move Your Shadow: South Africa, Black and White

GREAT SOUL

Not yet a mahatma, 1906

Twenty-five years later, 1931

GREAT SOUL

*Mahatma Gandhi
and His Struggle with India*

JOSEPH LELYVELD

ALFRED A. KNOPF   NEW YORK   2011

THIS IS A BORZOI BOOK
PUBLISHED BY ALFRED A. KNOPF

Library of Congress Cataloging-in-Publication Data

Lelyveld, Joseph.
Great soul : Mahatma Gandhi and his struggle with India / Joseph Lelyveld.—1st ed.
p. cm.
"This is a Borzoi book"—T.p. verso.
Includes bibliographical references and index.
ISBN 978-0-307-26958-4
1. Gandhi, Mahatma, 1869–1948. 2. Statesmen—India—Biography. 3. Nationalists—India—Biography. 4. India—Politics and government—1919–1947. 5. South Africa—Politics and government—1836–1909. I. Title.
DS481.G3L337 2011
954.03'5092—dc22
[B]   2010034252

Jacket illustration:
Haynes Archive/Popperfoto/Getty Images
Jacket design by Darren Haggar

Manufactured in the United States of America
First Edition

FOR JANNY

I do not know whether you have seen the world as it really is. For myself I can say I perceive the world in its grim reality every moment. (1918)

I deny being a visionary. I do not accept the claim of saintliness. I am of the earth, earthy . . . I am prone to as many weaknesses as you are. But I have seen the world. I have lived in the world with my eyes open. (1920)

I am not a quick despairer. (1922)

For men like me, you have to measure them not by the rare moments of greatness in their lives, but by the amount of dust they collect on their feet in the course of life's journey. (1947)

—MOHANDAS KARAMCHAND GANDHI, 1869–1948

CONTENTS

AUTHOR'S NOTE

THE MAHATMA had been gone for half a century, but there were still Gandhis at the Phoenix Settlement, outside Durban on South Africa's Indian Ocean coast, when I visited there the first time in 1965. A little boy, identified as a great-grandson, toddled across the room. He was living with his grandmother, widow of Manilal Gandhi, second of Gandhi's four sons, who'd stayed on in South Africa to edit *Indian Opinion*, the weekly paper his father had started, and thereby keep alive the settlement and its values. The patriarch had chosen to be father to a whole community, so he turned the farm into a kind of commune where he could gather an extended family of followers, European as well as Indian, nephews and cousins, and, finally, with no special status, his own wife and sons.

I was not a pilgrim, just a reporter looking for a story. By the time of my visit, Gandhi had been dead for nearly eighteen years, Manilal for nine, and *Indian Opinion* for five. There wasn't a lot to see besides the simple buildings they'd inhabited. On one of them, the brass nameplate still read "M. K. Gandhi." The great work of racial separation—what the white authorities called apartheid—had already begun. Small Indian plot holders, who'd once lived and farmed among Zulus, now crowded onto the settlement's one hundred acres. I wrote about the visit in a mournful vein, noting that Indians and other South Africans no longer believed that Gandhian passive resistance could accomplish anything in their land. "Passive resistance doesn't stand a chance against this government," a trustee of the settlement said. "It's too brutal and persevering."

If my next assignment as a foreign correspondent hadn't been India, where I lived for a few years in the late 1960s, that afternoon might not have stuck in my mind as a reminder of a subject to which I'd need to return. For me the South African Gandhi would always be more than an antecedent, an extended footnote to the fully fledged Mahatma. Having looked at the green hills of Africa from his front porch, I thought, in the simplifying way reporters think, that he was the story.

The maelstroms of India could obscure but never dislodge that intuition. The more I delved into Indian politics, the more I found myself pondering the seeming disconnect between Gandhi's teachings on social issues and the priorities of the next generation of leaders who reverentially invoked his name. Often, in those days, these were people who'd actually encountered the Mahatma, who'd come into the national struggle fired by his example. So more than a patriotic ritual was involved when they claimed to be his heirs. Yet it was hard to say what remained of him beyond his nimbus.

An occasion for asking such questions occurred with the approach of the one hundredth anniversary of his birth in 1969. Setting out to report on the remnants of Gandhi's movement, I followed Vinoba Bhave, his last full-time apostle, as he trudged through the most impoverished parts of Bihar, then as now among the poorest of Indian states, trying to persuade landlords to cede some of their holdings to the landless. Vinoba collected deeds to thousands of acres of barren, untilled, and untillable land. The Mahatma's aging protégé seemed stoic, if not tragic, as he saw his doomed mission through to its largely inconsequential end.

"He became his admirers." That's Auden on Yeats. Three decades ago V. S. Naipaul used the line to characterize the decline of Gandhi's influence in his last years, when he was most revered. The combination of piety and disregard—hardly unique to India—lasted as a cultural reflex, surviving the explosion of India's first nuclear bomb.

Over time and at a distance, my experiences of South Africa and India ran together in my mind. Gandhi was an obvious link. I found myself thinking again about the Phoenix Settlement, to which I returned twice, the second time after it had been burned down in factional black-on-black violence accompanying the death throes of white supremacy, only to be restored with the blessing of a democratically chosen government eager to canonize Gandhi as a founding father of the new South Africa. I then found myself thinking about Gandhi himself, wondering how South Africa helped to form the man he became, how the man he became in South Africa struggled with the reality of India, how his initiation as a political leader on one side of the Indian Ocean foreshadowed his larger disappointments and occasional sense of failure on the other: whether, that is, there were clues to the end of his journey as leader in its beginning.

I'm hardly the first to raise such questions and won't be the last. But it seemed to me there was still a story to be uncovered and told, themes that could be traced from the beginning of Gandhi's political life in one country to its flourishing in another, with all the ambiguity of his legacy in each place. The temptation to retrace my own steps while retracing Gandhi's finally proved irresistible.

This isn't intended to be a retelling of the standard Gandhi narrative. I merely touch on or leave out crucial periods and episodes—Gandhi's childhood in the feudal Kathiawad region of Gujarat, his coming-of-age in nearly three formative years in London, his later interactions with British officials on three continents, the political ins and outs of the movement, the details and context of his seventeen fasts—in order to hew in this essay to specific narrative lines I've chosen. These have to do with Gandhi the social reformer, with his evolving sense of his constituency and social vision, a narrative that's usually subordinated to that of the struggle for independence. The Gandhi I've pursued is the one who claimed once to "have been trying all my life to identify myself with the most illiterate and downtrodden." At the risk of slighting his role as a political tactician, a field marshal of nonviolent resistance, or as a religious thinker and exemplar, I've tried to follow him at ground level as he struggled to impose his vision on an often recalcitrant India—especially recalcitrant, he found, when he tried not just its patience but its reverence for him with his harangues on the "crime" and "curse" of untouchability, or the need for the majority Hindus to accommodate the large Muslim minority.

Neither theme, it turns out, can be explained without reference to his long apprenticeship in South Africa, where he eventually defined himself as leader of a mass movement. My aim is to amplify rather than replace the standard narrative of the life Gandhi led on two subcontinents by dwelling on incidents and themes that have often been underplayed. It isn't to diminish a compelling figure now generally exalted as a spiritual pilgrim and secular saint. It's to take a fresh look, in an attempt to understand his life as he lived it. I'm more fascinated by the man himself, the long arc of his strenuous life, than by anything that can be distilled as doctrine.

Gandhi offered many overlapping and open-ended definitions of his

highest goal, which he sometimes defined as *poorna swaraj*.* He wasn't
the one who'd introduced *swaraj* into the political lexicon, a term usually
translated as "self-rule" while Gandhi still lived in South Africa. Later it
would be expanded to mean "independence." As used by Gandhi,
poorna swaraj put the goal on yet a higher plane. At his most utopian, it
was a goal not just for India but for each individual Indian; only then
could it be *poorna*, or complete. It meant a sloughing not only of British
rule but of British ways, a rejection of modern industrial society in favor
of a bottom-up renewal of India, starting in its villages, 700,000 of them,
according to the count he used for the country as it existed before its
partition in 1947. Gandhi was thus a revivalist as much as a political figure, in the sense that he wanted to instill values in India's most recalcitrant, impoverished precincts—values of social justice, self-reliance, and
public hygiene—that nurtured together would flower as a material and
spiritual renewal on a national scale.

Swaraj, said this man of many causes, was like a banyan tree, having
"innumerable trunks each of which is as important to the tree as the
original trunk." He meant it was bigger than the struggle for mere independence.

"He increasingly ceased to be a serious political leader," a prominent
British scholar has commented. Gandhi, who formally resigned from
the Indian National Congress as early as 1934 and never rejoined it,
might have agreed. If the leader succeeded in driving the colonists out
but his revival failed, he'd have to count himself a failure. Swaraj had to
be for all Indians, but in his most challenging formulations he said it
would be especially for "the starving toiling millions."

It meant, he said once, speaking in this vein, "the emancipation of
India's skeletons." Or again: "Poorna swaraj denotes a state of things in
which the dumb begin to speak and the lame begin to walk."

The Gandhi who held up this particular standard of social justice as an
ultimate goal wasn't always consistent or easy to follow in his discourse,
let alone his campaigns. But this is the Gandhi whose words still have a
power to resonate in India. And this vision, always with him a work in
progress, first shows up in South Africa.

Today most South Africans and Indians profess reverence for the
Mahatma, as do many others across the world. But like the restored
Phoenix Settlement, our various Gandhis tend to be replicas fenced off

---

*Indian and other foreign terms are italicized on their first appearance and defined
in a glossary starting on page 351.

from our surroundings and his times. The original, with all his quirkiness, elusiveness, and genius for reinvention, his occasional cruelty and deep humanity, will always be worth pursuing. He never worshipped idols himself and generally seemed indifferent to the clouds of reverence that swirled around him. Always he demanded a response in the form of life changes. Even now, he doesn't let Indians—or, for that matter, the rest of us—off easy.

PART I

SOUTH AFRICA

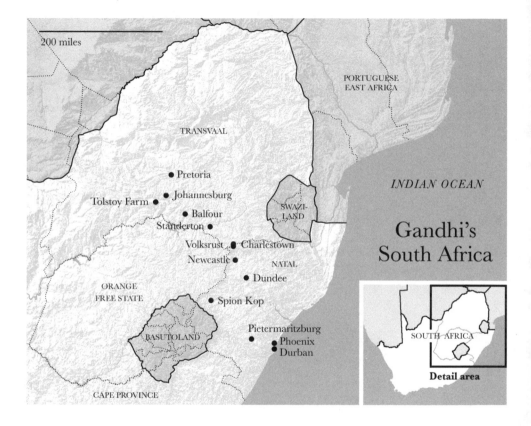

200 miles

PORTUGUESE
EAST AFRICA

TRANSVAAL

● Pretoria

● Johannesburg

Tolstoy Farm ●
● Balfour

Standerton ●

INDIAN OCEAN

SWAZI-
LAND

Gandhi's
South Africa

Volksrust ● Charlestown

Newcastle ●

NATAL

● Dundee

ORANGE
FREE STATE

● Spion Kop

Pietermaritzburg

BASUTOLAND

● Phoenix
Durban

SOUTH AFRICA

Detail area

CAPE PROVINCE

1

PROLOGUE:
AN UNWELCOME VISITOR

IT WAS A BRIEF only a briefless lawyer might have accepted. Mohandas Gandhi landed in South Africa as an untested, unknown twenty-three-year-old law clerk brought over from Bombay, where his effort to launch a legal career had been stalled for more than a year. His stay in the country was expected to be temporary, a year at most. Instead, a full twenty-one years elapsed before he made his final departure on July 14, 1914. By then, he was forty-four, a seasoned politician and negotiator, recently leader of a mass movement, author of a doctrine for such struggles, a pithy and prolific political pamphleteer, and more—a self-taught evangelist on matters spiritual, nutritional, even medical. That's to say, he was well on his way to becoming the Gandhi India would come to revere and, sporadically, follow.

None of that was part of the original job description. His only mission at the outset was to assist in a bitter civil suit between two Muslim trading firms with roots of their own in Porbandar, the small port on the Arabian Sea, in the northwest corner of today's India, where he was born. All the young lawyer brought to the case were his fluency in English and Gujarati, his first language, and his recent legal training at the Inner Temple in London; his lowly task was to function as an interpreter, culturally as well as linguistically, between the merchant who engaged him and the merchant's English attorney.

Up to this point there was no evidence of his ever having had a spontaneous political thought. During three years in London—and the nearly two years of trying to find his feet in India that followed—his causes were dietary and religious: vegetarianism and the mystical cult

known as Theosophy, which claimed to have absorbed the wisdom of
the East, in particular of Hinduism, about which Gandhi, looking for
footholds on a foreign shore, had more curiosity then than scriptural
knowledge himself. Never a mystic, he found fellowship in London
with other seekers on what amounted, metaphorically speaking, to a
small weedy fringe, which he took to be common ground between two
cultures.

South Africa, by contrast, challenged him from the start to explain
what he thought he was doing there in his brown skin. Or, more precisely, in his brown skin, natty frock coat, striped pants, and black turban, flattened in the style of his native Kathiawad region, which he wore
into a magistrate's court in Durban on May 23, 1893, the day after his
arrival. The magistrate took the headgear as a sign of disrespect and
ordered the unknown lawyer to remove it; instead, Gandhi stalked out
of the courtroom. The small confrontation was written up the next day
in *The Natal Advertiser* in a sardonic little article titled "An Unwelcome
Visitor." Gandhi immediately shot off a letter to the newspaper, the first
of dozens he'd write to deflect or deflate white sentiments. "Just as it is a
mark of respect amongst Europeans to take off their hats," he wrote, an
Indian shows respect by keeping his head covered. "In England, on
attending drawing-room meetings and evening parties, Indians always
keep the head-dress, and the English ladies and gentlemen seem to
appreciate the regard which we show thereby."

The letter saw print on what was only the fourth day the young
nonentity had been in the land. It's noteworthy because it comes nearly
two weeks *before* a jarring experience of racial insult, on a train heading
inland from the coast, that's generally held to have fired his spirit of
resistance. The letter to the *Advertiser* would seem to demonstrate that
Gandhi's spirit didn't need igniting; its undertone of teasing, of playful
jousting, would turn out to be characteristic. Yet it's the train incident
that's certified as transformative not only in Richard Attenborough's film
Gandhi or Philip Glass's opera *Satyagraha* but in Gandhi's own *Autobiography*, written three decades after the event.

If it wasn't character forming, it must have been character arousing
(or deepening) to be ejected, as Gandhi was at Pietermaritzburg, from a
first-class compartment because a white passenger objected to having to
share the space with a "coolie." What's regularly underplayed in the
countless renditions of the train incident is the fact that the agitated
young lawyer eventually got his way. The next morning he fired off
telegrams to the general manager of the railway and his sponsor in Dur-

ban. He raised enough of a commotion that he finally was allowed to reboard the same train from the same station the next night under the protection of the stationmaster, occupying a first-class berth.

The rail line didn't run all the way to Johannesburg in those days, so he had to complete the final leg of the trip by stagecoach. Again he fell into a clash that was overtly racial. Gandhi, who'd refrained from making a fuss about being seated outside on the coach box next to the driver, was dragged down at a rest stop by a white crewman who wanted the seat for himself. When he resisted, the crewman called him a "sammy"—a derisive South African epithet for Indians (derived from "swami," it's said)—and started thumping him. In Gandhi's retelling, his protests had the surprising effect of rousing sympathetic white passengers to intervene on his behalf. He manages to keep his seat and, when the coach stops for the night, shoots off a letter to the local supervisor of the stagecoach company, who then makes sure that the young foreigner is seated inside for the final stage of the journey.

All the newcomer's almost instantaneous retorts in letters and telegrams tell us that young Mohan, as he would have been called, brought his instinct for resistance (what the psychoanalyst Erik Erikson called his "eternal negative") with him to South Africa. Its alien environment would prove a perfect place for that instinct to flourish. In what was still largely a frontier society, the will to white domination had yet to produce a settled racial order. (It never would, in fact, though the attempt would be systematically made.) Gandhi would not have to seek conflict; it would find him.

In these bumpy first days in a new land, Mohan Gandhi comes across on first encounters as a wiry, engaging figure, soft-spoken but not at all reticent. His English is on its way to becoming impeccable, and he's as well dressed in a British manner as most whites he meets. He can stand his ground, but he's not assertive or restless in the sense of seeming unsettled. Later he would portray himself as having been shy at this stage in his life, but in fact he consistently demonstrates a poise that may have been a matter of heritage: he's the son and grandson of *diwans*, occupants of the top civil position in the courts of the tiny princely states that proliferated in the part of Gujarat where he grew up. A diwan was a cross between a chief minister and an estate manager. Gandhi's father evidently failed to dip into his rajah's coffers for his own benefit and remained a man of modest means. But he had status, dignity, and assurance to bequeath. These attributes in combination with his brown skin and his credentials as a London-trained barrister are enough to mark the son as unusual in that time and place in South Africa: for some, at least, a sympathetic, arresting figure.

He's susceptible to moral appeals and ameliorative doctrines but not particularly curious about his new surroundings or the tangle of moral issues that are as much part of the new land as its hardy flora. He has left a wife and two sons behind in India and has yet to import the string of nephews and cousins who'd later follow him to South Africa, so he's very much on his own. Because he failed to establish himself as a lawyer in Bombay, his temporary commission represents his entire livelihood and that of his family, so he can reasonably be assumed to be on the lookout for ways to jump-start a career. He wants his life to matter, but he's not sure where or how; in that sense, like most twenty-three-year-olds, he's vulnerable and unfinished. He's looking for something—a career, a sanctified way of life, preferably both—on which to fasten. You can't easily tell from the autobiography he'd dash off in weekly installments more than three decades later, but at this stage he's more the unsung hero of an East-West bildungsroman than the Mahatma in waiting he portrays who experiences few doubts or deviations after his first weeks in London before he turned twenty. The Gandhi who landed in South Africa doesn't seem a likely recipient of the spiritual honorific— "Mahatma" means "Great Soul"—that the poet Rabindranath Tagore affixed to his name years later, four years after his return to India. His transformation or self-invention—a process that's as much inward as outward—takes years, but once it's under way, he's never again static or predictable.

Toward the end of his life, when he could no longer command the movement he'd led in India, Gandhi found words in a Tagore song to express his abiding sense of his own singularity: "I believe in walking alone. I came alone in this world, I have walked alone in the valley of the shadow of death, and I shall quit alone, when the time comes." He wouldn't have put it quite so starkly when he landed in South Africa, but he felt himself to be walking alone in a way he could hardly have imagined had he remained in the cocoon of his Indian extended family.

He'd have other racial encounters of varying degrees of nastiness as he settled into a rough-and-ready South Africa where whites wrote the rules: in Johannesburg, the manager of the Grand National Hotel would look him over and only then discover there were no free rooms; in Pretoria, where there was actually a bylaw reserving sidewalks for the exclusive use of whites, a policeman on guard in front of President Paul Kruger's house would threaten to cuff the strolling newcomer into the road for transgressing on the pavement; a white barber there would refuse to cut his hair; in Durban the law society would object to his being registered as an advocate, a status hitherto reserved for whites; he would be denied admission to a worship service at an Anglican church.

It would take a full century for such practices to grind to a halt, for white minority rule finally to reach its inevitable and well-deserved end in South Africa. Now new monuments to Gandhi are scattered about the land, reflecting the heroic role attributed to him in the country's rewritten history. I saw such monuments not only at the Phoenix Settlement but in Durban, Pietermaritzburg, Ladysmith, and Dundee. Nearly always it was the elderly figure Winston Churchill scorned as "a seditious Middle Temple lawyer now posing as a fakir . . . striding half-naked" who was portrayed, not the tailored South African lawyer. (Probably that was because most of these statues and busts had been shipped from India, supplied by its government.) In Johannesburg, however, in a large urban space renamed Gandhi Square—formerly it bore the name of an Afrikaner bureaucrat—the South African Gandhi is shown in mufti, striding in the direction of the site of the now-demolished law court where he appeared both as attorney and as prisoner, his bronze lawyer's robe fluttering over a bronze Western suit. Gandhi Square is just around the corner from his old law office at the corner of Rissik and Anderson streets, where he received visitors under a tinctured image of Jesus Christ. The vegetarian restaurant, steps away, where he first encountered his closest white friends is long gone; hard by the place where it stood, perhaps exactly on the spot, a McDonald's now does a fairly brisk nonvegetarian trade. But it's not entirely far-fetched for the new South Africa to claim Gandhi as its own, even if he failed to foresee it for most of his time in the country. In finding his feet there, he formed the persona he would inhabit in India in the final thirty-three years of his life, when he set an example that colonized peoples across the globe, including South Africans, would find inspiring.

One of the new Gandhi memorials sits on a platform of the handsome old railway station in Pietermaritzburg—Maritzburg for short—close to the spot where the newcomer detrained, under a corrugated iron roof trimmed with what appears to be the original Victorian filigree. The plaque says his ejection from the train "changed the course" of Gandhi's life. "He took up the fight against racial oppression," it proclaims. "His active non-violence started from that day."

That's an inspirational paraphrase of Gandhi's *Autobiography*, but it's squishy as history. Gandhi claims in the *Autobiography* to have called a meeting on arrival in Pretoria to rally local Indians and inspire them to face up to the racial situation. If he did, little came of it. In that first year, he had yet to assume a mantle of leadership; he was not even seen as a resident, just a junior lawyer imported from Bombay on temporary assignment. His undemanding legal work left him with time on his hands, which he devoted more to religion than to politics; in this new environment, he became an even more serious and eclectic spiritual seeker than he'd been in London. This was a matter of chance as well as inclination. The attorney he was supposed to assist turned out to be an evangelical Christian with a more intense interest in Gandhi's soul than in the commercial case on which they were supposed to be working. Gandhi spent much of his time in a prolonged engagement with white evangelicals who found in him a likely convert. He even attended daily prayer meetings, which regularly included prayers that the light would shine for him.

He told his new friends, all whites, that he was spiritually uncommitted but nearly always denied thereafter that he'd ever seriously contemplated conversion. However, according to the scholar who has made the closest study of Gandhi's involvement with missionaries, it took him two years to resolve the question in his own mind. On one occasion Gandhi acknowledged as much to Millie Polak, the wife of a British lawyer who was part of his inner circle for his last ten years in South Africa. "I did once seriously think of embracing Christianity," she quoted him as having said. "I was tremendously attracted to Christianity, but eventually I came to the conclusion that there was nothing really in your scriptures that we had not got in ours, and that to be a good Hindu also meant I would be a good Christian."

Late in 1894 we find this free-floating, ecumenical novice flirting, or so it sometimes seemed, with several religious sects at once, writing to *The Natal Mercury* on behalf of a movement called the Esoteric Christian Union, a synthesizing school of belief, as he explained it, that sought to reconcile all religions by showing that each represents the same eternal truths. (It's a theme Gandhi would repeat at prayer meetings in the last years and months of his life, more than a half century later, where the spirit was so all-embracing that "O God, Our Help in Ages Past" had its place among chanted Hindu and Muslim prayers.) In an advertisement for a selection of tracts meant to accompany a letter to the editor

he wrote in 1894, he identified himself proudly as an "Agent for the Esoteric Christian Union and the London Vegetarian Society."

Judging from his autobiographical writings, it seems possible, even
likely, that Gandhi spent more time in Pretoria with his evangelical well-
wishers than with his Muslim patrons. In any case, these were his two
circles, and they didn't overlap, nor did they represent any kind of
microcosm of the country South Africa was fast becoming. By necessity
as much as choice, he would remain an outsider. The abrasiveness of
some of his early confrontations with whites made it obvious that
searching for footholds in this new land could bring him into conflict.
To stake a claim for ordinary citizenship was to cross a boundary into
politics. Within two months after settling in Pretoria, Gandhi was busy
writing letters on political themes to the English-language papers,
putting himself forward but, as yet, representing only himself.

On September 5, scarcely three months after he arrived in the country, the *Transvaal Advertiser* carried the first of these, a longish screed
that already has implicit in it political arguments Gandhi would later
advance as a spokesman for the community. Here he was responding to
the use of the word "coolie" as an epithet commonly attached to all
brown-skinned immigrants from British India. He doesn't mind it being
applied to contract laborers, impoverished Indians transported en masse
under contracts of indenture, or servitude, usually to cut sugarcane.
Starting in 1860, it was the way most Indians had come to the country,
part of a human traffic, a step up from slavery, that also carried Indians
by the tens of thousands to Mauritius, Fiji, and the West Indies. The
word "coolie," after all, appears to have been derived from a peasant
group in India's western regions, the Kolis, with a reputation for lawlessness and enough group cohesion to win recognition as a subcaste. But,
Gandhi argues, former indentured laborers who don't make the return
trip home to India at the end of their contracts but stay on to stand on
their own feet, as well as Indian traders who had initially paid their own
passage, shouldn't be denigrated that way. "It is clear that Indian is the
most proper word for both the classes," he writes. "No Indian is a coolie
by birth."

This is not a proposition that would have come easily to him had he
remained in India. The alien environment, it's fair to speculate, had
stirred in him the impulse to stand outside the community and explain.
Implicit in this—the first nationalist declaration of his life—is a class
distinction. He speaks for Indians here but not for coolies. Between the

lines he seems to be saying that the best that can be said for them is that
their status isn't necessarily permanent. Nowhere in the letter does he
comment on the harsh terms of their servitude.

He concedes that coolies may sometimes be disorderly, may even
steal. He knows but doesn't make a point of saying that most of those he
has now agreed to call coolies are of lower-caste backgrounds. If anything, caste is a subject he avoids. He doesn't say that coolies are fundamentally different from other Indians. They can become good citizens
when their contracts end. For now, however, their poverty and despera-
tion do not conspicuously engage his sympathies. Temporarily, at least,
he doesn't identify with them.

The South Africa confronted by young Mohan was counted as four different states or territories by its white inhabitants and the Colonial
Office in London. (There was also Zululand, which was under British
supervision and had yet to be fully merged into Natal, the self-
governing territory that surrounded it. In the view of whites, settlers and
colonial officials alike, the subcontinent's surviving African kingdoms
existed only on sufferance, remote from the main paths of commerce,
with nothing approaching sovereign status.) The states that were
deemed to count were those with white governments. The two coastal
territories were British crown colonies: the Cape, at the very tip of
Africa, where whites first settled in the seventeenth century and where
the Atlantic and Indian oceans meet; and Natal, on the continent's ver-
dant east coast. Inland were two landlocked, quasi-independent Boer
(meaning Afrikaner) republics, the Orange Free State and what was
called the South African Republic, a culturally introverted frontier settlement in the territory known as the Transvaal. That republic, created
as a Zion for an indigenous white population of *trekboers*, farmers of
mainly Dutch and Huguenot descent who had fled British rule in its two
colonies, had been all but overwhelmed by a recent influx of mostly
British aliens (called Uitlanders in the simplified Dutch dialect that was
just beginning to be recognized as a language in its own right, henceforth known as Afrikaans). For it was in the Transvaal, beyond formal
British control but temptingly within its reach, that the world's richest
gold-bearing reef had been discovered in 1886, only seven years before
the fledgling Indian barrister inauspiciously disembarked at Durban.

· · ·

The South Africa from which Gandhi sailed all those years later had become something more than a geographic designation for a random collection of colonies, kingdoms, and republics. It was now a single sovereign state, a colony no longer, calling itself the Union of South Africa. And it was firmly under indigenous white control, with the result that a lawyerly spokesman for a nonwhite immigrant community, which was what Gandhi had become, could no longer expect to get anywhere by addressing petitions or leading missions to Whitehall. To this great political transformation he'd been little more than a bystander. But it had the effect of sweeping his best argument for equal Indian rights off the table. Originally, Gandhi had based his case on his own idealistic reading of an 1858 proclamation by Queen Victoria that formally extended British sovereignty over India, promising its inhabitants the same protections and privileges as all her subjects. He called it "the Magna Charta of the Indians," quoting a passage in which her distant majesty had proclaimed her wish that her Indian subjects, "of whatever race or creed, be freely and impartially admitted to offices in our service." It was Gandhi's argument that those rights should attach themselves to "British Indians" who traveled from their homeland to outposts of the empire such as the British-ruled portions of South Africa. That wasn't quite what the queen's advisers had in mind, but it was an awkward argument to have to work around. In the new South Africa, which came into existence in 1910, it counted for nothing. To achieve less and less, Gandhi found in the course of two decades, his tactics had to become more and more confrontational.

This transformation and practically everything South African that coincided with his earliest political activities were ultimately traceable to gold and all that the new mines brought in their train—high finance, industrial strife, and the twentieth century's first major experience of a type of warfare that could be classed as an anticolonial or a counterinsurgency struggle, even though the combatants on both sides were mainly whites. This was the Anglo-Boer War, which seared its brutal course across South Africa's mostly treeless grasslands and hillsides from 1899 to 1902. It took an army of 450,000 (including thousands, British and Indian, brought across the Indian Ocean under British command from the Raj) to finally subdue the Boer commandos, militia units that never numbered as many as 75,000 at any given time. About 47,000 soldiers perished on the two sides; in addition, nearly 40,000—mainly Afrikaner children and women but also their black farmhands and servants—died of dysentery and infectious diseases like measles in segregated stockades where they'd been massed as the army forcibly cleared the countryside. Coining a functional, antiseptic term for these open-air reservoirs of misery, the British called them concentration camps.

Gandhi briefly played a bit part. The man who would emerge within the next two decades as the modern era's best-known champion of non-violence saw action himself in the early stages of the war as a uniformed noncommissioned officer, leading for about six weeks a corps of some eleven hundred noncombatant Indian stretcher bearers. Then thirty and already recognized as a spokesman for Natal's small but growing Indian community—amounting at that time to scarcely 100,000 but soon to outnumber the colony's whites—Gandhi went to war to score a parochial point with the colony's white leaders: that Indians, whatever the color of their skins, saw themselves and should be seen as full citizens of the British Empire, ready to shoulder its obligations and deserving of whatever rights it had to bestow.

Once the British got the upper hand in Natal and the war moved inland, the Indian stretcher bearers disbanded, ending the war for Gandhi. His point had been made, but in no time at all it was brushed aside by the whites he'd hoped to impress. Natal's racial elite persisted in enacting new laws to restrict property rights for Indians and banish from the voters' rolls the few hundred who'd managed to have their names inscribed there. The Transvaal could be said to have shown the way. In 1885, claiming sovereignty as the South African Republic, it had passed a law putting basic citizenship rights off limits to Indians; that was eight years before Gandhi landed in its capital, Pretoria.

At first he allowed himself to imagine that the hard-wrung British victory, uniting the two colonies and Boer republics under imperial rule, could only benefit "British Indians." What happened was the opposite of what he imagined. Within eight years, a national government had been formed, led by defeated Boer generals who won at the negotiating table most of their important war aims, accepting something less than full sovereignty in foreign affairs in exchange for a virtual guarantee that whites alone would chart the new Union of South Africa's political and racial future. Some "natives" and other nonwhites protested. Gandhi, still looking to strike a tolerable bargain for Indians, was silent except for a few terse asides in the pages of *Indian Opinion*, the weekly paper that had been his megaphone since 1903, his instrument for sounding themes, binding the community together. His few comments in its pages on the new structure of government showed he wasn't blind to what was actually happening. Generally speaking, however, it was as if none of this larger South African context and all it portended—the blatant attempt to postpone indefinitely any thought, any possibility, of an eventual settlement with the country's black majority—had the slightest relevance to his cause, had been allowed to impinge on his consciousness. In the many thousands of words he wrote and uttered in South Africa, only a few hundred reflect awareness of an impending racial conflict or concern about its outcome.

Yet if the forty-four-year-old Gandhi who later sailed from Cape Town to Southampton on the eve of a world war seemed deliberately oblivious of the transformation of the country in which he'd passed nearly all his adult life up to that point, there was probably no single individual in it who'd changed more than he had. The novice lawyer had established a flourishing legal practice, first in Durban and then, after a quickly aborted attempt to move back to India, in Johannesburg. In the process, he'd moved his family from India to South Africa, then back to India, then back to South Africa, then finally to the Phoenix Settlement outside Durban, which he'd established on an ethic of rural self-sufficiency adapted from his reading of Tolstoy and Ruskin. Their teachings, as interpreted by him, were then translated into a litany of vows for an austere, vegetarian, sexually abstemious, prayerful, back-to-the-earth, self-sustaining way of life. Later, all but abandoning his wife and sons at Phoenix, Gandhi stayed on in Johannesburg for a period that stretched to more than six years.

By the time of his departure from South Africa, he'd spent only nine of twenty-one years in the same household with his wife and family. By his own revised standards, he could no longer be expected to put his family ahead of the wider community. Instead of concentrating on Phoenix, he started a second communal settlement called Tolstoy Farm in 1910, on the bare side of a rocky *koppie*, or hill, southwest of Johannesburg, all the while carrying on his unending campaign to fend off the barrage of anti-Indian laws and regulations that South Africa at every level of government—local, provincial, and national—continued to fire at his people. What inspired these restrictions was an unreasoning but not altogether ungrounded fear of a huge transfer of population, a siphoning of masses, across the Indian Ocean from one subcontinent to the other, under the sponsorship of an empire that could be deemed to have an interest in easing population pressures that made India hard to govern.

Sage, spokesman, pamphleteer, petitioner, agitator, seer, pilgrim, dietitian, nurse, and scold—Gandhi tirelessly inhabited each of these roles until they blended into a recognizable whole. His continuous self-invention ran in parallel with his unofficial position as leader of the community. At first he spoke only for the mainly Muslim business interests that had hired him, the tiny upper crust of a struggling immigrant community; at least one of his patrons, a land and property owner named Dawad Mahomed, employed indentured laborers, presumably on the same exploitative terms as their white masters. Gandhi himself belonged to a Hindu trading subcaste, the Modh Banias, a prosperous group but only one of numerous Bania, or merchant, subcastes that have been counted in India. The Modh Banias still discouraged and sometimes forbade—as he himself had discovered when he first traveled to London—journeys across the *kala pani*, or black water, to foreign shores where members of the caste could fall into the snares of dietary and sexual temptation. That's why there were still few fellow Banias on this side of the Indian Ocean. It also helps explain the early predominance of Muslims among the Gujarati merchants who ventured to South Africa. So it was that the first political speeches of Gandhi's life were given in South African mosques, a fact of huge and obvious relevance to his unwavering refusal, later in India, to countenance communal differences. One of the high points of Gandhi's South African epic occurred outside the Hamidia Mosque in Fordsburg, a neighborhood at the edge of downtown Johannesburg where Indians settled. There, on August 16, 1908, more than three thousand Indians gathered to hear him speak and burn their permits to reside in the Transvaal in a big cauldron, a nonviolent protest against the latest racial law restricting further Indian immigration. (Half a century later, in the apartheid era, black nationalists launched a similar form of resistance, setting fire to their passes—internal passports they were required to carry. Historians have searched the documentary record for evidence that the Gandhian example inspired them. So far, the record has been silent.) Today in the new South Africa, in a Fordsburg once proclaimed "white" under apartheid, the refurbished mosque gleams in a setting of overall dinginess and decay. Outside, an iron sculpture in the form of a cauldron sitting on a tripod commemorates Gandhi's protest.

Such symbols resonate not only with later South African struggles but also with Gandhi's campaigns in India. When Johannesburg Muslims wanted to send humble greetings to a new Ottoman emperor in what was still Constantinople, they relied on their Hindu mouthpiece to compose the letter and convey it through the proper diplomatic channels in London. Later, in the aftermath of a world war in which the Ottoman Empire had allied itself with the losing side, Gandhi rallied Indian Muslims to the national cause by proclaiming the preservation of the emperor's role as caliph and protector of the Muslim holy places to be one of the most pressing aims of the Indian national struggle. On one level, this was a sensitive reading of the emotional tides sweeping through the Muslim community; on another, a breathtaking piece of political opportunism. Either way, it would never have occurred to a Hindu politician who lacked Gandhi's experience of trying to bind together a small and diverse overseas community of Indians that was inclined to pull apart.

If the Johannesburg Gandhi could speak comfortably for Muslims, he could speak for all Indians, he concluded. "We are not and ought not to be Tamils or Calcutta men, Mahomedans or Hindus, Brahmans or Banias but simply and solely British Indians," he lectured his people, seeking from the start to overcome their evident divisions. In India, he observed in 1906, the colonial masters exploited Hindu-Muslim, regional, and language differences. "Here in South Africa," he said, "these groups are small in number. We are all confronted with the same disabilities. We are moreover free from certain restrictions from which our people suffer in India. We can therefore easily essay an experiment in achieving unity." Several years later, he would claim prematurely that the holy grail of unity had been won: "The Hindu-Mahomedan problem has been solved in South Africa. We realize that the one cannot do without the other."

In other words, what Indians in South Africa had accomplished could now be presented as a successful demonstration project, as a model for India. For an upstart situated obscurely on another continent, far beyond the farthest border of British India, it was an audacious, even grandiose claim. At first, it made no discernible impression outside the actual halls in which it was voiced; later, it would be one of his major themes when he succeeded in making himself dominant in the national movement in India. For a brief time then, Muslim support would make the difference between victory for Gandhi and a position in the second tier of leaders; it would guarantee his ascendance in India.

But that was probably still beyond Gandhi's own imagining. Events would soon show that the ideal of unity wasn't so easily clinched in South Africa, either. Hindu and Muslim revivalists arrived from India with messages that tended to polarize the two communities and under-cut Gandhi's insistence on unity. By sheer force of personality, he managed to smooth over rifts in his final months in the country—a temporary fix that allowed him to claim with pardonable exaggeration, as he would for years to come, that his South African unity demonstration was an achievement for India to copy. It was also, of course, his own offshore tryout, his great rehearsal.

Gandhi's really big idea—initially it was termed "passive resistance"—came in 1906 with a call for defiance of a new piece of anti-Indian legislation in the Transvaal called the Asiatic Law Amendment Ordinance. Gandhi lambasted it as the "Black Act." It required Indians—only Indians—to register in the Transvaal, where their numbers were still relatively minuscule, under ten thousand: to apply, in other words, for rights of residence they thought they already possessed as "British Indians," British law having been imposed on the territory as a consequence of the recently concluded war. Under this discriminatory act, registration would involve fingerprinting—all ten fingers—of every man, woman, and child over the age of eight. Thereafter certificates had to be available for checking by the police, who were authorized to go into any residence for that purpose. "I saw nothing in it except hatred of Indians," Gandhi later wrote. Calling on the community to resist, he said the law was "designed to strike at the very root of our existence in South Africa." And, of course, that was exactly the case.

The resistance he had in mind was refusing to register under the law. He said as much at a packed meeting in the Empire Theater in Johannesburg on September 11, 1906 (an earlier 9/11, with a significance quite the contrary of the one we know). The all-male crowd probably numbered fewer than the figure of three thousand that has been sanctified by careless repetition; the Empire—which burned down that same night, hours after the Indians had dispersed—couldn't have held that many. Gandhi spoke in Gujarati and Hindi; translators repeated what he said in Tamil and Telugu for the sake of the South Indian contingent. The next speaker was a Muslim trader named Hadji Habib, who hailed, like Gandhi, from Porbandar. He said he would take an oath before God never to submit to the new law.

The lawyer in Gandhi was "at once startled and put on my guard," he would say, by this nonnegotiable position, which on its face didn't seem all that different from the one he had just taken himself. The spiritual seeker that he also was couldn't think of such a vow as mere politics. The whole subject of vows, their weight and worth, was at the front of his consciousness. During the previous month, Gandhi himself had taken a vow of *brahmacharya*, meaning that this father of four sons pledged to be

Burning registration certificates at the mosque

celibate for the rest of his days (as he had presumably been, after all, during all the years of separation from his wife in London and South Africa). He'd discussed his vow with some of his associates at Phoenix but not yet publicly. He'd simply announced it to his wife, Kasturba, assuming it called for no sacrifice on her part. In his mind, he was dedicating himself to a life of meditation and poverty like an Indian *sannyasi*, or holy man, who has renounced all worldly ties, only Gandhi gives the concept an unorthodox twist; he will remain in the world to be of service to his people. "To give one's life in service to one's fellow human beings," he'd later say, "is as good a thing as living in a cave." Now, in his view, Hadji Habib had suddenly gone beyond him, putting the vow to defy the registration act on the same plane. So it wasn't a matter of tactics or even conscience; it had become a sacred duty.

Speaking for a second time that evening in the Empire, Gandhi warned that they might go to jail, face hard labor, "be flogged by rude warders," lose all their property, get deported. "Opulent today," he said, "we might be reduced to abject poverty tomorrow." He himself would keep the pledge, he promised, "even if everyone else flinched leaving me alone to face the music." For each of them, he said, it would be a "pledge even unto death, no matter what others do." Here Gandhi hits a note of fervor that to the ear of a secular Westerner sounds religious, almost born-again. Unsympathetic British officials would later portray him as a fanatic in dispatches to Whitehall; one of his leading academic biographers comes close to endorsing that view. But Gandhi was not speaking that night to an audience of secular Westerners. It's also unlikely that Hadji Habib or the overwhelming majority of his audience had any inkling of his distinctly Hindu vow of brahmacharya. The idea of civil disobedience was original with neither man. It had lately been tried by suffragettes in London. The idea that it might call for chastity was Gandhi's alone.

In his own mind, his two vows were now bound together, almost inextricable. Gandhi held to a traditional Hindu idea that a man is weakened by any loss of semen—a view aspiring boxers and their trainers are sometimes said to share—and so for him his vows, from the outset, were all about discipline, about strength. "A man who deliberately and intelligently takes a pledge and then breaks it," he said that night in the Empire Theater, "forfeits his manhood." Such a man, he went on, "becomes a man of straw." Years later, upon learning that his son Harilal's wife was pregnant again, Gandhi chided him for giving in to "this weakening passion." If he learned to overcome it, the father promised, "you will have new strength." Later still, when he'd become the established leader of the Indian national movement, he'd write that sex leads to a "criminal waste of the vital fluid" and "an equally criminal waste of precious energy" that ought to be transmuted into "the highest form of energy for the benefit of society."

After a while, he sought an Indian term to replace "passive resistance." He didn't like the adjective "passive," which seemed to connote weakness. *Indian Opinion* held a contest. A nephew suggested *sadagraha*, meaning "firmness in the cause." Gandhi, by then accustomed to having the last word, changed it to *satyagraha*, normally translated as "truth force" or sometimes, more literally, as "firmness in truth," or "clinging to truth." To stand for truth was to stand for justice, and to do so nonviolently, offering a form of resistance that would eventually move even the oppressor to see that his position depended on the opposite, on untruth and force. Thereafter the movement had a name, a tactic, and a doctrine. These too he would bring home.

Gandhi kept changing, experiencing a new epiphany every two years or so—Phoenix (1904), brahmacharya (1906), satyagraha (1908), Tolstoy Farm (1910)—each representing a milestone on the path he was blazing for himself. South Africa had become a laboratory for what he'd later call, in the subtitle of his *Autobiography*, "My Experiments with Truth," an opaque phrase that suggests to me that the subject being tested was himself, the pursuer of "truth." The family man gives up family; the lawyer gives up the practice of law. Gandhi would eventually take on garb similar to that of a wandering Hindu holy man, a *sadhu* off on his own lonely pilgrimage, but he would always be the opposite of a dropout. In his own mind, his simple handwoven loincloth was a signal not of sanctity but of his feeling for the plight of India's poor. "I did not suggest," he would later write, "that I could identify myself with the poor by merely wearing one garment. But I do say that even that little thing is something." Of course he was aware, politician that he was, that it could be read in more than one way. His idea of a life of service also meant staying in the world and having a cause, usually several at a time.

The householder takes to the land and settles on a farm. "Our ambition," one of his colleagues explains, "is to live the life of the poorest people." He was a political man, but he was surprisingly free in Africa, as he would not have been in India, to go his own way. Family and communal ties, less binding in the new environment, had to be reinvented anyway; he had room to "experiment." And, of course, there were no offices to seek. Whites had them all.

It's not easy to pinpoint the moment in South Africa when the ambitious, transplanted barrister becomes recognizable as the Gandhi who would be called Mahatma. But it had happened by 1908, fifteen years after his arrival in the land. Still called *bhai*, or brother, he sat that year for a series of interviews by his first biographer, a white Baptist preacher in Johannesburg named Joseph Doke who, not incidentally, still harbored the ambition of converting his subject. It doesn't demean Doke's well-written tract to call it hagiography, for that's distinctly its genre. Its main character is defined by saintly qualities. "Our Indian friend lives on a higher plane than most men do," Doke writes. Other Indians "wonder at him, grow angry at his strange unselfishness." It also doesn't demean Doke to note that Gandhi himself took over the marketing of the book. He bought up the entire first edition in London in order, he said with false modesty, to save Doke from "a fiasco" but actually to have volumes to distribute to members of Parliament and ship to India; later he arranged for publication of an Indian edition by his friend G. A. Natesan, a Madras editor; and every week for years to come he ran house ads in *Indian Opinion* inviting mail orders. In Gandhi's hands, Doke's book becomes a campaign biography for a campaign as yet unlaunched.

He's still wearing a necktie and a Western suit in the group portrait for which a garlanded Gandhi and Kasturba posed on the docks in Cape Town on their last day in the country, but if you look closely, there's what may be a tiny foreshadowing in his shaved head and the hand-crafted sandals on his feet of a sartorial makeover he'd already experimented with on several occasions and that he'd display on his arrival in Bombay six months later and then adapt over the following six years until he had reduced his garb to the utter, literally bare simplicity of the homespun loincloth and shawl. In the Bombay arrival pictures, suit and tie have been banished for good; he wears a turban, the loose-fitting tunic called a *kurta* on top of what appears to be a lungi, or wraparound skirt. The lungi would soon be replaced by a *dhoti*, a wide enveloping loincloth, which in later years, in its most abbreviated form, would sometimes be all he wore. He wanted, he would teasingly say in rejoinder to Churchill's gibe, to be "as naked as possible."

Viewed as if in a digitally manipulated tracking shot over time, Gandhi the South African lawyer who goes through these changes seamlessly morphs into the future Indian Mahatma. In this long view, an extraordinary, heroic story unfolds: Within the brief span of five and a half years after landing in his vast home country, though still largely unknown to the broad population that hasn't yet had a taste of modern politics, he takes over the Indian National Congress—up to then a usually sedate debating club embodying the aspirations of a small Anglicized elite, mostly lawyers—and turns it into the century's first anticolonial mass movement, raising a clamor in favor of a relatively unfamiliar idea, that of an independent India. Against all the obstacles of illiteracy and an absolute dearth of modern communications reaching down to the 700,000 villages where most Indians lived in the period before partition, he wins broad acceptance, at least for a time, as the authentic exemplar of national renewal and unity.

That outcome, of course, was not foreordained. If the earlier frames are frozen and the South African Gandhi is viewed up close, as he might easily have been seen a year or two before the end of his African sojourn, it's not a mahatma who comes into focus; it's a former lawyer, political spokesman, and utopian seeker. In this view, Gandhi shows up as a singularly impressive character. But in the political realm, he's nothing more than a local leader with a weakening hold on a small immigrant community, facing an array of adherents, critics, and rivals. In such a perspective, if we had to guess, it would seem likeliest that his trajectory would end in a smallish settlement or ashram, a transplanted Phoenix, lost somewhere in the vastness of India; there he'd be surrounded by family and followers engaged with him on a quest as much religious as political. In other words, instead of ending up on pedestals in India as Father of the Nation, the leading figure in a mistily viewed national epic and subject for legions of biographers, scholars, and thinkers who have made him perhaps the most written-about person of the last hundred years, the South African Gandhi could have become another Indian guru whose scattered devotees might have remembered him for a generation or two at best. In South Africa itself he might even have been remembered as a failure rather than held up for reverence, as he is there today, in the fading glow of the advent of democratic, supposedly nonracial government, as one of the founding fathers of the new South Africa.

In fact, the South African Gandhi was explicitly written off as a failure a little more than a year before he left the country by the irascible editor of a weekly newspaper in Durban that competed—sometimes respectfully, sometimes spitefully—with Gandhi's *Indian Opinion* for Indian readers. *African Chronicle* was aimed mainly at readers of Tamil origin, among whom Gandhi found most of his staunchest supporters. "Mr. Gandhi's ephemeral fame and popularity in India and elsewhere rest on no glorious achievement for his countrymen, but on a series of failures, which has resulted in causing endless misery, loss of wealth, and deprivation of existing rights," fumed P. S. Aiyar in a series of scattershot attacks. His leadership over twenty years had "resulted in no tangible good to anyone." He and his associates had made themselves "an object of ridicule and hatred among all sections of the community in South Africa."

There was some basis for Aiyar's tirade. Gandhi's support had been dwindling for some time; the nonviolent army of Indians willing to step forward yet again and volunteer for the "self-suffering" that came with service as willing *satyagrahis*—offering themselves as fodder, that is, for his campaigns of civil disobedience against unjust racial laws, by courting arrest, going to jail, thereby losing jobs, seeing businesses fail—had visibly shrunk to the point that it hardly exceeded his own family and a band of loyal Tamil supporters in Johannesburg, members of what was called the Tamil Benefit Society. The campaigns had pushed the government into compromises, but these fell many leagues short of the aspirations of the more emboldened Indians for rights of full citizenship; and the authorities had repeatedly stalled and reneged on the meager promises they'd made.

For all that, 1913 was to prove a turning point. Gandhi's experience over two decades in Africa is replete with turning points in his inner life, but this is the one in his public life, in the political sphere, that best explains his subsequent readiness and ability to reach for national leadership in India. He might have faded into semi-oblivion if he'd returned to India in 1912. His final ten months in South Africa, though, transformed his sense of what was possible for him and those he led.

It was only then that he allowed himself to engage directly with the "coolies" he'd described twenty years earlier in his first letter to a newspaper in Pretoria. These were the most oppressed Indians working on sugar plantations, in the coal mines, and on the railroad under renewable five-year contracts of indenture that gave them rights and privileges only slightly less flimsy than those of chattel. A colonial officer with the title "Protector of Immigrants" had a statutory duty to make sure that these "semi-slaves," as Gandhi termed them, were not overworked or underfed in violation of the letter of their labor contracts. But the records show that the putative protector more commonly served as an enforcer on behalf of plantation owners and other contract holders. Under the indenture system, it was a crime for a laborer to leave his place of employment without authorization: not only could he lose his job; he could be clapped in jail and even flogged. Yet, for a spell of only several weeks in November 1913, in a collective spasm of resentment and hope, what had been unthinkable happened: thousands of these indentured Indians walked off the mines, plantations, and railroad to follow Gandhi in the greatest and last of his campaigns of nonviolent resistance in South Africa.

For their leader it was a sudden and radical change in tactics, a calculated risk: in part a result of events accelerating out of his control, transforming and renewing his own sense of his constituency, his sense of who it was he actually represented, for whom it was he actually spoke. If Gandhi had gone home at the start of that year as he'd originally hoped, it's questionable whether he would ever have been able to conceive of, let alone effect, such a mass mobilization. Instead, he returned to India in 1915 with an experience no other Indian leader had yet known.

He hadn't seen it coming. In June 1913 he outlined his expectations for this final struggle in a letter to Gopal Krishna Gokhale, the statesmanlike and moderate Indian leader whom he'd taken as a mentor years before and to whom he was now hoping to apprentice himself on his return. Gokhale had just visited South Africa, where he'd been hailed by whites as well as Indians as a tribune of the empire. "So far as I can judge at present 100 men and 30 women will start the struggle," Gandhi wrote. "As time goes on, we may have more." (Reminiscing, many years later, he would remark that the number with whom he actually started was only 16.) As late as October 1913, *Indian Opinion* flatly declared: "The indentured Indians will not be invited to join the general struggle."

Then, just two days after the date on that issue, Gandhi showed up in the coal-mining town of Newcastle in northern Natal to address indentured laborers who'd already started to leave the mines. He had shaved his head, and for the first time at a political event in South Africa the former lawyer dressed in Indian garb, showing his allegiance to the laborers by donning their attire.

"It was a bold, dangerous and momentous step," *Indian Opinion* commented a week later. "Such concerted action had not been tried before with men who are more or less ignorant. But with passive resistance nothing is too dangerous or too bold so long as it involves suffering by themselves and so long as in their methods they do not use physical force." This sounds like a passage Gandhi himself may have dictated in the full flush of the movement. The condescending reference to the ignorance of the strikers is a consistent Gandhian note. Later, back in India, he would regularly speak of the "dumb millions" in summoning the national movement to work for the poorest of the poor, or, on an occasion when he contemplated with some irony the scope of his influence, of "the numberless men and women who have childlike faith in my wisdom." On this South African test run for satyagraha as a form of mass mobilization, the hint of concern that the dumb and childlike could lapse into violence foreshadows the Gandhi who would write, after his first call for a national movement of noncooperation with British rule in India ended in a spasm of arson and killing, "I know that the only thing that the Government dreads is the huge majority I seem to command. They little know that I dread it more than they."

Of course, in South Africa, he didn't command a majority. Here the huge majority was black. In his fixation on winning for Indians what he deemed to be their rights as citizens of the British Empire, he never posed the question about how or when that majority could be mobilized. Considering what a leap of faith it was for him to call out even Indian indentured laborers in Natal in 1913, it's clear that mass mobilization would remain for him a dangerous political weapon, tempting but risky. He would try it on a national scale in India on only a roughly decennial basis—in 1921, 1930, and 1942—as if he and the country required years to recuperate in each case. Yet this time in South Africa—because he desperately needed reinforcements on the front line of nonviolent resistance at a moment when his support among his people had dwindled, because his most devoted followers whom he'd trained for disciplined resistance wanted him to seize the opportunity—the Mahatma-to-be found the political steel, the will, to grasp the weapon. He was fighting for his people but also for his own political survival. The prospect of returning to India as the retiring head of an exhausted and defeated movement had little appeal; it may even have been a goad to action. Not to have seized the moment would have been to acknowledge the possibility that he might fade from the scene. "The poor have no fears," he later wrote wonderingly, looking back on the wildfire of strikes that spread across Natal after he and his comrades lit the fuse. It was an important discovery.

What had he known of the indentured laborers? Maureen Swan, author of a pioneering study that filled in and thereby demythologized the received narrative of Gandhi's time in South Africa, notes significantly that he'd never previously tried to organize the indentured, that he'd waited until 1913 before addressing the grievances of "the Natal underclasses." The received narrative, of course, was Gandhi's own, based on the reminiscences he later set down in India; there they were serialized on a weekly basis, in the newspaper published from his ashram, as parables or lessons in satyagraha, until eventually they could be collected as autobiography. The scholar Swan speaks and works in the language of class. Her social analysis doesn't touch on the categories by which Indians who came to South Africa were accustomed to viewing themselves. I mean those of region and caste or—to be a little more specific without plunging into a maze of overlapping but not synonymous social categories—*jati* and subcaste, the groupings by which poor Indians would commonly identify themselves. That her "underclasses" were heavily lower caste was not relevant to her argument. But it may have some relevance to the way Gandhi saw them, for he'd come, by his own peculiar route, early in his time in South Africa, to a position of moral outrage on the injustice of caste discrimination by Indians, against so-called untouchables especially.

Gandhi's ideas of social equality kept evolving during his time in South Africa and later, after he confronted the turbulent Indian scene. He'd struggled for the legal equality of Indians and whites. This had led him, inevitably, to the issue of equality between Indian and Indian. He crossed the caste boundary before he crossed the class boundary, but all these categories would eventually blur and come to be overlaid on one another in his mind so that years later, in 1927, it would seem natural to him to refer back to his South Africa struggle when campaigning in India against untouchability: "I believe implicitly that all men are born equal . . . I have fought this doctrine of superiority in South Africa inch by inch, and it is because of that inherent belief that I delight in calling myself a scavenger, a spinner, a weaver, a farmer and a laborer." Here he echoes his half-jesting suggestion to his biographer Doke, twenty years earlier in Johannesburg, that the first study of his life could be titled "A Scavenger." On another occasion, he'd say that "uplift of Harijans"—a term meaning "children of God" he tried to popularize for untouchables— first struck him as an idea and a mission in South Africa. "The idea did occur to me in South Africa and in the South African setting," he told his faithful secretary Mahadev Desai. If he was referring to his political life—to actions he took in the world and not simply to values he'd come to hold inwardly—there's little in all Gandhi's South African experience besides the 1913 campaign that could stand as a basis for the assertion.

Talk of scavengers and other untouchables is not the vocabulary of class struggle used by a revolutionary like Mao Zedong. But it's radical in its own terms—its own Indian terms—and makes the link between the struggles he later waged in India against untouchability and the strikes of indentured laborers he found himself leading, despite obvious misgivings, in 1913 in the coal-mining district of northern Natal.

Long before he thought of deploying the indentured in his struggle, Gandhi was alive to their oppression. When he made it a cause, he didn't make explicit the connection, the overlap, between the indentured and the untouchables. Still, he had to be aware of it. It was a subject generally to be avoided, but all Indians in South Africa knew it was lurking in their new world. They had mostly come to South Africa as indentured laborers, or were descended from indentured laborers. And most indentured laborers were low caste; the proportion of those deemed to be untouchable seems certain to have been significantly higher in South Africa than in India, where it was estimated, at the time, to be about 12 percent nationally, as high as 20 percent in some regions. One of the appeals for the indenture system made by recruiters who canvassed for volunteers in South India and on the Gangetic plain had been that it could lighten the load carried by oppressed laborers held to be outcastes. Crossing an ocean, even on a contract of indenture, made it easier to change one's name, religion, or occupation: in effect, to pass. Even if these remained unchanged, caste could be expected to recede as a touchstone and social imperative in the new country. Yet it was there. Because Gandhi himself was liberated on caste issues, he could finally conceive of leading indentured laborers, just as it came easily for him to conceive of Hindus and Muslims, Tamils and Gujaratis, as one people in the setting of an immigrant community where they were all thrown together as they seldom were in India.

At this point in South Africa, the political Gandhi and the religious Gandhi merge, not for the first or last time. At the end of his life, just before India's independence and in its aftermath, a heartsick Mahatma would verge on seeing himself as a failure. He saw Hindus and Muslims caught up in a paroxysm of mutual slaughter, what we later learned to call "ethnic cleansing." Untouchables were still untouchable in the villages, where they mostly dwelled; the commitment to liberate them as part of the achievement of freedom, which he'd tried to instill among Hindus, seemed to have become a matter for lip service, whatever new laws proclaimed. No individual, no matter how inspiring or saintly, could have accomplished the wholesale renewal of India in only two generations, the time that had passed since Gandhi had started to conceive it as his mission while still in South Africa. It was there, Gandhi later wrote in his summing-up, *Satyagraha in South Africa*, that he'd "realized my vocation in life."

Those who depend on what he called "truth force" were "strangers to disappointment and defeat," he claimed in that book's last line. Yet here he was, at the end of his days, expressing chronic disappointment and, sometimes, a sense of defeat. He'd had more to do with India's independence than any other individual—in declaring the goal and making it seem attainable, in convincing the nation that it was a nation—but he was not among those who celebrated that day. Instead, he fasted. The celebrations were, he said, "a sorry affair."

In our own time, the word "tragedy" inevitably gets tagged to any disastrous event. A highway pileup or a killer tornado that claims lives, a shooting binge in a post office or an act of terrorism—all will promptly be labeled "tragic" on the evening news as if tragedy were simply a synonym for calamity or baleful fate. Naipaul once wrote that Indians lack a tragic sense; he didn't specifically mention Gandhi in that connection, but probably, if asked, he would have. Yet in the deeper meaning of the word—connecting it to character and inescapable mortality rather than chance—there's a tragic element in Gandhi's life, not because he was assassinated, nor because his noblest qualities inflamed the hatred in his killer's heart. The tragic element is that he was ultimately forced, like Lear, to see the limits of his ambition to remake his world. In that sense, the play was already being written when he boarded the steamship in Cape Town in 1914.

"The saint has left our shores, I sincerely hope forever," wrote his leading South African antagonist and occasional negotiating foil, Jan Christian Smuts, then the defense minister. An "unwelcome visitor" at the beginning of his long sojourn, a "saint" at the end but obviously still unwelcome, it wasn't easy to say what Gandhi had accomplished beyond his remarkable self-creation and the example he'd set. A top British official worried that he might have shown South Africa's blacks "that they have an instrument in their hands—this is, combination and passive resistance—of which they had not previously thought." It would be years before that hypothesis would be seriously tested.

But for Gandhi himself, South Africa had been more than an overture. Between his arrival and his departure, he'd acquired some ideas to which he was committed, others that he'd only begun to try out. Satyagraha as a means of active struggle to achieve a national goal belonged to the first category; satyagraha involving the poorest of the poor fit the second. These were what he carried in his otherwise meager baggage when, finally, he came out of Africa.

Another conceivable variation on this theme—struggle not only involving the poorest but specifically for their benefit—never quite materialized in South Africa. It would prove even harder to conceive of in the circumstances of the India to which he returned.

To understand how Gandhi's time in South Africa set him on his brilliantly original, ultimately problematic course, we need to delve deeper into some of the episodes that made up this long tryout, to see how his experiences there shaped his convictions, how those convictions shaped a sense of mission and of himself that was close to fully formed by the time he headed home for good.

2

NO-TOUCHISM

". . . the least Indian of Indian leaders."

V. S. NAIPAUL'S WORDS were intentionally surprising, even startling. What a way to describe the iconic figure in a loincloth
whom the Cambridge-educated Nehru called "the quintessence
of the conscious and subconscious will" of village India. How could
Gandhi be at once "the least Indian" and "the quintessence" of the
country's deepest impulses? I was newly arrived in India toward the end
of 1966 when I came upon Naipaul's line. For me it was the most memorable in his scorching, sometimes hilarious first book on India, *An Area
of Darkness*, published in 1964. It spoke to Gandhi's time in South
Africa, to the question of how it had shaped him.

I'd landed as a correspondent in New Delhi, coming from South
Africa via London myself, just as Gandhi had in 1915, which may suggest why I was susceptible to the flattering argument that outsiders saw
the country more clearly than its most sophisticated inhabitants. In the
first generation after independence, it was insolent if not heretical for
any Indian, especially one born in Trinidad and resident in London, to
argue that India's father figure, its beloved Bapu, as he was called in his
ashrams and beyond, had come into his own overseas—in Africa, of all
places—and had been forever changed by the traumatic but unavoidable
experience of having to look on his motherland through what had
become foreign eyes. In other words, the way Naipaul himself saw India.
The writer was blunt. He didn't waste words; that was an essential part
of his genius. Basically, he was saying that Gandhi was appalled by the
country he'd later get credit for liberating. It was the social oppression
of India and its filth—the sight of people blithely squatting in public
places to move their bowels and then, just as blithely, leaving their turds

behind for human scavengers to remove—that accounted for the Mahatma-to-be's reforming zeal. "He looked at India as no Indian was able to," the young Naipaul wrote; "his vision was direct, and this directness was, and is, revolutionary."

Naipaul found supporting evidence in the *Autobiography*, a book he would continue to mine every decade or so for new insights into "the many-sided Gandhi." In this earliest excavation, he concentrated on a visit by Gandhi to Calcutta on a return home in 1901 that he'd originally intended to make permanent. Gandhi doesn't know it yet, but he still has a dozen years ahead of him in South Africa. Within a year, he'll allow himself to be summoned back from India. This is the pre-satyagraha Gandhi, still only thirty-two, the writer of lawyerly petitions to remote officials, not yet a leader of mass protests. Gandhi is in Calcutta—now called Kolkata—to attend his very first annual meeting of the Indian National Congress, a movement he'd one day transform and dominate but that, at this stage, hardly knows his name.

Naipaul doesn't waste words on context, but a little helps. Calcutta, at the start of the last century, is "the packed and pestilential town" Kipling described, but it's also in those days still the seat of the viceroy, capital of the Raj, "second city" of the empire, and capital as well of an undivided Bengal (a Muslim-majority area by a thin margin, taking in the entire Ganges delta including all the present Bangladesh and the Indian state of West Bengal). Not just that, it has been an important seedbed of Hindu reform movements and is now on the verge of a period of ferment that might be called prerevolutionary. In these respects, it's India's St. Petersburg. A political newcomer, Gandhi has been granted a scant five minutes to speak about the situation Indians confront in far-off South Africa. In nobody's eyes but his own is the arrival of this lawyer, lately from Durban, a big deal. He's as central to the proceedings as a delegate from Guam or Samoa at an American political convention.

But look what happens. Naipaul brilliantly swoops in on three paragraphs in the *Autobiography*. They need no magnification. Twenty-five years later, when Gandhi wrote about this first encounter with the Congress, he still sounded astonished, really aghast. "I was face to face with untouchability," he said, describing the precautions high-caste Hindus from South India felt they had to take in Calcutta in order to dine without being polluted by the sight of others. "A special kitchen had to be made for them . . . walled in by wicker-work . . . a kitchen, dining room, washroom, all in one—a close safe with no outlet . . . If, I said to myself, there was such untouchability between the delegates of the Congress, one could well imagine the extent to which it existed amongst their constituents."

And then there was the problem of shit, which was not unconnected, since sweepers, scavengers, Bhangis, call them what you will, were deemed to be the lowest, most untouchable of all outcastes. Here's Gandhi again:

> There were only a few latrines, and the recollection of their stink still oppresses me. I pointed it out to the volunteers. They said pointblank, "That is not our work, it is the scavenger's work." I asked for a broom. The man stared at me in wonder. I procured one and cleaned the latrine . . . Some of the delegates did not scruple to use the verandahs outside their rooms for calls of nature at night . . . No one was ready to undertake the cleaning, and I found no one to share the honour with me of doing it.

If the Congress had stayed in session, Gandhi concludes tartly, conditions would have been "quite favourable for the outbreak of an epidemic." A quarter of a century lies between the Calcutta meeting and his rendering of this memory. Conditions have improved but not enough. "Even today," he says, in his insistent, hectoring way, "thoughtless delegates are not wanting who disfigure the Congress camp . . . wherever they want." (Forty years later, when I attended my first session of the All India Congress Committee, the party—in power then for a generation—had discovered the Indian equivalent of the Porta-Potty.)

Naipaul considers Gandhi's fierce feelings about sanitation and caste an obvious by-product of his time in South Africa. He doesn't go further into their genesis. Gandhi tells another story, but it's incomplete; it doesn't begin to explain his readiness to do the scavenger's job in the Calcutta latrine, his eventual readiness to make this one of his signature causes. He says he has been opposed to untouchability since the age of twelve, when his mother chided him for brushing shoulders with a young Bhangi named Uka and insisted he undergo "purification." Even as a boy, he says in his various renditions of this incident, he could find no logic in his mother's demand, though, he adds, he "naturally obeyed."

The memory isn't unique to Gandhi or his era. Indians living today, when the practice of untouchability has been forbidden by law for more than sixty years and now is more or less disowned by most educated Indians, can recall similar lessons in distancing from their childhoods. This is true among Indians even in South Africa, where the existence of untouchability was seldom acknowledged and never became an issue of open debate. On a recent visit to Durban, I heard a story like Gandhi's from an elderly lawyer friend who recalled his mother refusing to serve tea to one of his schoolboy pals whom she identified as a Pariah. (Yes, that outcaste South Indian group gave us the English word.) But Gandhi's experience as a boy doesn't explain his behavior in Calcutta. At the age of twelve, he didn't think of helping Uka empty the Gandhi family's latrine, and his readiness to shrug off untouchability didn't instantly mature into a passion to see it abolished. The path he followed to the Calcutta meeting has twists and turns and leads ultimately through South Africa. But it starts in India, where untouchability was coming into disrepute among enlightened Hindus well before Gandhi made himself heard on the subject. Coming into disrepute, that is, among a smallish sector of an Anglicized elite that had been educated to one degree or another in English. At the same time, according to persuasive recent scholarship, the actual practice of untouchability was becoming more rigid and oppressive in the villages where the elite seldom ventured. This happened as upwardly mobile subcastes sought to secure their own status and privileges by drawing a firm line between themselves and dependent groups they conveniently branded as "unclean" but systematically exploited. Just as racial segregation became more rigid and formally codified in the Jim Crow era in the American South and the apartheid years in South Africa, the barriers of untouchability were, in general, not lowered but raised even higher in colonial India, according to this line of interpretation.

What outsiders and many Indians think they know and understand about the caste system and the phenomenon of untouchability owes much to colonial taxonomy: the unstinting efforts of British classifiers—district officials called commissioners, census takers, and scholars—to catalog its multiplicity of subgroupings and pin them down the way Linnaeus defined the order of plants. Outlining the system, they tended to freeze it, imagining they had finally uncovered some ancient structure undergirding and explaining the constant flux, jostling, and blur of contending Indian social groups and sects. But the fixed system they thought they had delineated could not be pinned down; shot through with all the inconsistencies, ambiguities, and clashing aspirations of the actual India, not to mention its undeniable oppressiveness, it kept shifting and moving. Not all very poor Indians were regarded as untouchable, but nearly all those who came to be classed as untouchable were wretchedly poor. Shudras, peasants in the lowest caste order, could be looked down upon, exploited, and shunned on social occasions without being considered polluting by their betters. Some untouchable groups practiced untouchability toward other untouchable groups. If one group could be considered more polluting than another, untouchability could be a matter of degree. Still, to be born an untouchable was almost surely to receive a life sentence to an existence beyond the pale, though the location of what the scholar Susan Bayly calls the "pollution barrier"— the boundary between "clean" Hindu groups and those deemed to be "unclean" or polluting—might shift from place to place or time to time. In some regions, South India in particular, contact with even the shadow of an untouchable could be regarded as polluting. In few regions, however, were supposedly untouchable women secure from sexual exploitation by supposedly "clean" higher-caste men.

Some outcaste groups managed, over a stretch of generations, to promote themselves out of untouchability by ceasing to practice trades that were regarded as polluting such as picking up night soil or handling dead carcasses or working in leather. Others found they could distance themselves from their lowly origins by converting to Christianity and Islam. (Among Christians, in a shadowy carryover belying missionary promises, not to mention the Sermon on the Mount, some Indian Christians continued to treat others as untouchable.) Practices varied from region to region, as did the authority of high-caste Brahmans, the priestly types who rationalized the system and were, usually, its chief beneficiaries. The British and the missionaries who followed in their train taught members of the broad spectrum of various overlapping sects, devoted to various gods, that they belonged to a great encompassing collective called Hinduism. Simultaneously and more important, Indians were making the discovery for themselves. (Ancient Persians described "Hindus" more than two millennia before the British arrived; and recent scholarship suggests that the coinage "Hinduism" was first accomplished by an Indian, early in the nineteenth century.) Similarly, members of specific groups that were targets of untouchability— Chamars, Mahars, Malas, Raegars, Dusadhs, Bhangis, Doms, Dheds, and many more—learned they were all members of a larger group called untouchables. In short order, some began to draw the conclusion that they could make common cause for their own advancement.

Before Gandhi made his final return from South Africa to India, Brahmans were running schools in Maharashtra for the education of untouchables. They didn't necessarily, however, make a practice of eating with those they were uplifting. A movement called the Arya Samaj, concerned about the number of untouchables converting to Christianity and—given the then-theoretical possibility that votes might one day be counted in India—even more concerned about the number converting to Islam, instituted a ritual of *shuddi*, or purification, for untouchables who could be lured into "the Hindu fold" (as Gandhi would later describe it). Here again the equality they offered was strictly limited; followers of the movement were not even consistent on the question of whether the "purified," or reconverted untouchables, should be allowed to draw their water from wells used by higher castes. Perhaps it would be just as well if they were given their own separate but equal wells. It was enough not to consider the practitioners of polluting trades polluted. Higher-caste reformers saw no need for them to undertake such dirty, distasteful tasks themselves.

In later years, Gandhi displays at least a passing familiarity with this reformist history without ever acknowledging it influenced his own thinking. The theme of a memoir subtitled "The Story of My Experiments with Truth"—in the literary sense, its conceit—is that he had always been an independent operator, fearlessly making his own discoveries based almost entirely on his own experience. In the political realm, he never really portrays himself as a follower, even when he writes about his close ties to Gokhale, the Indian leader who cleared a path for his return to India, seeing Gandhi as a potential heir, and whom he acknowledged as a political guru. In the religious realm, he also acknowledged one guru, a philosophizing Jain poet (and diamond merchant) in Bombay named Shrimad Rajchandra, from whom he sought guidance when feeling pressed by Christian missionaries in his Pretoria days. But Rajchandra, who died early, in 1901, was no social reformer. Gandhi posed a series of questions to this sage. Included in his response was advice on what's called *varnashrama dharma*, the rules of proper caste conduct. Gandhi was then warned not to eat with members of different castes and, in particular, to shun Muslims as dining companions.

Much as he admired, even revered, Rajchandra, these strictures against out-of-caste dining gave him no pause. It took years for members of Gandhi's own household who remained orthodox to become accustomed to nonsectarian dining. "My mother and aunt would purify brass utensils used by Muslim friends of Gandhiji by putting them in the fire," recalled a young cousin who grew up on the Phoenix Settlement. "It was also a problem for my father to eat with Muslims." Later, back in India, Gandhi sometimes argued that the reluctance of Hindus to eat with Muslims was just another offshoot of the untouchability he deplored. "Why should Hindus have any difficulty in mixing with Mussalmans and Christians?" he asked in 1934. "Untouchability creates a bar not only between Hindu and Hindu but between man and man."

The question of how he came upon his independent views still needs some untangling. In Gandhi's own telling, after being warned against physical contact with the untouchable Uka at age twelve, he was not confronted with caste as a significant question until he resolved to go to London to study law. Then the *mahajans*, or elders, of the Modh Banias—the merchant subcaste to which all Hindu Gandhis belong—summoned him to a formal hearing in Bombay, now Mumbai, where he was spoken to severely and warned that he'd face what amounted to excommunication if he insisted on crossing the "black water," thereby subjecting himself to all the temptations of flesh (principally, meat, wine, and women) that can be assumed to beckon in foreign parts. If he went, he was told, he'd be the first member of the subcaste to defy this ban. Then only nineteen, he stood up to the elders, telling them they could do their worst.

We can surmise that the mahajans were already fairly toothless, for Gandhi's orthodox mother and elder brother Laxmidas supported him: in part, because he solemnly took three vows in front of a Jain priest to live abroad as a Bania would at home, in part because his legal training was seen as a key to the extended family's financial security. What we cannot do is conclude that this younger Gandhi was already in open rebellion against the caste system. In asserting his independence, he stopped well short of renouncing the caste that had just effectively declared him untouchable, warning its members that dining or close contact with him would be polluting. Three years later, when he returned from London, a docile Gandhi traveled with Laxmidas to Nasik, a sacred place in Maharashtra, to submit to a "purification" ritual that involved immersion in the Godavari River under the supervision of a priest who then issued certificates, which Gandhi preserved, saying he had performed his ablutions. The Bania in Gandhi, who always kept a frugal eye on accounts and expenditures, made a point of complaining to his first biographer, Doke, nearly two decades later, that the priest had charged fifty rupees.

And that wasn't the end of his purification. The Gandhi family then had to give a banquet for caste members in the Gujarati town of Rajkot, where he spent much of his childhood and where his wife and son had been stashed all the time he was abroad. The dinner itself included a ritual of submission. The prodigal son was expected to strip to the waist and serve all the guests personally. Gandhi—whose torso would be naked above the waist throughout the latter part of his life—submitted. Most members of his jati were mollified, but some, including his wife's family, never again ran the risk of allowing themselves to be seen eating in the presence of one so wayward, even after he became the recognized leader of the country. Gandhi went out of his way not to embarrass the holdouts, some of whom signaled that they were ready to ignore the ban in the privacy of their homes. He preferred to shame them. "I would not so much as drink water at their houses," he tells us, lauding himself for his own "non-resistance," which won him the affection and political support of those Banias who still regarded him as excommunicated.

Or so he claims. The line between humility and sanctimoniousness can be a fine one, and Gandhi occasionally crossed it. On display here is his tendency to turn his life into a series of parables, as he dashed off his memoir in the 1920s and, as he grew older, in his everyday discourse. The fact is he'd defied the caste elders and then, even after he'd gone through the purification ceremony, ostentatiously refused to evade the ancient prohibition in collusion with anyone who worried it might still be valid. His handling of the matter might be seen as passive-aggressive: in the arena of family, a precursor of satyagraha. It's Gandhi's way of seizing higher ground. All that came later. On his return from London, he had strong practical reasons for getting back on good terms with his caste. His standing with the Modh Banias was bound to have a bearing on his prospects as a lawyer, for it was among them that he would expect to find most of his clients.

The purification ceremony in Nasik and the banquet in Rajkot show that he was far from being a rebel against the strictures of caste in the interim between his return from London and his departure for South Africa. Whatever his private views, the newly minted barrister's stand on caste and its place in Indian society was still basically conformist. The experience of becoming untouchable in his own relatively privileged subcaste had given Gandhi no particular insight into the life of the downtrodden. At most, it insinuated the notion that caste might not be an impermeable barrier. It was just a step, then, on the way to Calcutta in 1901. Naipaul is almost certainly right: that encounter might never have occurred the way it did had he not gone to South Africa. If we look closely at Gandhi's early experience there, several critical moments of consciousness-raising appear to converge in a period of roughly half a year, starting in the latter part of 1894 as he was setting up a law practice in Durban.

Could his engagement with Christian missionaries in that period have had something to do with the sprouting of a social conscience? It's clear enough that British and American missionaries helped insinuate a notion of social equality into Indian thought. The thin edge of their wedge, it was always implicit and sometimes explicit in their general critique of a social order they considered wicked and in their more specific attack on the authority of Brahmans. The priestly caste was portrayed in Christian tracts as self-serving and corrupt. ("Wherever you see men, they have two hands, two feet, two eyes, two ears, one nose and one mouth, whatever their kind or country," a letter in a missionary newspaper noted nearly three decades before Gandhi was born. "Then God could not have had it in mind to create many castes among men. And the system of caste, that is only practised in India, is caused by the Brahmans to maintain their superiority.") However, it's less clear that discussions of caste and social equality came up in discussions between Gandhi and the missionaries who competed for his soul in Pretoria and Durban. Everything about the newcomer's first experiences in the emerging racial order suggests that such matters should have and may have arisen. But these evangelicals had salvation, not social reform, on their minds. From all that we actually know of their conversations with Gandhi, they were consistently otherworldly.

Enter Tolstoy, from the steppes. At some point in 1894, apparently in his last weeks in Pretoria, Gandhi received a packet in the mail from one of his well-wishers in Britain. This was Edward Maitland, leader of the tiny Esoteric Christianity spin-off from the Theosophist movement. Inside was the newly published Constance Garnett translation of *The Kingdom of God Is Within You*, the great novelist's late-life confession of a passionate Christian creed, founded on the individual conscience and a doctrine of radical nonviolence. Ten years later, Gandhi would come upon Ruskin and a few years after that on Thoreau. Subsequently, he would correspond with Tolstoy himself. But if there is a single seminal experience in his intellectual development, it starts with his unwrapping that package in Pretoria. The author of *War and Peace*, a book the young lawyer would have found less compelling, excoriates the high culture of the educated classes, which profess to believe in the brotherhood of man, condemning in the course of his argument all the institutions of church and state in czarist Russia. What they have in common, he rages, is bedrock hypocrisy, never more so than when they're declaiming on the subject of brotherhood:

We are all brothers, but I live on a salary paid me for prosecuting, judging, and condemning the thief or the prostitute whose existence the whole tenor of my life brings about . . . We are all brothers, but I live on the salary I gain by collecting taxes from needy laborers to be spent on the luxuries of the rich and idle. We are all brothers, but I take a stipend for preaching a false Christian religion, which I do not myself believe in, and which only serves to hinder men from understanding true Christianity.

And this: "We are all brothers—and yet every morning a brother or a sister must empty the bedroom slops for me."

Here we begin to get a clear view of how the social conscience that Gandhi would bring to Calcutta in 1901 was formed. It was not just living in South Africa that inspired it. It was musing about India while living in South Africa and reading Tolstoy there as he would continue to do in the coming years. By the time he got to the Calcutta meeting, Gandhi had read Tolstoy's subsequent jeremiad, *What Is to Be Done?* Here Tolstoy, continuing in his full-throated prophetic vein, tells the educated classes how they can save themselves—through an uncompromising rejection of materialism, a life of simple living, and physical labor to provide for their own necessities. ("Body labor" and "bread labor," he calls it, language Gandhi eventually appropriates for his own use.) In this context, Tolstoy, now determined to shed the privileges of a Russian aristocrat, returns to the question of human feces. The laws of God will be fulfilled, he writes, "when men of our circle, and after them all the great majority of working-people, will no longer consider it shameful to clean latrines, but will consider it shameful to fill them up in order that other men, *our brethren*, may carry their contents away."

The deep impression Tolstoy etched on Gandhi's soul was sufficiently conspicuous for one of his Indian critics to seize on it, years later, as proof of his essential foreignness. This was Sri Aurobindo, a brilliant Bengali revolutionary who advocated terrorism under the name Aurobindo Ghose, then lived out his long life as an ashram mystic and guru in the tiny French enclave of Pondicherry in South India. "Gandhi," Aurobindo said in 1926, "is a European—truly a Russian Christian in an Indian body." Gandhi, by then all but undisputed leader of the nationalist movement in India, might plausibly have retorted that Aurobindo was a Russian anarchist in an Indian body, but the Bengali's remark either passed him by or was beneath his notice.

The younger Gandhi, the South African lawyer and petitioner, immediately saw the contradiction between Tolstoy's prophetic teachings and the values prevailing among Indians of his station. Evidence that he has been more than shaken soon begins to accumulate. In May 1894, he travels to Durban, presumably to close out his year in South Africa and board a ship for home. Gandhi's account of what happened then has been accepted by most biographers: how at a farewell party his eye happened to fall on a brief newspaper item on the progress of a bill to disenfranchise Natal's Indians, how he called it to the attention of the community and was then prevailed upon to stay and lead a fight against the legislation. But an Indian scholar and Gandhi enthusiast, T. K. Mahadevan, noting that the bill had by then been progressing in stages through the colonial legislature for more than half a year, devoted a whole book to exposing Gandhi's "fictionalizing" and "mendacity" in his recounting of this episode in the *Autobiography*. With all the vehemence of a trial lawyer addressing a jury, the scholar concluded that the young barrister was mainly looking out for himself. Rather than return to an uncertain future in India, according to Mahadevan, he wanted to establish a legal practice in Durban.

It's more generous and probably more accurate to allow for the possibility of mixed motives, of altruism and ambition each playing its part in the cancellation of his voyage home. In any case, by August 1894 he has thrown himself into a life of what would now be called public service, drafting petitions and, early on, a constitution for the Natal Indian Congress, a newly formed association of better-off Indians, mostly traders and merchants and, in the Durban of that time, mostly Muslim. And here for the first time, at the very outset of his career in politics, he notices and mentions poor Indians. With Tolstoy hovering at his shoulder, or so we can reasonably surmise, Gandhi lists among the seven "objects" of the new Congress two for which it's hard to find any other inspiration in his reading or experience: "To inquire into the conditions of Indentured Indians and to take proper steps to alleviate their sufferings . . . [and] to help the poor and helpless in every reasonable way." He may have done little for or with the indentured until late in his stay in South Africa, but clearly they were on his mind and conscience from his earliest days in politics.

Such "objects" remained words, floating for years into a realm of high-flown aspiration, stopping far short of a program. Gandhi doesn't immediately travel to the sugar plantations and mines to make an on-the-spot inquiry. Years later, back in India, he would attribute his hesitation to his own social anxieties. "I lived in South Africa for 20 years," he

In 1895, with founders of the Natal Indian Congress, mostly Muslim merchants

said then, "but never once thought of going to see the diamond mines there, partly because I was afraid lest as an 'untouchable' I should be refused admission and insulted." By then, his equation of British racism and Indian casteism—the notion that all Indians were untouchable in British eyes—had become the rhetorical cutting edge of his argument as a social reformer. It worked for him as a nationalist, too.

But that was not where he started. Initially, his goal was social equality within the empire for his benefactors and clients, the higher-class Indian merchants. Indentured Indians thus weren't invited to join the Natal Indian Congress. Its annual membership fee of three pounds was far beyond their means. Their sufferings remained unalleviated, but several months later Gandhi had his first notable encounter with an indentured laborer; it's a case of reality crashing in. A Tamil gardener named Balasundaram, indentured to a well-known Durban white, turns up in Gandhi's recently opened law office, where one of the clerks, also a Tamil, interprets his story. The man is weeping, bleeding from the mouth; two of his teeth have been broken. His master has beaten him, he says. Gandhi sends him to a doctor, then takes him to a magistrate.

That's the version of the encounter he gives in the *Autobiography*, what deserves to be belittled as its movie treatment. None of his biographers seem to notice how far this account, written after the passage of three decades, strays from one he wrote just two years after the event. In the earlier one, the laborer has already gone on his own to the official known as the protector of immigrants, who conveys him to a magistrate, who, in turn, arranges for him to be hospitalized for "a few days." Only then does he land on Gandhi's doorstep. His wounds have been treated, he is no longer bleeding, but his mouth is so sore he can't speak. Surprisingly, he's able to write down his request in Tamil. He wants the lawyer to have his indenture canceled. Gandhi asks whether he'd be willing to have it transferred to someone other than his employer if cancellation can't be arranged. It takes half a year, but finally Gandhi arranges for Balasundaram to be indentured to a Wesleyan minister of his acquaintance, whose services Gandhi has been attending most Sundays.

Balasundaram is hardly a typical indentured laborer. Instead of toiling on a sugar plantation or mine, where laborers in large numbers are confined to compounds, the gardener lives in the city, where he knows his way around well enough to be able to get to the protector and Durban's one Indian lawyer on his own. That he's at least semiliterate suggests that he may not be an untouchable. Gandhi, later claiming more credit than he seems to have deserved, describes the case as a turning point. "It reached the ears of every indentured laborer, and I came to be regarded as their friend," he says in the *Autobiography*. "A regular stream of indentured labourers began to pour into my office." He says he got to know their "joys and sorrows." These broad claims have been widely accepted. ("He emerged virtually as a one-man legal aid society for these poor Indians," a respected Indian scholar, Nagindas Sanghavi, wrote.) Evidence from this period to support them, however, is less than slight. Gandhi himself doesn't go on to mention any subsequent cases involving indentured laborers; if there were records of such cases, they've long since disappeared. Apart from sketchy reports of two weekend forays late in 1895 to pass the hat for the Natal Indian Congress, there's nothing to indicate he went out of his way to meet the indentured in his Durban years.

On October 26, 1895, he's said to have visited shanties near the Point Road where Indian dockworkers and fishermen lived, collecting only five pounds. (Point Road, the thoroughfare he first traveled on landing in Durban, has lately, in the new South Africa, been renamed Mahatma Gandhi Road, a well-meant tribute that has discomfited local Indians, given its reputation for prostitution.) The next weekend he ventured north with some Congress members to the sugar country, but, barred from speaking to laborers at the Tongaat estate, he concentrated on local Indian traders. A British estate owner was asked by a magistrate in Durban to report on Gandhi's activities. The planter was no clairvoyant. This is what he wrote: "He will cause some trouble I have no doubt, but he is not the man to lead a big movement. He has a weak face."

Gandhi's real attitude to the indentured in this period is made plain by the arguments he advanced on the first of his losing causes in South Africa: that of protecting the voting rights of literate, propertied Indians. Such Indians, he wrote in December that year, "have no wish to see ignorant Indians who cannot possibly be expected to understand the value of a vote being placed on the Voters' List."

If the thought of following Tolstoy's teaching on his brief foray to the sugar country on Natal's north coast so much as crossed his mind, it hadn't yet carried him to the conclusion that he needed to do physical labor with his own hands. Nor, it seems, did he try again to penetrate the plantations, having failed the first time. So for anyone looking for the origins of his passion on untouchability—so evident by the time he reaches Calcutta in 1901—the Balasundaram case sheds little light. The most that can be said is that it might have helped set the stage for his next revelation, which came not from actual encounters with poor Indians but from finding himself on the short end of an argument with whites. At virtually the same time, probably no more than a few weeks after the gardener's arrival in his office, Gandhi the lawyer and petitioner was pulled up short by an editorial in a Johannesburg paper called *The Critic.*

The editorial chews over Gandhi's first venture in political pamphleteering, an open letter to the members of the colonial legislature in Natal, published at the end of 1894. In it, Gandhi took on "the Indian question as a whole," asking why Indians were so despised and hated in the country. "If that hatred is simply based upon his color," the twenty-five-year-old neophyte wrote, "then, of course, he has no hope. The sooner he leaves the Colony the better. No matter what he does, he will never have the white skin." But if the hatred was a result of misunderstanding, then maybe his letter would spread some appreciation of the richness of Indian culture and the thrifty hard work that made Indian citizens so useful. The case was different, Gandhi conceded, with indentured laborers, imported by the thousands on starvation wages, held under bondage, and lacking anything that can be described as "moral education." In finely honed understatement, so understated it probably passed over the heads of most white readers, Gandhi writes: "I confess my inability to prove that they are more than human." He's saying: Sure, they're unsanitary and degraded, but what can you expect, given the conditions in which you confine them? Maybe the image of Balasundaram, the only indentured laborer he'd met up to that point, flitted through his mind.

The Critic seizes on that argument and turns it around. It was the caste system and not the laws of Natal that condemned Indian laborers to be "a servile race," it said. "The class of Hindoos which swarms in Natal and elsewhere is necessarily of the lowest caste and, under the circumstances, do what they will, they can never raise themselves into positions which command respect, even of their fellows." Gandhi, the newspaper said, should "begin his work at home."

It's Gandhi's authorized biographer and longtime secretary, Pyarelal, who brings this passage to our attention. That may mean he has come upon a clipping Gandhi—a great hoarder and indexer of clippings all through his career—had saved from his South Africa days. Or, since Pyarelal was at Gandhi's side for nearly thirty years, from boyhood on, it may also mean that he has discussed the editorial with the man he called his "Master." Pyarelal is given to flowery hyperbole. But writing of the editorial in *The Critic*, he seems sure of his ground as he describes an epiphany:

> The barbed shaft penetrated to the core of Gandhiji's heart. The truth burst upon his heart with the force of revelation that so long as India allowed a section of her people to be treated as pariahs, so long must her sons be prepared to be treated as pariahs abroad.

The shaft flung by an English editorial writer in Johannesburg would become a fixture in Gandhi's own arsenal of arguments. ("Has not a just Nemesis overtaken us for the crime of untouchability?" he would ask in 1931. "Have we not reaped as we have sown? . . . We have segregated the 'pariah' and we are in turn segregated in the British colonies . . . There is no charge that the 'pariah' cannot fling in our faces and which we do not fling in the faces of Englishmen.")

Gandhi would testify that the point made by the editorial writer in Johannesburg was one he regularly had to confront. "During my campaigns in South Africa, the whites used to ask me what right we had to demand better treatment from them when we were guilty of ill-treating the untouchables among us." Whether the point was made routinely or just once, it left a permanent impression.

Ultimately, he did "begin his work at home," if under "his work" we include his Tolstoyan preoccupation with sanitation and the cleaning of latrines. He returned to India in 1896 with the aim of gathering his family and bringing it back to Durban. Soon after he arrived in Rajkot, there was an outbreak of plague in Bombay. Put on a sanitation committee in Rajkot, he made the inspection of latrines his special task. In the homes of the wealthy—and even in a Hindu temple—they were "dark and stinking and reeking with filth and worms." He then went into the untouchables' quarter: "the first visit in my life to such a locality," he acknowledged. Only one member of the committee was ready to go along. It turned out the untouchables had no latrines. "Latrines are for you big people," they told him, or so Gandhi recalled. They relieved themselves in the open, but, to his surprise, they kept the hovels where they lived cleaner than the more substantial homes of their social betters. Henceforth for Gandhi, sanitation and hygiene were at or near the top of his reform agenda.

The first overt sign that he has started to connect his passion for latrine cleaning with his convictions about untouchability crops up back in Durban, a year or so later. By his own account, Gandhi turns vicious in an argument with his long-suffering wife, Kasturba, over the emptying of a chamber pot. Here for the first time we find the categorical imperative of "body labor," derived from Tolstoy, brought into action against the very Indian practice of untouchability which Gandhi has now learned to abhor on grounds that it undercuts the case he has been making for Indian equality in South Africa. The chamber pot in question had been used by Vincent Lawrence, one of Gandhi's law clerks, whom he describes as "a Christian, born of *Panchama* parents." A Panchama is an untouchable. Lawrence had been recently staying as a houseguest in the lawyer's two-story villa on Beach Grove, steps from Durban Bay. A submissive Hindu wife, in her husband's portrayal, the illiterate Kasturba, normally called just Ba, had reluctantly learned to share with him the unspeakable duty of cleaning chamber pots. "But to clean those used by one who had been a Panchama seemed to her to be the limit," says Gandhi. She carries the clerk's pot but does so under vehement protest, weeping and upbraiding her husband, who responds by demanding sternly that she do her duty without complaining.

"I will not stand this nonsense in my house," he shouts, according to his own account.

"Keep your house to yourself and let me go," she replies.

The future Mahatma is now in a fury. "I caught her by the hand, dragged the helpless woman to the gate . . . and proceeded to open it with the intention of pushing her out." She then sues for peace, and he admits to remorse. Thirty years later he either doesn't remember or chooses not to say who finally emptied the chamber pot.

Here we have a clear prelude to the Calcutta scene on which Naipaul fastened. It shows that Gandhi didn't have to travel back to India to be confronted by the persistence of untouchability. He could bully his own wife on that score but must have known he had yet to convert her. As late as 1938, he erupts in a similar fury upon learning that Ba has entered a temple in Puri that still bars untouchables. His pique becomes an occasion for a fast, and he loses five pounds. What's somewhat unreadable, still, after the first incident in Durban, is the question of his own attitude to the very poor, the Panchamas and other low-caste Indians oppressed by the practice he abhors. His Christian law clerk is too easy an example. He is educated, an upstanding citizen in a starched collar. What about the indentured laborers on the sugar plantations with whom he doesn't mix, for whom he sometimes apologizes, those who fit a white man's stereotype of a "servile race"? Does he care about them in only an abstract, self-regarding sort of way, because he objects to the impression they leave of Indians? Or does he actually care about them?

A few lines in the *Autobiography* suggest that a positive answer came during the Durban years. Gandhi, who developed what he describes as a "passion" for nursing while caring for a dying brother-in-law in Rajkot, started putting in an hour or two most mornings as a volunteer in a small charitable hospital. This brought him, he says, into "close touch with suffering Indians, most of them indentured Tamil, Telugu or North India men." But that's all he says. It's a remark made in passing. We don't know how long this volunteer nursing went on, only that he counted it as good preparation for the Boer War, when the stretcher bearers he led sometimes nursed wounded British troops. These "body snatchers," as they were called by the troops, were themselves mostly indentured laborers. It was the war, rather than the volunteer nursing, that actually gave him his most conspicuous engagement with the poorest Indians before the final satyagraha campaign in his last year in South Africa.

Of the eleven hundred stretcher bearers nominally under his command, more than eight hundred were indentured, recruits from the sugar plantations on a stipend of one pound a week (double what most of them normally earned). The indentured, Gandhi makes clear, remained "under the charge of English overseers." Technically, they were volunteers, but they'd actually been drafted as a result of an official government request to their employers passed along by the so-called protector of immigrants. Rounded up on the plantations where they were indentured, these "semi-slaves," as Gandhi called them, were then marched off under the command of their usual overseers. It would be an overstatement, but not altogether inaccurate, to describe Gandhi as a convenient front man in this transaction. In a revealing passage, he later acknowledged he had nothing to do with recruiting most of the stretcher bearers: "The Indians were not entitled to the credit for the inclusion of the indentured laborers in the Corps, which should rightly have gone to the planters. But there is no doubt that the free Indians, that is to say the Indian community, deserved credit for the excellent management of the Corps."

Here again he's plainly saying that "free Indians" are members of the community; Indian indentured laborers are not. So while he has told us in the pages of the *Autobiography* that he was now recognized as "a friend," a man who knew their "joys and sorrows," his claim to have "got into closer touch" with the indentured with whom he served on the fringes of Boer War battlefields rings a little hollow. He speaks of no individuals, no incidents, just "a greater awakening amongst them," a realization that "Hindus, Musalmans, Christians, Tamilians, Gujaratis and Sindhis were all Indians and children of the same motherland." The awakening is "amongst *them*." We can almost picture his captive audience nodding while he speaks, even though many of them—the Tamils in particular—have no common language with him. But, as a matter of fact, we're not sure he delivered such speeches at the time. More likely, these words are directed to a different audience, in a different place, at a later time: convinced Gandhians in India who follow from week to week the installments of his memoirs in his newspaper. Long after the events he relates, Gandhi the Indian politician shapes and reshapes the experience of Gandhi the South African lawyer in order to advance his nationalist agenda and values at home.

Part of that reshaping involves his memory of valor in the face of danger. The original understanding was that the Indians would not be exposed to battlefield fire and risks. But when the British found themselves falling back from a severe reversal, according to Gandhi, their commander paused to reopen the question with the Indians in the most tactful and sensitive way. "General Buller had no intention of forcing us to work under fire if we were not prepared to take such risk," he wrote, "but if we undertook it voluntarily, it would be greatly appreciated. We were only too willing to enter the danger zone." In later years, Gandhi habitually used martial metaphors to summon the valor of his volunteers for nonviolent resistance. Perhaps that's what he's doing in this passage. But the impression he leaves is exaggerated. He never met General Redvers Buller; it's less than clear that the general knew his name. What he's talking about are orders and dispatches issued in the commanding officer's name. And his stretcher bearers never really operated on battlefields. They were at their greatest peril when, briefly, they were asked to carry their burdens over a pontoon bridge and pathways known to be in range of Boer artillery. But the guns remained silent, and no Indians were wounded or killed, even though the early Natal battles to which they were dispatched—Colenso in mid-December 1899 and Spion Kop a month later—quickly became charnel houses for the British, with the total of killed, wounded, and captured amounting to 1,127 in the first case and 1,733 in the second. The fact that not a single member of the ambulance corps fell to a Boer marksman or shell makes clear that their arduous, certainly stressful labors in the "danger zone" couldn't have been all that dangerous.

In describing these events, Gandhi cultivates the manly, modest voice of a leader who doesn't want to boast. On a rereading, there comes to seem a touch of the mock-heroic in that voice as well; his small ambiguities seem more calculated than careless. Yet biographers make the most of them. Here's Louis Fischer, one of the earliest and still one of the most readable, on the stretcher bearers: "For days they worked under the fire of enemy guns." Pyarelal, the apostle turned biographer, describes Gandhi's role in carrying General Edward Woodgate, the mortally wounded commander at Spion Kop, to the base hospital. "The agony of the General was excruciating during the march and the bearers had to hurry through the heat and dust." Two months were to pass before Woodgate finally died from his wounds. It's possible he was conscious as the stretcher or, more likely, curtained palanquin in which he was evacuated bumped along across the Tugela River valley for a little more than four miles to the base hospital at Spearman's Camp, where General Buller had established his headquarters. Physical details of the evacuation are sparse in Gandhi's account. Whether he accompanied the wounded commander for the whole distance is never entirely clear.

Spion Kop was a strategic hilltop that Woodgate had led his troops to capture in the middle of the night, only to discover in the morning that he'd neglected to secure the highest ground. Their trenches were half-dug when the Boers opened fire. Recklessly standing outside the trenches, Woodgate was shot through the head as soon as the morning mist lifted. He had to be pulled into a trench filled with dead and dying Lancashire fusiliers, then evacuated to "the first dressing station" by a squad of his troops, next hauled down the hillside to a "field hospital" by British stretcher bearers before his body could be handed over to the Indians. The contemporaneous *"Times" History of the War in South Africa* has a detailed narrative of these events, even naming one Lieutenant Stansfield as head of the squad that got Woodgate's body down the hill. The narrative doesn't mention the Indians, nor did a young British correspondent who climbed the hill late in the day after "the long, dragging hours of hell fire" had wound down.

"Streams of wounded met us and obstructed the path," Winston Churchill wrote in his dispatch to the *The Morning Post*. "Corpses lay here and there. Many of the wounds were of a horrible nature." At the base of the hill, "a village of ambulance wagons grew up." Gandhi and Churchill were seldom again on the same side. They wouldn't actually meet until a brief official encounter in London in 1906, which proved to be their only one. It's intriguing to think they may have crossed paths at Spion Kop. What's especially striking is the complete absence from Gandhi's accounts of the picture Churchill described. Either he saw very little of it, or, somehow, the impression it left soon faded.

Thirty educated Indians from Durban had been designated as "leaders" and given uniforms (paid for by the Muslim traders, none of whom volunteered). Leaders also got tents. The recruits from the ranks of the indentured had to sleep on open ground, often without blankets, at least in the early weeks. Gandhi was leader of the "leaders." It's never entirely clear that the leaders actually carried stretchers. In his several accounts Gandhi leaves the point vague. It's at least as likely that they supervised the work, marching along and setting the pace (though Gandhi's first biographer, Doke, came away from his interviews with the impression that his subject actually hauled stretchers). When it was all over, Gandhi wrote a beseeching letter to the colonial secretary noting that a gift of "the Queen's Chocolate"—held out as more than a gift, a royal beneficence—had just been distributed to British troops in Natal. He asked that the chocolate go as well to the uniformed leaders of the ambulance corps who had served their brief tours without compensation. He made no request on behalf of the much larger number of indentured laborers whom he had not personally recruited. In the event, no

Indians got "the Queen's Chocolate." The exchange makes a pathetic coda. The official replied stiffly. The chocolate was intended only for enlisted men and noncommissioned officers, he said; only for whites, he might just as well have said, for that's how Gandhi, scrounging for some small recognition of common citizenship, no matter how symbolic, would have read it. Eight Indians, including Gandhi, got medals. None of the other stretcher bearers got any recognition except a letter from Gandhi himself accompanied by a modest unspecified gift.

Vincent Lawrence, the outcaste clerk whose chamber pot had disgusted Kasturba Gandhi, was among the "leaders" sleeping in tents, which shows that for Gandhi the great social divide had become a matter of class, not caste. The idea of crossing that divide is presented only retrospectively. At the time he finds it remarkable that the stretcher bearers got along well with British soldiers they encountered, considering that the indentured laborers were "rather uncouth."

The fastidiousness is Gandhi's. He'd not always be this fussy. Much later, in India, after he'd crossed the social divide, Gandhi adopted an untouchable girl as his daughter. She was named Lakshmi. Years after his death, when the writer Ved Mehta sought her out, Lakshmi described Gandhi's obsession with the system of sanitation he established in his ashram: how his followers were trained to pass stool and urine into separate whitewashed buckets in a whitewashed latrine, then cover the stool with earth, eventually emptying the stool buckets in a distant trench, covering what was disposed there with cut grass, and then using the urine to rinse the bucket out. "Bapu had found a use even for urine," Lakshmi said. Ved Mehta doesn't indicate whether this was said with pride, irony, or some measure of each. Maybe she was simply matter-of-fact, in which case she sets an example for anyone trying to understand his thinking on such matters now.

The ashram and the refinements of its sanitation system were still to come when Gandhi reached Calcutta in 1901. But the impulse to experience India as the mass of rural Indians did, more or less the way Tolstoy sought to experience the Russia his former serfs inhabited, was now breaking through. Perhaps the spectacle of South Indian Brahmans shielding themselves from pollution behind wicker walls was what triggered it. The boundaries of caste were obviously more firmly drawn in India, even in the precincts of the Indian National Congress, than they had been in South Africa. There, among the indentured at least, intercaste relationships, sometimes sanctified as marriages, were not uncommon, an adaptation to a shortage of females resulting from the decision of colonial officials to import only two women for every three men. A laborer on a particular estate could hardly be sure of finding a mate from his specific subcaste and region there. He might not even care about these categories anymore. In a contemporary send-up of the recruiting agents for the distant plantations who operated in the most depressed parts of India, the promise that caste restrictions could be loosened or abandoned in the new land is part of the pitch of a "sweet-tongued talker." In this lightly satiric version, the agent promises high wages, light workloads, and no priests "to call on you to conform to the customs of caste traditions." The laborer will be able to eat, drink, or lie down "with any lass you may love and no one demurs or disputes your rights."

In fact, an 1885 judicial commission looking into conditions on the sugar plantations in Natal found "high-caste men married to low-caste women, Mahommedans to Hindus, men from Northern India to Tamil women from the South." Later, when the contracts of indenture ran out, upwardly mobile ex-indentured Indians who'd elected to stay in South Africa and make a life there soon started to reerect the barriers that had been taken down. In 1909, fifteen years after Gandhi had first come forward as a spokesman for the Indians of Natal, twenty-nine Hindus sent a petition to the protector of immigrants, demanding the immediate dismissal of two Pariahs who'd been appointed as constables in their community. "These two Indians are sent out to execute writs," the petitioners complained, "and at other times to search our houses . . . What we wish to point out is that if a pariah touches our things or makes an arrest we [are] polluted They also put on airs."

Today, five or six generations later, marriages between persons of South and North Indian extraction, not to mention Hindus and Muslims, are still likely to provoke family tensions in South Africa. Marital Web sites tend to be less pointed about caste requirements, however, than they still are in India, but there are sometimes veiled allusions. In marital ads in India today, there are occasional explicit references to Dalits, the preferred name for the former untouchables in recent decades. In South Africa today, such up-front, unashamed allusions to untouchability seem to be beyond the scope of marital ads aimed at the Indian minority. Untouchability is never mentioned. Except for a rare academic study, it may not have been acknowledged in print since a single mention a long lifetime ago in *The Star* of Johannesburg. The headline on a small article on June 18, 1933, nearly two decades after Gandhi left South Africa, said: UNTOUCHABILITY IN JOHANNESBURG REMOVED.

The elders of the Hindu temple in a neighborhood called Melrose, the article said, had decided to admit untouchables to worship there, in response to a fast against the practice that the Mahatma had ended in India three weeks earlier. Without acknowledging it in so many words, the article thus confirmed that there had long been Indians deemed to be untouchable by other Indians in South Africa and that they'd been barred from the temple throughout Gandhi's time there.

Gandhi must have known this. But since it was not in the open, untouchability never had to be named as a particular target of his reforming zeal, much as he'd come to abhor it. Even if he had the impulse to launch a campaign among South African Indians against it, how could he have done so without reinforcing anti-Indian sentiments among whites or splitting his small community? Calcutta at the end of 1901 was a different story. At the Congress session untouchability was blatantly in the open as an unquestioned social practice. Not only did Gandhi see it with a foreign eye; he reacted.

When the Congress ended, he stayed on in Calcutta for a month, lodging for most of that time with his political guru, Gokhale, and calling on prominent figures, including Swami Vivekananda, a Hindu reformer known to his followers as "the Seraphic Master." An overnight sensation at the World's Parliament of Religions held in Chicago in conjunction with the World's Fair in 1893 when he was just thirty, Vivekananda had been hailed as a prodigy, even prophet, in some religious circles in the West. But when the colonial lawyer came to call, he was on his deathbed at the age of thirty-nine and not receiving visitors. There's no way of knowing whether Gandhi wanted to talk about religion or India. For both men, these were never unrelated subjects. Vivekananda's central theme was the liberation of the soul through a hierarchy of yogic disciplines and states of consciousness, starting with some Gandhi would later profess: nonviolence, chastity, and voluntary poverty. He also spoke scathingly about the involuntary poverty to which Indians by the millions were subjected, saying it was futile to preach religion to the Indian masses "without first trying to remove their poverty and their sufferings." When Gandhi mentioned Vivekananda in speeches later, it was almost always to haul out a favorite quotation about the evil of untouchability. The swami could be down-to-earth as well as mystical. He condemned India's "morbid no-touchism." And, in the phrase Gandhi regularly used, he played on the official designation of India's lowest and poorest as "depressed classes." What they really should be called, Vivekananda said before Gandhi came on the scene, was "the suppressed classes." Their suppression depresses all Indians, Gandhi would always add.

On leaving Calcutta at the end of January 1902, Gandhi resolved to travel alone across India by train on a third-class ticket in order to experience firsthand the crowding, squalor, and filth that were the lot of the poorest travelers. With a rhetorical flourish but no direct reference to anything his Master said then or later, Pyarelal wrote that Gandhi wanted to bring himself "into intimate touch with a wide cross-section of the Indian humanity with whom it was his ambition to merge himself." He bought a blanket, a rough wool coat, a small canvas bag, and a water jug for his expedition.

His resolve to travel third-class from Calcutta may not have become as celebrated as his resistance to being expelled from a first-class compartment on the other side of the Indian Ocean nearly nine years earlier. But it's not far-fetched to see it as a turning point that's equally laden with portents. If he hadn't crossed the social divide in his own mind and heart before, he did so now. It wasn't a political gesture, something done to attract attention, for no one was paying him any except Gokhale, who, after reacting incredulously to the unheard-of notion of an upper-caste lawyer in third class, finally was touched by Gandhi's earnestness, so touched he accompanied his protégé to the station, bringing him some food for the journey and saying, "I should not have come if you had gone first-class but now I had to." That, at least, was the way Gandhi remembered his send-off. Gokhale's admiration for his would-be apprentice, who was only three years younger, grew into a kind of reverence. "A purer, a nobler, a braver and more exalted spirit," he would tell a crowd of Punjabis in 1909, while Gandhi was still in South Africa, "has never moved on the earth."

After that trip across India in early 1902, Gandhi made it a rule—it might even be called a fetish—always to travel third-class in India (even when, as sometimes happened in later years, the railway laid on entire cars and even trains for the exclusive use of his entourage, inspiring the poet Sarojini Naidu's loving jibe: "You will never know how much it costs us to keep that saint, that wonderful old man, in poverty"). On this first outing, he found the noise unbearable, the habits of the passengers disgusting, their language foul. Chewing betel and tobacco, they "converted the whole carriage into a spittoon," he said. Getting into "intimate touch" with Indian humanity proved to be a nasty experience, but, Pyarelal wrote, "in retrospect, Gandhi even enjoyed it." Presumably he means that Gandhi got a kick out of the thought that he was doing something completely original for an aspiring Indian politician. In South Africa, he noted, third-class accommodations, used mainly by blacks, were more comfortable with cushioned rather than hard wooden seats and railway officials not as completely indifferent to overcrowding as they were in India. But in South Africa he had mostly traveled first-class until then. Merging with indentured Indians there wasn't yet part of his program, and they weren't often on trains; merging with blacks never occurred to him.

3

AMONG ZULUS

Fʀᴏᴍ ʜɪs ꜰɪʀsᴛ ᴍᴏɴᴛʜs in South Africa, the young Mohandas Gandhi was acutely sensitive to the casual racism that dripped and oozed from the epithet "coolie." Never could he get over the shock of seeing the word used as a synonym for "Indian" in official documents or courtroom proceedings; making that translation in reverse—defining himself on behalf of the whole community as an Indian rather than as a Hindu, Gujarati, or Bania—was his first nationalist impulse. Years later he could be freshly affronted by the memory of having been called a "coolie lawyer." Yet it took him more than fifteen years to learn that the word "kaffir" had similar connotations for the people he occasionally recognized as the original owners of the land, the "natives," as he otherwise called them, or Africans, or blacks.

Gandhi is likely to have heard the term in India. Originally derived from the Arabic word for infidel, it was sometimes used by Muslims there to describe Hindus. Its range of meanings in the speech of white South Africans would have been new to him. In Afrikaans and English, whites used "kaffir" in a variety of compounds and contexts. The Kaffir Wars of the early nineteenth century were fought by white settlers against black tribes who inhabited territory known as Kaffirland or Kaffraria. Kaffir corn was the grain used in their mealie porridge and beer. Anything with the word attached to it was normally deemed to be inferior, backward, or uncivilized. In its most polite usage, as a noun, it signified a primitive being. When it came with a sneer, it amounted to "nigger." *Kafferboetie* was an abusive term in Afrikaans for anyone who liked or sympathized with blacks; a fair translation was "nigger lover." It was something Gandhi was never called.

Here he is in early 1908, reporting on his first experience of prison as an inmate:

> We were then marched off to a prison intended for Kaffirs . . . We could understand not being classed with the whites, but to be placed on the same level as the Natives seemed too much to put up with. It is indubitably right that Indians should have separate cells. Kaffirs are as a rule uncivilized—the convicts even more so. They are troublesome, very dirty and live almost like animals.

Indians sentenced to hard labor were routinely placed in the same cells with blacks, an experience Gandhi would have himself the next time he went to prison, later that same year.

Much happened in the eight months between these two prison experiences. Initially, he'd urged Indians to refuse to register in the Transvaal as the "Black Act" required; then he'd quixotically struck a deal with Smuts under which, as he understood it, Indians would register "voluntarily" and then, in recognition of their easy compliance, the law requiring them to do so would be repealed. As Gandhi saw it, the removal from the statute books of a racial law defining Indians as second-class citizens had to be welcomed even if little or nothing changed in their actual lives. Similarly, he would later demand changes in a law called the Asiatic Act (enacted in 1907 by the all-white new provincial legislature, as soon as self-rule was restored to the former South African Republic) that barred Indian immigrants to the Transvaal with no history of previous residence there. Gandhi wanted six, just six, highly educated Indians to be admitted annually as permanent residents, even if they had no ties to the territory. By Gandhi's puzzling, legalistic standard, the admission of half a dozen Indians a year would cancel any suggestion that they were innately unequal and unworthy of citizenship. It could also be interpreted as a sly tactical maneuver designed to establish or, rather, insinuate a precedent or right, which is precisely why the new white government resisted the demand. "The spirit of fanaticism which actuates a portion of the Indian community" made it inadvisable, Prime Minister Louis Botha explained to a British official, suggesting it would be an invitation to further Gandhian resistance. What the prime minister really meant was that even six Indians a year—one every two months—would be enough to inflame whites, for whom, of course, there had never been numerical quotas or educational standards. It would violate one of their regularly proclaimed demands: that a lid be placed absolutely on the number of Indians. "Resolved," a group calling itself the White League had formally declared as early as 1903, "that all Asiatics should be prevented from coming into the Transvaal." In Botha's view, that was reasonable, not "fanatical."

The registration issue came first; and for the first but not last time, Gandhi's instinct for compromise, for sticking to a principle even if it meant gaining little in practice, confused and upset followers, to the point that he was waylaid and severely beaten on the day he himself went to register by burly Pathans, Muslims from the frontier area of what's now Pakistan who'd been brought over during the war to serve in various noncombatant roles. The Pathans were quick to conclude that Gandhi's supposed deal was a betrayal. The distinction between being fingerprinted voluntarily and being fingerprinted under duress was not apparent to them. Reacting in horror to the assault on their leader, who was now beginning to be recognized as a spiritual pilgrim as well as a lawyer and spokesman, the broader Indian community finally heeded his appeal and registered. But, in a further twist, the "Black Act" wasn't repealed as he'd assured them it would be. A nonplussed Gandhi said he'd been double-crossed. As his grandson and biographer Rajmohan Gandhi observes, he then "for the first time permitted himself the use of racial language," saying Indians would never again "submit to insult from insolent whites." Satyagraha resumed with the aroused mass meeting at the Hamidia Mosque in Johannesburg, where, following Gandhi's example, Transvaal Indians flung their certificates into the iron cauldron, where they were promptly doused with paraffin, set aflame, and incinerated.

So Gandhi had no certificate to present when, in October, he led dozens of similarly undocumented Indians from Natal into the Transvaal border town of Volksrust, where, refusing to be fingerprinted, he was arrested and sentenced to two months of hard labor. Brought to Johannesburg under guard and wearing the garb of ordinary black convicts ("marked all over with the broad arrow," in Doke's contemporaneous description), the well-known lawyer was paraded through the streets from Park Station to the Fort, Johannesburg's earliest prison, where he was tossed into an overcrowded holding cell in the segregated "native jail," full of black and other nonwhite criminals. This too is commemorated: the skeleton of the old Park Station, all elegant fretwork and filigree open to the elements under a pitched metal roof, sits today as a monument on a bluff above the rail yards in downtown Johannesburg; the communal holding cell at the Fort has been converted into a permanent Gandhi exhibition where his reedy voice, recorded in an old BBC interview, can be heard complaining a dozen or so times an hour about being belittled as "a coolie lawyer." The prison, where Nelson Mandela and many other political prisoners were subsequently jailed, has been converted into a museum preserving the memory of past oppression and struggle. Hard by its thick ramparts stand the open, airy chambers of South Africa's new Constitutional Court, pledged to uphold a legal order guaranteeing equal rights for all South Africa's peoples: an imaginative juxtaposition intended as an act of architectural restitution and rebalancing, meant to enshrine, not just symbolize, a living ideal.

All that—the dedication of the new court building, the renaming of the prison precincts as Constitution Hill—came ninety-six years after Gandhi's first imprisonment there in 1908. His experience, recounted to Doke and subsequently written up in *Indian Opinion*, more than confirmed his earlier fears. The future Mahatma was mocked and taunted by a black inmate, then by a Chinese one, who finally turned away, going to "a Native lying in bed," where "the two exchanged obscene jokes, uncovering one another's genitals." Gandhi, who tells us that both men were murderers, admits to having felt uneasy and finding it hard to fall asleep for a while; the Baptist preacher Doke, with whom he spoke the next day, is instantly horror-struck. "This refined Indian gentleman was obliged to keep himself awake all night, to resist possible assaults upon himself, such as he saw perpetrated around him," Doke writes. "That night can never be forgotten." The man who didn't have the experience is more vivid in this instance than the one who did, probably, we may surmise, because of the immediacy, the sense of looming violation, with which the badly shaken prisoner related it to him as compared to the cool indifference Gandhi attempted to affect two months later, when he got around to writing about that evening himself.

On that second day in the holding cell at the Fort, as Gandhi was starting to use a prison latrine, so he later wrote, "a strong, heavily built, fearful-looking Native" demanded that Gandhi step aside so he could go first. "I said I would leave very soon. Instantly he lifted me up in his arms and threw me out." He was not injured, Gandhi tells us, "but one or two Indian prisoners who saw what happened started weeping," out of shame over their inability to defend their leader. "They felt helpless and miserable," he says. Here again Gandhi doesn't say how he felt. It was the fourth assault on his person in South Africa, the first by a black. Yet he writes about it only once, doesn't dwell on it even then. He's not shocked, he leads us to infer, not even surprised.

Writing after the passage of two months, he draws a conclusion that's not about jail life. It's about ordinary relations between Indians and the black majority. "We may entertain no aversion to Natives," he says, "but we cannot ignore the fact that there is no common ground between them and us in the daily affairs of life." This time he doesn't say "kaffirs." But the sentiment isn't conspicuously different from what a refined Brahman in that era—or, for that matter, most Banias—might have voiced about untouchables. Is that, as some Indian scholars suggested to me, really how Gandhi saw Africans, as people who should be deemed untouchable? In strict interpretation of caste, any non-Hindu or foreigner, white or black, is an outcaste by definition, unsuitable as a dining companion, or for partnering of a more intimate kind. Then and later, other South African Hindus found it natural to apply the strictures of untouchability to black servants, not allowing them to have contact with their food or dishes or persons. Gandhi himself had for years eaten with non-Indian vegetarians, all whites. At this stage in his life, he was actually living with a non-Indian, a Jewish architect of Lithuanian background by way of East Prussia named Hermann Kallenbach. So when we think it through, the question becomes this: whether, on account of race, he put hard-living, uneducated, meat-eating Africans in a separate category of humans from that of hard-living, uneducated, meat-eating Indian "coolies," or the third-class passengers whose behavior appalled him on Indian trains; in other words, whether for him, race was a defining characteristic or, finally, as incidental as caste.

It's in this context that we must view Gandhi's early reflections on jail life from the same year. I've not highlighted them because they're especially shocking or revealing of his feelings about race. There are passages sprinkled among Gandhi's writings of earlier years in South Africa that sound—in, as well as out of, context—even more condescending to Africans, sound, frankly, racist. As early as 1894, in an open letter to the Natal legislature, he complained that "the Indian is being dragged down to the position of the raw Kaffir." Two years later he was still going on about "the raw Kaffir, whose occupation is hunting and whose sole ambition is to collect a number of cattle to buy a wife, and then pass his life in indolence and nakedness." (The very proper young lawyer Gandhi then was plainly had no premonition of the day he'd teasingly vow to be "as naked as possible" himself.) In 1904, during an outbreak of plague in Johannesburg, he asks the official medical officer why the so-called Indian location—the area where the city's Indians were mostly required to live—had been "chosen for dumping down all the Kaffirs of the town." Hammering his point further, he declares what's only obvious: "About the mixing of the Kaffirs with the Indians, I must confess I feel most strongly." And there's Gandhi the eager racial theorist who had written a couple of months earlier: "If there is one thing the Indian cherishes more than any other, it is purity of type." And a couple of months before that: "We believe as much in the purity of races as we think they [the whites] do."

All that can be said by way of extenuation about such passages is that they were addressed to whites. If we want to give him any benefit of the doubt, we might say that the eager-to-please advocate was maybe playing to his audience, seeking to advance his argument that so-called British Indians could safely be acknowledged as cultural and political equals of whites, worthy citizens bound to them by their common imperial ties—that equality of sorts for Indians would not, in the near or far future, undermine the dominance of whites. But he was up against the color bar. For many whites, color was all that mattered; in this view, Indians had to be classed first and foremost as "non-white" if white dominance was to be maintained as the basic premise of social order. To concede that there could be "British Indians"—Indians who met standards that could be acknowledged as "civilized"—was a step away from admitting the unthinkable, the possibility of "British" or "civilized" Africans. It was an attitude that had riled Gandhi practically from the time he set foot in the country. In his fifth month in South Africa he clipped and saved a snatch of racist verse from a humor column in a Transvaal newspaper:

> Oh, say have you seen
> On our market so clean
> Where the greens are exposed to the view,
> A thing black and lean,
> And a long way from clean,
> Which they call the accursed Hindoo.

Insisting that Indians were British was one way of resisting the easy classification that blackness suggested to colonial minds, and not just colonial minds but Indian minds as well, as Gandhi himself, having returned to India, acknowledged years later in these reflections on race:

A fair complexion and a pointed nose represent our ideal of beauty. If we discard this superstition for a moment, we feel that the Creator did not spare Himself in fashioning the Zulu to perfection . . . It is a law of nature that the skin of races living near the equator should be black. And if we believe there must be beauty in everything fashioned by nature . . . we in India would be free from the improper sense of shame and dislike which we feel for our own complexion if it is anything but fair.

Back now to those 1908 reflections on race and the mixing of races that jail inspired in Gandhi's own mind: it's not their content but the timing that makes them stand out, for they happen to frame the single most farsighted and enlightened thing Gandhi would say on the subject during his many years in Africa. In May 1908—scarcely four months after his first imprisonment ended, a little more than four months before his second began—the recently sprung barrister was asked to argue the negative side in a formal debate before the YMCA in Johannesburg. The issue was tailor-made: "Are Asiatic and Colored races a menace to the Empire?"

"In a well-ordered society," Gandhi begins, "industrious and intelligent men can never be a menace." Immediately he makes it plain that he's speaking of Africans as well as Indians (and the mixed-race people known in South Africa as Coloreds). "We can hardly think of South Africa without the African races . . . South Africa would probably be a howling wilderness without the Africans," he says. The ugly racial stereotype of the "raw Kaffir" has been discarded. Africans are described as being among "the world's learners." Nothing special has to be done for them, "able-bodied and intelligent" as they are. But "they are entitled to justice" and what he calls "a fair field." He makes the same claim for indentured Indians, brought to the country as "semi-slaves." It's not a question of political rights, he carefully insists. It's a question of being able to own land, live and trade where they want, move freely from province to province, without regard to color, so they are no longer barred from having "their being on God's earth in South Africa with any degree of freedom, self-respect and manliness." Implicitly, for the first time, indentured Indians and Africans coming into the colonial labor market are put on the same plane.

So far what's new here is that the debater has bracketed Africans with Indians. Otherwise it's his standard trope, his appeal for equality of opportunity for his people. But as he starts to wrap up, he takes a further step. He has always said it's not a question of political rights, but now he breaks out of that straitjacket. On this one occasion, he allows himself to talk about "free institutions" and "self-government" and the duty of the British to lift "subject races" to "equality with themselves." Surprisingly, in this imperial context, he finds a vision of something like "the rainbow nation" the multiracial South Africa of today aspires, or at least claims, to be:

> If we look into the future, is it not a heritage we have to leave to posterity, that all the different races commingle and produce a civilization that perhaps the world has not yet seen? There are differences and misunderstandings, but I do believe, in the words of the sacred hymn, "We shall know each other better when the mists have rolled away."

How do we reconcile these two contrasting Gandhis, each circa 1908 in South Africa—this debater and visionary with the narrow racial pleader who, earlier and afterward that same year, spoke in such a different vein? Can one be seen as more real or enduring than the other? Put another way, can what he says to a white audience be taken as more genuine than what he says to Indians? The answer is so far from being obvious that the only possible conclusion seems to be that Gandhi's views on race—on blacks in particular—were now contradictory and unsettled. Considering what they had been, this has to be seen as an advance.

If Gandhi was in flux, so was the country. An all-white national convention was about to set a constitutional course. Standing apart with their list of grievances against the Transvaal, Indians were in no position to influence the debate. In fact, there was no national Indian organization. Gandhi himself was all that connected the Transvaal British Indian Association to the Natal Indian Congress. Less and less did they seem like different faces of a single movement. (It wasn't till 1923, nine years after Gandhi left South Africa, that a national Indian organization finally came into being, calling itself the South African Indian Congress; by then, the organizations he led were dormant.)

Even the courageous band of Transvaal protesters courting arrest—his "self-suffering" satyagrahis—were sometimes less united than he might have wished. This became evident, he later acknowledged, in the tight quarters of a jail. "Indians of all communities and castes lived together in the jail, which gave us an opportunity to observe how backward we are in the matter of self-government." Some Hindus refused to eat food prepared by Muslims or fellow prisoners of lower caste. One satyagrahi objected to sleeping near another from the scavenger subcaste; he was afraid his own caste would punish him, perhaps even brand him as outcaste if it learned of his propinquity to an untouchable. Speaking about caste in a specifically South African context for the first

On the building site of Kallenbach's new home

time, Gandhi denounced "these hypocritical distinctions of high and low" and the "caste tyranny" that lay behind them. So both forms of government—"self-government" (meaning how Indians treated Indians) and national government for South Africa (meaning whites ruling everyone else)—were on his mind when he spoke to the YMCA in Johannesburg between his first two jail experiences. At its heart, each held for him the issue of equality. In that sense, he now saw the issue through different ends of one telescope. On this occasion at least, in taking the long view, Gandhi managed to include Africans in his vision of "a civilization that perhaps the world has not yet seen."

But outside prison walls, who were the Africans in his life? What, after fifteen years in the country, did he actually know of them? The historical record has remarkably little to say on that score. There is a photograph taken in early 1910 of a dapper, neatly groomed Gandhi, in shirtsleeves and tie, sleeves rolled up, casually sitting on a hillside, where a big tent has been pitched, with a few of the pioneers who would form the nucleus of his nascent utopian community. Standing off to the side, very much apart, are two black men. Possibly these are "Native Isaac" and "Native Jacob," whose monthly wages of one pound each are

detailed in the diary of Gandhi's friend and fellow settler Hermann
Kallenbach, the architect who purchased the land for what became
known as Tolstoy Farm and later functioned as its treasurer. Gandhi
would propose, in a set of rules drafted for this new commune and boot
camp for nonviolent resisters, that it employ no servants. "It is understood that the ideal is not to employ native labor and not to use machin-
ery," he'd written. But Isaac and Jacob remained on Kallenbach's books
until the end of its brief life of two and a half years. Gandhi himself later
came close to portraying these low-paid farmhands as noble savages in a
paean to the life of physical labor in the fields of Tolstoy Farm: "I regard
the Kaffirs, with whom I constantly work these days, as superior to us.
What they do in their ignorance we have to do knowingly." (Rajmohan
Gandhi, his grandson, suggests this may have been his last use of the
epithet "kaffir.")

Other Africans from the neighborhood may have visited Tolstoy
Farm—as Zulus living near the Phoenix Settlement visited there—but
no such visitors, nor the seemingly indispensable Isaac and Jacob, were
invited into the mixed group of Indians and whites that made up the
company of Gandhian recruits. Their leader couldn't have passed many
days in his two decades in Africa without seeing ordinary Africans,
legions of them. But the question of how much contact he had with
them, like the question posed earlier of how much actual contact he had
with indentured Indians toiling on the plantations and in the mines,
finds no ready answer. It can only be inferred from what he wrote. He
had a fair amount to say about indentured Indians—about their miserable circumstances, about caste—before he finally became involved
with them. Few and far between were his reflections on Africans. Calling
him ethnocentric doesn't cover the case. He had plenty to say to—and
about—whites.

In the several thousand pages Gandhi wrote in South Africa, or later
about South Africa, the names of only three Africans are mentioned. Of
the three, he acknowledges having met only one. And when it comes to
that one African, what documentary evidence there is covers only two
meetings with Gandhi—seven years apart—leaving to our imaginations
the question of whether they ever met again.

His name was John Langalibalele Dube. A Zulu aristocrat descended
from Zulu chiefs, he'd been raised at the American Zulu Mission station
in Inanda, where his father, James Dube, had become one of the first

converts and, eventually, a pastor as well as a prosperous farmer, so prosperous that he had thirty gold sovereigns to invest in sending his son
off in the company of an American missionary to Oberlin College in
Ohio. John Dube thus took a cultural leap as long as the one Gandhi
managed when he crossed the black water to be trained as a lawyer in
London. Later Dube returned to America to be ordained in Brooklyn as
a Congregational minister and raise funds for an industrial school mod-
eled on Booker T. Washington's Tuskegee Institute. Dube called Washington, to whom he made a pilgrimage in 1897, "my patron saint . . . my
guiding star."

In 1900 he founded an organization called the Natal Native Congress,
in hopes of giving a voice to Zulus on issues of land, labor, and rights
where the traditional chiefs seemed unprepared to engage white authorities. The new group's name strongly suggested that it found its model in
Gandhi's own Natal Indian Congress. Twelve years later, John Dube
became the first president—president-general he was called—of the
South African Native National Congress, which later simplified its
nomenclature, calling itself the African National Congress, the name
under which it finally took power in 1994 after the country's first experience of nonracial universal suffrage. In homage to John Dube's standing
as a founding father, Nelson Mandela made a point of casting his own
first vote in Inanda at Dube's school, the Ohlange Institute. The place
has since been known as First Vote.

So if Gandhi was to know only one African of his own generation,
John Dube, just two years his junior, was probably the one to know. That
is exactly what Gandhi himself concluded after hearing Dube speak in
1905 at the home of a white planter and civic leader named Marshall
Campbell. "This Mr. Dubey [*sic*] is a Negro of whom one should know,"
he wrote in *Indian Opinion*. The article had an unfortunate headline:
THE KAFFIRS OF NATAL. And Gandhi called Dube the leader of "educated Kaffirs," which demonstrates that for him the word applied to all
blacks, including Congregational ministers and headmasters, not merely
unlettered tribal Africans. Still, his summary of the speaker's remarks—
more than likely the first speech he'd ever heard by an educated African
and quite possibly the last—was respectful and sympathetic:

> They worked hard and without them the whites could not carry on for
> a moment. They made loyal subjects, and Natal was the land of their
> birth. For them there was no country other than South Africa; and to
> deprive them of their rights over lands, etc., was like banishing them
> from their home.

What's striking here is that Gandhi had to travel the several miles to the Campbell residence in Mount Edgecombe to meet Dube. The two men were near neighbors; the Ohlange Institute in Inanda was (and is) less than a mile from the Phoenix Settlement, its buildings visible to this day from the veranda of Gandhi's cottage. A brisk walker like Gandhi could have crossed the narrow valley that separated them in less than half an hour.

Only one such visit surfaces in the written record. Just as disappointing is the absolute lack of any correspondence, even a brief note, indicating they kept in touch or were used to addressing one another with familiarity. Gandhi was absent from Phoenix much more than he was present there in the eight years following its founding; and when he was there, often for a matter only of days, his routine was to focus on the settlers, going door-to-door to visit families, holding prayer meetings, gathering the children around him. And there was always *Indian Opinion* with its weekly demand for more copy from its proprietor and guiding light. Even so, it's surprising how little turns up linking him to his Zulu neighbor. We know that Gopal Krishna Gokhale, the Indian leader who toured South Africa in Gandhi's company in 1912, was taken to Dube's school during a stay of less than forty-eight hours at Phoenix. But only in Dube's Zulu-language newspaper, *Ilanga lase Natal* (Sun of Natal) do we find evidence that Gandhi accompanied him. We know also that *Ilanga* was printed for a brief time on the hand-operated press at the Phoenix Settlement; that the Ohlange Institute came into being just three years before Gandhi's Phoenix; and that *Indian Opinion* was just months older than *Ilanga*. But tantalizing as these parallels are, they continue to run on in parallel without yielding any firm evidence of a crossing of paths by Gandhi and John Dube beyond their somewhat formal encounters at the white plantation owner's spacious residence and years later, on the occasion of the Gokhale visit.

There's another Gandhi who later became a regular visitor at the Ohlange Institute, stopping by now and then on his daily walks. That Gandhi also got to know Isaiah Shembe, called by his followers the Prophet. In 1911 the Prophet founded the Nazareth Church—the largest movement among Zulu Christians, with more than two million adherents today—at Ekuphakameni, which lies between Inanda and Phoenix. (The Nazareth Church was called independent, meaning it was unaffiliated to any white denomination.) Shembe had a bigger impact on South Africa, it can be argued, than the founder of the Phoenix Settlement ever had. The other Gandhi, the one who took the trouble to cultivate the acquaintance of these two significant African leaders, was Manilal, the mainstay of Phoenix after his father returned to India. When John Dube died in 1946 at seventy-five, the headline on his obituary in *Indian Opinion* read A GREAT ZULU DEAD. "To us at the Phoenix Settlement from the days of Mahatma Gandhi," the obituary said, "he has been a kindly neighbor."

Sparse as this record is, the names Gandhi, Dube, and Shembe are hallowed today as a kind of Inanda troika, if not trinity, by the publicists and popular historians responsible for weaving a teachable heritage for the new South Africa out of the disparate movements that struggled into existence under oppressive white rule. The fact that three leaders of such consequence emerged in rural Natal in the same decade, within an area of less than two square miles, is too resonant with possibilities to be overlooked. It has to be more than a coincidence. And so we find the man who became the new South Africa's third president elected by universal franchise, Jacob Zuma, celebrating "the solidarity between the Indians and Africans" that came into being in Inanda. "What is also remarkable about the history of the Indo-African community in this area is the link that existed between three great men: Gandhi, John Langal-ibalele Dube and the prophet Isaiah Shembe of the Nazareth Church." A tourist brochure urges visitors to follow the "Inanda Heritage Route" from Gandhi's settlement to the Dube school and finally to Shembe's church. ("Inanda where there is more history per square centimeter than anywhere in South Africa!" the brochure gushes, making no allusion to the sad, sometimes alarming state of what might otherwise be seen as a hard-pressed rural slum, except for the telltale caution that it not be visited without "a guide who knows the area well.")

On my last visit to Inanda, banners stamped with Dube's face were streaming from lampposts on the Kwa Mashu Highway, which cuts through the district, alternating with lampposts bearing Gandhi banners. Such sanctification of their imagined alliance rests on little more than the political convenience of the moment and a wispy oral tradition. Lulu Dube, the last surviving child of the Zulu patriarch, grew up with the notion that her father kept in touch with Gandhi. "In fact, they were friends, they were neighbors and their mission was one," she said in a chat on the veranda of Dube's house, which was declared a national monument at the time of the first democratic election, then left to rot (to the point that eighty-year-old Lulu, fearful of a roof collapse, had moved into a trailer nearby). Born sixteen years after Gandhi left the country, she's at best a link in a chain, not a witness. Ela Gandhi, keeper of her grandfather's flame in Durban as head of the Gandhi Trust, inherited a similar impression. She was raised at Phoenix but decades after her grandfather departed. She was only eight when he was killed. A member of the African National Congress, she's aware that, politically and historically, this is treacherous ground, so she chooses her words with care. "They were each concerned with dignity, particularly the dignity of their own people," she said of the two men on the banners.

What the real history, as opposed to heritage mythmaking, seems to disclose is a deliberate distancing of each other by Gandhi and John Dube, a recognition, on rare occasions, that they might have common interests but a determination to pursue them separately. If there could ever have been a possibility of their making common cause, it may well have been stalled for a generation by Gandhi's calculated reaction to a spasm of Zulu resistance in 1906—the year after they met—that was instantly characterized as a "rebellion" and brutally suppressed by Natal's white settlers and colonial authorities.

The immediate provocation for the rising was a new head tax on "natives," called a poll tax, and the severe penalties imposed on those who failed to pay up promptly. The broader provocation was a sense among Zulus—those still bound by tradition and those adapting to imported ways and faiths—that they were losing what was left of their land and autonomy. Numbers as much as race always had to be factored into these South African conflicts. Altogether the Zulus of Natal outnumbered the whites by about ten to one in that era (outnumbered the whites and Indians combined by about five to one). Gandhi's instant reflex, as at the time of the Anglo-Boer War seven years earlier, had been to side with English-speaking whites who identified themselves with British authority in their struggle with Afrikaans-speaking whites who resisted it. Here again he offered to raise a corps of stretcher bearers—another gesture of Indian fealty to the empire, which in his view was the ultimate guarantor of Indian rights, however circumscribed they proved in practice. It was a line of reasoning few Zulus were likely to appreciate.

The story isn't a simple one. Gandhi and Dube, each in his own way, were men of divided loyalties at the time of what came to be known as the Bhambatha Rebellion. Martial law was declared by trigger-happy colonial whites confronting Zulus armed mainly with assegais, or spears, before anything like a rebellion got under way. The spark was a face-off in early February between a group of protesting Zulu artisans from a small independent church and a police detachment sent to arrest its leaders. One of the policemen pulled a revolver, spears were thrown, and before the smoke cleared, two of the officers had been killed. The protesters were then rounded up and twelve of them sentenced to death. The British cabinet tried at first to have the executions postponed, but the condemned men were lined up at the edge of freshly dug graves and shot on April 2. A few days later, a chief named Bhambatha, who was being sought for refusal to pay the tax, took to the deepest, thorniest bush in the hills of Zululand with some 150 warriors. A thousand troops were sent in hot pursuit, homesteads were raked with machine-gun fire, shelled, and then burned. More warriors took to the hills. Against this background, under the leadership of the man who would one day be called a mahatma, the Indian community offered its support to the governing whites in the fight against the so-called rebels. The least temperate of his many justifications for this stand is worth quoting at length, for it's revealing on several levels:

> For the Indian community, going to the battlefield should be an easy matter; for, whether Muslim or Hindu, we are men with profound faith in God . . . We are not overcome by fear when hundreds of thousands die of famine or plague in our country. What is more, when we are told our duty, we continue to be indifferent, keep our houses dirty, lie hugging our hoarded wealth. Thus, we live a wretched life, acquiescing in a long, tormented process ending in death. Why then should we fear the death that may overtake us on the battlefield? We have much to learn from what the whites are doing in Natal. There is hardly any family from which someone has not gone to fight the Kaffir rebels.

Obviously, what we have here is a rant. Gandhi's irony is out of control; his inclination to scold undermines his desire to persuade. He has lost the thread of his argument about duty and citizenship. What comes across is revulsion, barely contained anger over the cultural inertia of his own community, its resistance to the social code he hopes to inculcate. If it offers nothing else, he seems to feel, the battlefield promises discipline.

The war posed a different set of conflicts for John Dube, the Congregational minister seeking to arm young Zulus not with spears but with the Protestant work ethic and basic skills that could win them a foothold in a trading economy. The rebels were, on the other hand, his people, and in the final stages of the conflict it was the chiefdom from which he descended that was attacked. The Christian in Dube, not to mention the pragmatist, could not endorse the rising, but the mercilessness of the

Sergeant Major Gandhi with stretcher bearers, 1906

repression shook his faith in the chances for racial peace. Cautiously, in the columns of his newspaper, he questioned the heavy-handedness of the whites. Soon he was summoned to appear before the governor and warned that the martial law regulations applied to him and his paper. Somewhat chastened, he later wrote that the grievances of the rebels were real but "at a time like this we should all refrain from discussing them."

What was said to be the severed head of Chief Bhambatha had been displayed and the rebellion all but crushed by June 22, when Gandhi finally left Durban for the struggle for which he'd been beating the drums in the columns of *Indian Opinion* for two months. This time the community had managed to restrain its enthusiasm for what he proposed as a patriotic duty and opportunity. Gandhi had the rank of sergeant major but a much smaller band of stretcher bearers under his nominal command than he'd had at the start of the Anglo-Boer War: nineteen as opposed to eleven hundred in the earlier conflict; of the nineteen, thirteen were former indentured laborers; this time just four of twenty, counting Gandhi himself, could be classed as "educated." In the next few weeks, in the sporadic final clashes of the conflict, the colonial troops were told to take no prisoners. What Gandhi and his men got to witness were the consequences of the mopping up, the worst part of the repression. At this stage of the conflict, there were few white wounded. Mostly the Indians ended up treating Zulu prisoners with terrible suppurating lacerations, not warriors with bullet wounds, but villagers who'd been flogged beyond submission.

Gandhi later wrote that the suffering Zulus, many of whom had been untreated for days, were grateful for the ministrations of the Indians, and maybe that was so. White medics wouldn't touch them. But back at Phoenix, roughly forty miles from these scenes, Gandhi's relatives and followers were seized by the fear that the Zulus in their neighborhood would rise against them in retaliation for the choice he'd made. He'd deposited Kasturba and two of his four sons there before leaving for the so-called front. "I do not remember other things but that atmosphere of fear is very vivid in my mind," Prabhudas Gandhi, a cousin who was a youngster at the time, would later write. "Today when I read about the Zulu people's rebellion, the anxious face of Kasturba comes before my eyes." No reprisals materialized, but signs of Zulu resentment over Gandhi's decision to side with the whites were not lacking. Africans would not forget, said an article reprinted in another Zulu newspaper, *Izwi Labantu*, "that Indians had volunteered to serve with the English savages in Natal who massacred thousands of Zulus in order to steal their land." That article was by an American. *Izwi* offered no comment of its own. But it did say: "The countrymen of Gandhi . . . are extremely self-centered, selfish and alien in feeling and outlook." In London, an exile Indian publication called *The Indian Sociologist*, which tacitly supported terrorist violence in the struggle for Indian freedom, found Gandhi's readiness to join up with the whites at the time of the Zulu uprising "disgusting."

As the Zulu paper implied, Gandhi's own outlook may have initially been alien and, in that sense, self-centered. But he was profoundly moved by the evidence of white brutality and Zulu suffering that he witnessed. Here again is Joseph Doke, his Baptist hagiographer: "Mr. Gandhi speaks with great reserve of this experience. What he saw he will never divulge . . . It was almost intolerable for him to be so closely in touch with this expedition. At times, he doubted whether his position was right." The biographer seems to hint unwittingly at taboos of untouchability that Sergeant Major Gandhi's small band had to overcome. "It was no trifle," he writes, for these Indians "to become voluntary nurses to men not yet emerged from the most degraded state." Eventually, Gandhi did divulge what he saw—in his *Autobiography*, composed two decades after the event, and in conversations in his last years with his inner circle. "My heart was with the Zulus," he then said. As late as 1943, during his final imprisonment, Sushila Nayar tells us, he was still recounting "the atrocities committed on the Zulus."

"What has Hitler done worse than that?" he asked Nayar, a physician who was attending his dying wife and himself. Gandhi, who'd tried writing to Hitler on the eve of world war in an attempt to soften his heart, never quite realized, or at least acknowledged, that the führer represented a destructive force beyond anything he'd experienced.

By his own account, the horror over what he'd seen in Natal and the soul-searching over his unpopular decision to side with the whites produced the major turning point of his life spiritually. Gandhi drew a straight line from his battlefield reflections to his vow of perfect celibacy—necessary, he felt, to clear the way for a life of service and voluntary poverty—and from that vow to the one he offered at the Empire Theater in Johannesburg on September 11, 1906. All this happened in little more than two months: marching off to support the whites, swearing off sex for the rest of his life, and following up that life-transforming promise to himself with his vow of nonviolent resistance to the Transvaal "Black Act," which then became his first exercise of the strategy later called satyagraha. Gandhi's testimony of cause and effect is irrefutable as far as it goes, but, as Erik Erikson noted, it doesn't carry us to anything approaching a full understanding. "These themes, were they to be clarified," the psychoanalyst wrote, "might more directly connect the two decisions of avoiding both sexual intercourse and killing. For it would seem that the experience of witnessing the outrages perpetrated on black bodies by white he-men aroused in Gandhi both a deeper identification with the maltreated, and a stronger aversion against all male sadism—including such sexual sadism as he had probably felt from childhood on to be part of all exploitation of women by men."

What was not aroused in Gandhi in the immediate aftermath of the Bhambatha Rebellion—not, at least, as far as we can discern—was a deepened curiosity about black Africans or sympathy for them that reached further than pity. Two years later, when he started writing about his first experience of jail, they were still "kaffirs," too uncivilized and dirty to be incarcerated with Indians, let alone to be seen as potential allies. In part, this may have been because of a change in context: leaving Natal and returning to his base in Johannesburg, having left his family behind at Phoenix, Gandhi also left behind whatever opportunities he might still have had to build bridges and, ultimately, deepen contacts with a Zulu leader like John Dube who spoke for a small Christianized, landowning black elite, sometimes called in the language of urban Zulus the *amarespectables*.

In part, it was also due to Gandhi's continued reluctance to let go of the idea that his so-called British Indians were naturally the allies of whites, just another kind of settler. If indentured Indian "coolies" were still seen, in his view, as too ill-bred, unlettered, and backward to be citizens, then what could he do about "kaffirs" except put them out of mind? Gandhi kept his distance and apparently found it easy to do so. A tacit alliance between blacks and Indians was the opposite of what he'd all along been seeking. If he thought about it at all, he would have known that such an alliance could only deepen white racial hysteria. He must have understood, too, that it would not have been an easy sell in his own community. Much later he knit together a rationalization out of such disparate reflections. Asked long after he returned to India by a visiting delegation of black Americans whether he'd ever made common cause with blacks during his time in South Africa, Gandhi replied, implying he had to resist the impulse: "No, I purposely did not invite them. It would have endangered their cause." A few years later, a quarter of a century after he returned home, he told a black South African, "Yours is a far bigger issue."

This Gandhi, the full-blown Mahatma of 1939, is doing some retrospective tidying up. In 1907, the Gandhi who actually resided in South Africa, the barrister and community leader, sent a letter to Sir Henry McCullum, the colonial governor who had imposed martial law on the restive Zulus the previous year. The letter is written a year after Gandhi's vows. The doctrine of nonviolent resistance has now been proclaimed, but "the many-sided Gandhi," as Naipaul called him, is arguing that the time had come to give Indians an opportunity for service in the colonial militia, a force whose most obvious function—as he had to know, given his experience the previous year—was to keep Zulu power in check.

"I venture to trust," the special pleader pleads, "that as the work done by the Corps had proved satisfactory, the Indian community will be found some scope in the Natal Militia. If such a thing is done, I think it will be mutually advantageous and it will bind the Indians, who are already a part of the body politic in Natal, closer to the Colony."

Gandhi knew in his heart that he'd taken the wrong side at the time of the rebellion, but he was still ready to claim a dividend from the white authorities for services rendered, just as he'd sought "the Queen's Chocolate" as a reward for his service with the "body snatchers" on a couple of the early battlefields of the Anglo-Boer War.

The strain on the Reverend John Dube, who imbibed a strategy of accommodation from his exemplar Booker T. Washington, was even more severe. In the aftermath of the rebellion, the Oberlin graduate and Congregational minister positioned himself as a defender and supporter of the Zulu king, Dinuzulu, who had been put on trial for high treason. He had spoken of the need to raise "the native people out of the slough of ignorance, idleness, poverty and superstition." In later years, at a ceremony honoring white missionaries, he sounded almost fawning in his expression of a gratitude that had to be genuine, for he was a missionary himself. "Who was it," he asked his white audience, "who taught us the benefits and decency of wearing clothes? Who was it who taught us that every disease is not caused by witchcraft . . . that a message can be transmitted by writing on a piece of paper?" But now in the aftermath of the 1906 conflict, he showed that he was prepared to exempt some tribal traditions from such broadsides. Dube remained close to the Zulu royal house and thus immersed in ethnic politics for the rest of his life. He also spoke for a broader nationalism as the first leader of the movement that became the African National Congress. But the straddle between these two kinds of politics—urban-based mass politics and aristocratic tribal politics—became increasingly difficult. In 1917, the first Congress president was eased out. The accommodationist in him had expressed a willingness to accept the principle of racial separation that the white government was pushing in exchange for an expansion of the so-called native reserves. To secure a bigger Zululand, he was prepared to bow reluctantly to a law that reserved most of Natal for whites. This was too much for younger Africans rising in the movement.

The law was the Natives Land Act, passed in 1913 by the white parliament, just three years after white hegemony had been formally built into the new Union of South Africa. A huge, blatant land grab, the law made it illegal for blacks to own land in 92 percent of the entire country. Dube was eloquent in denouncing it. So, strikingly, was Gandhi, in what was really his first serious engagement with any measure weighing on Africans. "Every other question, not excluding the Indian question, pales into insignificance before the great Native question," he now wrote in *Indian Opinion*. "This land is theirs by birth and this Act of confiscation—for such it is—is likely to give rise to serious consequences unless the Government take care." The date was August 30, 1913. Gandhi was already in his last year in the country when he wrote those words. Not only that, he was already laying the strategy for his last, most radical campaign there, his first on behalf of indentured laborers. Suddenly, it seems, he is less parochial, able for the moment, at least on paper, to take something approaching a national view.

It's tempting to try to imagine what the two neighbors, each a religiously inclined political leader—a Congregationalist Zulu and a neo-Christian Hindu—might have had to say to each other had they met to exchange views at this time. It's not impossible that there was such an encounter, but, more likely, each was aware at a distance of what the other was saying and doing. *Indian Opinion* reprinted a portion of an appeal John Dube addressed to the British public. "You must know that every one of us was born in this land, and we have no other," he said. "You must know that for untold generations this land was solely ours—long before your father had put a foot on our shores." That could have moved Gandhi.

For his part, John Dube professed to have been struck by the example of nonviolent resistance that Gandhi's followers were about to furnish. Decades later a memoir appeared in the Gujarati language describing an encounter between Dube and a British cleric in which the African described an instance of nonviolent resistance that he said he'd witnessed himself at Phoenix in late 1913:

> About five hundred Indians were sitting together in a group. They had come there after going on a strike in their factory. They were surrounded from all sides by white managers, their staff and white police . . . Whiplashes began to descend on the backs of the Indians sitting there, in quick rapidity, without stop. The whites beat them with lathis and said, "Get up, do your work. Will you do your duty or not?" But nobody rose. They sat, quite motionless . . . When whips and lathis failed, gun butts came to be used.

The Gujarati was translated into Hindi, the Hindi back into English. It would be a miracle if those were Dube's exact words, but some such conversation may have occurred. Dube may even have expressed admiration for the fortitude of the Indians who followed Gandhi, though probably not in the words attributed to him in this Gujarati reminiscence, which has the Zulu expressing wonder over their "divine power" and "Himalayan firmness." Or all this may be little more than rosy self-congratulation on the part of an Indian witness with a hazy memory.

What Dube is known to have said is less admiring. While Zulus fought among themselves, he observed in 1912, "people like Indians have come into our land and lorded it over us, as though we who belong to the country were mere nonentities." Heather Hughes, a Dube biographer, writes of "his pronounced anti-Indianism." She quotes a Dube article headlined "The Indian Invasion" that ran in *Ilanga:* "We know from sad experience how beneath our very eyes, our children's bread is taken by these Asiatics."

Perhaps it is just as well that, as far as we can tell, the two neighbors never had that searching conversation. Even if there was a moment after the new white regime imposed the Natives Land Act when they appear to have been more or less aligned, they were moving in different directions. For more than six years after the 1906 Zulu rising, Gandhi had devoted most of his time and energy to the Transvaal. At the start of 1913, he abruptly shifted back to Natal. Within months, he was laying plans for a new satyagraha campaign, with the repeal of a three-pound head tax ex-indentured Indians were required to pay annually if they wanted to stay on in the country as one of its main demands.

Dube, meanwhile, was consumed by the land issue, by the dispossession of his people. Later a Zulu newspaper would portray the Reverend John Dube sitting in his Chevrolet, a mere onlooker, as the police marched a group of black Communist organizers to jail in Durban. If Gandhi had stayed on in South Africa, he might have been similarly sidelined. As leaders of the African National Congress made their first tentative international contacts, they came into touch with Jawaharlal Nehru and other leaders of the Indian independence movement that had grown up in Gandhi's shadow. In 1927, Nehru and Josiah Gumede, then ANC president, twice crossed paths—at an anti-imperialism conference in Brussels and in Moscow at the tenth-anniversary celebration of the Bolshevik Revolution. Nehru and his circle were quick to take the view, from afar, that Indians in South Africa should stand together with blacks there. Gandhi himself held out. "However much one may sympathize with the Bantus," he wrote as late as 1939, "Indians cannot make common cause with them." Two years later, in 1941, an antithetical political message was personally delivered in Durban by the young Indira Nehru—later to be known by her married name, Gandhi—who stopped off in South Africa on her way home from Oxford, having been forced by the outbreak of war to take the Cape route. "Indians and Africans must act together," she said. "Common oppression must be met with the united and organized power of all the exploited people." That night, according to one reminiscence, Gandhi's son Manilal endorsed "a united front of all non-Europeans" for the first time in his life.

Manilal's father by this time was more than a quarter of a century removed from South Africa. Perhaps, reflecting back over all the years and miles he'd traveled since his jail experiences there in the aftermath of the Bhambatha Rebellion, he sensed there were grounds for conflict between Indians and Africans in Natal. A year after Gandhi's death, in January 1949, communal rioting, sometimes characterized as a Zulu "pogrom" against Indians, engulfed Durban. The violence had been sparked by a scuffle with a young Zulu in an Indian shop. By the time it burned out, 142 persons had been listed as killed—the majority, as a result of police fire, African migrant laborers—and more than 1,700 injured. The violence exposed the long-standing African resentment of the relatively privileged status of Indians in the racial hierarchy, of Indian shopkeepers in particular. A hangover of fear and mutual suspicion lingered for years.

Yet three years later Indian and African activists in South Africa finally succeeded in coming together politically to make common cause against apartheid, a program for comprehensive racial separation and white dominance that neither Dube nor Gandhi lived to see. In 1952, the African National Congress and the South African Indian Congress agreed on what was called the Defiance Campaign Against Unjust Laws.

The nonviolent campaign could be seen as self-consciously Gandhian in tactics and strategy. But few African leaders were ready to embrace him as their patron saint. From the other side of the Indian Ocean, shortly before his assassination, the Mahatma had finally given his highly qualified support to the idea of Indians throwing in their lot with Africans. "The inclusion of all the races while logically correct," he said, "is fraught with grave danger if the struggle is not kept at the highest level." Between the lines, he seems to be expressing his doubts that blacks would hew to nonviolent principles. For his part, the young Nelson Mandela had to overcome his own doubts about an alliance with Indians. "Many of our grassroots African supporters saw Indians as exploiters of black labor in their role as shopkeepers and merchants," he later said.

Manilal Gandhi, the faithful second son, briefly lent his name to the Defiance Campaign, but he was mostly out of step. Following his father's example, he endured fasts of increasing duration against apartheid; in his case, however, their impact was not great. Repeatedly, he courted arrest by going to the white section of the library or post office in Durban, but the police had instructions to merely take down his name. Finally, at the end of the year, in the company of other whites and Indians, he managed to get arrested by entering a black "location" in the Transvaal town of Germiston. He was then sentenced to fifty days in jail for the crimes of "meeting with Africans" and "incitement to break laws." But Manilal had no organized following of his own and remained an independent operator, standing "outside the organized struggle," his granddaughter and biographer, Uma Dhupelia-Mesthrie, acknowledges. The movement had become more radical than Manilal, who was suspicious of the influence of Communists, would ever be. And its commitment to nonviolence was merely tactical. At one meeting, as Manilal, seeking to be "worthy of Bapu and serve as he served," sermonized at length on the ethical discipline of satyagraha, the young Nelson Mandela rattled his teacup to signal his impatience.

The first Gandhi in South Africa never had to face the kind of retaliation the Afrikaner nationalist regime now rolled out in the form of repressive new security laws, allowing arbitrary arrest, preventive detention at the hands of an emboldened security police, and bannings, not only of organizations, but of individuals (making it illegal for their words to appear in print or for them to meet more than one person at a time); eventually, as the struggle intensified, the white regime would resort to torture, "disappearances," bombings, and assassination. The colonial regime in India had been repressive, regularly jailing Gandhi and his followers, but it had never imagined it could remove them permanently from the scene, that it could purge India of the Indian national movement. The Afrikaner regime had exactly that ambition when it came to the sponsors of the Defiance Campaign. Long before the movement was driven underground, younger leaders like Mandela and Oliver Tambo reappraised their tactical embrace of the Gandhian code of nonviolence.

But satyagraha did get its trial in a national cause, the cause of nonracial justice. For a brief time, it was no longer parochially Indian in its appeal. And a much older, more mellow Mandela himself would later claim, once he'd emerged from his long imprisonment and stepped into the role of father of the nation, that the model for the mass action campaigns he'd witnessed in his youth had been the nonviolent campaign the original Gandhi led in 1913. "The principle was not so important that the strategy should be used even when it was self-defeating," Mandela said then, explaining how he'd deployed his own interpretation of

Gandhi against Gandhi's son. "I called for nonviolent protest for as long as it was effective." As an interpreter of Gandhian doctrines, Mandela was decidedly less rigorous about means and ends than their originator. Still, no one was better qualified to certify that Gandhi was indeed a founding father in the country he adopted temporarily, as well as in his own.

Doke's Gandhi, 1908

4

UPPER HOUSE

THE REVEREND DOKE, the first of Gandhi's many hagiographers, took a snapshot of the pensive barrister as he recuperated in 1908 from his beating at the hands of the Pathans. His subject bears little resemblance to the Gandhi the world would come to know. Lean and slouching in casual Western clothes, he gazes past the lens with an expression that's inward and contemplative, not kindly or twinkling in the manner of the loincloth-clad public man who'd evoke a mass following in India within little more than a decade. Yet he'd already laid out essential components of his thought and leadership strategy. Ecumenical and open-minded in his approach to religion and relations between sects of all description, loyal by his own lights to the British Empire and to values embedded in the British legal system, yet aggressive in his resistance to unjust colonial laws that system not infrequently upheld, the Johannesburg Gandhi now claimed the right to follow his conscience—what he would variously identify as his "inner voice" or, simply, "truth"—in every sphere of life. Yet he was still Gandhiji or Gandhibhai—the suffixes indicating respect for an elder or leader and fraternal feeling for a relative or friend—and not yet canonized as a mahatma, still engaged in self-creation, finding his way to a grounded sense of himself and his mission. In his own mind, we may infer, self and mission both felt incomplete as he closed in on his late thirties.

Celibacy as a spiritual discipline was now a preoccupation of his daily life but not, as yet, a theme of his public discourse; his interviews with his Baptist Boswell never, or so it appears from Doke's book, got around to the delicate subject of brahmacharya. Probably the politician in him understood that this was the least appealing side of his evolving doctrine.

He'd experienced sexual passion but could never condone it or, having made his choice, simply drop the subject. "Marriage is not only not a necessity but positively a hindrance to public and humanitarian work," he'd later write. Those, like himself and Kasturba, who'd fallen into the coils of matrimony could save themselves by living together chastely as brother and sister. "No man or woman living the physical or animal life can possibly understand the spiritual or ethical." Gandhi doted on children but regarded childbirth as prima facie evidence of a moral lapse. With distressing regularity, he'd nag his daughters-in-law and others close to him to mend their ways and not do it again.

His vegetarianism was still in his early Johannesburg years a matter of moral preference, hygiene, and heritage, but apart from eschewing meat and grinding his own grain, he hadn't yet placed severe strictures on his diet, hadn't yet arrived at the conviction that the curbing of one appetite was dependent on the curbing of another, that sexual abstinence and diet were closely linked. He still drank milk, still enjoyed spicy food in convivial settings. Such indulgences would soon be brought to an abrupt end. The vegetarian would try for a time to become a fruitarian, having concluded that milk, other dairy products, and most spices have aphrodisiac qualities; he'd also give up salt, cooked food, and seconds, eventually measuring his intake in ounces and thoroughly chewing each spare mouthful of carefully blended and pounded mush—lemons, honey, and almonds were usually part of the mix along with grains and leaves—in order to derive as much nourishment from as little food as possible. Mastication would thus become one of his many lesser disciplines and causes.

"Meagerness," he'd later write, was the ethical standard by which diet should be measured, according to "God's economy" and Gandhi's own reading of a Hindu scripture, the Bhagavad Gita. That standard enjoined a perpetual "partial fast," which would require "a grim fight against the inherited and acquired habit of eating for pleasure." Grim was the word for it. A full meal, Gandhi would write, was "a crime against God and man . . . because the full-mealers deprive their neighbors of their portion." There you have the Gandhi of 1933, not 1906. The rule-giving ashram dweller who'd finally decide that delicious food was an invitation to gluttony, who'd find wry satisfaction in being portrayed as a faddist and crank, who'd bring his conviction that less is more to his solitary repasts, had yet to make his entrance. He may have felt driven to distance himself from his wife and sons, but he was still a social being in the early stage of his Johannesburg years, when he is reported to have gone on picnics and ridden a bicycle.

The inner change is harder to trace with any exactitude in the six and a half formative years he spent in Johannesburg after witnessing the brutal reprisals against Zulus in Natal—a period that stretches from August 1906 to January 1913—but it's at least as significant as the well-documented evolution of the public man. For five of those years he lived in the Transvaal without family. Gandhi insists in his *Autobiography* that he'd intended from the first to settle at Phoenix himself, give up his law practice, and support himself and the settlement through manual labor. But his emotional need for distance, for not being hemmed in by customary obligations, seems as obvious and important in anchoring him in Johannesburg as the ongoing satyagraha campaign against the Transvaal's racial legislation. Gandhi treated the Transvaal as the main arena because that's where the campaign against discriminatory legislation had been launched. If satyagraha was his most important "experiment with truth," the Transvaal was now the favored workstation in his laboratory. His obligations to the local community were heavy; he was locked into a test of will with the white provincial government, personified by Jan Christian Smuts, the onetime Boer general, now provincial minister of the interior.

That's all obvious. But the Transvaal was also where he needed or wanted to be for his own purposes. He could have made a case for basing himself in Natal, which by then was clearly the center of Indian life in South Africa. Its Indian community outnumbered the Transvaal's by about ten to one (110,000 to 11,000 by 1908). He had established the Phoenix Settlement there. It was where *Indian Opinion* was edited and printed. Also, Natal was where nearly all Indians under the indenture system still labored, in conditions he'd described as "semi-slavery." In fact, the number of Indians still under indenture in Natal in that period was more than three times the Transvaal's total Indian population. And in those same years—before racial issues were nationalized with the creation in 1910 of the Union of South Africa—the legislative assembly in English-speaking Natal could hardly be said to lag in its drive to stiffen existing anti-Indian statutes and pass new ones.

With Gandhi mostly absent and looking the other way, the white political class of Natal proved itself to be at least as inventive in coming up with new racial measures and as relentless as the Afrikaans-speaking Transvaalers. The dueling white supremacists may have fought on opposing sides in the recently concluded Anglo-Boer War, but there was no choosing between them when it came to their mutual hostility to the idea of equal citizenship for the Indian minority. Colonial Natal was a place where the leading newspaper, *The Natal Mercury*, was happy to publish a letter signed with the nom de plume "Anti-Coolie." The letter said it was a disgrace that Indian shops were allowed to do business in the center of Durban. (The *Mercury* continues to publish in post-apartheid South Africa. Today in its lobby, a larger-than-life-size portrait of Gandhi, matching an equally large portrait of Mandela, peers down on journalists and their visitors, a guardian angel blessing their endeavors.)

The Natal of Gandhi's day had a pressing economic need for indentured Indian labor; so argued the plantation and mine owners whose mouthpiece the *Mercury* was. But it wasn't ready to be outdone when it came to restrictions on free Indian immigration. Sir Henry McCallum, the governor to whom Gandhi had appealed for militia places for Indians in recognition of their service at the time of the Zulu rising, saw "no reason why we should be swamped by *black matter* in the wrong place," just because of the demand for field labor. So a new immigration act, passed as early as 1903, in the immediate aftermath of the Anglo-Boer War, made it easy to bar any immigrant who couldn't fill out an application in a European language to the loosely defined satisfaction of officials. Year after year, Indians were turned back on this basis by the thousands. Next came a municipal corporations act designed to eliminate Indian voting rights at the local level—the final disenfranchising step backward on what had been, fourteen years earlier, Gandhi's first South African issue; and just as regularly legal screws were tightened to restrict licenses for Indian shopkeepers. Any indentured laborers or former indentured laborers—or their descendants in perpetuity—were classed for purposes of these acts as belonging to "uncivilized races." In order to keep them that way, public funds were cut off for Indian secondary schools. Finally, in 1908, came a bill designed to make it impossible for any "Asiatics" to hold trading licenses in Natal after 1918, even those whose families by then would have been trading in the province for two generations.

Yet Gandhi remained stuck in the Transvaal, following his own path. In 1907 he came to Durban three times to address monthly meetings of the Natal Indian Congress. Each time he harangued his listeners on the need to support the campaign in the Transvaal. Only occasionally did he comment in his paper, usually from afar, on developments in Natal. By

1909, as the final diplomatic and parliamentary steps were being taken to form the new Union under an all-white Parliament—making it, in essence, a color-coded democracy for the white minority only—the Indian communities of the Transvaal and Natal sent parallel delegations to London to lobby on their parochial issues rather than the national one. Gandhi, whose influence in Natal was by then conspicuously waning, headed the Transvaal team.

Yes, he was preoccupied with the satyagraha campaign. But he was also working out a new sense of family in these years. "I fail to understand what you mean by the word 'family,' " he'd written in 1907 to his elder brother Laxmidas not quite a year after he'd deposited his wife and sons at Phoenix. Laxmidas had complained that he was failing to meet his family obligations on two continents. "If I could say so without arrogance," he now replied, "I would say that my family now comprises all living beings."

He'd been sending money to his brother for more than a decade to pay off various debts and fulfill his role as the extended family's primary earner, which he undertook when he sailed to Britain for legal training. Laxmidas had a continuing claim on his income, Gandhi now acknowledged. But there was a catch—he no longer viewed himself as having a personal income. He didn't deny that his law practice still raked in money, only that he put it to his own use. "I use all the money that God gives me for the public good," he explained breezily. Basically the "public good" in this context meant covering the losses of the weekly *Indian Opinion* and helping to keep the Phoenix Settlement afloat. (It would have been "both a loss and a disgrace," Gandhi later wrote, if the paper had been allowed to die. "So I kept pouring out all my money until ultimately I was practically sinking all my savings in it.") In effect, Gandhi was presenting a seemingly secular—some would say heretical—take on the traditional Hindu concept of the sannyasi, the religious wanderer who turns his back on the joys, distractions, and obligations of family life in order to devote himself wholly to spiritual discipline in the form of meditation and prayer. Self-invented, one of a kind, he henceforth presents himself as the sannyasi as social worker.

His own visits to the Phoenix Settlement in these years proved to be irregular and usually brief, so much so that they took on the air of royal visitations or command inspections. "One day news came that Gandhiji would be visiting Phoenix," wrote Prabhudas Gandhi, a nephew's son who grew up there. "The settlement became alive with excitement. The settlers began to tidy the press as well as their homes." Prabhudas cannot

Johannesburg attorney,
with Thambi Naidoo

remember "if Gandhiji ever stayed longer than a fortnight or a month." Sometimes he "did not come for months," and then it might be only for a matter of days. "I could stay there only for brief periods," Gandhi himself acknowledges. Considering that he'd kept Johannesburg as his base of operations, it's not altogether surprising that he didn't drop in more often, or that his erstwhile Durban followers didn't see more of him. The two centers, now an hour's flight distant from each other, were twenty-four hours apart by rail in that era; he'd leave Joburg one evening, arrive in Durban the next. We don't know exactly how often he made the trip, but it's plain he didn't make it as often as he might have. It's a pattern that would recur in Gandhi's life. Only sometimes would his travels be geared to the obvious needs of the movements that viewed him as their leader; frequently his whereabouts—in an ashram, on tour for a cause—would be dictated by a more personal agenda; his followers would understand that he was engaged with something else, or sense that he'd withdrawn. That sense began to spread among the Indians of Natal, especially among the Muslim merchant class whose members had been his earliest clients and supporters. They didn't appreciate his remoteness, or understand his readiness to compromise with Smuts on the "Black Act" after preaching that it was a "do or die" issue. At his first meeting in Durban in 1908, another Pathan rushed the platform brandishing a club. Someone doused the lights, saving Gandhi from yet another beating.

Meanwhile, he was assembling a surrogate family in Johannesburg, where his following remained avid, especially among Tamils, originally from South India, whose difficult Dravidian language he'd periodically set himself to learning when immobilized in prison or on an ocean voyage. The most stalwart of the Johannesburg Tamils was a builder and trader named Thambi Naidoo who'd come to South Africa from the Indian Ocean island of Mauritius, where his parents had been indentured. Naidoo was uneducated but spoke five languages (English, three South Indian languages, and the Hindustani of North India). Physically strong and quick-tempered, he'd be arrested fourteen times and serve ten jail sentences between 1907 and 1913 in the Transvaal satyagraha campaigns. According to Prema Naidoo, a grandson who became an elected city councillor in Johannesburg after the end of white rule nearly nine decades later, this patriarchal resister never fully recovered from blows to the head he took trying to protect Gandhi from the Pathans at the time of their 1908 attack, suffering dizzy spells for the rest of his life. "If Thambi Naidoo had not been rash and if he had been free from anger," Gandhi later wrote, "this brave man could easily have assumed the leadership of the community in the Transvaal."

But Gandhi's surrogate kin in this Johannesburg period didn't turn out to be Tamils. They were Westerners, mostly nonobservant Jews, who like Gandhi had dipped into the murky waters of Theosophy. "Mine would be considered an essentially heterogeneous family," he wrote in his *Autobiography*, referring to this period, "where people of all kinds and temperaments were freely admitted. When we think of it, the distinction between heterogeneous and homogeneous is discovered to be merely imaginary. We are all one family." This was the ultimate rejection of caste, but Gandhi didn't put it in those terms. By strictest Hindu standards, the Westerners in his circle, some of whom now joined his household, were untouchable; all black and white South Africans were.

In 1904, Gandhi had met Henry Polak, a young copy editor on *The Critic*, the newspaper, at Ada Bissicks's vegetarian teahouse on Rissik Street, across from Gandhi's law office. Polak, just turned twenty-one then and in his first year in South Africa, had been struck by a letter Gandhi had written to a paper on the wretched sanitary conditions in an Indian area where there had been an outbreak of plague. Their conversation ranged widely, and soon they discovered a mutual reverence for Tolstoy and shared enthusiasm for German nature cures involving mud packs. Months later Polak made John Ruskin another such enthusiasm, lending Gandhi a copy of the tract *Unto This Last*, which in one overnight reading on a train instantly inspired the idea of the Phoenix

Settlement. It's a eureka moment that says more about Gandhi and his activist reflexes than it does about Ruskin, who'd inveighed against the skewed values of industrial society, with its focus on capital formation and undervaluing of physical labor, but hadn't imagined the founding of idealistic rural communes as a response. Gandhi, preoccupied with the costs of running *Indian Opinion* from Durban, instantly took that leap. Giving Ruskin's ideal of sturdy husbandry a Tolstoyan twist, he found an answer to his immediate practical problem: he could save his paper by moving it to a self-sustaining rural settlement. In that instant the patriarch chose to be father to a whole community—later it would be a nation—so he gathered an extended family of followers, Westerners as well as Indians, nephews and cousins, and, finally, his own wife and sons. So when he wrote to his brother two years later about his redefinition of "family," it was a fait accompli. Workers on the farm were expected to double as pressmen and simultaneously feed themselves. Hand labor, thereafter, would be the reflexive Gandhian answer to various problems, from colonial exploitation to rural underemployment and poverty. He would elevate it into a moral imperative.

Within a year of first meeting Gandhi, Henry Polak was living with the barrister's family in a spacious rented house, graced by a deep upstairs veranda, in a then-upscale white Johannesburg neighborhood called Troyeville, where some neighbors objected to the proximity of an Indian family, possibly the only one within a couple of miles. Most Indians were relegated by law to a "location"—prefiguring the segregated townships and "group areas" of the apartheid era—at the other end of town. It's noteworthy that the barrister gave no thought to moving in there, preferring to set himself up among whites, in a house suitable by their standards to his professional standing and income. Gandhi's house still stands in what's now a racially mixed, slightly rundown Troyeville, half a block down Albermarle Street from another house that mistakenly bears a plaque saying it's the one where Gandhi lived. Polak was married there to an English non-Jew, Millie Downs, the day she arrived in South Africa at the end of 1905, with Gandhi as best man. "His voice was soft, rather musical, and almost boyishly fresh," Millie told a BBC interviewer much later, recalling her first impressions of the Johannesburg Gandhi, who instantly welcomed her to his extended family. Months later Henry was dispatched to edit *Indian Opinion*, until Millie, whom he'd met at an Ethical Society meeting in London, decided she'd had enough of Phoenix and the dignity of rural labor. So the tables were turned later in 1906, when Gandhi, having moved out of Troyeville, returned without family to Joburg from the front of the so-called war with the Zulus and moved in with the Polaks, in a tiny house in a neighborhood called Belleville West. Later they shifted to an area called Highland, taking their revered boarder with them. Kasturba commented sourly from her place of exile in Natal that Gandhi treated Polak as his "eldest son." In fact, he signed his letters to Polak "Bhai," meaning brother.

Ba was obviously alluding to the sense of neglect their actual eldest, Harilal, was already feeling, had probably always felt, given that he'd gotten to live with his father less than two of his first eight years. When Harilal was married in Gujarat in 1906, shortly before his eighteenth birthday, a disapproving Gandhi had written from South Africa: "I have ceased to think of him as a son." Several years later when a wealthy supporter made funds available so one of his sons could study in Britain as he had himself, Gandhi passed over Harilal, considered sending Manilal, his next born, but finally sent a nephew instead. He was giving up on Western ways and professions and wanted his sons to follow him in his transformation, gathering what education they could in Gujarati, rather than English, while doing manual labor at Phoenix and dedicating their lives to satyagraha and service. In a will drafted in 1909, he said it was his wish that his sons "should devote their lifetime" to Phoenix or similar projects. For a while Harilal bent every effort to win his remote, usually absent father's approbation by proving himself the perfect satyagrahi; in the Transvaal campaign he went to jail six times, for a total of nineteen months in a twenty-seven-month period. Then, making a break, he set off on his own in 1911 for India, where, years later, the pathos of his intermittent rebellion culminated in alcoholic free fall and a short-lived conversion to Islam. Father and son had a meeting before he left Johannesburg. "He feels that I have always kept all the four boys very much suppressed . . . always put them and Ba last," Gandhi wrote, offering a dispassionate summary of his son's bitter complaint.

Clearly, he'd not put them first. Not putting them first was by then a matter of duty for Gandhi, even creed, as his 1906 letter to Laxmidas had shown. In fact, Gandhi had moved in with the Polaks just as Harilal arrived in Johannesburg without his new bride to join his father's struggle. There was no room for Harilal in their little household, and he was soon sent down to Phoenix. When the arrival of a baby made quarters at the Polak residence too cramped for Gandhi's modest needs, he moved in with the architect Hermann Kallenbach in what became, it can reasonably be said, the most intimate, also ambiguous, relationship of his lifetime.

"They were a couple," Tridip Suhrud, a Gandhi scholar, said when I met him in the Gujarati capital of Gandhinagar. That's a succinct way of summing up the obvious—Kallenbach later remarked that they'd lived together "almost in the same bed"—but what kind of couple were they? Gandhi early on made a point of destroying what he called Kallenbach's "logical and charming love notes" to him, in the belief that he was honoring his friend's wish that they be seen by no other eyes. But the architect saved all of Gandhi's, and his descendants, decades after his death and Gandhi's, put them up for auction. Only then were the letters acquired by the National Archives of India and, finally, published. It was too late for the psychoanalyst Erik Erikson to take them into account, and most recent Gandhi studies tend to deal with them warily, if at all. One respected Gandhi scholar characterized the relationship as "clearly homoerotic" rather than homosexual, intending through that choice of words to describe a strong mutual attraction, nothing more. The conclusions passed on by word of mouth in South Africa's small Indian community were sometimes less nuanced. It was no secret then, or later, that Gandhi, leaving his wife behind, had gone to live with a man.

In an age when the concept of Platonic love gains little credence, selectively chosen details of the relationship and quotations from letters can easily be arranged to suggest a conclusion. Kallenbach, who was raised and educated in East Prussia, was a lifetime bachelor, gymnast, and bodybuilder, "having received physical training at the hands of Sandow," as Gandhi himself later boasted. This was an allusion to Eugen Sandow, a strongman still celebrated as "the father of modern bodybuilding," who turns out to have been a contemporary of Kallenbach's in what was then called Königsberg (and is now the city of Kaliningrad in a Russian enclave on the Baltic fastened to Poland). Gandhi was preoccupied throughout his life with physiology, especially as it pertained to appetites, but never, it hardly needs saying, with bodybuilding. His taut torso—he'd weigh in later at 106 to 118 pounds, depending on how recently he'd fasted, on a frame of not quite five feet seven inches in height—would eventually become better known than Sandow's. But in his heyday, it was the overdeveloped strongman who was the international pinup, the precursor of Charles Atlas and Arnold Schwarzenegger (becoming enough of a household name to pop several times into Leopold Bloom's mind in Joyce's *Ulysses*).

The son of a timber merchant, Kallenbach had served a year in the German army and then trained as an architect in Stuttgart before arriving in Johannesburg in 1895 at the age of twenty-four. He'd thus been in South Africa for nearly a decade when Sandow, who'd been discovered and turned into an international star by Flo Ziegfeld, brought his act, a form of male striptease, to Johannesburg in 1904. It's hard to imagine Kallenbach, who'd yet to meet Gandhi, bypassing the chance to become reacquainted with his fellow Königsberger.

If not infatuated, Gandhi was clearly drawn to the architect. In a letter from London in 1909, he writes: "Your portrait (the only one) stands on my mantelpiece in the bedroom. The mantelpiece is opposite to the bed." Cotton wool and Vaseline, he then says, "are a constant reminder." The point, he goes on, "is to show to you and me how completely you have taken possession of my body. This is slavery with a vengeance." What are we to make of the word "possession" or the reference to petroleum jelly, then as now a salve with many commonplace uses? The most plausible guesses are that the Vaseline in the London hotel room may have to do with enemas, to which he regularly resorted, or may in some other way foreshadow the geriatric Gandhi's enthusiasm for massage, which would become a widely known part of the daily routine in his Indian ashrams, arousing gossip that has never quite died down, once it became clear that he mostly relied on the women in his entourage for its administration.

Two years later, the lawyer Gandhi drafts a mock-serious agreement for his friend to sign, using the teasing pet names and epistolary salutations that Gandhi, easily the wittier and more humorous of the two, almost certainly coined. Kallenbach, two years the younger, has come to be addressed as "Lower House" in the parliamentary sense (a jocular allusion, it seems, to his role as the source of appropriations). Gandhi is "Upper House" (and therefore gets to vote down excessive spending). Lower House can pronounce on matters of physical fitness and everything that's literally down-to-earth on the communal settlement, known as Tolstoy Farm, they'd by then established. Upper House gets to think deep thoughts, strategize, and direct the moral development of his other half in this touching bicameral relationship. In the agreement dated July 29, 1911, on the eve of a trip Kallenbach is about to make to Europe, Upper House makes Lower House promise "not to contract any marriage tie during his absence" nor "look lustfully upon any woman." The two Houses then mutually pledge "more love, and yet more love . . . such love as they hope the world has not yet seen." By then, except for time subtracted by Gandhi's jail terms in 1908 and trip to London in 1909, the two had been together more than three years.

Remember, we have only Gandhi's letters (invariably starting, "Dear Lower House"). So it's Gandhi who provides the playful undertone that might easily be ascribed to a lover, especially if we ignore what else his letters contain and their broader context. Interpretation can go two ways here. We can indulge in speculation, or look more closely at what the two men actually say about their mutual efforts to repress sexual urges in this period.

A 1908 letter from Kallenbach to his brother Simon in Germany, shortly after Gandhi moved in with him, shows that he'd been under his lodger's influence for some time. "For the last two years I have given up meat eating; for the last year I also did not touch fish any more," he writes, "and for the last 18 months, I have given up my sex life . . . I have changed my daily life in order to simplify it." Later it is Kallenbach who points out to Gandhi the insidious tendency milk has to enhance arousal. Gandhi, ever the extremist in dietary experiments, extends the prohibition to chocolates. "I see death in chocolates," he lectures Polak, who isn't in this period involved in the food trials that Kallenbach readily undergoes. Few foods are so "heating," meaning likely to stimulate forbidden appetites. He sends Kallenbach a verse on nonattachment to "bodily pleasures." We have bodies, according to this message, in order to learn "self control."

The Jewish architect from Kaliningrad on the Baltic and the Bania lawyer from Porbandar on the Arabian Sea first lived together in Orchards, one of Johannesburg's older northern suburbs, in a house called the Kraal, a Dutch word originally for homestead, now broadly applied to rural African enclosures. The inspiration for the design was African as well. Kallenbach took the rondavel—a round thatched structure with thick clay walls, sometimes whitewashed—as his prototype for 15 Pine Street, where he cohabited with Gandhi for a year and a half; it still stands (and was recently purchased by a French company with plans to turn it into a tourist attraction, yet another Gandhi museum). It's actually two rondavels, cleverly joined and set back behind a high fence with a sign, omnipresent these days on the walls and fences of the northern suburbs, warning intruders of an "armed response." Obviously, the warning isn't Gandhian. When he discovered that Kallenbach had appointed himself bodyguard and started packing a revolver after the Pathan attack, Gandhi insisted he get rid of it.

The couple then moved to an area called Linksfield, where Kallenbach was building a bigger house called Mountain View, over which Gandhi had predictable misgivings. One of his self-imposed missions in this period was to drill his housemate in the discipline of self-denial. He nagged him to rid himself of a new car and live up to the vow of poverty both had taken by slashing his personal spending. "My hope is that we will not this time have aristocratic simplicity but simple simplicity," he writes before work on the new house has actually begun. For a time in 1910, they live on the building site in a tent. What he really wants, it emerges, is for Kallenbach to shut down his architecture practice—just as he at this point is preparing to give up the law—and return with him to a shared life of service at Phoenix. "It appears," Gandhi writes hopefully in a laudatory profile of his companion in *Indian Opinion*, "that Mr. Kallenbach will gradually give up his work as architect and live in complete poverty."

Kallenbach professes to be tempted, but he's not yet sold. His office remains open and active. At one point he competes simultaneously for commissions on a new synagogue, a Christian Science church, and a Greek Orthodox one. Tolstoy Farm, all eleven hundred acres of it, which he purchased, is the big spender's way of proving he's serious about voluntary poverty. Both he and Gandhi write to the dying Tolstoy to tell him of their plans. The farm meets an immediate need confronting Gandhi. He now has a place to house the families of passive resisters who have gone to jail as part of the fading satyagraha campaign, a place where he can also train new resisters. Also, it's a place where he can test the pedagogical and small-economy precepts he'd just propounded in the most important piece of sustained argument he would ever write, a tract called *Hind Swaraj*. The title translates as "Indian Self-Rule" or, more loosely, "India's Freedom." Gandhi dashed it off in ten days on a ship called the *Kildonan Castle*, sailing home in 1909 from his last futile attempt at lobbying in Whitehall.

In the form of a Socratic dialogue, this powerfully original little book encapsulates in one place his disappointment in the imperial system, the West in general, and modern industrial societies everywhere; also his rejection of violence as a political tactic; and his romantic feeling for the Indian village, of which he had, until then, little firsthand experience. His blanket rejection of modern ways includes modern medicine, lawyers (like himself), railroads (on which he'd rely for the rest of his life), and parliamentary politics (which Indian nationalists wanted for themselves). Capping its complicated and eclectic provenance is the surprising discovery that its immediate inspiration came not from Tolstoy or Ruskin but from the prolific Anglo-Catholic man of letters G. K. Chesterton, who, in a column in *The Illustrated London News* that Gandhi happened to see in London, asked what a real Indian nationalist, "an authentic Indian," would say to an imperialist trying to establish British-style institutions and ways of thought under the Raj.

"Life is very short; a man must live somehow and die somewhere," the English writer's authentic Indian declares in response to this rhetorical question. "The amount of bodily comfort a peasant gets under your best Republic is not so much more than mine. If you do not like our sort of spiritual comfort, we never asked you to. Go, and leave us with it." In *Hind Swaraj*, the character Gandhi inhabits, called "the Editor," steps forward as that authentic Indian. Chesterton hasn't given Gandhi new ideas but has shown him how the ideas he has been gradually gathering to himself can be made to define a persona. What he does in these pages, he will soon do in life; the Editor will become the Mahatma who, twelve years later, in his first noncooperation campaign in India will act out one of the book's themes. "The English have not taken India," the Editor declares. "We have given it to them." His answer is to "cease to play the ruled." This is more than a foreshadowing of Gandhi's later campaigns. It's a declaration of their basic theme.

Although written as he sails to Cape Town from a failed mission to London bearing on Indian rights in the Transvaal, the words "South Africa" never show up in *Hind Swaraj*. In his own mind, he has already started to repatriate himself to India, where the tract was promptly branded subversive and banned. It's actually more subversive of the pre-Gandhi Indian national movement, with its Anglicized leadership and imported values, than it is of British colonial rule. "Those in whose name we speak we do not know, nor do they know us," its author, who has spent fewer than five of the previous twenty years in India, boldly asserts, implicitly setting a challenge for himself. But his critique can also be applied to the movement he has led in South Africa generally, particularly Natal. An explicit part of the purpose of Tolstoy Farm is to enable Gandhi and Kallenbach—the first person to be shown the manuscript of *Hind Swaraj*—to close the social gap among Indians that he has finally come to recognize. Six months after he returns from London, Gandhi drafts the first of his informal contracts with Kallenbach, setting up what amounts to a basic law for the new community. "The primary object of going to the Farm so far as K. and G. are concerned," this document decrees, "is to make themselves into working farm hands." Nearly a year later, in May 1911, with the farm up and running, Gandhi tells Polak: "I should like to slip out of the public gaze . . . to bury myself in the farm and to devote my attention to farming and educating." The farming gives him a new appreciation for the aptitudes of Africans and Indians, like the indentured, who work the land. "They are more useful than any of us," he writes in *Indian Opinion*, making an explicit contrast between field laborers and a second generation of white-collar Indian clerks that's starting to criticize his leadership. "If the great Native races should stop working for a week, we should probably be starving."

But it's the school he runs six afternoons a week and every evening into which he pours most of his energy in the latter half of 1911. "That is my predominant occupation," he writes to Kallenbach on September 9. The enrollment is small. Gandhi has one dietary requirement that helps keep it low. Students must commit themselves to a saltless diet, for he has discovered that salt "makes us eat more and arouses the senses." Two decades later, in a notable demonstration of ideological flexibility, he'd declare salt to be one of life's necessities, making it the focus of his single most successful exercise in militant nonviolence, the Salt March of 1930. Now, when he eases up on his stricture against salt at Tolstoy Farm, allowing it back into the diet in modest amounts, enrollment shoots up to twenty-five, eight of them, he notes proudly, Muslims. The curriculum includes a course in sandal making. Gandhi had sent Kallenbach to a Trappist monastery near Phoenix to learn the craft; the architect then taught the lawyer, and the lawyer then taught the students. Soon they'd turned out fifty pairs, he reported, one of which he sent to his political sparring partner Jan Smuts.

Tolstoy Farm, with Gandhi serving as schoolmaster and chief medical officer, was now for a time the foreground of his life; the fading satyagraha campaign against the racial legislation of the Transvaal receded into the background. Gandhi carried on a desultory negotiation with Smuts, now minister of defense and also mines in the new Union government, but his focus was on developing a curriculum using Indian languages and texts, as well as on diet and nature cures as wholesome alternatives to aggressive modern medicine. Kallenbach is more involved in these "experiments" than political foot soldiers like Thambi Naidoo or Polak who lead conventional married lives. His commitment to Gandhian values, as they evolve, seems wholehearted, not selective.

Kallenbach, 1912, striding

He is more than an acolyte, less than an equal. Never, as far as we can tell, does he present an intellectual challenge to the spiritual explorer who has become his companion.

The original agreement specified that K. would live apart from the settlers and that G. would mostly stay with him. Then Mrs. Gandhi moves up to Tolstoy Farm from Phoenix for a period of more than a year. It's not clear what effect this has. By then, Ba and her husband have been sleeping in separate quarters for more than five years. At Tolstoy Farm, they sleep on separate verandas, each surrounded by students from Gandhi's school.

What's easy to miss in accounts of Gandhi's life at Tolstoy Farm is how powerful a factor his feeling for Kallenbach has become in the inward turning he has taken. Not only is he bent on reforming this partner, he strives to make their association permanent. The architect wavers. He is living life on two planes. While at Tolstoy Farm with Gandhi, he has also become a Zionist and a more observant Jew; he takes Gandhi to synagogue on Passover and introduces him to matzoh. Some weeks, in preparation for a move to India, he studies Hindi; other weeks, when he wonders how much of Gandhi's time he'll be able to own in a still unimaginable Indian future, he studies Hebrew in preparation for a new life in Palestine. On a day-by-day basis, the surest index to the architect's changeable mood is which language he's studying, Hindi or Hebrew. He's disconsolate, if not jealous, when Gandhi lavishes admiration and time on someone else. Persisting, Gandhi puts up with all this for more than two years, all the time seeking to preserve their bond.

Kallenbach's ups and downs can be traced in an appointments and account book he kept for 1912 and 1913, which can be viewed in the archive of Gandhi's Sabarmati Ashram in Ahmedabad, India. For the sake of frugality and fitness, Kallenbach and Gandhi made a regular practice of walking the twenty-one miles from the farm, near a rail stop called Lawley, to the center of Johannesburg, following a route across a great expanse of veldt that much later, in the apartheid era, was turned into the sprawling black township of Soweto. On each occasion, Kallenbach records the times. When he walks with Gandhi, often starting as early as 4:00 a.m., it takes a little more than five and a half hours to reach their respective offices in the center of Johannesburg; on his own, he usually manages to lop an hour off. On every single mention, Gandhi in these pages isn't Upper House but "Mr. Gandhi." The formality seems to acknowledge that their relationship, however it's understood, isn't one of equals.

Today Lawley still functions as a rail stop. Next to it sprawls a large postapartheid shantytown of corrugated metal and mud huts squeezed together on virtually every square foot of some long-defunct white farm. When an attempt was made to restore Tolstoy Farm and erect a memorial there, the squatters from the shantytown soon stripped the place bare. When I visited it in 2008 there was not even a sign. All that was left were some banked brick benches, the foundation of an old farmhouse, the well-fenced dwellings of a few white stakeholders who work at an adjacent brick kiln, some burned-over eucalyptus trees, and a few fruit trees, progeny perhaps of the scores Kallenbach planted a century ago, and, finally, a view across the townships and mining slime dams to a Johannesburg Gandhi would scarcely recognize.

In their day, Gandhi and Kallenbach continued to experiment with diet, limiting their daily intake at one stage to a single carefully rationed evening meal. And every month or so Kallenbach recorded another "long discussion" with Mr. Gandhi. Details are completely absent, but sometimes these conversations provoke resolutions on Kallenbach's side to step up his Hindi studies and come to a decision on leaving his profession. Then someone else comes into the picture, competing for his soul mate's attention, and a fresh shower of doubts rains down on him. The most personal and intriguing note in the diary is recorded on August 27, 1913, eight months after Gandhi has finally moved back to Phoenix. Tolstoy Farm has been wound up, Kallenbach is back at Mountain View, and Gandhi, on a visit, is staying with him. Then another of the Jews in Gandhi's Johannesburg circle, Sonja Schlesin, his feisty secretary, shows up. By some accounts, it was Kallenbach who introduced Schlesin, seventeen years his junior, to Gandhi in 1905; their families had been close in the old country. But he has come to consider her high-handed in her claims on Gandhi's time and, in some sense, to view her as a rival. "On account of Miss Schlesin's coming to Mountain View walked alone to office," Kallenbach writes. "Discussions about her brought about Mr. Gandhi's vow. It has been an exceedingly trying day for me."

If this entry were an ancient cuneiform inscription, it would hardly be more difficult to decipher. Is he alluding to Gandhi's vow of brahmacharya, or the recent vow that led to a fast the previous month over some carnal doings that surfaced at Phoenix? (In Gandhi's mind, there could be no such thing as innocent sexual play; earlier he'd complained about a case of "excessive tickling" at Phoenix.) Neither of those vows seems to be what Kallenbach has in mind. Probably he's referring to a vow known only to K. and G. The context is obscure, but Kallenbach's feelings, for once, leap off the page. Rivalries and jealousies of this sort would become chronic in Gandhi's entourage in later years. But Kallenbach is special. In leaving Joburg, Gandhi appears to have left him behind, to have broken free. In fact, he made the move at the start of 1913 on the assumption that his dearest friend would eventually follow. Recognizing that Kallenbach is "on the fence," he asks him in a tone that's at once wheedling and passive-aggressive "to consider the joint life as we have lived it." But the clearest clue to his feelings is this: in packing up his own things for shipment to Phoenix, it turns out, he has also packed and shipped Kallenbach's books and tools. Upper House is wounded when Lower House requests their return; even then he doesn't give up. As we will see, this isn't the end. Kallenbach eventually plunges into Gandhi's last and greatest satyagraha campaign in South Africa, then seems to pull back again, thrown off balance by Gandhi's newfound fondness for a British clergyman, Charles F. Andrews. "Though I love and almost adore Andrews so," Gandhi writes, "I would not exchange you for him. You still remain the dearest and nearest to me . . . I know that in my lonely journey through the world, you will be the last (if even that) to say good-bye to me. What right had I to expect so much from you!"

So much of what, we're left to wonder. The answers can only be love, devotion, unquestioning support. In Gandhi's words, Kallenbach was "a man of strong feelings, wide sympathies and childlike simplicity." On another occasion, he complained of his friend's "morbid sensitiveness," meaning, it seems, his jealousy and susceptibility to other influences. Three months before he leaves South Africa, Gandhi again reassures his Jewish soul mate: "You will always be you and you alone to me. I have told you you will have to desert me and not I you." Finally Kallenbach succumbs. He sails with Gandhi when he leaves the country with the intention, soon thwarted, of accompanying him all the way to India.

The several ties that bound Gandhi to the Transvaal—the satyagraha campaign, Tolstoy Farm, and Kallenbach—cannot easily be disentangled. But by January 9, 1913—the day Kallenbach jotted in his diary, "Mr. Gandhi and balance of Tolstoy Farm occupants left for Phoenix"— the strongest of these was the personal one to the architect. Only when it's factored into consideration can Gandhi's prolonged abstention from Indian politics in Natal be plausibly explained.

The timing of Gandhi's departure from the Transvaal and his return to Phoenix had little or nothing to do with Indian politics in Natal, from which he'd been conspicuously removed for a decade. It was dictated by a pledge that his staunch admirer and presumptive guru, Gopal Krishna Gokhale, had wrung from him at the end of his triumphal five-week tour of South Africa in 1912. The Indian leader's visit, organized with all the pomp and circumstance usually reserved in South Africa for visits by British cabinet ministers—a blur of public tributes, crowded procession routes, and civic receptions attended by dignitaries who in that era were, by definition, nearly all white—had brought Gandhi out of his retreat at Tolstoy Farm. At its end, when Gokhale sailed for home, Gandhi and Kallenbach accompanied him as far as Zanzibar. When Indian communities at East African ports along the way turned out to welcome the leaders, they found the lawyer from Johannesburg in Indian garb for the first time in southern Africa since the London-returned dandy wore a turban into a Durban courtroom, the day after he arrived from India, now nearly twenty years earlier. The older man ("whose eyes were always on me," so Gandhi later wrote) used the time on board to talk earnest politics. "In these conversations Gokhale prepared me for India," Gandhi said. When they parted in Zanzibar, Gokhale exhorted, all but commanded, Gandhi to prepare to put South Africa behind him within a year and come home to fulfill his destiny. Gandhi, it appears, promised to try. Back at Tolstoy Farm by mid-December 1912, it took him just four weeks to wind up that particular experiment with truth and move his base back to Phoenix. In his own mind, this was just the start of a longer eastward journey that had always been inevitable. "I shall be there when the time comes," he'd written when the subject of his repatriation came up. His "inner voice," it seemed, would help him know when his "withdrawal," as he termed it in a letter to Kallenbach, should occur.

There was unfinished business he still needed to clear. Gandhi believed he'd reached a compromise with Smuts in early 1911 that would enable him to write finis to the satyagraha campaign that had been his ostensible reason for camping in the Transvaal. That was a year after South Africa's first national government—all white, of course— had come into being. In truth, the compromise Gandhi had been ready to embrace would have made only a slight difference in the real circumstances of beleaguered Indian communities. The "Black Act" requiring Indian registration in the Transvaal would have been repealed by the new white Parliament (for whatever that was worth, now that practically all Indians had registered), and an immigration law that was explicitly anti-Asian would have been replaced by one that was seemingly nonracial in terminology, only implicitly and functionally anti-Asian. (By means, for instance, of literacy tests in European languages, with Yiddish being included on the list of languages in which an immigrant could be tested but not, of course, Hindi, Tamil, or any other Indian language.) Absurdly, as a gesture to the principle of equality, it would retain the provision from earlier drafts that six "educated" Indians (meaning Indians who'd followed an English curriculum) could be admitted to the Transvaal annually, a way around the likelihood that even Indians who were proficient by Western standards would still be effectively barred.

Seen in a broader context, as a second generation of Indians born in South Africa was beginning to do, the "compromise" didn't promise much. If it went through, Indians would still lack a vote; their rights to own land or open businesses could still be subject to severe restrictions; the indentured labor system would be left standing; and educational opportunities for Indian children would remain entirely at the discretion of antagonistic white authorities. Still, for a few months in 1911, there seemed to be a deal. Then the government introduced bills supposed to embody the extremely limited aims of the Gandhi-Smuts bargain, and once the arcane language and obscure cross-references to provisions in other laws had been parsed, traced, and decoded, the only thing that was obvious was that Gandhi's good faith had yet again been exploited. What one provision appeared to grant, another provision took away. If anything, the draft legislation worsened conditions for Indian residents and raised the barrier to immigration even higher. Threatening renewed resistance, Gandhi himself had now to acknowledge that the immigration reform over which he'd bargained had yielded a new "Asiatic Expulsion Bill." New drafts were then promised, withdrawn, and promised again as the authorities waited him out, testing Indian resolve. Nearly five years after the start of satyagraha, he had nothing to show for the resistance his leadership had inspired. Indians had courted arrest and gone to jail more than two thousand times, serving sentences of up to six months at hard labor; some, like Thambi Naidoo and Gandhi's son Harilal, doing so repeatedly. Hundreds of other resisters had been deported back to India. The world had fleetingly taken notice—India, especially—but the new white government had outmaneuvered Gandhi. Disillusion was building, especially in the Natal to which he returned at the start of 1913.

Then he did something remarkable, upping the ante. He added a new demand and put it at the top of his list, one that had more heft, that spoke directly and clearly to the central question of whether the Indian community in South Africa was to be regarded as temporary or permanent, a demand that carried radical implications, bearing as it did on the prospects of the poorest Indians, the indentured laborers of Natal who toiled in a system Gandhi had long since identified as "a substitute for slavery." Seemingly all of a sudden, Gandhi made the abolition of Natal's annual three-pound head tax on former indentured laborers the main object of the new satyagraha campaign he'd been threatening for two years.

This is usually portrayed as the logical and inevitable culmination of Gandhi's opposition over nearly two decades to the indentured labor system and to the tax—now called by Gandhi "the blood tax"—which had been adopted in 1895 as a means of forcing indentured laborers to return to India at the end of their contracts, or reenlist by signing a new contract.

The story is more complicated. The original proposal had been to put a head tax of twenty-five pounds on each former indentured laborer, a levy that exceeded his annual income and therefore would be impossible for him to scrimp together. Gandhi himself had drafted the original protest lodged by the Natal Indian Congress, and after the issue had been carried to the imperial authorities in Whitehall, the tax had been reduced to three pounds on each man, woman, and child, onerous still for workers who counted themselves fortunate if they earned a pound in a month. Collection over the years had been spotty, but as fines piled up on former indentured laborers who failed to pay, white magistrates took this as a pretext for jailing them on contempt charges. Early on, no one was more eloquent in calling attention to the plight of the indentured and former indentured than Gandhi. "To a starving man there is virtually no home," he wrote in 1903. "His home is where he can keep body and soul together." By this standard, Natal was a more plausible "home" than the impoverished Indian villages the laborers had fled.

But indentured laborers were never a preoccupation of Gandhi's during his Transvaal years. They and their sufferings were located in Natal, generally removed from his field of vision. When a group of second-generation Natal-born Indians started to agitate in Durban for the removal of the tax in 1911, the absent Gandhi, in retreat on Tolstoy Farm, seemed impervious to appeals for his support. Perhaps he calculated that in throwing his weight behind a new movement with new demands, he might sink his chances for the already pending deal with Smuts. Or perhaps, egotistically, he now sensed a challenge from younger would-be leaders. Whatever his motives, he plainly didn't have any liking for the prime mover of the agitation against the tax. This was P. S. Aiyar, the rambunctiously independent editor of *African Chronicle*, whose own attitude to Gandhi—as expressed in print in his weekly paper—ran an unpredictable gamut from reverential to critical and from critical to wrathful. *Indian Opinion* carried a brief item mentioning the formation of a committee to launch a campaign against the head tax, with Aiyar as secretary. The movement against the three-pound head tax then lurched on for months with petitions and meetings, the sorts of things Gandhi's paper routinely recorded when they bore on Indian interests. But Aiyar's committee garnered no further mention in its pages. Afterward, Polak apparently made the mistake of writing something favorable about Aiyar to Gandhi, who replied: "In spite of your remarks in one of your letters, I still very much distrust Aiyar's good faith. He is a man of the moment. He will write one thing today, and just the opposite tomorrow." In addition to showing how unaccustomed the Johannesburg Gandhi could still be to criticism coming not from whites but from one of his own, the letter proves he was a reader of *African Chronicle*.

Aiyar's agitation never got very far. He seems to have had little organizing talent and no stomach for the sort of personal sacrifice that could land him in jail. But his agitation did put the tax issue back on Gandhi's mind. The most Gandhi had been hoping for was the repeal of the tax on women, not as a result of Indian agitation, but as a gesture by Smuts to show the good faith of whites. It was an idea they'd apparently discussed. Gandhi was unreceptive to ideas about a more active approach. The possibility of his starting a movement of his own against the tax was suggested to him by the editor in that period of *Indian Opinion*, an Englishman named Albert West. But that would have meant leaving Tolstoy Farm and coming to Durban. It was late 1911, and Gandhi wasn't ready for that. Uncharacteristically, he shrugged off the suggestion. "I am not just now in a position to feel the pulse of the community there," he wrote. "If I felt like being free to head the movement, I should plunge without a moment's hesitation, but, just now, I am not in that condition at all." Maybe West should start a movement himself, he countered, an unlikely suggestion for him to offer the Englishman. But if he does, he "should not in any way clash with what Aiyar is doing." Apparently, Aiyar had been seeking support from West or Gandhi or both. Gandhi referred to "the Aiyar correspondence," which he returned to West, saying he didn't want to keep it. Still, he couldn't let the matter drop. A week later he wrote to West again asking him to collect statistics on the tax that might be used to steer white opinion, so that passive resistance on the issue could be avoided.

For nearly a year Gandhi then remains at Tolstoy Farm doing basically nothing about the three-pound tax after writing a flurry of pieces on the subject in *Indian Opinion*, which were notable mostly for their failure to allude to the sputtering campaign in Durban. Aiyar, who'd only recently described Gandhi as "our revered and respected leader" and "that selfless, noble soul," first fumes, then burns.

The maverick editor had stood by the aloof and absent leader when he came under attack from a swami named Shankaranand, recently arrived from India, who couldn't abide Gandhi's emphasis on harmony with Muslims. The supposed holy man was getting a hearing from local Hindus, showing how easy it could be for a newcomer to reignite communal tensions, despite Gandhi's wishful boast that they'd been surmounted by Indians in South Africa under his leadership. Hindus needed "an absolute Hindu as their leader instead of a Tolstoyan," the swami had preached, putting himself forward. Aiyar instantly rose to Gandhi's defense. He wrote that the newcomer had shown himself to be a politician "sheltering himself under the cloak of a hermit." If the swami imagined he could "step into the shoes of Mr. Gandhi," he said, "it is our pleasant or unpleasant duty to say this is an impossible dream."

Just ten months later Aiyar accused Gandhi and *Indian Opinion* of having done "all in their power to smother the £3 tax committee." In full cry against "the great sage of Phoenix," the *African Chronicle* editor now used his pages to assert, bitterly but not implausibly, that the movement he'd tried himself to start had gotten no recognition from Gandhi "simply because it did not emanate from him." His fulminations became uncontrollable. His invective is something to behold. He railed against Gandhi's "cosmopolitan followers," an obvious allusion to the Jewish backgrounds of Polak and Kallenbach, whom he derided as the leader's "trusted Prime Ministers." Why, he asked, baring his own disappointment and apparent jealousy, had Gandhi found it so hard to depend on Indians?

"Mr. Gandhi may have been a good man prior to his assuming the role of a saint," Aiyar eventually reflected, "but since he has attained this new state by himself without being ordained by a holy preceptor, he seems to be indifferent though not callous to human sufferings and human defects." By the time this was written at the start of 1914, seven months before Gandhi sailed from the country, the final satyagraha campaign had briefly brought Natal's mines and plantations to a standstill, and the abolition of the head tax—the issue Aiyar himself had struggled to bring to the fore—was about to be secured by the man who'd become his nemesis. By then thoroughly alienated, the editor plainly felt that Gandhi had stolen his issue and the portion of glory that might have been his due.

The turning point came on November 14, 1912, when Gopal Krishna Gokhale, toward the end of his South African tour, had an audience with the former Boer commanders Louis Botha and Jan Smuts in the prime minister's office in Pretoria. Gokhale had campaigned in India for the abolition of the indenture system. He grasped the practical and symbolic importance of the tax that had been designed to drive former indentured laborers back to the impoverished villages in India from which they'd fled. He told the two Afrikaners that it was ineffective, unjust, poisoning relations between India and South Africa, and therefore ought to be scrapped. Eager to please, offering no defense, they left their visitor with the impression that they would do the political work necessary to win over Natal's whites. Gokhale thought this amounted to a commitment.

It's not impossible that Gokhale had this exchange on his own initiative, but it's more likely that Gandhi, who was at his side every day of the tour, put him up to it. Though they'd agreed that the meeting with the ministers would go better if Gandhi, their old antagonist, were not present, they'd spent the previous evening together prepping for the encounter. Some days earlier, P. S. Aiyar also had a chance to lobby Gokhale in public and private on the three-pound head tax despite, so he wrote, the "jolly good care" taken by the Gandhi "clique" to insulate the visitor from gadflies like himself. Possibly Aiyar's persistence on a subject that, as he said, "has been dear to me since a considerable length of time" counted for something after all. In any event, the Gandhi of Tolstoy Farm who didn't feel free to "plunge" into an agitation against the tax a year earlier was now on the verge of returning to Natal. If he was not exactly spoiling for a fight, the prospect of getting the question resolved at the top must have appealed to him as a way of trumping the irritating Aiyar and, more important, as a demonstration that he'd never given up on an issue of such magnitude to the poorest Indians.

Beyond the clash of egos and considerations about his reputation in India, there was the issue itself. Fifteen years after the fact, Gandhi would write that a "fresh fight" would have been necessary to abolish the head tax even if Smuts had honored his end of the original compromise, in which it hadn't featured at all. Nothing indicates that he felt that combative at the time. In fact, with conspicuous remorse, he would soon acknowledge that he and other free Indians had shelved the issues of indenture and the head tax for too long. "Are we not to blame for all this?" a distraught-sounding Gandhi would ask, after returning to Natal and reviewing the prison sentences meted out to former indentured laborers prosecuted for walking out on their contracts or not paying the head tax. "We did not hear the cry for help at our own doors! Who can tell how much of the burden [of guilt] we have to bear? It's enjoined by all religions that we should share in the suffering that we see around us. We have failed to do so."

The Gandhi who returned from Johannesburg to Phoenix came to this realization reluctantly. He didn't seize the tax issue. It can almost be said to have seized him. But it was the right issue, after all, for the climax of his last act in South Africa. If he wasn't going to spend the rest of his life battling for equal rights there, he could at least try to keep faith with the indentured. Everything he'd learned—about caste and untouchabil-ity, about "high and low," about the dignity of physical labor—had armed him for the struggle. Originally, it was mostly book learning, the earnest barrister's distillations from Tolstoy and Ruskin. Now, after the experiences of war, jail, and Tolstoy Farm, the long hikes across the veldt with Kallenbach to and from the city center at dawn and sometimes twi-light, the detachment from family as commonly defined, the lawyer and petitioner had given way to the spiritual pilgrim with a strategy of mass action.

As a memoirist, Gandhi had, like many writers in our own day, the knack of total recall for conversations that had occurred a decade or two earlier. As if he'd taped it, he has Gokhale telling him following his ses-sion with Botha and Smuts: "You must return to India in a year. Every-thing has been settled . . . The £3 tax will be abolished."

"I doubt it very much," Gandhi has himself replying. "You do not know the ministers as I do. Being an optimist myself, I love your opti-mism, but having frequent disappointments, I am not as hopeful in the matter as you are."

"You must return to India within twelve months, and I will not have any of your excuses," Gokhale says again in his version.

In some such way, the stage was set once Smuts rose in the white Par-liament in April 1913 to present his latest attempt to codify his supposed agreements with Gandhi and Gokhale. The head tax would no longer have to be paid on Indian women and children, but it would be retained for indentured men who did not re-indenture or repatriate themselves at the end of their contracts: in other words, men who tried to assume some of the attributes of freedom. The minister said there had never been a commitment to abolish the tax totally. Gandhi said this was an insult to Gokhale and, therefore, to India. Without great confidence that it would amount to much, he began to plan his final South African campaign.

5

LEADING THE INDENTURED

THE GREAT SATYAGRAHA CAMPAIGN of 1913 is a conspicuous milestone on Gandhi's road, a biographical episode that can't be lightly passed by. The campaign became his model or prototype for effective political action. Had it never occurred, the spiritual pilgrim into whom he'd transformed himself might never have had the fortitude—or spirit—to reach for mass leadership in India. Yet in the angry, fractious white politics of the Union of South Africa, then in its infancy as a nation-state, satyagraha was little more than a sideshow—at most, a temporary distraction. The status of Indians, Smuts would later say, was "an entirely subordinate question." He meant that rights for Indians could not be disentangled from the larger question of rights for blacks, and that rights for blacks were simply unthinkable. "The whole basis of our system in South Africa rests on inequality," he said with an easy candor that may now seem brazen but, at the time, took for granted the self-evident soundness of his reasoning.

In the political history of white South Africa, 1913 doesn't stand out as the year that Indians marched for the abolition of a now-forgotten tax. It was the year that the Boer War generals then governing the country clashed among themselves over South Africa's proper place in the British Empire and over which whites specifically should hold power in the land. Smuts and his prime minister, Louis Botha, embraced the British program of "reconciliation," implying unity between Afrikaners and English-speaking whites as well as continued deference to Whitehall on imperial and international issues. Under the slogan "South Africa First," which really meant Afrikaners first, another faction wanted the Boer War's losers to defer to no one and to embark on a more rigorous program of racial segregation. The Nationalists, as they would call themselves when they broke away in November that year, would prove to be the wave of the future until a greater nationalism, that of the suppressed African majority, finally came crashing in.

In 1913, white restlessness and infighting weren't confined to the former generals at the top. The foundations of the new industrial society, based on the hugely profitable gold mines, had been severely shaken by a brief general strike by white mine workers in July; six months later, white railway men called another. In the first strike, involving nascent trade unions and, so it was alleged, allied anarchist conspirators, thousands of white miners took over the center of Johannesburg. They set fire to the railway station and to the offices of *The Star*, a newspaper known for following the line of the mine owners. They next turned their attention to the Rand Club, the stuffy preserve of those same interests. This was class warfare, but on behalf of whites only. (The same color-coded radicalism, a decade later, during another supposed general strike, would express itself in a priceless slogan adapted from Marx and Engels: "Workers of the world, fight and unite for a white South Africa.")

In 1913, Smuts had yet to build his army. The former Boer commander had to rely on two regiments of mounted imperial—that's to say, British—troops to suppress the strikers, some of whom would have fought in the Boer War, under his or Botha's command, against those same regiments. The troops saved the Rand Club, killing twenty-one strikers, but couldn't contain the rioting, which stopped only when Botha and Smuts arrived personally on the scene without a security escort and succumbed to the miners' demands. It was "a deep humiliation," Smuts said.

It's in this period of turmoil—between two whites-only general strikes, as the governing party started to break apart—that Gandhi launched his campaign, which he later chronicled as if it had happened in a vacuum, as if the land had been inhabited by only Indians and white autocrats. His numerous biographers have generally followed his lead, paying little or no attention to the South African context. It wasn't that Gandhi failed to register what was going on. He wrote a long piece for *Indian Opinion* summing up the whites versus whites class struggle. Using what the editors of his collected writings helpfully footnote as "a Gujarati saying," he said it was a mountain being made out of a mustard seed. (Student of the New Testament that he was, Gandhi himself probably knew it was Matthew 17:20.) If the spectacle of white unrest had any implications for South African Indians, he failed to spell them out. But by then, in a steady stream of telegrams from Phoenix to ministers and members of the white Parliament, he'd already started to threaten a new round of passive resistance if the government held firm on the three-pound head tax and on its restrictive new immigration bill, which seemed to turn virtually all Indians into "prohibited aliens."

As if these grievances weren't enough, yet another controversy burst out following a judicial ruling in Cape Province that traditional Indian marriages—Hindu, Muslim, and Parsi—had no standing in South African law, which recognized only weddings performed by judges, other officials sanctioned by the state, or Christian clerics. This meant all Indian wives, except a small number of Indian Christians, were living out of wedlock and all their children were illegitimate in the eyes of the law of their adopted country, further undermining their already tenuous residence rights.

The marriage question helped jolt Indians in South Africa out of the despondency and resignation that seemed to have settled on the community during the years of Gandhi's withdrawal to Tolstoy Farm. Mass meetings were held in Johannesburg in April and May, though Gandhi himself, now back in Natal, was absent. The marriage issue even made an activist out of Gandhi's hitherto-retiring wife, according to an account he gave at the time. "Then I am not your wife according to the laws of this country," he quoted Kasturba as saying in April after the matter had been explained to her. "Let us go to India." Her husband replied that they couldn't back off the struggle. She then volunteered to join it by courting arrest. Or so the story went in his telling. The idea of women doing that hadn't previously occurred to Gandhi. Soon he had a female flying squad ready to follow Kasturba to jail, on his signal. "We congratulate our plucky sisters who have dared to fight the Government rather than submit to the insult," he wrote after forty Johannesburg wives signed a petition to the interior minister that was probably drafted by Gandhi himself (certainly not by Kasturba, who was illiterate).

Part of Gandhi's inspiration for his earliest passive resistance campaigns had come from the example of suffragette demonstrations he'd witnessed in London. That example may have had something to do with his openness now to the idea of Indian women courting arrest, which was novel to the point of being countercultural. It was also a sign that Gandhi was beginning to think tactically and politically again. His attention had been diverted first to Tolstoy Farm and then, after his return to the Phoenix Settlement at the start of the year, to proselytizing for his latest discoveries in matters of health and diet. In thirty-three weekly installments, ending in August, Gandhi held forth in *Indian Opinion* on the efficacy of cold baths and mud packs, on the danger of vaccination against smallpox, and on the perils of sexual indulgence. But even before winding up the series, he dropped hints that the next campaign wouldn't be a simple reprise of the last. "I have sketched out an elaborate program which I have not the time to set forth here," he remarked in a letter to Hermann Kallenbach at the end of April. Two months later, in another letter to his confidant, he says he's "resolving in my own mind the idea of doing something for the indentured men." The scholar Maureen Swan seizes on this sentence as a harbinger, a turning point. "Never before," she writes, "had Gandhi addressed himself to the Natal underclasses." But what was that "something" he was thinking of doing? And did doing it *for* the indentured entail or even imply, in his early strategizing, that it might also be done *with* them? In letters and articles written in the months leading up to the 1913 campaign, there's nothing besides these suggestive but vague sentences to hint that it might have. But fifteen years later, when, back in India, Gandhi got around to writing his own narrative of the period, everything fell tidily, retrospectively, into place. Here, without acknowledging that he'd dodged pleas to join an earlier campaign against the head tax, he says the "insult" to Gokhale and, by extension, all Indians over the tax issue had thrown open the door to mobilizing the indentured.

"When this tax thus fell within the scope of the struggle," Gandhi wrote in a second autobiographical volume, *Satyagraha in South Africa*, "the indentured Indians had an opportunity of participating in it . . . thusfar this class had been kept out of the fray." It's reasonable to read this as acknowledging they had been "kept out of the fray" as a considered choice made by none other than himself. Though the indentured were illiterate, he then recalled, they turned out to understand issues better than he'd have imagined. How many of them would actually join in, he goes on, remained a mystery to which he had no clues. From this we can surmise that the idea of calling out the indentured may indeed have lodged in Gandhi's mind months before the campaign kicked off in September, but he had little confidence they'd respond.

There's circumstantial evidence that a turning point in his thinking may have come in the days leading up to the violent white miners' strike in Johannesburg, which broke out on July 3, soon after Gandhi dropped his tantalizing aside to Kallenbach about "doing something for the indentured." Gandhi had then traveled up to Johannesburg on June 30 for negotiations on his long-pending, or rather slow-fading, compromise with Smuts. The government was too preoccupied with its own dissension and the rising white militancy on the mines for those talks to go anywhere. But Gandhi stayed on, settling down in Kallenbach's Mountain View house for a week or so. On consecutive days, Kallenbach dutifully noted in his diary, they then went to lunch at the home of Thambi Naidoo, the Tamil leader who'd proved himself to be Gandhi's single most dedicated satyagrahi; on the third day, they took dinner there. Kallenbach tells us nothing else; and there's no other record. But these meals are unusual enough to command attention. The fussy ascetic that Gandhi had become by 1913 had long since ceased to dine out, even in vegetarian households. And even when he'd had a social life of sorts, it had been largely with his European friends and soul mates, not the Naidoos. Three days in a row suggests these could have been meals with a purpose, an impromptu satyagraha summit or skull session—what today might be called a retreat.

An impression has lingered in the oral tradition of South African Tamils that Thambi Naidoo sometimes had to press his leader to lead. Could this have been such an occasion? On July 5, the day of the shootings by the troops guarding the Rand Club, Gandhi and Kallenbach walked into town from Mountain View and back. Kallenbach takes terse note of the shootings, saying only that there were "many more deaths." That evening he and Gandhi have "another long discussion." Did it involve the day's events? We'll never know. At roughly the same time, Botha and Smuts arrived on the scene downtown and, unable to do anything else, bowed to the workers' demands. Word of their retreat would have gotten around, even without the burned-out and crippled *Star* to spread it. The idea that the Boer War generals had bent under pressure couldn't be contained.

Could the example of the white mine workers have served as Thambi Naidoo's "mustard seed"? He wouldn't have had to be told that indentured Indian mine workers in the coal districts of Natal were mostly Tamils. Given the fact that his meetings with Gandhi in Johannesburg coincided with the rising of the white working class there, it's not far-fetched to think that he drew some inspiration from the white proletariat. What we do know is that on October 11, when eleven Indian women—ten of them Tamils, including Thambi Naidoo's wife—courted arrest by illegally crossing into Natal from the Transvaal border town of Volksrust, they were accompanied by Naidoo; and when they

Arriving in Newcastle October 1913, at the
start of strikes on the coal mines

reached the coal-mining center of Newcastle two days later and
implored the Indian miners to strike, Naidoo was still their guide. *The
Natal Witness,* published in the provincial capital of Pietermaritzburg,
identified Thambi Naidoo as the "ringleader."

Gandhi had used the threat of a strike by the indentured to badger the
government. Just two weeks earlier he'd written to the minister of the
interior warning that "the step we are about to take . . . is fraught with
danger." That step, as the letter defined it, involved "asking those who
are now serving indenture and who will, therefore, be liable to pay the

After the strikes, possibly in Durban

£3 tax on completion of their indenture, to strike until the tax is withdrawn." In the immediate aftermath of the strike he also acknowledged
there had been a "plan" to send the Tamil women to Newcastle to agitate among the indentured Tamil coal miners "and persuade them to go
on strike on the issue of the £3 tax." The signal for the start of the walkout was to have been Gandhi's own arrival in town, some days afterward,
once the women had prepared the way. "But the mere presence of these
women," Gandhi wrote, "was like a match to dry fuel . . . By the time I
reached there Indians in two coal mines had already stopped work."

Gandhi had solemnly warned the interior minister: "It may be difficult to control the spread of the movement beyond the limits one may
set." Here we see in action the passive-aggressive in passive resistance.
Years later, writing as memoirist rather than activist, he said he'd been

"as much perplexed as I was pleased" by the early outbreak of the strikes. "I was not prepared for this marvelous awakening," he recalled. In his mind, though he'd hatched the movement and foretold its spreading, he was not responsible for the course it now took. Responsibility, he'd say, lay with the government for rebuffing his reasonable demands for the removal of the head tax as promised. This can be interpreted as self-delusion, opportunism, or cunning, all of which were part of the leader's makeup in shifting proportions. It can also be interpreted as political genius. Gandhi may actually have been surprised that things worked out as he'd warned the authorities they might. But he had no hesitation exploiting the outcome he'd foreseen, even if he hadn't fully believed his forecast.

He was not therefore a prisoner of events when he arrived in Newcastle on October 17, 1913. For the first time in his life, he found himself the leader of a mass movement. In Durban recently, Hassim Seedat, a lawyer whose avocations include the study of Gandhi's life and the collection of Gandhi materials, showed me a photograph of Gandhi as he disembarked that day. In it, the advocate turned leader is once again in Indian dress as he'd last been in Zanzibar, ten months earlier, bidding farewell to the homeward-bound Gokhale. The point of the costume change was to stress his identification with the indentured by adopting their garb. Hermann Kallenbach, his architecture practice now on hold, was there to greet him. He'd arrived the day before and had already gone on mine visits with Thambi Naidoo. Natal's attorney general reported that "a Jew Kallenbach . . . appears to be agitating."

Gandhi immediately called for the walkout to be extended to collieries still in operation. The strikes quickly spread beyond the mines. GANDHI CAUSES TROUBLE, a headline over a Reuters dispatch from Newcastle announced the next morning on the front page of *The Natal Witness* of Pietermaritzburg. "A peculiar position has arisen here," the dispatch began. "Hotels are without waiters and the mines are without labor."

As the message spread beyond the two collieries that had already shut down, the roster of closed mines lengthened: Ballengeich, Fairleigh, Durban Navigation, Hattingspruit, Ramsey, St. George's, Newcastle, Cambrian, and Glencoe. Within a week, all nine had been at least partly crippled by the walkout of indentured Indian mine workers. Two thousand strikers were believed to be waiting for their leader's next command.

Most of the strikers were still in mine compounds, still being fed by

their increasingly anxious employers, still refusing to work. The strike
next spread to Durban, where most services halted as indentured Indian
bellmen, waiters, and sweepers, municipal menials of all sorts, stopped
working. Thambi Naidoo was eventually arrested in a railway barracks
in the process of enlisting even more indentured workers, threatening
the shipment of coal to the gold mines and ports.

For a week, Gandhi himself was a self-propelled whirlwind, in constant motion from meeting to meeting, rally to rally, riding up and down
the rail line he'd had his first fateful venture on in 1893. From Newcastle he traveled to Durban, where he faced a meeting on October 19 of
restive Indian businessmen who made up the leadership of the Natal
Indian Congress, the organization he once spearheaded, whose charter
he'd single-handedly drafted, in whose name he'd sent all his early pleadings to colonial and imperial authorities. Frightened by the radical turn
in Gandhi's movement that his call to the indentured seemed to represent, the Congress passed what amounted to a motion of no-confidence,
effectively expelling him. (A Gandhian rump soon regrouped as the
Natal Indian Association.) The leader had lost the support of most,
though not all, of the Muslim traders who'd been his original backers,
but he had little time now to mend fences.

Not surprisingly, it was P. S. Aiyar, the maverick editor of *African
Chronicle*, who gave doubts about Gandhi's new course their most can-
tankerous expression. "Any precipitate step we might take in regard to
the £3 tax," he wrote with some foresight, "will not be conducive to
improving the lot of these thousands of poor, half-starving people."
Aiyar urged Gandhi to call a national conference of South African Indians and heed any consensus on tactics it reached. Gandhi brushed the
suggestion aside, saying he could accept the idea only so long as the
result didn't conflict with his conscience. This was too much for Aiyar.
"We are not aware," he erupted, "of any responsible politician in any
part of the globe making such a stupid reply." In effect, he said, Gandhi
was presenting himself as "such a soul of perfection . . . [that his] superior conscience was pervading everywhere."

No such sideline mutterings could slow Gandhi now. From Durban
he shot back to Newcastle to tour some mine compounds, then scooted
off to Johannesburg to rally white supporters, then went back again to
Durban to face the owners of the mines. In six days, he spent at least
seventy-two hours on trains. Everywhere, in speeches and written statements, he held out hope for an early end to the disruptions, even as his
lieutenants worked to draw more indentured laborers into the still

spreading protest. The aims of the strikers, soothing passages in his written statements and speeches seemed to say, couldn't be more modest; all the government needed to do was honor its pledge to banish the head tax, and fix the marriage law while they were at it. The workers were not striking for improved working conditions, he told the mine owners. The quarrel was not with them. Nor was it political. "Indians do not fight for equal political rights," he declared in a communiqué to Reuters really meant for the authorities. "They recognize that, in view of existing prejudice, fresh immigration from India should be strictly limited."

Despite all these signals and assurances, some of the mine executives voiced their deepest fear: that in addition to calling out his indentured countrymen, he'd seek, finally, to widen the stoppage by involving African workers. Gandhi denied having any such intention. "We do not believe in such methods," he told a reporter from *The Natal Mercury*.

John Dube's *Ilanga*, reacting to the Indian strikes, slyly took note of white fears that Africans might follow this example. The first of several commentaries ended with a Zulu expression that can be translated, "We wish you the best, Gandhi!" or even, "Go for it, Gandhi!" Later, when it seemed likely that the agitation might gain some privileges denied Africans from a white Parliament simultaneously engaged in passing the egregious Natives Land Act, an undertone of resentment crept in.

By October 26, the leader had landed back in the coalfields. All the women he'd dispatched to the area to win over the indentured had by then been arrested and sentenced to prison terms of up to three months, including his wife—along with scores of strikers identified by mine supervisors as "ringleaders," many of whom would eventually be deported back to India—but an unfazed and completely focused leader was now ready to stay put with the strikers, to take over as field commander of what *The Star*, in a small headline, sneeringly mislabeled MR. GHANDI'S ARMY. In the next eleven days, until he himself was finally locked up on November 11, Gandhi would have his most prolonged and intense engagement with indentured laborers in his two decades in South Africa.

Within a day of his return to Newcastle, Gandhi hit on a tactic for bringing the conflict to a head. It involved forcing the authorities to contemplate mass arrests, far beyond the capacity of the prisons to hold those it detained. With this end in view, Gandhi urged the miners to leave the compounds and court arrest by marching across the Transvaal border at Volksrust. It was "improper," he said, for them to be consum-

With Kallenbach, during 1913 strikes.
Gandhi's secretary, Sonja Schlesin, center.

ing the rations of the mining companies when they had no intention of working until the head tax had been abolished. Another point probably counted for more but was left unstated: as long as the strikers were at the mines, there was a danger they could be sealed off in the compounds, limiting the possibility of communication and further mass action. On October 28, the first batch of marchers set out from Newcastle in the direction of the provincial border. The next day Gandhi himself led another two hundred from the Ballengeich mine. The procession, according to a tabulation he made later, reached five hundred, including sixty women, voicing religious chants as they marched: "Victory to Ramchandra!" "Victory to Dwarkanath!" "Vande Mataram!" Ramchandra and Dwarkanath were other names for the gods Rama and Krishna, heroes of the great Hindu epics. The last cry meant "Hail, Mother!" or, more specifically, Mother India, fusing high-flown religious and political connotations. "They struck not as indentured laborers but as servants of India," Gandhi wrote. "They were taking part in a religious war."

By November 2, about two thousand miners and other indentured laborers had assembled at Charlestown, the Natal railway terminus, where the young Gandhi had boarded a stagecoach on his first journey to the Transvaal in 1893. Charlestown is thirty-four miles from Newcastle, mostly uphill, sometimes steeply. Here a reporter for the *Sunday Times* found Gandhi in shirtsleeves in "the evil-smelling backyard of a tin shanty . . . sitting on an upturned milk case." Next to him was a galvanized tub "full of an unsavory concoction which I took to be soup," also sacks containing hundreds of bread loaves. The future Mahatma, working with "incredible rapidity," was serving as quartermaster, cutting the loaves into three-inch hunks, then, according to this description, digging with his thumb a small hole into each hunk, which he then filled with coarse sugar as the men filed by in successive batches of a dozen strikers each.

It's a picture to fix in the mind: Gandhi, in the thick of his struggle, feeding his followers—described by another reporter on the scene as "consisting mostly of the very lowest castes of Hindus," plus "the merest smattering of Mohammedans"—with his own hands. That a certain proportion of the strikers (maybe 20 percent, maybe more) were once considered untouchable in the Tamil villages from which they originally hailed is no longer, for Gandhi, something to be remarked upon. In his own mind, feeding them one by one in this way is basic logistics, not a display of sanctity. But for however many hundreds or thousands who received their food directly from his hands, he set a new standard for Indian leadership, for political leadership anywhere. Later he wrote that he'd made serving food in Charlestown his "sole responsibility" because only he could persuade the strikers that portions had to be tiny if all were to eat. "Bread and sugar constituted our sole ration," he said.

On November 5, he tried to get through to Smuts in Pretoria by phone in order to give him one last chance to renew his pledge on the tax. By then, Smuts was flatly denying that there had ever been such a pledge. Gandhi was curtly rebuffed by the minister's private secretary. "General Smuts will have nothing to do with you," he was told. Then and now, the provincial border consisted of a little stream on the edge of Volksrust. (Under majority rule, names have changed. What was Natal is now KwaZulu-Natal; that portion of the Transvaal is now Mpumalanga.) The geography of this hinterland was familiar to Gandhi, who'd

On march through Volksrust.

Strikers march into the Transvaal at Volksrust

been arrested in 1908, at this same point, for crossing the same provincial border without a permit.

On the morning of November 6, shortly after dawn, he set out from Charlestown with 2,037 men, 127 women, and 57 children. Gandhi told them that their destination was Tolstoy Farm, a distance of about 150 miles. A small police detachment was waiting for them at the border, but the "pilgrims," as Gandhi had taken to calling them, swarmed across. Volksrust's Afrikaners, who'd threatened to fire on the marchers, looked on passively as the procession passed through the town in regular ranks. Their first encampment was eight miles down the road. There, that night, Gandhi was arrested and taken back to Volksrust to appear before a magistrate who granted the retired barrister's professionally argued request for bail. The sequence of arrest, arraignment, and bail was repeated the next day, so twice in two days he was able to rejoin the marchers. On November 9, with the procession already past the Transvaal town of Standerton, more than halfway to Tolstoy Farm, their leader was arrested for a third time in four days. Denied bail this time, he was hauled back to Natal where, two days later in Dundee, yet another coal-mining town with a British antecedent, he was found guilty in a small whitewashed courtroom—still in use in the postapartheid era—on three counts relating to his having led indentured laborers out of their mine compounds and out of the province. As always, Gandhi eagerly pleaded guilty to each charge. The sentence—welcomed by Gandhi, who was never truer to his principles than when he found himself in the dock—was nine months of hard labor.

If the authorities calculated that the detention of Gandhi and his Jewish lieutenants, Polak and Kallenbach, would be enough to break the back of the strike, they soon discovered that it had a momentum all its own. The indentured mine workers from Natal got within fifty miles of Johannesburg before a mass arrest could be organized. They had to be reminded by Polak that satyagraha ruled out active resistance to arrest. It took two days to pack them into three special trains that were waiting for them in the town of Balfour. Unlike Gandhi, the authorities made no provision for feeding the strikers, who were immediately prosecuted when they got back to Natal for the statutory crimes of abandoning their workplaces and illegally crossing the provincial border. They were then sentenced to hard labor underground at the mines, which had been conveniently certified as annexes to the overflowing Newcastle and Dundee jails—"outstations," they were called—with their white foremen deputized as warders. Hard labor meant there would be no pay for the six months the sentences would last. Beatings with sticks and *sjamboks*, whips made out of rhino or hippo hide, were among the methods used to herd the strikers back to work.

At the Ballengeich mine, the source of the first coal miners to march with Gandhi, the indentured laborers had been absent from the compound for nearly two weeks by the time they were returned. Goolam Vahed and Ashwin Desai, two South African scholars who have written a comprehensive account of the repression that followed the strike, offer the testimony a laborer named Madhar Saib later gave to the so-called protector about his encounter with a white mine captain named Johnston: "He gave me strokes with a sjambok on the posterior, the Kaffir policeman holding me by one of my hands. He then told me to go to work . . . [then] tripped me with his foot and I fell down, whereupon he placed his foot on my throat and gave me another stroke which caught me on the penis. When I urine it hurts."

Having discovered that hunger and exhaustion wouldn't be enough to break the strikes, the authorities had now determined on a crackdown. "Any government worth its salt would put its foot down," said Smuts, noting with scathing accuracy that the demand for the repeal of the head tax on former indentured workers had been "an afterthought" for Gandhi. His elevation of the head tax as an add-on to his earlier list of demands, Smuts said in a telegram to the mine owners, was a political maneuver "intended to influence Natal Indians, to whom the real grounds which he started the passive resistance movement, and which never included this tax, do not appeal."

The mine owners, disillusioned by the losses they'd suffered after listening to Gandhi's sweet talk, were now pressing for action. The Natal Coal Owners Association said the time had come for the strikers to be arrested. Taking their cues, editorial writers demanded to know why the government's response had been so feeble. *The Star,* which never bothered to dispatch a reporter to the scene, called on it to end its "shilly-shallying" in an editorial that ran under a headline that shouted COOLIE INVASION. How was it possible, the newspaper asked, that "a handful of fanatics, however conscientious," could get away with preaching "defiance of the laws of the Union"?

Adding to the gathering pressure for a crackdown was the spread of the strike's seeming flood tide even after Gandhi and his lieutenants had been locked up, even after the Natal strikers had been shipped back to the coal mines as not merely indentured laborers but prisoners of the state. From the coalfields in the hinterland it now reached the sugar lands on the Indian Ocean coast, leading at the height of the harvest season to a seemingly spontaneous succession of walkouts from the plantations and sugar refineries where indentured Indians still amounted to three-quarters of the workforce, taking in places where Gandhi had never campaigned.

The first walkout from a sugar estate appears to have come on November 5, at Avoca on the north shore, not far from Phoenix. By November 8, sugar refineries on the south shore had been hit, and by the middle of the month, when a stoppage by Indian street cleaners, water carriers, household servants, railway men, and boatmen briefly paralyzed Durban, there were probably more than ten thousand indentured Indians on strike in the province. In Durban, the strike was "practically universal," the chief magistrate reported on November 17. Sporadic incidents of sugarcane fields being set ablaze spread panic among the planters, some of whom bundled their wives and children off to safer precincts in the city.

The authorities now found themselves spread thin. Detachments of British troops had to be rushed from as far away as King William's Town in the Eastern Cape and Pretoria. At the height of the unrest, Durban found that its only detectives who could speak Hindustani or Tamil had been dispatched to Dundee to work on the case against the imprisoned

Gandhi, who by then had been moved to Bloemfontein in the Orange Free State, where Indians were basically banned. Rajmohan Gandhi suggests that this was done "so that no Indian could see Gandhi or carry messages from him."

The impression that this resistance and strife in the sugar country was spontaneous, that Gandhi the prisoner had willed or organized none of it, seems plausible on its face. How and when could he have done so? Nevertheless, there are scattered hints that the idea of calling out the plantation workers had crossed his mind. Before his own arrest on November 10, Hermann Kallenbach said as much in an interview in Johannesburg. "The leaders of the movement will not have the least compunction about asking all Indians on the sugar plantations to come out," he was reported to have said, at least two weeks before any had done so. The Indians could "get work on the farms anywhere," the report of his musings continued, "because they were more intelligent than the natives." In five years at Gandhi's side, the architect appears not to have learned how the indenture system, with its binding contracts, operated, or what he was supposed to think about the mental capacity of Africans. Perhaps his words were just bluster, intended merely to add to the pressure on the authorities. Nevertheless, Vahed and Desai found evidence that Gandhi's followers in the newly formed Natal Indian Association were sufficiently on top of events, despite the spreading turmoil, to ship food to striking laborers on a north-coast sugar estate after their employers had cut off rations.

The plantation to which the food aid was shipped happened to be at Mount Edgecombe, where Gandhi had encountered the African leader John Dube under the auspices of its owner, Marshall Campbell, eight years earlier. Campbell had been sympathetic to Gandhi's movement up to this point. He'd given a lunch honoring Gokhale the previous year; he was also a consistent opponent of the three-pound tax on former indentured workers. After his release from prison, Gandhi would write to him to say how sorry he was that Campbell's plantation was one of the first hit. He'd told his supporters in Durban, Gandhi's letter said, that "your men should be the last to be called out," acknowledging plainly enough that before being jailed, he'd been in on a discussion of tactics for extending the strike to the coastal sugar lands. "Had I been free and assisted in calling out the men," Gandhi told Campbell, "I must freely admit that I would have endeavored to call out your men also; but, as I have already stated, yours would have been the last estate."

For Campbell the letter was a last straw. His estates had seen weeks of turmoil. Gandhi's fine words about nonviolence were contradicted, he replied, by "grave threats of personal violence made by persons whom I believe to be your agents." Campbell writes as one who's sure of his facts. He'd actually been away from Natal and is relying on the testimony of his son William, who was relying in turn on that of his youngest brother, Colin. "The men will not listen to anybody but Ghandi [*sic*] or the gun," William wrote to his father who stopped short of calling Gandhi a hypocrite but lectured him severely on the harm done to defenseless Indians he was purporting to lead:

> You have admittedly started a movement which grew . . . till it was entirely beyond your control, and has culminated in riot, turbulence, and bloodshed, and the sufferers in this carnival of violence have been, and will be the ignorant laborers . . . and the intelligent Natal Indians . . . More and more of those you lead are realizing the weakness of your policy . . . and are coming to the conclusion that to use a large body of, in the main, contented but ignorant people . . . as a tool for procuring political rights by which most of them will never benefit, even if they are attained . . . is not a policy dictated by wisdom and far-sightedness.

In a second letter noticeably less apologetic than his first, Gandhi replied with the perfunctory distress of a field commander who has been informed of civilian casualties in an operation he ordered. Passive resistance, he reminded Campbell starchily, was the community's "only weapon." Obviously, its use over a wide area would have caused "much greater suffering" than earlier satyagraha campaigns. It could not have been otherwise. As he said in his first letter to Campbell, "In all our struggles of this nature, the innocent as well as the guilty suffer."

Neither Gandhi nor the plantation owner makes the slightest allusion to the role played by Campbell's son Colin in the deadliest of the confrontations at Mount Edgecombe. The account eventually accepted by a magistrate acknowledged that the violence had its origins in an attempt by the younger Campbell to force the striking laborers back to work with the support of mounted police. It also acknowledged that Colin Campbell drew his revolver and fired four shots. By his own testimony—accepted without question by the police, the magistrate, and the white press—the shooting came when he was already under attack; because his horse was agitated, he said, his shots went wild. Indians testified that he fired the first shots, killing an indentured worker named Patchappen, one of eight Indians killed or mortally wounded on the morning of November 17, and wounding another. Though Gandhi later mourned indentured workers who lost their lives in such confrontations as martyrs, he refrained from laying blame only on the side of the whites. On his farewell tour of South Africa a half year later, making his final rounds on Natal's north coast, he sounded as if he'd come to accept some of the elder Campbell's strictures. Fighting with sticks and burning fields of sugarcane were not passive resistance, he told an audience of indentured cane workers, according to a paraphrase of his remarks that ran in *Indian Opinion*. If he'd not been in jail, he'd "have repudiated them entirely and allowed his head to be broken rather than permit them to use a single stick against their opponents." It wasn't a point Gandhi often made on his farewell tour, which took on a triumphalist air, but it may have lodged in his consciousness. Later, in India, much to the dismay of his lieutenants in the nationalist movement, he regularly put the brakes on satyagraha campaigns at the first sign that the discipline of nonviolence was giving way.

The tone of Campbell's letters had been patronizing in a colonial way but not as hostile as might have been expected, considering all that had gone on at Mount Edgecombe. The Indians had refused to cut sugarcane for two weeks before the shootings. Local planters soon were calling for a show of force by mounted police to contain the agitation. Within a couple of days, bands of striking indentured laborers were reported to be roaming the neighborhood, armed with clubs and the long, razor-sharp knives used for cutting cane, stopping at residences of planters and their white managers to demand that Indian house servants come out and join the struggle. Or so the Durban newspapers reported.

A detachment of police, "both European and Native, galloped to Mount Edgecomb" from neighboring Verulam on November 17, *The Natal Advertiser* said. The "native police . . . quickly got in among their natural enemies," meaning the indentured Indians, until they had to be restrained. The Africans were armed with assegais, or spears, and the heavy Zulu war club known as a knobkerrie, a carved staff ending in a bulbous hardwood head that could be wielded like a medieval mace.

In reports by journalists and officials on clashes on the mines and in the sugar lands in these weeks, a standard story line unfolds. The forces of law and order are portrayed as restrained as long as they're kept under firm white command. The Indians are easily agitated, soon beyond reason, uncontrollable, nearly crazed, even when confronted by a well-armed constabulary with drawn firearms. The Indians fought with sticks and stones, the reports said; a handful are described as brandishing cane knives. These themes are regularly reflected in headlines in the English-language press. POLICE SHOW EXEMPLARY PATIENCE, the *Transvaal Leader* assured its readers, even as COOLIES RUN AMUCK.

Here's a judicial commission's eventual explanation of why Indian strikers had to be gunned down in the clashes at Mount Edgecombe: "The Indians were very excited and violent, and so determined were they that, though one of their number had been killed and several wounded . . . they had not been intimidated." A failure to use firearms, the commission concluded on the basis of testimony by militia officers, "might eventually have led to greater bloodshed." Ballistic evidence, it maintained, contradicted testimony by Indians who said the first shots had been fired by Campbell's son. The mounted police had to be called out, it explained, to deal with laborers committing the crime of disobeying a lawful order to return to work.

The police, members of the South African Mounted Rifles, had been "overwhelmed in numbers by the coolies" who charged "with all the suddenness characteristic of the Asiatic variableness of temper," the *Transvaal Leader* told its readers, hewing to the official line. The commission that looked into the Mount Edgecombe clashes also looked into a disturbance on November 21 at the Beneva Sugar Estates near Esperanza, where four strikers were killed after a display of Indian "variableness" forced the police to choose between using their weapons and leaving unarmed whites, including nearby women and children, "at the mercy of an excited crowd of almost two hundred Indians." The indentured cane cutters, in the official account, had resisted a police order to march to a nearby magistrate so they could be charged with desertion in an orderly way. Instead, they'd fallen supine and lain on their backs. "Get off your horses and come cut our throats," one of them unaccountably cries out in the official version, which the commissioners easily swallowed. When the police then approach on horseback, a seemingly possessed Indian leaps to his feet and smacks a trooper's horse with a stick, so hard that the animal falls down. Then, as the troopers withdraw, some with their revolvers unholstered, they're pursued by laborers with sticks. A witness told Reuters the Indians fought like "dervishes."

The Indians are regularly described as demented or nearly so, but when press accounts and official judgments get down to explaining the origins of the violence, it's always the same story. On the sugar estates, as well as the mines, clashes had less to do with the "variableness" of the Indian temper than with orders to police and military units to use force

in rounding up "ringleaders" and charging them with desertion if that
was what it took to break the strike and get the indentured Indians back
to work. With foremen on the mines and estates deputized as warders
and given authority to swear in Africans as "special constables," the line
between law enforcement and vigilantism soon blurred. An indentured
laborer named Soorzai sought refuge at the Phoenix Settlement, having
run off from a nearby plantation where he'd been thrashed. He soon
died. In all of Natal only one white, a planter named Armstrong, was
later charged with having gone too far. Seemingly at random, he'd
picked out two Indians—neither in his employ, both Muslims, one said
to be an imam—and had two of his African workers tear off their
clothes, then hold them while he beat them repeatedly with sjambok and
fists. Later he pursued the two already-battered men, repeating the
whole performance not once but twice. The Armstrong case caught
Fleet Street's attention. Downing Street then requested a report. Eventually, Armstrong was fined a hundred pounds. He was trying, he testified before sentencing, "to teach the whole tribe a lesson."

The reports on the crackdown that reached London also reached
India, where the viceroy, Lord Hardinge, took it upon himself in a
speech in Madras to voice India's "deep and burning sympathy" for
Gandhi's followers "in their resistance to invidious and unjust laws."
The viceroy followed the speech up with a cable urging a judicial commission to look into the shootings. Since the indenture system couldn't
have existed without the Raj's agreement, the viceroy's intervention carried weight. The British governor-general in South Africa, more or less
the viceroy's opposite number on this other side of the Indian Ocean,
reacted furiously. Lord Gladstone—youngest son of the Victorian
prime minister—praised the "great forbearance" of Botha and Smuts
and fumed in a cable to London over "official credence being given to
outrageous charges." The governor-general wanted nothing less than
the viceroy's dismissal. By the time of this clash in the stratosphere of the
empire, the strike was all but over. By December 10, according to official
statistics relayed to London, 24,004 "coolies" were back at work, 1,069
in jail, only 621 still striking. (Of those counted as strikers, some may
have found themselves suddenly jobless and therefore vulnerable to
deportation. Employers were now hiring Africans to fill jobs Indians had
held. At the Model Dairy, a popular Durban café, "white girls" had
replaced Indian waiters who struck.)

None of this was conveyed to the man who'd started it all. By his own
description, instead of the hard labor to which he'd been sentenced,

Gandhi was enjoying a respite in the special-status quarters reserved for him in the Bloemfontein jail. Most of his spare time, he wrote, was being devoted to the study of Tamil, the language of most of the indentured strikers, which had been eluding him for more than a decade. The spillover of the strike from the coalfields to the sugar lands combined with the bad press his response had won Smuts at home and abroad— for its initial restraint among his domestic critics, then, in London and elsewhere in the empire, for the shootings and floggings that the crack-down entailed—led him to recognize that this tussle with Gandhi had spun out of his control, that it had become too costly. He needed a face-saving way to back down and found it in the proposal for the judicial commission, which had two tasks, judging from the outcome. One was to whitewash the shootings, the other to propose a settlement forth-coming enough to close the book on Gandhi's satyagraha campaigns in South Africa.

Within a week of the viceroy's speech, the commission composed of three white men (one a longtime antagonist in Durban of Gandhi and the Indian community) had come into existence. Within a week of its appointment, it recommended that Gandhi, Kallenbach, and Polak be released, though they had nearly eight months to go on the sentences they'd received for lighting the fuse on the strikes.

Gandhi emerged from his five weeks of a meditative life in prison in a fighting mood. He didn't at first grasp that his campaigning days in South Africa were already at an end, that he was now only a month away from being able to claim victory in his struggle. Freed in Pretoria on December 18, he spoke that evening to supporters at the Gaiety Theater on Kort Street in Johannesburg. He said he'd miss the solitude and peace of jail, the opportunity it gave him for reflection. But he was ready to resume "the work on which he was engaged when he was convicted." Two days later, back in Durban, he told *The Natal Mercury* he'd seek "re-arrest and re-imprisonment" unless the judicial commission were enlarged to include "appointments from the European nationality known to possess no anti-Asiatic bias." That might not seem a huge demand; he wasn't asking, after all, for anything so precedent shattering as the appointment of an actual Indian to the panel considering the grievances of Indians; he was saying simply that Indian sentiments ought to be respected by at least some of its members. But in the Union of South Africa in 1913, it was a radical proposal, one the government instantly slapped down.

A day later he appeared at the Durban racecourse with his head shaved, dressed again like an indentured Indian laborer—a long loose kurta worn over baggy pants—before a crowd much larger than any he could have drawn in the city before the heroic march and his jailing. Bouquets were thrust into his hands, full-throated cheers engulfed him. There may still have been pockets of dissenters, especially among the merchants in the old Natal Indian Congress, but the size of the crowd— around six thousand, the largest he'd ever faced—made it clear that the conspicuous erosion of support for Gandhi among Natal's Indians in the months and years before his last campaign had now been more than reversed. If not unchallenged, he was once again clearly preeminent. The march had been the crowning experience of his time in Africa; this rally now crowned the march.

Gandhi used it to prepare his supporters for more struggle, urging them to get "ready again to suffer battle, again to suffer imprisonment, to march out . . . to strike, even though this may mean death." He explained that he'd put on the garments of a laborer in mourning for those who'd been shot down. The bullets that killed the indentured, he said, had pierced his heart too. So went the *Mercury*'s lengthy summary of his remarks. "How glorious it would have been if one of those bullets had struck him also, because might he not be a murderer himself . . . having advised Indians to strike?" Here he was, possibly for the first time, certainly not for the last, anticipating the end he'd meet thirty-four years later. "The struggle for human liberty," by Gandhi's now standard definition, was "a religious struggle." At this point, the newspaper's white reporter interpolated the throng's cries of "Hear, hear" in his account. It was a struggle, said Gandhi, "even unto death."

Despite his play on the word "murderer," the leader here is as solemn and free from self-reproach as a head of state laying a wreath at a war cemetery. He's offering a demonstration of what he had been saying about satyagraha ever since 1906, even before he coined the word: that the resistance he offered might provoke violence even, or especially, if it succeeded in maintaining the discipline of nonviolence, that it demanded "self-suffering" and, sometimes, martyrs. Gandhi is saying that he himself might eventually be among them. He's not saying that the indentured laborers who fell in the Natal shootings paid too high a price or expressing much concern about the indentured who survived who were now back at the plantations and mines, if anything, even poorer and less free. Calling it a religious struggle took care of all that. As always, he was not speaking in sectarian or communal terms. He was too much of an ecumenicist to imply that it was a Hindu struggle, or a

Hindu and Muslim struggle, or a struggle against people who happened to be Christians. He called it a religious struggle because of the sacrifice his followers, his satyagrahis, were prepared to make. It was another way of insisting that their motives were pure and disinterested, that they rose up not for themselves but for a future in which they might or might not have a share. If Gandhi ever thought of the possibility, even probability, that the indentured might have an actual stake in the strike—that some of them may have realized that their futures in South Africa could turn on the rollback of the head tax—he never found public words for the thought. Satyagraha was self-sacrifice, in his view, not self-advancement.

Gandhi is showing himself at this moment of symbolic near triumph and practical near stalemate to be anything but tenderhearted. He's an unconventional politician, but what he's saying is quite conventional for a leader in a conflict that remains unresolved. With the usual melodrama, he's saying that if more deaths were needed, Indians stood ready to pay the price. A couple of weeks later, reflecting on the death in jail of a seventy-year-old indentured laborer named Hurbatsingh, Gandhi elaborated on the theme. "I saw that it was no matter for grief if an old Indian like Hurbatsingh went to jail for India's sake and died while in prison," he said. It was a kind of fulfillment.

In donning the garb of the indentured and vowing to eat only one meal a day for as long as "this religious struggle" continued, he did more than declare himself to be in mourning. He completed the synthesis he'd been seeking throughout his two decades in South Africa between his public role and his questing inner self. The well-tailored attorney who went on retreats with Christian missionaries and immersed himself in Tolstoy had evolved step-by-step over those years into the leader of a movement that could capture mass support and, however fleetingly, international attention in an age when mass communications still depended on the printing press and the telegraph. As he'd later say himself, he'd found his vocation. His ongoing self-creation was now more or less complete.

Part of it was a new regard for the poorest Indians, which in South Africa meant the indentured. Soon he'd be scolding them again on their "addictions" to meat eating, tobacco, and drink. But fresh out of jail, he was "astonished," he wrote in a cablegram to Gokhale, "at the unlooked-for ability shown by indentured Indians without effective leadership to act with determination and discipline." They had shown "unexpected powers of endurance and suffering."

He still had to deal with the reality of white-ruled South Africa. The outcome would not be clear-cut. Gandhi put on the clothes of the indentured, downtrodden, and outcaste, but they formed only a small portion of his audience at the Durban racecourse. He could speak of them and for them, but, mostly, he wasn't speaking to them. His words wouldn't reach thousands who'd followed his lead without ever having heard or glimpsed him and who now were doing hard time back on the mines and the sugar estates. They'd chanted religious and patriotic slogans when they marched to the Transvaal, so he had some basis for calling it a religious struggle. And he'd never promised to deliver a change in their living standard or terms of employment. It was a point he later illustrated with an anecdote drawn from the early days of the march, offered as a kind of parable. One of the strikers had asked Gandhi for a hand-rolled cigarette known as a *bidi*. "I explained that they had come out, not as indentured laborers, but as servants of India. They were taking part in a religious war and at such a time they must abandon addictions such as drinking and smoking . . . the good men accepted this advice. I was never again asked for money to buy a bidi."

In assigning to the strikers a purely religious motive for their rising— and assuming for himself sole authority to declare when the movement had attained its ends—Gandhi was short-circuiting normal politics, including protest politics. In the perspective of his long life, of the struggles he had yet to undertake, this too could be called typically Gandhian. One day soon he'd leave South Africa, and those who'd followed him there would be left with his word that something important had been achieved, left with the pride of having stood up and having not been cowed when they answered his call. Not a small thing, most of them may well have concluded. Meanwhile, while the leader was being lionized at the racecourse, prosecutions of his followers were continuing across the province. On the day of his release, thirty-two passive resisters, including five women, had been sentenced to three months in jail for illegally entering the Transvaal.

With Gandhi's resurgence, the readership of P. S. Aiyar's *African Chronicle* took a dive. Among Indians there was no longer much of a market for sharp, independent criticism of the leader. Still Aiyar battled on. Of the Durban speech, he wrote: "Mr. Gandhi's performance of penance is a poor consolation for those who have lost their bread winners and dear ones." Called on to end his carping, the editor vowed he'd "keep silent when he is in the grave and even there too our spirit will not be dead."

As the calendar turned to 1914, Gandhi made a show of boycotting the judicial commission but slipped comfortably into renewed negotiations with Smuts. Before long the outlines of an agreement foreshadowed in their discussions became the commission's formal recommendations. Under this latest compromise the three-pound head tax on former indentured laborers would finally be scrapped; the marriage law would be amended to make room for traditional Indian marriage customs except polygamy as practiced by Muslims, which would be neither legalized nor banned; immigration would be eased for a relatively small number of Indians with a record of prior residence in South Africa; and a tiny number of "educated" Indians would be admitted so that the color bar would not be absolute. In broader—but hopelessly vague—terms was the government's formal pledge that the laws would be administered justly. In little more than a month after Gandhi's release from jail, he and Smuts reached their latest and last accord. By the end of June, the white Parliament had enacted the Indian Relief Act. Gandhi then declared his eight-year, on-and-off satyagraha campaign ended. The new law, he said, was a "magna carta for Indians" (the same phrase he'd used twenty years earlier to characterize Queen Victoria's more sweeping proclamation, which now counted for nothing in the new Union of South Africa). Continuing on his verbal binge, he also termed it "a charter of our freedom" and "a final settlement."

Soon he was having to amend, if not swallow, such high-flown words as dissenters like P. S. Aiyar pointed out how far short of the legal equality for which Gandhi had once struggled his "final settlement" now fell. What had been true before the last campaign remained true afterward: not only would Indians still be without political rights, but they'd still require permits to travel from one South African province to another; still not be allowed to settle in the Orange Free State or expand their numbers in the Transvaal, where they'd still have to register under what Gandhi once decried as the "Black Act"; and they would still be subject to a tangle of local laws and regulations saying where they could own land or set up businesses. Nothing in the Indian Relief Act relieved the situation of indentured laborers still under contract who'd been the main body of strikers and marchers.

Nevertheless, the indenture system itself was clearly on its last legs. Natal had stopped importing contract laborers from India as early as 1911. The only way to keep the system going, then, was to persuade those still working off their indentures to sign new contracts when their five-year commitments were up. Now the head tax no longer figured in such deals, no longer hung over the heads of the indentured. It may be said that Gandhi deserved a measure of credit for India's eventual decision in 1917 to shut the system down altogether by halting the shipment of indentured laborers to island colonies like Fiji and Mauritius, which had continued recruiting them after South Africa stopped, that his campaigns in South Africa had helped force the Raj's hand by arousing indignation among Indians. But the end of the indenture system hadn't ever been one of the declared aims of those campaigns.

In a farewell letter to South African Indians, Gandhi conceded there were unmet goals, which he listed as the right to trade, travel, or own land anywhere in the country. These could be achieved, he said, within fifteen years if Indians "cultivated" white public opinion. On political rights, his farewell letter looked to no distant horizon. This was a subject to be shelved. "We need not fight for votes or for freedom of entry for fresh immigrants from India," it advised. "My firm conviction is that passive resistance is infinitely superior to the vote," he told the *Transvaal Leader*. Speaking here was the Gandhi of *Hind Swaraj* who frankly scorned the parliamentary institutions for which most Indian nationalists thought they were fighting. Finally, he had to concede that the "final settlement" was not really final. While "it was final in the sense that it closed the great struggle," he rephrased himself, awkwardly blurring the operative adjective, "it was not final in the sense that it gave to Indians all that they were entitled to."

Smuts, who'd allowed himself to hope that he'd shelved the "Indian question" for the foreseeable future, considered Gandhi's reformulation a betrayal of their understanding. Gandhi couldn't express himself with his usual plainness on the question of how final the "final settlement" was because his "truth," in this instance, wasn't simple: the struggle had to end because he was leaving; he'd gotten all he could get. No one said it in so many words, but his departure was part of the deal.

White public opinion continued to harden, and Gandhi's rosy forecasts proved far off the mark. The situation of Indians in South Africa got worse, not better, after he turned his attention to India. They were no better than second-class citizens and often less than that. Under apartheid, Indians were more relentlessly ghettoized and segregated than ever before, though never as severely oppressed and discriminated against as Africans. It took sixty years before they could travel freely in the only country nearly all of them had ever known, more than seventy years before the last restriction on Indian landholding had been repealed. Equal political rights came eventually—a full century after Gandhi first sought them. In the years immediately following his departure, the white government dangled promises of free passage and bonuses to induce Indians to follow him home. Between 1914 and 1940, nearly forty thousand took the bait. Immigration had been halted, but the number of Indians continued to rise by natural increase. And naturally, then, the vast majority had only faint hand-me-down memories of the mother country. In 1990, as the apartheid system was collapsing, the Indian population of South Africa was estimated to have passed one million. In Nelson Mandela's first cabinet, four of the ministers were Indian.

Though the future for the next several generations of South African Indians would prove bleak, the leader himself was almost free. His very tentative plan had been to sail directly to India with an entourage of about twenty and settle in Poona (now spelled Pune) in western India so as to be near the ailing Gopal Krishna Gokhale. They had an understanding that Gandhi would keep a perfect silence on Indian issues for an entire year (as Gandhi put it, "keep his ears open and his mouth shut"). Gandhi now offered to nurse Gokhale and serve him as secretary. But Gokhale headed for Europe, specifically Vichy, in hopes that the waters there might be good for his failing heart. He asked Gandhi to meet him in London.

All he had to do before sailing for Southampton was complete a round of farewells. In Johannesburg, Mrs. Thambi Naidoo, who'd had the courage to go to the mines in Natal to appeal to the indentured mine workers to strike before Gandhi arrived on the scene, was said to have fallen over in a faint when her husband rose at a dinner and asked his old comrade-not-in-arms to adopt the four Naidoo sons and take them with him to India. She'd not been consulted. Gandhi thanked the "old jailbirds" for their "precious gift." As his departure day neared, the indentured laborers with whom he'd marched became a preoccupation. He ended his farewell letter to the Indians of South Africa by penning these words above his signature: "I am, as ever, the community's indentured laborer." In Durban, he addressed indentured laborers as "brothers and sisters," then pledged: "I am under indenture with you for all the rest of my life."

Speaking for the last time to his most loyal supporters, the Tamils of Johannesburg, Gandhi concluded by dwelling on matters of caste. The Tamils had "shown so much pluck, so much faith, so much devotion to duty and such noble simplicity," he said. They'd "sustained the struggle for the last eight years." But after all that had been acknowledged, there was "one thing more." He knew that they had carried over caste distinctions from India. If they "drew those distinctions and called one another high and low and so on, those things would be their ruin. They should remember that they were not high caste and low caste but all Indians, all Tamils."

It's impossible at this distance to know what had prompted this admonition on that occasion in that setting, this hauling into the open of a question even Gandhi had mostly allowed to recede for much of his time in South Africa. Had some Tamils on the great march, or even at this farewell gathering, shown their fear of ritual pollution? Or was he thinking ahead to what he would face in India? The exact connections are hard to pin down, but in a more general sense they seem obvious. For Gandhi, the phenomenon of indentured labor, a system of semi-slavery, as he branded it, had fused in his South African years with that of caste discrimination. Whatever the underlying demographic facts showing the proportions of high caste, low caste, and untouchable among the indentured, these were no longer two things in his mind but one, a hydra-headed social monster that still needed to be taken on.

Finally, on the dock in Cape Town, as he was about to board the SS *Kinfauns Castle* on July 18, 1914, he put a hand on Hermann Kallenbach's shoulder and told his well-wishers: "I carry away with me not my blood brother, but my European brother. Is that not sufficient earnest of what South Africa has given me, and is it possible for me to forget South Africa for a single moment?" They traveled third-class. Kallenbach brought with him two pairs of binoculars to use on deck. Gandhi, seizing on them as a gross self-indulgence, a backsliding into luxury by his friend, tossed them overboard. "The Atlantic," Rajmohan Gandhi, his grandson, writes, "was enriched." Fatefully, the *Kinfauns Castle* docked the day after the outbreak of a world war. Kallenbach moved with the Gandhis into a boardinghouse for Indian students and, in preparation for a new life with Gandhi in India, tried to concentrate on his Hindi and Gujarati studies. Gandhi sent off letters to Pretoria, New Delhi, and Whitehall, searching for a chink in a bureaucratic wall that threatened to keep him from realizing his dream of having the Jewish architect at his side in India. No one was willing or able to authorize a German passport holder to take up residence there in wartime. The viceroy wouldn't run "the risk." Gandhi delayed his own departure, but still the door stayed slammed. Eventually, Kallenbach was detained in a camp for enemy aliens on the Isle of Man, only to be returned to East Prussia in a prisoner swap in 1917. It was 1937 before the two men met again. "I have no Kallenbach," Gandhi lamented in his fifth year back in India.

The Gandhis leaving South Africa

Six months later arriving in Bombay

PART II

INDIA

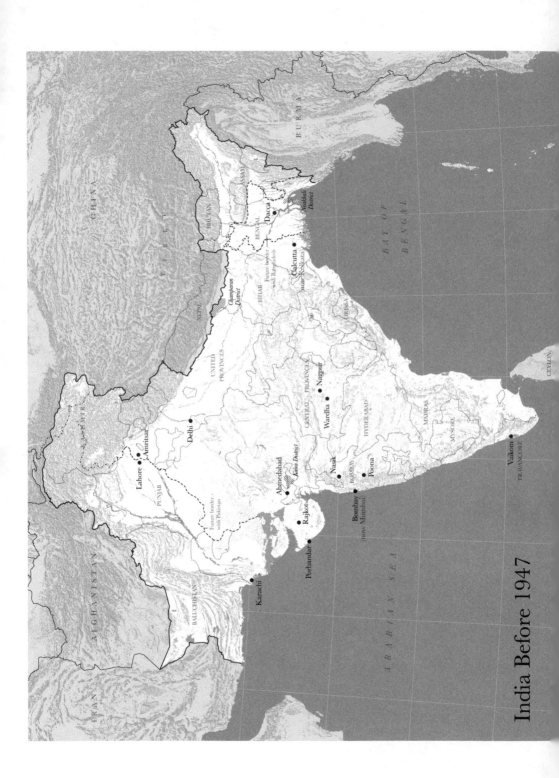

India Before 1947

6

WAKING INDIA

GANDHI HAD TAKEN A VOW to spend his first year back in India readjusting to the swirl of Indian life. He'd promised his political mentor, Gokhale, that he'd make no political pronouncements in that time, take no sides, plunge into no movements. He'd travel the land, establish contacts, make himself known, listen, and observe. In loftier terms, he could be seen as trying to embrace as much of the illimitable Indian reality as he could. That proved to be quite a lot, more than any other political figure on the Indian scene had ever attempted.

Welcomed at first as an outsider, he became an itinerant guest of honor at civic luncheons and tea parties, hailed wherever he landed for his struggles in South Africa. His standard response was to protest, with becoming but not overly insistent modesty, that the "real heroes" on that other subcontinent had been the indentured laborers, the poorest of the poor, who had continued striking even after he'd been jailed. He was more "at home" with them, he claimed in the first of these talks, than he was with the audience he was now facing, Bombay's political elite and smart set. In obvious ways, it was a questionable claim, but it described Gandhi, from his first pronouncements in India, as a figure focused on the masses. It was also about as provocative as he allowed himself to be over the course of 1915, his first year home. He could have taken Gokhale's death, just five weeks after that speech, as a release from his vow but refrained from advancing anything like a leadership claim of his own. But then, with his vow expiring in the first days of 1916, he made it plain that he had drawn some conclusions. "India needs to wake up," he told yet another civic reception, this one in the Gujarati town of Surat.

"Without an awakening, there can be no progress. To bring it about in the country, one must place some program before it."

Once again he drew explicitly on his experience in the Natal strikes, two years earlier. To move the nation, he would need to bring education to the poorest—just as he now claims to have done with the indentured in South Africa—to "teach them why India is growing more and more abject." Already, he's on his way to turning his South African experience into a parable, editing out unfortunate details such as the outbreaks of violence in the sugar country, or the ambiguity of the movement's results, especially the glaring shortfall in actual benefits for the indentured. Seasoned campaigner that he is, he's now looking forward, not back, to the advent of mass politics in India. However flawed his analogy to South Africa, he's declaring his ambition to jolt India with a program. It's too soon to say what content he may give to that program, but it's foreshadowed in some of the preoccupations he has carried with him, notably his concern for Hindu-Muslim unity and his condemnation of untouchability as a curse on India. The obvious difference is that from here on, he won't just be striving to carve out some breathing room for a marginalized minority in a system he has little or no hope of changing. In India, he'll have the opportunity and burden of trying to carry the majority with him, in an effort to overturn and replace the colonial rulers. Though he never voices an ambition to participate in government himself, he'll have much to say about the direction of society under the leaders he'd eventually designate, its need for reform.

Remarkably, it takes less than six years for the repatriated politician, starting on this vastly enlarged stage with no organization or following beyond his immediate entourage, to accomplish some facsimile of the "awakening" he sought. His audacious goal, ratified by a national movement that had been revitalized—practically reinvented in his image—is captured in a slogan: "Swaraj within a year." Swaraj, in Gandhi's reinterpretation, remains a fuzzy goal, some form of self-government approaching but not necessarily including full independence. What's radical is the promise that mass mobilization can make it a reality in just a year. And that fateful one year was to be 1921.

By then, Gandhi had come to be seen in a whole new light. No longer was he a guest of honor at tea parties. In the space of only two years—from the start of the hot season in April 1917, when he took up the cause of exploited peasants on indigo plantations in a backwater of northern Bihar, until April 1919, when he called his first nonviolent national strike—he had made his mark on India. Now, when he travels to promote his swaraj, massive throngs turn out numbering in the thousands and tens of thousands, crowds that were ten, even twenty times the throng he'd faced at the Durban racecourse. He makes a point of speaking in the vernacular, Gujarati or his still less than fluent Hindi—later, reaching for the broadest common denominator, he'd specify the demotic Hindustani as his preferred lingua franca—but he can usually be heard only in the front ranks of the crowds; and, when he barnstorms beyond North India, he's forced to speak in a language that's little or not at all understood by most of those within the sound of his voice.

It seems not to matter; the crowds keep swelling. The peculiarly Indian point of the commotion he inspires is, after all, not to hear but to view him: to gain or experience *darshan*, the merit or uplift that accrues to those who enter the spiritual force field of a *rishi*, or sage. For some in these crowds the vision of Gandhi is literally an apotheosis. They think they're seeing not a mere mortal but an actual avatar of a god from the crowded Hindu pantheon. By the second half of 1921, as the clock runs out on his premature promise of swaraj, the prophet finds it necessary to protest his own deification. "I should have thought," he writes, "that I had in the strongest sense repudiated all claim to divinity. I claim to be a humble servant of India and humanity, and would like to die in the discharge of such service." It's no time for avatars, he insists. "In India, what we want now is not hero-worship, but service."

Early on, he'd expressed his own skepticism about these ephemeral transactions between leader and those who want to bask passively in his afterglow: "I do not believe that people profit in any way by having darshan. The condition of him who gives it is even worse." But he allowed it to become an almost daily, sometimes nightly, feature of his life. Not just at his public appearances but often when he worked and slept outside his ashrams, there were usually stupefied congregations of piously staring onlookers, ignoring his determination to ignore them.

Occasionally, the adulation, expressed in the surge of crowds pressing forward—their members reaching out to graze the leader's feet with their fingertips, in a mark of humility and reverence—gets to be more than Gandhi can stand. In the English-language version of his weekly newspaper *Young India*—reincarnating *Indian Opinion*, still being printed in South Africa at the Phoenix Settlement—he complains of "the malady of foot-touching." Later, he warns: "In the mere touch of my feet lies nothing but the man's degradation." There's plenty of such degradation to be had. "At night," Louis Fischer reports, "his feet and shins were covered with scratches from people who had bowed low and touched him; his feet had to be rubbed with Vaseline." Later, his devoted English follower Madeleine Slade, renamed by him Mirabehn, was reported by a Fleet Street journalist to "actually shampoo his legs every night."

Gandhi's first Indian Boswell and faithful secretary in these years, Mahadev Desai, sees in the clamoring throngs a reflection of "the people's love-mad insolence." He's writing in his diary about a specific incident in February 1921 at the last of a succession of rural train stops between Gorakhpur and Benares. At each, a crowd had been waiting, blocking the tracks, demanding to see Gandhi, who'd addressed nearly 100,000 earlier that day in Patna. "We have come for the darshan of the Lord," one man tells Mahadev, who has gone so far at one stop as to impersonate Gandhi in a vain effort to get his adherents, who have never seen an image of their hero, to back off.

Now it's well past midnight. Yet another big crowd, after waiting for hours, converges on Gandhi's third-class carriage. The touring Mahatma isn't scheduled or inclined to speak. Mahadev pleads for silence so he can catch some sleep after a strenuous day, but deafening cries of "*Gandhi ki jai*"—"Glory to Gandhi"—rent the night sky. At last, a suddenly imperious Gandhi rises in a rage, his face twisted in an angry scowl Mahadev has never before seen. Once again, a clamorous mob made up of his supposed followers is hanging from the footboards of the train, preventing it from moving on. The apostle of nonviolence later admitted that he felt an urge to beat someone at that moment; instead of lashing out verbally, he beats and smacks his own forehead in full view of the crowd. Again he does it, then a third time. "The people got frightened," he wrote. "They asked me to forgive them, became quiet and requested me to go to sleep."

This picture of an infuriated Mahatma assaulting himself in order to turn back an idolatrous, overwhelmingly rural crowd in the early hours of the morning obviously raises questions about the fundamental nature of his appeal. Gandhi by now had spelled out the program he seemed to promise in Surat. Practically all of it had been at the forefront of his thinking when he left South Africa, or is easily traceable to his preoccupations at Tolstoy Farm. Swaraj would come when India solidified an unbreakable alliance between Muslims and Hindus; wiped out untouchability; accepted the discipline of nonviolence as more than a tactic, as a way of life; and promoted homespun yarn and handwoven fabrics as self-sustaining cottage industries in its numberless villages. He would call these "the four pillars on which the structure of swaraj would ever rest." And the national movement—more to please him than out of conviction—would formally adopt his program as its own. In Ahmedabad in December 1921, as the year he'd given himself and India to achieve swaraj expired, the Indian National Congress would give no thought to spurning him as a failed prophet. Instead, it would vote to assign Gandhi "sole executive authority" over the movement, making him, in effect, a one-man Politburo in a period when most of his lieutenants and former rivals had been removed from the scene, having been jailed by the British authorities (who hadn't quite figured out how to handle the Mahatma himself). The revivalist in him had been tirelessly pushing the four-part program forward in his writing and itinerant preaching, declaring each part in its turn to be absolutely necessary for swaraj, its very essence. The logical connections are sometimes clear only to him. Gandhi is capable of arguing that Hindu-Muslim unity cannot be achieved without spinning. Other times the banishment of untouchability becomes the highest priority. Not everyone understands, but his words become a creed for a growing band of activists spread across the land in places he has visited. Meanwhile, by 1921, the newly empowered political tactician is threatening civil disobedience. As an expression of the discipline and mission Gandhi had taken on himself, his program offered a coherent vision. As practical politics, it could be, to put it mildly, a tricky if not impossible juggling act.

But the crowd at that one, now nameless, rail siding on the Gangetic plain hadn't stayed on by the thousands through a long night to express its enthusiasm for Gandhi's four pillars or its fellow feeling for Muslims or untouchables or even to enlist in his next nonviolent campaign. It had come to pay homage to the man, more than that, to a saint. The idea that he cared for them in a new and unusual manner had been communicated only too well. The idea that he had demands to make on them had gotten across in a wispy, vague, and incidental way, if at all. Gandhi's actual goals could verge on the utopian, but they could also be, in this teeming Indian context, beside the point—sometimes, not nearly acceptable in the real world he meant to change. The throngs that turned out for him had their own ideas about what he was promising; often they seemed to be waiting for a messiah to usher in a golden age in which debts and taxes and the prevailing scarcities would cease to weigh on them. Sometimes they would call this dawning era of ease and sufficiency, if not plenty, the Gandhi Raj. Regularly speaking past his adherents, Gandhi found himself a prisoner of the expectations he aroused.

In his own supple, rationalizing mind there was seldom tension between his two roles, that of spiritual pilgrim and that of mass leader—spearhead of a national movement, tribune of a united India that had come into being first in his own imagining. When conflict did arise between the Gandhi personae, it was almost invariably the mass leader, not the spiritual pilgrim, who retreated. His career is punctuated by periods of seeming withdrawal from active leadership, similar to his withdrawal to Tolstoy Farm in South Africa between 1910 and 1912. But his retreats from politics were never final. Given India's poverty, he would argue, the only fulfillment for a religiously motivated person was in service through politics. "No Indian who aspires to follow the ideal of true religion can afford to remain aloof from politics," he said. This was Gandhi's distinctive interpretation of *dharma*, the duty of a righteous man. Judith Brown, a British scholar, puts it well when she writes that for him it was "morality in action."

Those Gandhi called "political *sannyasis*," religious seekers who renounced the comforts of the world but lived in the world to make it better, had a duty "to mix with the masses and work among them like one of themselves." That meant, first of all, speaking their languages rather than the language of the colonial oppressor, in which Gandhi himself happened to excel. The emphasis is original with him. It can be called Gandhian. It's the self-invented Gandhi who came out of Africa, the Gandhi of *Hind Swaraj*, who took it on himself to dole out rations of bread and sugar to indentured miners in Natal about to court mass arrest by following him across a forbidden border.

On the Indian scene, all this seemed at first to push him to the periphery, an exotic and isolated creature. The Gandhian emphasis on speaking to the rural poor in their own languages left him instantly swimming against the tide in a largely Anglicized national movement that conducted most of its business in English. A president of the Indian National Congress, which Gandhi would eventually take over, had recently spoken warmly of "the spread of English education" as "perhaps [Britain's] greatest gift to the people of India." It had, this pre-Gandhian said, "instructed our minds and inspired us with new hopes and aspirations." His assessment was a kind of fulfillment of the vision of Thomas B. Macaulay, the great British historian, who had argued in his landmark "Minute on Indian Education," written in 1835, that the British could only rule India if they succeeded in forming "a class who may be interpreters between us and the millions whom we govern; a class of persons, Indian in blood and colour, but English in taste, in opinions, in morals, and in intellect."

As a product of the Inner Temple in London, Gandhi might himself have been counted as a member of that class. Instead, he rebelled against the dominance of the colonialist's language. Macaulay, in an ensuing, less-quoted passage, had also said it would be the responsibility of this Anglicized new class "to refine the vernacular dialects . . . and to render them by degrees fit vehicles for conveying knowledge to the great mass of the population." There was an injunction that would have resonated with the populist in Gandhi. Whenever he could, he shunned English, though he'd been functioning in the language of India's rulers for most of his adult life. Fewer than 1 million of India's population then of 300 million, he pointed out sharply, "have any understanding of English. "All the existing agitation is confined to an infinitesimal section of our people who are a mere speck in the firmament," he would say.

Such home truths went down hard. Even Gokhale may have backed off. He'd found *Hind Swaraj* regressive and unpalatable but nevertheless seems to have regarded Gandhi as a possible successor as leader of a tiny reformist vanguard, known as the Servants of India Society, he'd founded with the aim of infiltrating a cadre of totally disciplined, totally selfless nationalists into Indian public life. But before the great man's death, it dawned on the newcomer that he might not fit in there. He was too singular; his history of strikes and passive resistance, his tendency to make himself the sole arbiter of the "truth" that gave force to satyagraha, his stand on the language issue, all set him apart even before he cast his lot in Indian politics. In other words, he came with his own doctrine, and it was not that of the Servants of India Society.

He showed his grief for Gokhale by walking barefoot everywhere he went for weeks after his guru's demise. Pious and heartfelt as it was, the gesture also underscored Gandhi's singularity, as if he were claiming a place for himself as Gokhale's chief mourner. Seen that way, it was more likely to put off than to touch the surviving members of the Servants of India Society who found him, as he later said, "a disturbing factor." Writing to Hermann Kallenbach four months after he returned home and shortly after his application to the Servants of India Society had finally been rebuffed, the newcomer acknowledged that his views, the ones he arrived with, were "too firmly fixed to be altered."

"I am passing through a curious phase," he went on. "I see around me on the surface nothing but hypocrisy, humbug and degradation and yet underneath it I trace a divinity I missed [in South Africa] as elsewhere.

This is my India. It may be my blind love or ignorance or a picture of my own imagination. Anyway it gives me peace and happiness." The same letter reports the establishment of his first Indian ashram on the outskirts of Ahmedabad, in Gujarat, his home region. "I am an outsider and belong to no party," he remarked a year later.

The Kochrab Ashram had only two cottages and a total population of under fifty. But Gandhi had large ambitions for it. "We want to run our institution for the whole of India," he wrote. Characteristically, in his self-assigned role of rule giver, he'd also drafted an eight-page constitution, which can be read as a redrafting, with a decidedly Gandhian twist, of the rules his guru had laid down for the Servants of India Society. At Gokhale's death, only two dozen candidates had successfully completed a rigorous five-year training program under the stern tutelage of the "First Member," as the founder referred to himself. They took seven vows, one involving a promise to live on a subsistence wage.

Gandhi, who declared himself his ashram's "Chief Controller" in his draft of its constitution, promulgated vows that were more numerous and far-reaching. He demanded total celibacy of all "inmates," even those who were married; "control of the palate" (on the understanding that "eating is only for sustaining the body"); a "vow of non-possession" (meaning that "if one can do without chairs, one should do so"); and a "vow against untouchability" (involving a commitment to "regard the untouchable communities as touchable"). Members were to speak their own Indian languages and learn new ones. They were also to take up spinning and handloom weaving. To the extent that these rules—written down within five months of his arrival in Bombay—were closely observed, the ashram could be expected to turn out a steady supply of replica Gandhis. About half its original intake included relatives and adherents who'd followed Gandhi from South Africa, including Thambi Naidoo's sons and a Muslim cleric from Johannesburg, Imam Abdul Kader Bawazir.

"The object of the Ashram," Gandhi wrote, "is to learn how to serve the motherland one's whole life." So much self-denial was built into the lessons he proposed to give those he classed as "novitiates" that the appeal was sure to be severely limited on both sides of the communal divide. Meat-eating Muslims were bound to see the ashram as a Hindu retreat; that was, after all, the meaning of the word. Hindus had to wrestle with Gandhi's views on untouchability, not to mention sex. (Celibate now for more than a decade, Gandhi was getting ever more crotchety on the subject. "I cannot imagine a thing as ugly as the intercourse of man and woman," he would counsel his second son, Manilal, who found self-denial a trial.) Neither Muslims nor Hindus were inclined to fall in line with Gandhi when it came to the problem of human excrement and his Tolstoyan insistence that its removal be seen as a universal social obligation. Simply put, mass appeal was never going to be a prospect, or problem, for the ashram.

Even before its modest beginning in May 1915, Gandhi had his first encounters with an emerging Muslim leadership. His first week back, in fact, Mohammed Ali Jinnah, the future founder of Pakistan, presided and gave the speech of welcome at a reception Bombay Gujaratis held for their native son. On the surface, the two men had much in common. Their families came from the same part of Gujarat, the coastal Kathiawad region, now more commonly known as Saurashtra; both were lawyers trained in London. But the parallel ended there. Jinnah's grandfather was a Hindu who converted to Islam. Dapper in a bespoke suit, Jinnah welcomed the new arrival in the well-turned English sentences of a colonial gentleman. Gandhi, dressed like a Gujarati villager in vest, kurta, dhoti, and flattened turban, replied colloquially in his native language, already insinuating, without putting it in so many words, that the Anglicized professional elite could not by itself achieve India's freedom.

At the time of this encounter, Jinnah was a rising figure in the Indian Congress, the national movement Gandhi had yet to join. To put it mildly, he wasn't much given to religious enthusiasms, then or later. In politics, he would have insisted at the time, he was an Indian nationalist; he too had drawn close to Gokhale. Yet two years later he was persuaded to take out membership as well in the Muslim League, the movement he'd eventually lead out of India, impelled by injured pride and a somewhat cynical but undoubtedly effective argument—that Gandhi had turned the Congress into "an instrument for the revival of Hinduism and for the establishment of Hindu Raj." The path to India's partition would have many twists and turns, none harder to map than this: one of those who brought Jinnah the nationalist into the staunchly sectarian Muslim League was a Pan-Islamist named Muhammad Ali who then became Gandhi's closest Muslim ally in the Congress.

Ali had a relatively humble background in the princely state of Rampur and an Oxford degree. With his elder brother, Shaukat, who'd won renown as a cricketer, he was already recognized among Muslims as a spokesman for beleaguered Islam within and beyond India. Specifically, the Ali brothers stoked and then gave voice to the community's mount-ing anxieties over the decline of the Ottoman empire in the years leading up to the world war. The slow erosion of authority that ultimately undermined the Mughal emperors in nineteenth-century India now seemed to be recurring in what was still Constantinople. In his religious role as caliph, the sultan was held to be the highest authority in Sunni Islam, suzerain still of the holy places on the Arabian Peninsula and a successor of the Prophet. Though few Indian Muslims actually visited Constantinople, they may have taken that connection more seriously than most Turks. The Ottoman sultanate became for them a symbol of Islam's standing in the modern world and therefore a cause for a minor-ity community anxious about its own status in India.

By the time Gandhi met Muhammad Ali in Delhi in April 1915, a month before his ashram opened, the Alis' passionate identification with the Ottoman cause had put them at cross-purposes with British power in India, which had cultivated and generally received the loyalty of Mus-lims who'd been educated in the English way. The sultan, after all, had just allied himself and his army with the German kaiser and the Austro-Hungarian Empire, against whom British Indian troops would soon be fighting, including many Muslims. Almost overnight, therefore, the Ali brothers had gone, in the eyes of the colonial authorities, from being seen as loyalists to potential agents of sedition. As the home ground shifted in response to far-off events, the Alis also found themselves closer to Indian nationalists who were overwhelmingly Hindu, among whom only one was in a position to intuit their feelings and identify with them. This was the newly arrived Gandhi, onetime mouthpiece for the Muslim merchant class of Durban and Johannesburg, a longtime vet-eran of political rallies in mosques. "I believe that Hindus should yield up to Mohammedans whatever the latter desire and that they should rejoice in so doing," the South African Gandhi had said in 1909. "We can expect unity only if such large-heartedness is displayed." The remark is recalled with some bitterness by Hindu nationalists to this day.

Muhammad Ali, a polished and sometimes florid polemicist in En-glish as well as Urdu, had written admiringly of "that long-suffering man, Mr. Gandhi," referring to his leadership in South Africa. He now welcomed Gandhi to Delhi, the former Mughal capital, newly desig-nated as capital of British India. It was, Gandhi said, "love at first sight." The two men wouldn't meet again for more than four years, for the Ali brothers were placed under confinement—a loose form of house arrest—soon after this first encounter. Gandhi then made appeals for the release of the brothers one of his earliest political commitments in India. He and Muhammad Ali kept up a correspondence. By the time the brothers were freed from detention, Gandhi and the Alis were ready to take up each other's causes.

That connection to Muslims would count soon enough. It would prove to be a crucial factor in Gandhi's takeover of the Indian National Congress. What matters here is the evidence that even before he had launched his first campaign in India, even before he joined the Congress, Gandhi had strong convictions about the need for Hindus to make common cause with Muslims if Indians were to be one people. No doubt he exaggerated the extent to which this had actually happened among Indians in South Africa, but it was the first political lesson he'd learned there and a touchstone of his nationalist creed.

His urgent feelings about untouchability also derived from lessons learned on that other subcontinent. The way whites there treated Indi ans, he'd long ago concluded, was no worse than the way India treated its Pariahs, scavengers, and other outcastes. In his own mind these feelings were only deepened by his passionate engagement with the indentured strikers in Natal. Strictly speaking, only a minority of them may have counted as untouchable, but they were mostly lower caste, and, in Gandhi's view, they were all sufficiently oppressed in a hierarchical system to make them virtual slaves. Caste lines blurred as they marched with him across the veldt. It was a contest of what he called "high and low," and he'd finally found a way to align himself with the "low."

The fresh memory of South Africa and the 1913 strikes, it can thus be argued, helped feed his feelings about untouchability when he returned to India. When he'd been home less than two months, he went to Hardwar in the Himalayan foothills at the time of the Kumbh Mela, a festival held every twelve years that draws masses of Hindu pilgrims, upwards of two million of them. The suffocating spectacle appalled him, not least because of his nagging preoccupation with sanitation and its opposite, which was everywhere on display. "I came to observe more of the pilgrims' absent-mindedness, hypocrisy and slovenliness, than of their piety," he later wrote. Soon he drafted the small entourage he'd transplanted from the Phoenix Settlement, who'd been staying nearby, to work as scavengers, scooping up excrement and shoveling dirt over the open-pit latrines used by the pilgrims. On a vastly larger scale, it was a reprise of his disillusioning first encounter with the Indian National Congress in Calcutta fourteen years earlier.

In his first real controversy in India, he defied the traditional injunctions against social pollution even more directly, creating a scandal. The controversy spilled out of his ashram a few months after it was established, provoked by Gandhi's acceptance of a Dhed as a resident there. Dheds traditionally deal with animal carcasses and hides—essentially they're tanners—which is enough to brand them and their offspring forevermore as untouchable whether they've anything to do with hides or not. The idea wasn't his own; it came in the form of a letter from a Gujarati reformer named A. V. Thakkar, usually called Thakkar Bapa, who'd remain Gandhi's right arm on the issue of untouchability over more than three decades. "A humble and honest untouchable family is desirous of joining your ashram," Thakkar wrote. "Will you accept them?"

For Gandhi there was only one possible answer. He called his Dhed "learned." Probably that just meant he was literate. He was named Dudabhai Malji Dafda, Duda for short. "Greater work than passive resistance has commenced," Gandhi wrote in one of his weekly letters to Hermann Kallenbach, who was still marooned in London by the war. "I have taken in a Pariah from these parts. This is an extreme step. This has caused a breach between Mrs. Gandhi and myself. I lost my temper. She tried it too much."

The first confrontation leads to another that, as Gandhi relates it a week later, comes close to replicating the scene in Durban in which the barrister Gandhi dragged his wife to the gate of his house after she objected to cleaning his formerly untouchable law clerk's chamber pot. Evidently, Ba's views on the issue hadn't much evolved over eighteen years. "I have told Mrs. Gandhi that she could leave me," he writes a week later. Two weeks after that, he's still complaining that "she's making my life hell." Finally, after more than a month, Gandhi finds a way to bend Ba to his will. He refuses to eat a staple of his highly restricted diet; that is, he gives up nuts. Nuts! "I had to undertake partial starvation," he tells Kallenbach, without a trace of irony. In context, he means to convey the full pathos of his situation as he experienced it.

The breakdown isn't just marital. Scarcely four months after starting the ashram—nine months after returning to India—Gandhi is faced with a virtual walkout by his disciples over the presence of the Dheds. "I have been deserted by most helpers," he complains, "and the burden is all falling on my shoulder assisted by two or three who are remaining staunch." Most will trickle back, but one who stays away permanently is Gandhi's own sister, Raliatbehn. "Your not being with me has given me a wound that will never heal," he later writes to her.

Contributions from Ahmedabad industrialists and merchants, on which he has been relying to keep the place going, suddenly dry up. Offended neighbors fend off not only Duda but all members of the ashram seeking to use nearby wells. The effect on Gandhi is to make him, once his year's vow of silence on Indian issues elapses, even more insistent in his condemnation of untouchability. He speaks of moving out himself—"shifting to some Dhed quarters and sharing their life." But an anonymous gift from the leading Ahmedabad industrialist, Ambalal Sarabhai, keeps the ashram running. Duda is joined by his wife, Dani, and finally, in complete surrender, Ba bows to Gandhi's request that they adopt Duda and Dani's daughter, Lakshmi, as their own. "She has beautifully resigned herself to things she used to fight," Gandhi says in a letter to Sonja Schlesin, his former secretary in South Africa. Ba's conversion, it turns out, was only on the surface. Seven years later Gandhi complains, "She cannot bring herself to love [Lakshmi] as I do." She's still surrounded, he says in 1924, by a "wall of prejudice."

The resistance the social reformer encountered to the admission of untouchables to his ashram didn't silence him. But if the shrewd politician that he also was had harbored any illusion that the fight against untouchability might be a popular cause, he now learned that a moral argument that could be uttered fairly easily from a platform in India's sophisticated precincts had the potential to backfire when words became deeds. In his earliest campaigns in rural India, Gandhi never ducked the question of untouchability. "This great and indelible crime," he called it, mincing no words. But mostly it remained incidental to whatever his immediate cause happened to be.

Take, for instance, that of the oppressed tenant farmers of the Champaran, in the Himalayan foothills of northern Bihar, who were forced by a corrupt combination of local law, taxation, chronic indebtedness, and crude force to devote a portion of the land they farmed to growing indigo plants on which they seldom earned a meaningful return. The indigo, in demand in Europe as a dye for fine fabrics, went to a class of British planters who leased the land, including whole villages, from large Indian landlords called *zamindars;* with the land came the tenants, who then had little or no bargaining power against the planters. It would be hard to argue that the state of these peasants, called *ryots,* was any better than that of the indentured laborers in South Africa; in many cases, it was probably worse. The system had grown up over nearly a century. "Not a chest of indigo reaches England without being stained with human blood," a British official once wrote.

Gandhi was invited into the Champaran in early 1917. He had never heard of the district; hardly anyone there had ever heard of him. Ordered to leave by the collector, the local representative of colonial authority, Gandhi politely defied the order, then stayed up nights sending missives in all directions until the national movement and everyone from the viceroy on down knew he was facing arrest. Crowds of rough, unlettered tenant farmers gathered to protect him; youthful nationalists made their way to the Champaran as would-be satyagrahis; and the viceroy intervened to cancel his expulsion.

Within weeks Gandhi himself was appointed to an official commission investigating the complaints of the tenant farmers—it would recommend they be freed from any compulsion to grow indigo—and newly minted Gandhian workers, some from the ashram near far-off Ahmedabad on the other side of India, were opening schools and giving lectures on sanitation in Champaran villages. "We have begun to convince the people," a Gandhian worker said in a letter to the Mahatma, "that there is no loss of prestige in at least covering the feces with earth by doing it ourselves for them." No record was kept on how many villagers took to doing it for themselves.

On their leader's insistence, the workers were also learning to ignore the usual rules against eating in the company of anyone from a lower caste. One of these early Gandhians, a young lawyer, left this testimony: "All of us who worked with him, and who, till then, had been observing this restriction and dining only with our caste people, gave it up and began to eat together—to eat not only with members of the so-called higher castes but even with people from whom even water was not acceptable. And the important thing is we did it openly and not in secrecy or privately. We used to do it surrounded by villagers who had come from distant places, and we took our food together in their presence." The young lawyer, Rajendra Prasad, passed up a position as a judge and stayed on as a Gandhian. Years later he became president of the Indian National Congress; in 1948 he became independent India's first president, its ceremonial head of state.

By sheer example and force of personality, Gandhi began to assemble the core of what would become a movement. It can't be said this happened spontaneously; he worked too hard, usually rising at four in the morning. His intense focus on the details of his various struggles and on the individuals who followed in his train, his prodigious program of writing and speaking, make it plain there was a driving force. But he was more method and example than plan in these early years back in India, going on short notice where he seemed to be wanted and needed. Defining himself in these improvised ventures, he found disciples like the youthful Prasad, some of whom would become leaders of a postcolonial India that was not yet on anyone's horizon, except perhaps Gandhi's. Months after Champaran came another rural campaign, this one against ruinous colonial taxes following crop-destroying rains in the Kheda district of Gujarat, which Gandhi assigned to another young lawyer he'd drawn to his side. Vallabhbhai Patel would be another future president of the Indian National Congress and a deputy prime minister after independence.

By one estimate, Gandhi spent 175 days in Bihar in 1917 working on the Champaran struggle. Later he would call it his "birthplace," meaning it was his first immersion in rural India. Referring back to the Natal strikes, he'd spoken of the need for educated Indians to work with "the poorest of the poor." Now he was finally doing it himself on home ground. India needed to adopt a "habit of fearlessness," he said. More than anything, that was what his new adherents saw in him. "The essence of his teaching was fearlessness and truth and action allied to these," Jawaharlal Nehru would write. It was also the essence of the man. "This voice was somehow different from others," Nehru said. "It was quiet and low, and yet it could be heard above the shouting of the multitude; it was soft and gentle, and yet there seemed to be steel hidden away somewhere in it . . . Behind the language of peace and friendship there was power and the quivering shadow of action and a determination not to submit to a wrong."

This preoccupation with "fearlessness" may explain another of the surprising, seemingly inexplicable twists in Gandhi's long career on two continents, a choice echoing the one he made in 1906 when he threw himself into the campaign to put down the Zulus. Gandhi has a way of repeating himself, of recycling old answers when confronting new questions. This time, seeming to brush aside the vows of nonviolence that he made his disciples take, he pledged to devote himself to recruiting Indian troops for the war in Europe, where they'd fill in the ranks of British forces depleted by the carnage. The staunchly pro-British Gandhi who'd voiced loyalty to the empire, who'd recruited stretcher bearers in two South African conflicts, had seemed to fade into the background after his last fruitless trip to London on behalf of the "British Indians" of the Transvaal in 1909. That Gandhi was altogether absent from the pages of *Hind Swaraj*, the nationalist tract written that year on the voyage back to South Africa, in which he likened the British parliament to a whore. Again in wartime, he now reappears, unctuously promising his loyal support as part of a political bargain that the Bania in him proposes in letters to the viceroy and the viceroy's secretary, at the end of April 1918, letters that recall his sometimes wheedling appeals to Smuts.

Gandhi is still, for all practical purposes, an independent operator in India, not yet head of a movement. Elsewhere he acknowledges at about the same time that he is "but a child of three" in Indian politics. Still, he writes with the conviction of one who now thinks he can speak for the country and its people. This is no pose but what he has recently come to believe. "I have traveled much," he'd said a month earlier, "and so come to know the mind of India." A few years later, on the strength of his Champaran and Kheda experiences and his subsequent traveling through rural India, he would make this boast even more emphatic: "Without any impertinence I may say I understand the mass mind better than anyone amongst the educated Indians." This was the end of 1920; he'd been back in India for not quite six years, actively campaigning in its villages for a little less than three. Yet the claim was accepted thereafter, perhaps because it had already become obvious that he'd made a connection in that relatively brief time with rural India that no politician with longer experience could begin to match. If so, it's only in the specific context of Champaran and Kheda that we can understand Nehru's observation that the former barrister, recently repatriated out of Africa, "did not descend from the top; he seemed to emerge from the millions of India." It wasn't sorcery but his willingness to take on obscure issues in obscure places, to act decisively on the conviction that what he'd learned in another place about building a mass movement could apply at home.

The political bargain he offered the viceroy, Lord Chelmsford, in April 1918 boiled down to this: if the Raj would allow some semblance of a positive outcome in the Kheda district, where it had been confiscating the land and livestock of peasants who'd taken a Gandhian pledge to withhold taxes on their property; and if it would show a new sensitivity to Muslim grievances that had deepened during the war, by allowing him to visit the Ali brothers, who were interned in central India, and by pressing the cause of what he called "the Mahomedan states" (meaning Turkey but not using the word because Turkey was now an enemy of Britain); if it did these things, gave him the gestures he needed, then the author of the doctrine of satyagraha, of unswerving nonviolence, would throw himself into the war effort as the viceroy's "recruiting agent-in-chief." The Bania insists that his support is "ungrudging and unequivocal," but then he lays down his conditions. "I love the English nation, and I wish to evoke in every Indian the loyalty of the Englishman," the special pleader now pleads.

The British are as adept as Smuts in exploiting Gandhi's eagerness for a deal without giving anything tangible in return. The Ali brothers remain interned; his appeal to see them goes unanswered. An order had already been transmitted down the chain of command to go easy on the Kheda confiscations, but this is done on the quiet, denying Gandhi and the civil disobedience campaign he fostered any obvious moment of victory or recognition of the role he has played. Gandhi, fobbed off with official expressions of gratitude for his loyal stand, is left to fulfill his pledge.

A depressing episode ensues. The recruiting agent in chief goes back to Kheda with the aim of enlisting twenty men from each of six hundred villages, a total of twelve thousand new soldiers. Where he was received as a savior months before, he's now sometimes heckled. Fearlessness is what he'd been trying to inculcate. What better means is there than military training, he now discovers, to "regain the fearless spirit"? His arguments, expressed in a series of leaflets and speeches as he trudges for the better part of three months through heat and dust and monsoon rain, from village to village, become far-fetched and contradictory. He implores wives to send their husbands to sacrifice themselves on behalf of the empire, blithely promising, "They will be yours in your next incarnation." Fighting for the empire, he now argues, is "the straightest way to swaraj." An India that has shown military prowess, his reasoning goes, will no longer need Britain to defend it. Fighting is a necessary step on the way to nonviolence. "It is clear that he who has lost the power to kill cannot practice non-killing." The Mahatma's powers of rationalization can still amaze and confound; they're inexhaustible, but he is not.

Finally, in August 1918, he collapses with dysentery after having admitted that he has enlisted "not a single recruit." He would later describe himself as "not a quick despairer." This time he struggles to draw a positive lesson from his experience. "My failure so far suggests that people are not ready to follow my advice. They are ready, however, to accept my services in a cause which suits them. This is as it should be," he writes to his fourth son, Devadas. It's a basic political lesson.

Eventually, he goes through the motions of submitting a list of about a hundred recruits, made up largely of co-workers, relatives, and members of the ashram; as he approaches his fiftieth birthday, his own name heads the list. But by then the war is practically at an end, and Gandhi, bedridden for months with dysentery and a gathering sense that he'd lost his way, is at a personal nadir. In this generally gloomy and weakened state, he also undergoes surgery for hemorrhoids and doesn't reenter politics until the following February. Slightly shamefaced, he attributes his recovery to a compromise of his dietary principles. A decade earlier he'd given up milk on account of the aphrodisiac qualities he attributed to it. Now he allows himself to be persuaded by Kasturba that he'd only taken a vow against cow's milk, not goat's milk. He gives in to her pressure, even though he suspects he's being self-serving in accepting her dubious rationale. Goat's milk proves to have hidden restorative powers. Within little more than a year, he reemerges as not simply the most intriguing and original figure in the nationalist movement but the dominant one, a leader who can sometimes be questioned and even circumvented but who henceforth can no longer be challenged.

Another key to this remarkable rebound—beyond the intense impressions of actual village conditions gathered in a brief period—is the tie he had taken care from the outset of his reimmersion in India to establish to Indian Muslims, his readiness to fight their battles on grounds that there could be no better way than that to promote national unity. The end of the world war relieved Gandhi of his self-imposed obligation to recruit troops. It also deepened the alienation into which Indian Muslims had been sinking over the Turkish question. In defeat, the Ottoman Empire faced dismemberment; its sultan, whom many of them recognized as their caliph—invested, in their view, with spiritual authority that was no less than papal—was being stripped in the war's aftermath of his control of Mecca and Medina and the other holy places. The struggle to save the caliphate, known on the subcontinent as the *Khilafat*, was portrayed in India's mosques as nothing less than a struggle for Islam, an occasion for *jihad* and even for *hijrat*, meaning voluntary migration to a truly Muslim country such as Afghanistan, if Lloyd George's imperial government remained impervious to the appeals of the subcontinent's faithful.

No one outside India seriously cared about the feelings of Indian Muslims on this issue or granted them any standing to be heard on it. This was true not only of the victorious Allies now dictating the peace but also of the Arab world, which was hardly sorry to be relieved of Turkish rule; it was even true of most Turks, who'd wearied of the sultan and his decadent court. To most Hindus as well, the future of the Khilafat would have been a matter of profound indifference had they not been exposed to Gandhi's tireless and ingenious rationalizations for making its preservation a primary goal of India's national movement. Even then, few understood what it was all about. Gandhi's knowledge of Islamic history derived from his reading in South Africa of Washington Irving's *Life of Mahomet* and an English translation of the Koran. He didn't try to make the case for the Khilafat. He offered a simple syllogism, telling Hindus it was of supreme importance to their Muslim brethren and, therefore, to national unity, and, therefore, to them. Using an Indian measure that stands for ten million, he asked, "How can twenty-two crore Hindus have peace and happiness if eight crore of their Muslim brethren are torn in anguish?"

Incomparably quixotic as it may appear today, the Indian struggle to preserve the authority of the Ottoman sultan became the preeminent Indian cause among Muslims. It's easy to say that it was doomed from the start, but that wasn't evident to them then. The coup de grâce wouldn't come until 1924, when Mustafa Kemal, known as Atatürk, formally dissolved the caliphate, driving the last sultan into exile. Still the Khilafat movement lingered on in India, channeling the passion and resentments it had aroused into new reformist groupings, some of which had an influence beyond India that played back into the Arab world in significant ways. One of these was a movement called the Tablighi Jamaat, or Society for the Propagation of the Muslim Faith, usually known as Tabligh, which from its start in India became "the most important element of re-Islamization worldwide," according to the French expert Gilles Kepel, "a striking example," he says, of "a fluid, transnational, informal Islamic movement." That may sound a little familiar: a complex religious and ideological lineage could be traced over nearly a century from Muhammad Ali and other Indian proponents of the cause to present-day Islamists, including Osama bin Laden, who made restoration of the caliphate one of Al Qaeda's war aims when he proclaimed his struggle against the United States.

Given that he deplored terrorism and was no Muslim, it would be simply wrong, not to say grotesque, to set Gandhi up as any kind of precursor to bin Laden. But the remote cause of the Khilafat was equally important in his rise. It was on his mind in 1918 when he wrote to the viceroy, on his mind a year later when he spoke in a Bombay mosque on the occasion of a national strike he'd called. The day of prayer and fasting was offered in April 1919 as a protest mainly against new legislation giving the colonial regime—in another haunting analogy to our own times—a slew of arbitrary powers it said it needed to combat terrorism. That supposedly nonviolent campaign quickly flared into riots in Bombay and Ahmedabad and "firings," confrontations in which the constabulary or military trained their weapons on surging unarmed crowds in the name of order. The first firing was in Delhi, where five were killed; another came two weeks later in the Sikh stronghold of Amritsar. There, on April 13, 1919, in the most notorious massacre of the Indian national struggle, 379 Indians taking part in an unauthorized but peaceful gathering were gunned down by Gurkha and Baluchi troops under British command in an enclosed square called Jallianwala Bagh for defying a ban on protests. By then, Gandhi was on the verge of calling off the national strike; he'd made a "Himalayan miscalculation," he said, in allowing himself to believe the masses were ready for satyagraha. To Swami Shraddhanand, an important Hindu spiritual leader in Delhi who questioned his bumpy, seemingly impulsive start-and-stop tactics, the Mahatma dismissively replied: "Bhai sahib! You will acknowledge that I'm an expert in the satyagraha business. I know what I'm about."

It took only six months for Gandhi to start paving the way to a resumed campaign. He had come up with a new tactic, which he named "non-cooperation." He outlined it first to Muslims involved in the gathering Khilafat campaign, then in Delhi to a joint conference of Hindus and Muslims, also on the Khilafat. The concept, which can be found in embryo in *Hind Swaraj*, was initially sketchy, but Gandhi soon filled it in. Noncooperation came to mean withdrawing participation, in stages, from colonial institutions, rendering them hollow and useless. Lawyers and judges would be asked to boycott the courts; would-be legislators would not take part in existing councils and provincial assemblies the British were promising; students would gradually abandon state schools, attending instead new ones to be improvised along Gandhian lines, with instruction, of course, in Indian languages instead of English; officials would surrender the status and security of their jobs; and, ultimately, Indians would learn to turn their backs on service in the armed forces, especially in Mesopotamia—soon to be known as Iraq—which the British had snatched from the sultan; those who'd received medals from the Raj would be called on to return them; honorary titles would be renounced. It was an exhilarating vision. One by one the props under British rule would be removed. The vision changed the lives of hundreds, maybe thousands, of Indians who joined the movement on a full-time basis. It inspired millions more.

Muslims didn't become unconditional converts to satyagraha as a doctrine. The Koran, after all, sanctions jihad in a just cause and doesn't rule out violence. But for the better part of two years, the Hindu Mahatma won acceptance as their campaign's chief tactician, the author of noncooperation. And with their support, he stepped to the fore for the first time in the national movement, on a unity platform embracing all his causes, among which the literally outlandish cause of preserving the caliphate in Constantinople for the Muslims of India regularly now emerged as first among equals. Gandhi had formed an ad hoc committee called the Satyagraha Sabha for his earlier agitation against the antiterrorism laws. Now, in December 1919, the month after the first Khilafat conference, he made what he later called "my real entry into Congress politics" at the movement's annual session in Amritsar.

There he was joined by the Ali brothers, Muhammad and Shaukat, just released from confinement. The Alis created a greater stir in Amritsar even than Gandhi. They were greeted, one scholar records, with "cheers, tears, embraces, and a veritable mountain of garlands." A rising tide of Hindu-Muslim unity was now in the offing, hard to imagine in an era in which predominantly Hindu India and predominantly Muslim Pakistan confront each other as nuclear powers. By design, three conferences were taking place simultaneously: in addition to the Indian National Congress, the Muslim League and the Khilafat Committee were meeting. In June the Central Khilafat Committee named an eight-man panel, including the Ali brothers, "to give practical effect" to a program of noncooperation. Gandhi, the only Hindu among the eight, was listed first.

The following September, Muslim votes ensured the adoption of Gandhi's noncooperation program by a narrow margin at a special Congress session in Calcutta, with the preservation of the caliphate now underscored as a primary goal of the national movement. "It is the duty of every non-Moslem Indian in every legitimate manner to assist his Mussulman brother, in his attempt to remove the religious calamity that has overtaken him," declared the resolution, written by Gandhi. Without Muslim votes, Gandhi's first challenge to the Congress to adopt satyagraha would almost certainly have foundered. The Mahatma hadn't won over the political elite; with the backing of the Alis, he'd swamped it. It was at Calcutta that he first held up the prospect of "swaraj within a year."

Soon-to-be Congress leader, 1920

Three months later, in December 1920, Shaukat Ali took the precaution of rounding up a flying force of burly "volunteers," Muslims uncommitted to nonviolence, to face down any anti-Gandhi demonstrators at the annual Congress meeting, held that year in the Marathi-speaking city of Nagpur in central India. The so-called volunteers weren't needed. Skepticism about noncooperation was still being voiced, but political opposition to Gandhi had melted away. His own example and relentlessness in argument, his mounting hold on the broader population and solid support from Muslims, all combined to make his leadership unassailable. The Nagpur Congress dutifully adopted Gandhi's draft of a new constitution, extending the movement's reach down to the villages for the first time, at least on paper. In another first engineered by him, it adopted the abolition of untouchability as a national goal. Swaraj would be impossible without it, Gandhi repeatedly said, but in fact the noncooperation campaign targeted two "wrongs" specifically attributed to the British—the threat to the Khilafat and their failure to punish those responsible for the Amritsar massacre. Untouchability might be, in Gandhi's words, a "putrid custom," but it was a Hindu wrong, an urgent issue, no doubt, but one without any obvious place on an agenda designed to rouse as many Indians as possible to nonviolent resistance to the colonial power.

There was one conspicuous dissenter. Mohammed Ali Jinnah was heckled when he referred drily in a speech to "Mister" rather than "Mahatma" Gandhi. He left the Congress after Nagpur, never to return, predicting that Gandhi's mass politics would lead to "complete disorganization and chaos." His departure, scarcely noted at the time, opened a tiny fissure in the nationalist ranks. It would become a gaping cleavage after orthodox Muslim elements drifted away from the movement with the waning of the Khilafat agitation. At this stage, it was not the nationalist goals of the Congress that had disillusioned Jinnah; he was still a convinced nationalist, an earnest believer in Hindu-Muslim reconciliation. Yet he was more a skeptic than a supporter of the Khilafat agitation. The readiness of Hindus—notably Gandhi—to exploit it was part of what alienated him.

At the start of 1921, the sway that the Anglicized Bombay lawyer Jinnah would come to have over India's Muslims could hardly have been foreseen, even by him. It was Muhammad Ali who then captured their imaginations, and Ali was still bound to the Mahatma. Understatement wasn't Ali's style. "After the Prophet, on whom be peace, I consider it my duty to carry out the commands of Gandhiji," he declared. (The one-syllable suffix, as we've noted, is a common Indian way of showing respect for an elder or sage. Even today, in conversation, Gandhi is commonly referred to as "Mahatmaji" or "Gandhiji.") For a time Muhammad Ali gave up eating beef as a gesture to Gandhi and all Hindus. Then, campaigning side by side with Gandhi across India, he took to wearing *khadi*, the homespun cloth the Mahatma embraced as a cottage industry, a means to *swadeshi*, or self-reliance, and, in the expanding Gandhian vision, as a mass self-employment scheme for village India and, therefore, its salvation. The weaving and wearing of khadi (sometimes called *khaddar*) would not only feed spinners, handloom operators, and their families; it would enable India to boycott imported cloth from British mills and thus stand as another form of noncooperation. The bearded *maulana*—an honorific given to a man learned in Islamic law—not only wore khadi; he became an evangelist for the *charkha*, or spinning wheel, in front of Muslim audiences. "We laid the foundation of our slavery by selling off the spinning wheel," Muhammad Ali preached. "If you want to do away with slavery, take up the wheel again." His support for such Gandhian tenets inevitably aroused criticism from fellow Muslims. Ultimately, the maulana had to defend himself against charges of "being a worshipper of Hindus and a Gandhi-worshipper."

The preservation of the caliphate remained Muhammad Ali's most urgent cause, but his readiness to stand with Gandhi on issues that meant little to Muslims—spinning and even cow protection—became a kind of validation of the Mahatma's rhetorical leaps, his constant juggling and merging of seemingly unconnected campaigns in an attempt to establish a stable common ground for Hindus and Muslims. Noncooperation was the most serious challenge the Raj had faced, and Gandhi was the movement's undisputed leader. But then the big tent of Hindu-Muslim unity he'd erected began to sag and, here and there, collapse as violence between the two communities, an endemic phenomenon on the subcontinent, appeared to give the lie to all the vows and pledges that had been offered up in India on behalf of the soon-to-exit caliph in Constantinople. The impressive coalition Gandhi had built and inspired was proving to be jerry-built. By August 1921, a still hopeful Gandhi had to acknowledge that some Hindus were "apathetic to the Khilafat cause" and that it was "not yet possible to induce Mussulmans to take interest in swaraj except in terms of the Khilafat."

By far the worst violence came that same month in the rural Malabar district on the Indian Ocean coast, where a community of Muslims known as Mappilas, also Moplahs, rose in rebellion, crying jihad and brandishing the Khilafat flag, after a couple of skirmishes with the police in which two British constables had been killed. Tiny Khilafat kingdoms were then proclaimed by the insurgents, and in some of these, Hindu homes and temples were set ablaze, women raped, and children slaughtered. The doctrine of nonviolence had never reached the Malabar district; political meetings had, in fact, been banned there. That was hardly an excuse for the gruesomeness or scale of the carnage: six hundred Hindus reported killed, twenty-five hundred forcibly converted to Islam. Gandhi and Muhammad Ali were denounced as infidels when they called on the insurgent leaders to disavow violence. The Raj dealt severely with the rising, blaming the noncooperation movement and hanging some two hundred rebels.

The next month Muhammad Ali was arrested on conspiracy charges at a train station in the Telugu-language region of southeastern India (today's Andhra Pradesh), including the charge of "conspiracy to commit mischief," while traveling with the Mahatma from Calcutta to

Madras. The British, who'd been looking for an occasion to re-exert their authority, found it in a series of statements by the maulana arguing that Islamic law forbade Muslims to enlist or serve in their army. Gandhi's reaction says a lot about the fecundity of his imagination, the range of his aspirations, and his adaptability as a political tactician. A week after seeing Ali hustled from the station by a police detachment, he appeared in the South Indian town of Madurai bare chested in a loin-cloth: in the attire, that is, that would be his unvarying guise for the rest of his life. It's the way he'd been dressing at the ashram on the Sabarmati River, outside Ahmedabad, for several years; in public, he'd continued to wear a kurta, dhoti, and cap. This was the first public outing of his new, very basic costume.

Being Gandhi, he hastened to explain the symbolic meaning of the change. His disrobing could be read in several ways: as a tribute to the imprisoned maulana and the other Khilafat leaders rounded up with him; or as a subtle shift of emphasis, a recognition that the Khilafat movement would soon be played out, at least as far as Hindus were con-cerned, that the larger national movement needed a new mobilizing tool. Gandhi had already seized on the spinning wheel for that purpose. For the goal of swadeshi to be achieved, he reasoned, there had to be enough hand spinning and hand weaving across India to replace the manufactured imported cloth being burned and boycotted as his cam-paign for swadeshi caught on. Without swadeshi and all it entailed, he now argued, there could be no swaraj. And only with swaraj—giving India the ability to engage diplomatically with the world—could there be any settlement of the Khilafat problem. Once the highest priority of the noncooperation movement, the preservation of the Khilafat was now to be seen as a potential by-product of its success. Gandhi was pointing the way to "full swadeshi" by showing the millions who were too poor to cover their whole bodies with newly woven homespun that it really wasn't necessary. "Let there be no prudery about dress," he now said. "India has never insisted on full covering of the body for males as a test of culture."

Later, he would explain the symbolism he invested in the loincloth by saying, "I wish to be in touch with the life of the poorest of the poor among Indians . . . It is our duty to dress them first and then dress our-selves, to feed them first and then feed ourselves."

If they could follow the winding path of his logic, Indian Muslims might see his wearing of the loincloth as proof of his continued devotion to the Khilafat cause. Otherwise there was a good chance they'd perceive

Gandhi to be drifting away from them. Muhammad Ali might have pointed out, were he not by this time in detention in Karachi, that the culture that Gandhi was describing so avidly was distinctly Hindu. "It is against our scriptures to keep the knees bare in this fashion," Maulana Abdul Bari, a leading religious authority who'd been prominent in the Khilafat agitation, subsequently informed the Mahatma.

Gandhi was starting a new variation on the fugue he was forever composing out of his various themes. Recalling perhaps how few South African Muslims were at his side when he marched across the Transvaal border in the 1913 satyagraha, he'd understood from the start of the noncooperation campaign that he could only speak to Muslims through other Muslims: Muhammad Ali, for instance. "I can wield no influence over the Mussulmans except through a Mussulman," he said. He'd also understood the improbability of the Khilafat as an Indian national cause. For him, it was less a cause than an investment: "the opportunity of a lifetime" for Hindus to demonstrate their stalwartness, their trustworthiness, to Muslims who, he kept suggesting, if not quite promising, would be likely to respond in kind by respecting the tender feelings of Hindus for the sacred cow. Ergo, according to this logic, preserving the Khilafat was the surest way to preserve the cow. Nothing like this opportunity would "recur for another hundred years." It was a cause for which he was "ready today to sacrifice my sons, my wife and my friends." In the short run, it was also a way to bind Muslims into the national movement that, thanks in no small measure to their support, he now led. The odds against it working were overwhelming, but who can now say, considering all that has happened since in confrontations between Hindus and Muslims, that Gandhi had his priorities wrong?

Gradually, he disengaged from the Khilafat agitation, which meant disengaging from Muslim politics, but Hindu-Muslim unity remained one of his main themes through to what might be called his tragic last act as Hindus and Muslims slaughtered each other at the time of partition. In September 1924, Gandhi fasted for the first but not last time against Hindu-Muslim violence following riots in Kohat, a frontier town south of Peshawar in what's now Pakistan. He said he was fasting for twenty-one days as a personal "penance." The flash point for this killing spree, which resulted in an official death count of thirty-six and the flight of Kohat's entire Hindu community, was a grossly blasphemous life of the Prophet written by a Hindu. While it had nothing to do with Gandhi, he held himself responsible in the sense that he'd been "instrumental in bringing into being the vast energy of the people" that had now turned "self-destructive." To demonstrate that the fast was not against Muslims or on behalf of Hindus, the main sufferers on this occasion, he made a point of camping in Muhammad Ali's Delhi bungalow during his starvation ritual. "I am striving to become the best cement between the two communities," he wrote. Twenty-four years later he'd fast again in Delhi with the same purpose. On each occasion, Hindu and Muslim leaders, fearful of losing that "cement," gathered at his bedside and vowed to work for peace. A shaky armistice would follow and hold until an obscure agitator, somewhere on the subcontinent, threw off the next spark.

Gandhi the politician retained a cool realist's grip on his own limitations in this highly charged sphere after the waning of the Khilafat cause. Never was it more clearly and coldly displayed than in 1926, when his second son, Manilal, now resettled in South Africa, realized he was in love with a young Muslim woman in Cape Town whose family had played host to his father in years gone by. Her name was Fatima Gool, and she was known as Timmie. When word of the interfaith love match reached Gandhi at his ashram in Gujarat, he wrote to his son telling him he was free to do as he wanted. Then, as his great-granddaughter Uma Dhupelia-Mesthrie observes in her finely wrought biography of Manilal, "the rest of the letter in fact closed the doors on free choice."

Generally speaking, Gandhi deplored marriage as a failure of self-restraint (ever since he unilaterally declared himself a *brahmachari*) and religious conversion as a failure of discipline (since he briefly contemplated it for himself in his Pretoria days). So he was hardly likely to celebrate intermarriage as a realization of Hindu-Muslim unity. His letter reads like a dry lawyer's brief, or a political consultant's memo, devoid of any expression of feeling for his son or the Gool family. Of its several arguments, the most forceful and hardest to refute is the politician's: "Your marriage will have a powerful impact on the Hindu-Muslim question . . . You cannot forget nor will society forget that you are my son." Persevering idealist though he was, he was seldom softhearted, least of all when it came to his sons.

Did the revivalist ever really believe that swaraj could come in a year, or that the caliphate could be preserved? The question is little different from asking whether modern political candidates believe the dreamy promises they make at the height of a campaign. For Gandhi, who was introducing modern politics to India, the question is especially fraught because he was seen by his own people in his own time and place as a religious figure, more saintly than prophetic, more inspiring than infallible. He could thus be expected to lay down unmeetable conditions to achieve unreachable goals. At a certain level of abstraction from what we're accustomed to calling reality, what he offered in 1920 and 1921 as a vision was obvious and inarguable, even and especially when it defied normal expectations. After all, if 100 million spinning wheels had produced enough yarn in a few months to clothe 300 million Indians, if state schools and courts had all emptied and colonial officials at every level found they had no one to ring for—if Hindu and Muslim India was that united and disciplined—then independence *would* have been within reach. Gandhi was telling his people that their fate was in their own hands; that much he surely believed. It was when these things failed to happen as he said they could that disillusion set in and the movement veered off course and slowed.

Shortly after the Mahatma donned his "symbolic disguise," as Robert Payne, one of his legion of biographers, termed his loincloth, he was challenged on the level of reality by Rabindranath Tagore, the great Bengali poet, a Nobel laureate by the time he met Gandhi in 1915, and, later, the admirer who first conferred on him the title Mahatma. Tagore now wrote that Gandhi had "won the heart of India with his love" but asked how he could justify the bonfires of foreign cloth promoted by his followers in a country where millions were half-clothed. The gist of Tagore's high-minded argument was that Indians needed to think for themselves and beware of blindly accepting such simplistic would-be solutions as the spinning wheel, even from a Mahatma they rightly revered. "Consider the burning of cloth, heaped before the very eyes of our motherland shivering and ashamed in her nakedness," he wrote. Gandhi swiftly replied with what may have been his most stirring prose in English, offering his retort on a less elevated level of reality, that of village India:

> To a people famishing and idle, the only acceptable form in which God can dare to appear is work and the promise of food as wages. God created man to work for his food, and said that those who ate without work were thieves. Eighty per cent of India are compulsory thieves half the year. Is it any wonder if India has become one vast prison? Hunger is the argument that is driving India to the spinning wheel ... The hungry millions ask for one poem—invigorating food. They cannot be given it. They can only earn it. And they can earn it only by the sweat of their brow.

Gandhi at his charkha, 1925

As far as the polemical exchange went, Gandhi may have bested Tagore, but soon he had to confront his own doubts. He was under pressure from impatient followers, Khilafat activists in particular, to launch an intensified campaign of mass civil disobedience that would fill colonial jails. Gandhi tried to defer the campaign or at least limit its scope. Unsure that he had enough disciplined workers under his command, he worried about seeing his nonviolent campaign spill over into mass rioting, as it had in 1919, once demonstrators finally confronted the police. The month after the exchange with Tagore, rioting in Bombay caused him to suspend civil disobedience. Less than three months later, it happened again.

The authorities had banned public meetings. This spelled opportunity for satyagraha; across India, Congress leaders and followers by the thousands defied the ban, got themselves arrested, and went to jail. As the prisons filled, Gandhi fired off congratulatory telegrams to the most prominent inmates, hailing them as one might hail a class of new graduates. Their jailing, his telegrams asserted, was wonderful news. Then a lethal clash at an obscure place in North India called Chauri Chaura moved Gandhi to order another suspension of his campaign—the third in less than three years—against the advice of close associates.

What happened in Chauri Chaura on February 5, 1922, fulfilled his worst fears. An angry crowd of roughly two thousand surrounded a small rural police station after having been fired on by a police detachment, which had then withdrawn and taken cover inside the building. The frustrated crowd, now a mob, soon set it ablaze. Driven out, policemen were hacked to death or thrown back into the flames; in all, twenty-two of them had been slaughtered with their assailants, so it was later said, shouting noncooperation catch-cries, including "*Mahatma Gandhi ki jai*"—"Glory to Mahatma Gandhi."

By Gandhi's standards, which derived from the Hindu value of *ahimsa*, or nonviolence, Chauri Chaura stood out as an abysmal, even frightening defeat. In his eyes, it showed that the country at large and the national movement in particular had never truly grasped the values of satyagraha. So, with more than fifteen thousand followers already in jail, he abruptly called a halt to civil disobedience, suspending it for more than ten months, until the end of 1922. It was only because he insisted on suspending the campaign that Congress leaders who'd not yet gone to jail went along with his decision. "I got the votes because I was Gandhi and not because people were convinced," he wrote with the self-lacerating candor he could be relied on to display in his lowest moments. As "penance" for the fact that "murders were committed in my name," he then fasted for five days.

Among those who expressed disappointment over the retreat were some, both Muslim and Hindu, who well understood that Gandhi was responding to what he deemed a moral imperative. If only they had a less exemplary, less principled leader, they seemed to say. "Our defeat is in proportion to the greatness of our leader" was the way Lajpat Rai, a Hindu and former Congress president, wryly put it. "To me," said Maulana Abdul Bari, the leading Muslim in the North Indian center of Lucknow, "Gandhi is like a paralytic whose limbs are not in his control but whose mind is still active." Neither statement was without a tinge of admiration, but each was more disillusioned than admiring. Gandhi had offered them satyagraha as a weapon; now, as the "expert in the satyagraha business," he was yanking it back.

With his usual industriousness, Gandhi churned out a series of letters and articles explaining his stand to key followers and the nation at large, promising that the suspension would not be permanent, that civil disobedience would eventually be resumed and swaraj achieved, if not in a year. The clearest statement of his position turned into a prophecy. No one, Gandhi included, could have realized that what he had to say in 1922 would accurately depict the circumstances of India's independence, still a quarter of a century in the future, or his own ambivalent reaction to its achievement. "I personally can never be a party to a movement half-violent and half non-violent," he said, "even though it may result in the attainment of so-called swaraj, for it will not be real swaraj as I have conceived it."

Even "so-called swaraj" was a long way off, a much bigger goal than any he had toiled for in South Africa. Swaraj as he had conceived it—a purer, cleansing independence, amounting to a social transformation—would never be within reach. It would survive as a permanent, ever-receding goal.

7

UNAPPROACHABILITY

SUPPOSE THAT MOHAN GANDHI, the young barrister who journeyed to South Africa in the last decade of the nineteenth century, had been persuaded by evangelical friends in Pretoria to convert to Christianity, that he'd then stayed on to build a profitable law practice in Johannesburg, living out his life there under apartheid, in a segregated township's largest house. Would relations between Hindus and Muslims on the Indian subcontinent be any different today? If different, would they be worse or better? The only point of proposing such a mind game is to underscore the role of chance and contingency, as well as character, in human affairs. Of course, the questions are unanswerable, but if we stay with the premise of a modern India minus Gandhi, it's not impossible to imagine a Mohammed Ali Jinnah who remained an Indian nationalist and brushed off the idea of Pakistan as the misbegotten dream of crackpots. Or a Jawaharlal Nehru who accepted Indian independence on behalf of an elitist movement, wearing a suit and tie rather than the khadi homespun that became mandatory for aspiring leaders after the advent of the Mahatma. This isn't to say that such scenarios would have been preferable to the one we designate as history, only to make the obvious point that other outcomes were possible. We can be reasonably certain at least that absent Gandhi, the cause of Hindu-Muslim unity wouldn't have flourished earlier, the way it did for a few brief years when he came close to achieving a merger between the national and the Khilafat movements, or the mirage of one. Most days of most years, Hindus and Muslims in most parts of India still live peacefully at close quarters, showing exemplary tolerance of each other's customs. Once, thanks to heavy lifting by Gandhi, their leaders were almost able to do so too.

Seen in perfect hindsight, powerful undercurrents all that time were carrying the two largest communities away from the reconciliation the leaders said they wanted. Such trends can be instructively traced in the life of a Hindu religious leader who was probably second only to Gandhi in stature in that era. This was Swami Shraddhanand, a revivalist in his own right, formerly known as Mahatma Munshi Ram, who loomed especially large in the Punjab and adjacent areas of North India. His views were close to Gandhi's; if anything, he was more uncompromising in his abhorrence of untouchability. Long before Gandhi, he had the nerve to voice his approval of intercaste dining and even marriage, and, beyond that, of all but abandoning the caste system itself in the name of a more generous and capacious Hinduism. Though the two mahatmas were in basic sympathy, they could seldom agree on tactics or their reading of Muslim intentions.

Shraddhanand, an impulsive man, a courageous one too, was prepared to follow Gandhi but not to subordinate his own judgment. His life offers two powerful punctuation points in an account of Gandhi's early efforts to bring Hindus and Muslims together. In the aftermath of Gandhi's first venture in nonviolent political action on a national scale, the strike of 1919, Shraddhanand was invited to preach from the pulpit in India's largest and most important mosque, Delhi's Jama Masjid. Days before, he'd become a hero to Delhi's Muslims as well as Hindus for baring his chest to troops attempting to turn back a march he was leading, daring them to fire. (Accounts differ on whether they were Gurkhas or Manipuris from the northeast.) No Hindu leader had ever before been invited to hold forth at the Jama Masjid, nor would this ecumenical invitation ever be repeated. In that instant, the swami, a hulking figure with a shaved head, wearing umber-colored robes, personified the unity for which Gandhi had tirelessly appealed. When he intoned a Sanskrit prayer for peace, Om Shanti, "the whole audience followed me with one reverberating voice," the swami wrote. Only six years later, he was shot and killed by a Muslim inflamed by Shraddhanand's later writings against what he deemed a Muslim conspiracy, thus becoming in death the personification of looming conflict.

"My heart refuses to grieve," Gandhi said upon learning of the murder. "It rather prays that all of us may be granted such a death." A "blessed death," a martyr's death, he called it, as if forecasting his own end.

The killer arrived at the door of the swami's Delhi bungalow on a December afternoon and managed to talk his way into the room where a convalescing Shraddhanand was bedridden, saying he had religious issues to discuss. The swami courteously invited him to return later when he hoped to be feeling stronger. The visitor then asked for a drink of water. Left alone with the great man, he pulled out a pistol and pumped two slugs into Shraddhanand's chest. The assassin turned out to be a Muslim calligrapher named Abdul Rashid. At his trial he explained that he blamed his victim for spreading blasphemies against the Prophet; then he was sentenced to hang, whereupon thousands of Muslims turned out for his funeral, hailing him, not his victim, as the true martyr. *The Times of India* spread a report that students and teachers at the celebrated Muslim seminary at Deoband recited the Koran five times over in order to ensure the assassin a place in "the seventh heaven."

Clearly, there'd been a communal mood swing in the years between the swami's unique exaltation at the Jama Masjid and the celebration of his killer's last rites. In those years, Shraddhanand had veered in and out of alliance with Gandhi. When they differed, it was because the swami thought Gandhi either was too soft on Muslims or had not lived up to his own pleadings on behalf of untouchables. In his view, the two failings were cause and effect.

The very idea that Gandhi's commitment to the struggle against untouchability could be challenged as halfhearted so early in his ascendancy over the national movement comes as a surprise. It's not part of the received narrative. Gandhi himself spoke and wrote as if he'd made the issue of what he called "high and low" one of his signature causes from his early South African years on. He could never get used to having his good intentions questioned in this area. Yet among Dalits in today's India the idea that Gandhi was a fair-weather friend, or no friend at all, has become a commonplace, one that's overdue for reevaluation. In that context, his relations with Shraddhanand offer a useful point of departure for the telling of a story that has been insufficiently explored, for all the studies of this much-studied life.

At first the bond between the two mahatmas seemed solid. Gandhi himself traced it back to 1913, when he received funds for his final satyagraha campaign in Natal and the Transvaal from students of Mahatma Munshi Ram at his school, the Gurukul, near the pilgrimage center of Hardwar in the foothills of the Himalayas. Munshi Ram had sent the students out to earn with the sweat of their brows funds to support the far-off indentured laborers marching as passive resisters. His covering letter addressed Gandhi as "My dear brother." Gandhi, who was twelve years younger and not yet known by that reverential honorific, never forgot this. It was to the Gurukul that he dispatched the first batch of his followers from the Phoenix Settlement when finally he pulled up stakes in South Africa. Within three months of his own arrival in India, Gandhi himself turned up there in 1915 for his first face-to-face encounter with Munshi Ram. Meeting the celebrated Hindu reformer in person was the real purpose of his visit to Hardwar; the mass spectacle of the Kumbh Mela (and all the fetid insanitation to which it gave rise, which so shocked his sensibilities) was incidental.

The swami had been keeping a deliberate distance from the national movement but got swept up in it in support of the Mahatma-to-be. In his view, Gandhi was leading a *dharma yudha*, a religious struggle. The start of the noncooperation campaign in April 1919 was the occasion for Tagore's call on Indians to recognize Gandhi as a mahatma. Yet shortly after Shraddhanand was hailed for his role in the campaign in Delhi, he quit the movement to protest the abruptness of Gandhi's decision to shut the campaign down. The swami agreed that the movement wasn't disciplined enough to prevent outbreaks of rioting in a vast land. It was more Gandhi's high-handed way of deciding than the decision itself that he was protesting. "Thousands of people have been inspired by their feeling of trust in you . . . and have given up all worldly worries," he wrote to Gandhi, resigning from the satyagraha committee. "The pity is that you at once bring out your pronouncements without even asking those people if they agree."

It was neither the first time nor would it be the last that Gandhi heard such a complaint from key supporters. Yet Shraddhanand very soon gave in to pleas from Gandhi and others and again threw himself back into the national movement, only to find himself regularly on the losing end of tactical disagreements with a leader used to consulting only himself. The most significant of these, in his own mind, were over the issue of untouchability, on which Gandhi had taken a consistent stand from his first months back in India. From Shraddhanand he then encountered for the first time the criticism that he was unwilling to back up his powerful exhortations with deeds. The swami could be even less malleable than Gandhi. For more than two decades, he'd been a stalwart promoter of the purification ceremonies called shuddi that were used to bring untouchables and low-caste Indians into a broad-based Hindu fold in which caste divisions would be downplayed if not eliminated. The man who'd spoken at the Jama Masjid had demonstrated his willingness to stand with Gandhi—and Muslims—in the Khilafat cause. But he bridled when he began to suspect that it was more of a priority for Gandhi than the struggle against untouchability.

So, in December 1919, at the Indian National Congress session in Amritsar, it was the swami, not Gandhi, who dwelled on the matter. "Is it not true," he asked provocatively, "that so many among you who make the loudest noises about the acquisition of political rights are not able to overcome your feelings of revulsion for those sixty millions of India who are suffering injustice whom you regard as untouchable? How many are there who take these wretched brothers of theirs to their hearts?" Nine months later at the special Congress session in Calcutta, Shraddhanand tried and failed to get the subject on the agenda. Gandhi was among those who felt that the discussion of the noncooperation campaign had more urgency, that anything else would be a digression. Given that the preservation of the caliphate was one of the campaign's declared aims, that amounted to saying the cause of the Muslims mattered more, for the moment at least, than the struggle against untouchability. "That was a grave mistake," the disappointed swami lamented. "Only at that time can non-cooperation with an enemy nation become a possibility, when full cooperation between ourselves has been achieved."

Gandhi made sure the Congress took up untouchability more or less in earnest at its regular annual meeting, held in Nagpur a few months after the Calcutta gathering. But Shraddhanand was not the only one who had started to worry that the Mahatma might be soft-pedaling the issue. The Anglican priest Charles F. Andrews, whom Gandhi addressed as "Charlie," had become close to Munshi Ram in India before meeting Gandhi in South Africa and had then brought the two together. Andrews wrote a "Dear Mohan" letter to Gandhi—he was the only one of the Mahatma's hundreds of correspondents who felt comfortable being so familiar—expressing his own fear that untouchability was slipping on his agenda. Gandhi was so upset by the criticism that he lay awake at two in the morning a month after the gathering at Nagpur and started framing his answer in his mind before rising at his usual hour of four to set down an emotional defense of his stand. Strong as the letter was, it confirmed the sense that he now saw untouchability as a cause that would have to wait its time. The Khilafat movement had priority because it was a prerequisite for unity between Hindus and Muslims, which was in turn a prerequisite for independence. But this was so, Gandhi argued with his usual capacity for disarming rationalization, not because untouchability was less important but because "it is a bigger problem than that of gaining Indian independence." He'd be able to "tackle it better," he said, if he gained independence "on the way." Therefore, he predicted, India "may free herself from English domination before India has become free of the curse of untouchability."

A quarter of a century later, when independence finally was conceded by a war-weary, battered Britain, that forecast proved to be more than half-true: the curse of untouchability lived on. But then Gandhi had little or no time left to "tackle" it. In the present tense of 1921 and 1922, Shraddhanand came to suspect that Gandhi's commitment to keeping Muslims in the national movement was stronger than his passion for uplifting the society's outcastes. Like Tagore, he objected to the campaign to burn foreign cloth that might have gone to the very poor. But he went a step further, asking how come Gandhi could go easy on Muslim leaders who, instead of having to burn imported cloth, were given a pass to ship it to their brethren in Turkey. "While Mahatmaji stood adamant and did not have the least regard for Hindu feeling when a question of principle was involved," he wrote, "for the Muslim dereliction of duty there was always a very soft corner in his heart."

Swami Shraddhanand had his own problems with orthodox Hindus. Appointed to a Congress committee to work on the untouchability issue, he found that sufficient funds were never appropriated for that purpose, his own initiatives and proposals mysteriously derailed. In his view, the Congress wasn't serious about what he deemed to be "the most important plank" in its program. So in January 1922—a little more than a month before Gandhi was arrested for the first time in India and jailed for nearly two years in order to head off another round of civil disobedience —the swami again resigned. On the rebound, he then threw himself into the Hindu Mahasabha, the party of Hindu supremacists. He imagined his new allies could not fail to grasp the urgency of his efforts to bring untouchables into the Hindu fold. Essentially, in his view, the outcastes were up for grabs. They would fall victim to Muslim proselytizers if caste Hindus failed to grant them justice. At stake, ultimately, was power on the subcontinent. "If all untouchables become Muslims," the swami wrote, "then Muslims will become equal to the Hindus and at the time of independence, they will not depend on Hindus, but will be able to stand on their own legs." But there was a catch. Shraddhanand's form of shuddi, or purification, demanded social equality. That was too much for the Mahasabha. The Congress had at least paid lip service to his goals. The Mahasabha turned him down flat, stranding him yet again.

With Gandhi still in jail, Muhammad Ali became president of the Congress. His proposal for preserving Hindu-Muslim unity from the bitter competition for untouchable souls—and eventual votes—was to cook a deal under which half the untouchables would become Muslims, half accepted as Hindus. Apparently, there would be no need to consult the untouchables themselves. To Shraddhanand this just demonstrated the Muslim lust for power. He was further incensed when Ali was quoted as having said that he prayed that Gandhi would see the light of Islam, that until then the most errant Muslim could be surer of salvation than the purest Hindu. This led to a public exchange of letters between the swami and the maulana, but each pulled back from the brink of confrontation; the exchange was more notable for its careful courtesy, expressions of esteem, and reiteration of religious platitudes than for its polemical firepower.

In this same period, the swami twice visited Gandhi to lobby him over the lagging anti-untouchability effort and, it appears, discuss Muslim intentions (once while Gandhi was still in Yeravda prison in August 1923 and again in early 1924 when he was recuperating from an appendectomy that had become the occasion for his release). In particular, he complained about Muslim *tabligh*, or proselytizing efforts. Gandhi gave his answer in print in *Young India*, blaming proselytizing on both sides, shuddi as well as tabligh, for much of the tensions between Hindus and Muslims. It was one thing to preach a creed out of burning faith, Gandhi said, another to misrepresent the other religion in a way that inevitably undermined national unity. "No propaganda can be allowed which reviles other religions," he wrote. "Intrepid and brave" as he was, Gandhi said, Shraddhanand spoke for the Hinduism of the Arya Samaj movement with which he'd long been identified, sharing its "narrow outlook and pugnacious habit."

The swami's political vicissitudes are worth dwelling on for the light they shed on Gandhi's dilemma. The younger Mahatma, now in his fifties and fully fledged as a national leader, usually spoke as if his campaigns for unity between Hindus and Muslims and for basic rights and justice for the tens of millions of oppressed untouchables were mutually reinforcing, the warp and woof of swaraj. In fact, they were often in conflict, not merely for his attention or primacy in the movement he led, but at a local level where proselytizers and religious reformers battled for souls. And, truth to tell, neither cause—that of Hindu-Muslim unity nor justice for untouchables—had much appeal to caste Hindus, especially rural caste Hindus, who were the backbone of the movement Gandhi and his lieutenants were building. His political revival may have articulated the nation's highest aspirations, but examined more closely at a regional or local level, it turned out to be a fragile coalition of competing, frequently clashing communal interests. Inspiring the movement was one of Gandhi's tasks; holding it together was another, one that Shraddhanand, a Hindu reformer bent on brooking little or no compromise, didn't have to shoulder. Bhimrao Ramji Ambedkar, who'd soon emerge as the modern leader of the untouchables, later called Shraddhanand their "greatest and most sincere champion." Ambedkar was drawing a contrast to the other Mahatma, whom he'd come to regard as devious and untrustworthy—in other words, as a crafty politician.

The swami himself usually allowed his hopes for Gandhi to outweigh his disappointments. So even after Gandhi had publicly castigated him for weakening national unity, Shraddhanand continued to press the Mahatma to focus more on the untouchability issue. It was a pressure Gandhi could not ignore and perhaps welcomed. His long article taking on Shraddhanand in the context of Hindu-Muslim tensions hadn't once alluded to the plight of the untouchables. Five months later, however, we find him replying to the swami, who'd asked, in particular, that he lend more open support and leadership to the first struggle on behalf of untouchables using his patented satyagraha methods. It targeted a long-standing ban on untouchables so much as walking on the roads approaching an ancient temple at Vaikom in the kingdom of Travancore, in what's now the South Indian state of Kerala. Although Gandhi had called the cause of the untouchables "a passion of my life," he'd been in the uncomfortable position of counseling the Vaikom demonstrators to go easy in their use of satyagraha methods he himself had inspired, on behalf of a cause he ostensibly championed. "I am trying to make the necessary arrangements for Vaikom," he now wrote to Shraddhanand, who may have urged him to go to Travancore, where he'd yet to set foot. If so, the response is noncommittal. "I hope help will reach the satyagrahis" is all Gandhi says.

The note to the sometimes obstreperous swami is written from Muhammad Ali's bungalow in Delhi, where Gandhi has just ended his twenty-one-day fast of "penance," provoked by a string of worsening clashes between Hindus and Muslims. It's late 1924, and he has been out of jail for half a year, but he's still struggling to bridge fissures that had opened in the national movement while he was passing his meditative two years in Yeravda prison—fissures not only between Hindus and Muslims but between those (known as No Changers) pledged to continue his earlier strategy of noncooperation and a political faction (called Swarajists) more impatient for the trappings of power in a colonial

Gandhi recuperating at Juhu Beach, after release from prison, 1924

framework. That faction had formed in the leader's absence and was now bent on taking part in legislative councils the movement had vowed to boycott. Trying to function as a one-man balance wheel, Gandhi in this time is not only weakened physically but nearly immobilized politically; his one consistent strategy for moving forward involves the charkha, or spinning wheel. Hindus, Muslims, No Changers, Swarajists, all are enjoined to achieve self-reliance through spinning. (In June 1924, a few months after the Vaikom demonstrations began, Gandhi actually proposed that each member of the Congress be required to do a minimum amount of daily spinning; the motion provoked a Swarajist walkout and was instantly a dead letter even though it was eventually watered down and passed so as not to humiliate the revered but no longer paramount leader.)

At this point, the isolated struggle in Vaikom, which Gandhi had yet to witness firsthand, was no longer getting his close attention. In all these ways, it was peripheral. Gandhi, from a distance, had championed the struggle in print in the pages of *Young India* but otherwise had done his best to keep it under his thumb. What's at issue for him in Vaikom is a question that will hover over his leadership for the rest of his life: Could he continue to function as a national leader, or has he been driven by the diversity and complexity of India, with all the clashing aspirations arising from its communal and caste divisions, to define himself as leader of the Hindus? Could he simultaneously lead a struggle for independence and a struggle for social justice if that meant taking on orthodox high-caste Hindus, which would inevitably strain and possibly splinter his movement? Behind that question lurked an even more unsettling and long-lasting one, a question still debated by Dalits and Indian social reformers: Granted that Gandhi did much to make the practice of untouchability disreputable among modernizing Indians, what exactly was he prepared to do for the untouchables themselves beyond preach to their oppressors? It was such questions that—acting from afar—he'd been trying to finesse at Vaikom, with the result that this first use of satyagraha against untouchability was now in danger of languishing.

Vaikom's Shiva temple sits in the center of a large walled compound, about the size of four football fields, reached on three sides by roads that cut through the bazaar of the smallish trading town southeast of Cochin, now Kochi. With the exception of a few shade-giving pipal trees, patches of grass, and a cement walk that can scald the bare feet of midday visitors required to shed their shoes or sandals at the gate, most of the area is packed earth that looks as if it's regularly swept. The temple itself is an oblong wooden structure with a latticed outer wall that sits on a stone platform under a sloping roof made of the same clay tiles traditionally used in Kerala's sturdier housing; at each of the four corners, a gold-painted statue of a bull—an animal symbolically associated with Shiva—reclines on its haunches. In the inner sanctum, Brahman priests assist worshippers making offerings to the deity. Today it's not uncommon for the worshippers to include Dalits, former untouchables, and other members of lower castes who would have been barred from the Shiva temple in 1924. Sometimes these groups are the majority of visitors to the compound, drawn by the free midday meals available at the temple.

Recently, a seemingly heretical question has become a matter of public debate: whether non-Brahmans should be allowed to perform the priestly function in violation of caste rules. Today's priests, after all, are civil servants, employed by a state government that calls itself Marxist and collects as revenue whatever remains after maintenance costs from the offerings worshippers bring. Such an issue would have been unimaginable at the time of the Vaikom Satyagraha when the temple was administered by four priestly families, known by the name of their subcaste as Namboodiris (sometimes spelled Nambuthiris). The revenues they collected went to the maharajah of Travancore, a princely state that survived throughout the colonial period under watchful British over-sight, occupying roughly the southern half of today's Kerala.

What Gandhi had learned about untouchability growing up in Gujarat, then viewing the subject from the other side of the Indian Ocean during his long sojourn in Africa, had scarcely prepared him for the mad intricacies of caste as practiced in Kerala. Untouchability was one thing, what were called "unapproachability" and even "unseeability" were something else. A Travancore Brahman was supposed to never have to set eyes on the lowest class of untouchables. It was as simple and categorical as that. If he did, he would have to consider himself polluted and perform a purification rite. A member of a landowning caste called Nairs would be polluted if he allowed an Ezhava—the pronunciation falls somewhere between *IRR-ava* and *ILL-ava*—to come within forty paces of him; the prescribed distance for a Pulaya, a much lower stratum of untouchable, was sixty paces. Until the beginning of the last century, Pulayas were literally barred from public roads. They were expected to ring bells, rap sticks, or make honking noises to warn any caste Hindu nearby of the danger of pollution. Their mobility was more constrained than that of a plantation slave; indeed, they were bonded to specific landowners as field hands. Ezhavas (an upwardly mobile group who'd been by tradition toddy tappers), Tiyyas (coconut pluckers), Pulayas, and other subcastes at the bottom of the Kerala pyramid were uniformly barred from setting foot in the sacrosanct precincts of a place where Brahmans worshipped such as the Shiva temple at Vaikom; if they did, the shrine itself would be considered polluted and have to be purified. Yet, amazingly, those who were barred constituted a majority of those counted as Hindus in what's now Kerala. The 1924 satyagraha was evi-dence that their tolerance of this oppressive state of affairs had worn very thin.

Due to his many years abroad, Gandhi wrote, he hadn't known "many things that as an Indian I should have known." Before the satyagraha campaign, he hadn't ever heard of unapproachability. Its existence, he said, "staggered and puzzled me." He was especially puzzled because Travancore had a well-justified reputation for promoting literacy and education. It could also be called worldly, if the Arabian Sea were taken to be the world. The watery coastal region of what's now Kerala—a land of bays, canals, lagoons, inland islands, glassy paddy fields reclaimed for large stretches from the sea—had been involved in the spice trade for centuries. Hindus, when untouchables were counted under that rubric, made up a bare majority of its population. Tallied together, Muslims and Christians amounted to 40 percent or more. There were even small communities of Jews, the newest of which had been settled near Cochin since the seventeenth century. Historians of a Marxist bent relate the oppression of untouchables in this riparian setting to the need to control field labor. By definition, the landowning castes didn't plow, plant, sow, or reap. Travancore may have looked idyllic, but only a small proportion of its population got to experience it that way.

Gandhi supplied the inspiration for the Vaikom campaign with his harping on the evil of untouchability. He'd also furnished its method of resistance; after all, he'd coined the word "satyagraha" years before in South Africa. ("To endure or bear hardships" was his latest definition of the term by the time it was taken up in Kerala.) But it was Ezhavas who eventually gave the movement its impetus, and for all his stature as national leader the Mahatma was decidedly not their Moses. They had their own. He was called Sri Narayan Guru, an Ezhava who'd founded a religious movement with its own temples, teachings, and social values. Narayan Guru might be seen as a Hindu Protestant. His impact on twentieth-century Kerala was as powerful as that of John Wesley on eighteenth-century England. "One caste, one religion, and one God for man" had been his mantra; he'd been preaching on that text since well before Gandhi returned to India. His followers revered him but didn't follow him all the way; specifically, they didn't admit Pulayas and other lower-down untouchables to their temples; part of their own self-promotion from untouchability was to treat these lower orders as untouchables irredeemably. According to his biographer M. K. Sanoo, Narayan Guru was at first ambivalent about the satyagraha at Vaikom, telling his people they should get their house in order by opening their own temples to untouchables before demanding that the Namboodiris and other higher castes make way for Ezhavas. But eventually he blessed the movement, supported it with money, and, in a rare political outing, even traveled to Vaikom and prayed for the demonstrators.

An ardent supporter of Narayan Guru appears to have been first to frame the idea of nonviolent resistance at Vaikom and, having made contact with Gandhi as early as 1921, followed up with the Indian National Congress and its branch in Kerala. His name was T. K. Madhavan, and it was at his initiative that an Untouchability Committee was formed in early 1924 under Congress auspices to spearhead the campaign. Madhavan was so grateful for support of the Congress that he impulsively named his son after its president, Muhammad Ali. Even in that heyday of Hindu-Muslim unity, the idea of giving the name of Islam's Prophet to a Hindu was too startling to be accepted and proved indigestible; no one in the Madhavan clan would use it. So when Gandhi finally visited Kerala, he was asked to rename the boy. Or so the aged man that the boy became, now far along in his ninth decade, told me when I visited him in the Kerala town of Harippad. Babu Vijayanath was sitting under a freshly garlanded portrait of Narayan Guru, who, he insisted, was his father's inspiration, far more than Gandhi.

Nowadays, a visitor is surprised to discover, Narayan Guru all but overshadows Gandhi in many Kerala precincts. But in early 1924 it was the Mahatma who had the stature and authority of national leader. In a program of political action carrying the Congress imprimatur, his word was law. But was this a program of political action, open to all supporters? Gandhi, the first to pose the question, surprised his followers by answering it in the negative, handing down an edict that said non-Hindus had no business taking part in the demonstration. This came hardly a week after the first attempt at satyagraha in Vaikom, which had already been scaled back, at Gandhi's urging, from the original plan of Madhavan's committee.

That plan, modest enough, hadn't been to attempt to enter the temple's walled compound, let alone approach the sanctum. It had been simply to march down the three approach roads and pray at the temple gates. This would mean ignoring, in a classic act of civil disobedience, official signs on each road about 150 yards from the compound forbidding the lowest castes and untouchables to proceed any farther. A moat in the form of a drainage ditch, stretches of which are still clearly visible, delineated the boundary that couldn't be crossed. The danger of spiritual pollution was deemed to be too great. (From the dark, bilious look of the water sitting stagnant in the ditch and in the large pool adjacent to the temple where worshippers still bathe, other kinds of pollution might more easily have been imagined.) The roads were deemed not to be public roads but to belong to the temple. Paradoxically they remained open to cows, dogs, Muslims, and Christians, including non-Hindus who were converted untouchables. The civic right to walk on public roads was more important to many of the participants in the campaign than the religious right to worship in a Brahman temple.

Gandhi had led a march of more than two thousand striking indentured laborers across a forbidden border in Africa ten years earlier. Now here he was—on an issue he called a "passion" of his life, one of the "four pillars" of swaraj—inventing arguments to keep a lid on mass

action, however nonviolent. Wary of the very idea of a march, he coun-
seled against any attempt to push past the roadside signs ordering potential carriers of pollution to turn back. In response to his signals, the plan
was changed in time for the first satyagraha demonstration at Vaikom
on March 30, 1924. The marchers stopped well short of the signs,
then three designated satyagrahis—a Nair, an Ezhava, and a Pulaya—
stepped forward to the invisible pollution barrier, where, after a time,
they sat and prayed until the Travancore authorities obliged them by
taking them into custody and sentencing them to six months each in jail.
Each succeeding day, three more volunteers stepped forward to take
their place, with the same results. The orthodox also were supposed to
believe in the Hindu value of ahimsa, or nonviolence, that Gandhi regularly cited. But it was not necessarily their practice. On more than one
occasion, the Travancore police didn't intervene when gangs of thugs,
operating on behalf of the orthodox, attacked the satyagrahis with sticks,
iron rods, and bricks. Some of the victims had sufficient caste status to
be eligible to enter the temple themselves, but they'd been infected with
the new thinking, inspired by Gandhi. One man, a Nair, was tied to a
tree and kicked in the groin. Another, a Brahman named Raman Ilay-
athu, had raw lime paste rubbed into his eyes, blinding him; an untouchable leader, a Pulaya named Amachal Thevan, was also reported to have
been blinded in this way.

From the beach bungalow where he was recuperating near Bombay,
Gandhi warmly praised the discipline and courage of the Vaikom satyagrahis. But he all but excommunicated the leader of the movement
he knew best. This was George Joseph, probably his most dedicated
follower among Indian Christians. A member of the Syrian Christian
community, which has been prominent in Kerala for more than a mil-
lennium, Joseph had given up a lucrative practice as a barrister to join
Gandhi's ashram near Ahmedabad; had been recruited by Motilal
Nehru, Jawaharlal's father, to edit a nationalist paper called the *Independent* in Allahabad; had then spent more than two years in jail before
understudying Gandhi as editor of *Young India* while the Mahatma himself went to prison. Now, after all that, he was being told by Gandhi to
back off, told that he had no place in the Vaikom Satyagraha because it
was a Hindu affair.

"I think you should let the Hindus do the work," Gandhi wrote. "It is
they who have to purify themselves. You can help by your sympathy and
by your pen, but not by organizing the movement and certainly not by
offering satyagraha."

The letter didn't reach George Joseph in time. By April 10, with Madhavan and others already arrested, this Christian leader found himself in charge of the campaign and faced with a tactical dilemma. The police had put up a barricade and, in an attempt to tamp down the negative publicity Travancore was getting, were no longer making arrests. Therefore, he telegraphed Gandhi, he'd told the demonstrators to start fasting. "Advise if change procedure necessary," his SOS said. "Urgent." The next day the police either revised their tactics again or made an exception for Joseph: he telegraphed to say he'd been arrested and to urge Gandhi to send a leader of stature, or perhaps his son Devadas, to take his place.

The Vaikom Satyagraha wasn't two weeks old by the time these crossed messages sorted themselves out. Gandhi, it finally became clear, not only was opposed to non-Hindus like Joseph playing any role. He also was opposed to using fasting as a weapon to force the pace. Fasts were to be used not coercively against those who opposed you politically, the rule giver in Gandhi now decreed, but only against allies and loved ones when they backslid on pledges. Gandhi thus set a standard from which, as we shall see, he'd eventually deviate himself. In this case, there were other strictures. He was also opposed to Congress supporters from outside Travancore flooding in as volunteers to bolster the campaign, though he himself had previously invited outsiders to support his own early efforts in Bihar and Gujarat. Some Sikhs who'd journeyed the length of the subcontinent, traveling from the Punjab to set up a kitchen to feed the satyagrahis, were urged to return home. And he dragged his heels on naming a leader from the outside; the leadership, he felt, ought to remain local. Despite the Congress support that Madhavan had painstakingly organized, Gandhi now took the view that the struggle at Vaikom could not be considered an appropriate Congress project. The national movement, he said, should not "come into the picture." It had as its goal the end of British rule, but, he reasoned, Travancore was outside the British imperium, being technically still an Indian princely state. Individual Congress members might take part, the leader ruled as if from on high, but only as individuals. The movement, which had so recently been mobilized nationally on the fate of the Khilafat in distant Constantinople, had to keep its hands off.

As usual, Gandhi came up with ingenious rationalizations for each of these stands, all pointing to one conclusion: righteous as he considered it to be, he wanted the Vaikom agitation to remain a small local affair; it could not be inflated into a test case for the anti-untouchability platform he himself had given the national movement, especially at a time when he felt his grip on the movement to be slipping.

His considerations were national and political, also religious. Under pressure to say where he stood on the issue of caste, he defined himself in orthodox terms, then added ambiguous qualifications and escape clauses that made his pronouncements suspect in the ears of the system's strict adherents. "I personally believe in *varnashrama*," he would say, meaning the four-way division of all Hindus according to their hereditary occupations as priests, warriors, merchants, or tillers; then he'd add, "Though it's true I have my own meaning for it." He wouldn't dwell on his "own meaning," because he was trying, for reasons more political than religious, to reassure high-caste Hindus without abandoning his basically reformist position.

The ambiguity was intentional. On a theoretical level, he drew his version of the four *varnas* more from John Ruskin than from the Hindu scriptures; in this view, they were roughly equal rather than hierarchical, a flexible framework for stability in the social cooperative that Gandhi wished Indian villages to be, which had little to do with what Indian villages actually were or had ever been. The villages were divided on the narrow lines of distinctive subcastes, where every tiny social advantage had to be fought for or guarded, not the broad categories of varna, which Gandhi somehow managed, later, to redefine as "true socialism." He would also argue that traditional varnashrama was "based on absolute equality of status" before conceding that such a caste system was "today non-existent in practice." Translated into secular terms, this was like saying that true capitalism would be utopian socialism. What Gandhi offered was a revivalist's vision; no such equality existed in actual villages. Whatever his deepest intention, it could easily be interpreted as a whitewashing of caste. Gandhi meant to coax the high caste, not confront them. In that way, he promised social stability, not upheaval. So he made a point of saying in this period that the abolition of untouchability would not entail caste Hindus having to dine with former untouchables, let alone marry their daughters to them, though he himself never hesitated to flout caste rules on dining. Beneath the ambiguity lay a seeming contradiction with which he'd wrestle for the next two decades: his insistence that it was possible to banish untouchability while retaining caste, with a little refurbishing, a humanizing makeover, as an organizing principle of Indian society.

Was this what he really thought, or was it a tactical feint? Years later, after the Mahatma's death, Jawaharlal Nehru would tell an interviewer that Gandhi had confided to him on more than one occasion that his ultimate aim in his fight against untouchability was to bring down the caste system once and for all. Here's Nehru's 1955 account:

> I spoke to Gandhi repeatedly: why don't you hit out at the caste system directly? He said that he did not believe in the caste system except in some idealized form . . . that the present caste system is thoroughly bad and must go. I am undermining it completely, he said, by my tackling untouchability. You see . . . he had a way of seizing one thing and concentrating on it. If untouchability goes, he said, the caste system goes; so, I am concentrating on that.

Nehru might be suspected of trying to gloss over the ambiguities in Gandhi's position here. But in a 1934 letter to an American, the Mahatma came close to using the words Nehru later ascribed to him. "The caste system, as it exists at present, is certainly the bane of Hindu life," he wrote. "The great movement of removal of untouchability is an attack on the evil underlying the caste system." He came even closer in conversation that same year with a member of his entourage. "If untouchability goes," he said, "the castes as we know them today go." Eventually, he'd shed his idealization of varna. In 1936 he said caste was "harmful both to spiritual and national growth." In 1942 he was quoted as saying he'd have "no interest left in life" if caste continued. Finally in 1945 he said the only remaining varna embraced *shudras*—traditionally the lowest order, basically the peasantry—and "*ati*-shudras, or Harijans or untouchables." Ati in this context meant beyond, lower down. Once again, he was saying it was sinful to believe in "high and low." He admitted that his views had changed, that he was no longer bent on putting an acceptable face on the caste system. He'd always maintained that the only reliable guide to his thinking on an issue was the last thing he'd said.

That may have been his final thought about caste, but it wasn't the burden of what he had to say eighteen years earlier at the time of the Vaikom Satyagraha. Then the contrast between Gandhi's words in condemning "the deep black ignorance of blind orthodoxy" and the severe restrictions he placed on those striving to adhere to his precepts so befuddled his Travancore followers that they dispatched two of their own to sit at the revered leader's feet and hear how he reconciled his preaching with the tactical restraints he'd been urging.

The meeting took place in the campaign's eighth week. Gandhi was asked why it was all right for Hindus to demonstrate in support of a distant Khilafat but not all right for non-Hindus to support the right of "unapproachables" to use a public road in Travancore; why untouchability and unapproachability had to be considered, in view of the Congress's pronouncements on the subject, a local Vaikom issue rather than a large national question; why if their maharajah was revered and loved as a benevolent ruler, his loyal subjects couldn't use fasting "to melt [his] heart and to conquer him through their sufferings" in accord with Gandhi's own teachings on satyagraha.

The Mahatma's answers pursue whatever tortuous logic comes to hand; they're also insistent and categorical; when he doesn't duck questions, he recasts them, then tosses them back without retreating an inch. "Outside help weakens the strength of your sacrifice," he declares. Similarly, "This is a purely Hindu question and, therefore, the non-Hindus have no place in the struggle."

It's not clear whether he's speaking here as leader of the Hindus or of the national movement. Since he's Gandhi, no one demands clarification on that score. In his solicitude for the feelings of orthodox Hindus, his answers can be read both ways. "Non-Hindu interference," he says, would "offend the orthodox section whom you have to convert and conquer through your love." Here Gandhi seems to speak as a Hindu. Even if the issues at Vaikom were to be viewed as national, he further argues, it would be "neither desirable nor practicable that the whole India or the central organization should fight out such questions. It will lead to chaos and confusion." Here he's the national leader suggesting, if not quite saying, that the Congress is divided enough already.

The two Travancore representatives who went to see Gandhi, both high-caste Hindus sympathetic to the cause of the untouchables, gained little clarity on a way forward for their movement, which Gandhi has effectively downgraded. On their return, they found the satyagraha camp in "utter confusion." So writes T. K. Ravindran, a Kerala historian who conducted extensive research in Travancore's Malayalam-language archives and then wrote the only narrative history of the movement based on such primary sources. In its efforts to interpret and abide by Gandhi's injunctions, the movement was sputtering. Swami Shraddhanand showed up to bless a joint gathering of thousands of low-caste Ezhavas and high-caste Nairs that set a new benchmark simply by happening. The meeting sent a delegation to the maharajah supporting the satyagraha and calling for reform.

Then, in August, the rajah died. Since his heir was a child, an aunt was installed as regent. Her first act was to free all those jailed over five

months for taking part in the satyagraha. The freed leaders threw themselves into gathering signatures from high-caste Hindus on petitions
"respectfully and humbly [praying] that Your Gracious Highness may be
pleased to command that all roads and all classes of public institutions
may be thrown open to all classes of Your Gracious Highness's humble
subjects without distinction of caste or creed." A cold official response
dashed such hopes. It was then that the unrelenting Swami Shraddhanand urged Gandhi not to let the Vaikom cause languish.

The Gandhi who finally arrived by motorboat at the Vaikom jetty on
March 9, 1925, nearly a year after the start of the satyagraha campaign
he'd been managing by remote control, had recently made a show of giving up his leadership of the national movement. It was the first of many
such supposed withdrawals from national politics by the Mahatma.
On his release from jail in February 1924, he'd offered the Indian
National Congress what he termed his "application for employment as
general." He meant, of course, commanding general. A general, he then
insisted, "must have soldiers who would obey." By the end of the year, he
was characterizing himself merely as "a non-violent soldier," acknowledging that he could no longer "command universal assent." Seen from
within the movement, he'd taken a step back, all but removing himself
from day-to-day politics. Seen from outside, he was still national leader.
In Kerala, his arrival was a huge event. A small armada of fishing boats
and flat-bottomed craft used for hauling rice and other freight con-
verged on the one bearing the leader, flanked by two long, ornate "snake
boats," outsize racing shells designed to carry dozens of rowers, helms-
men, even musicians on major ceremonial occasions. Obviously, this was
such an occasion.
Vaikom in those days had a population under five thousand. The
crowd that gathered at the jetty, now the site of a monument to the
Vaikom Satyagraha that wasn't opened until 2008, stretched for nearly
two miles, according to the report the next day in *Malayala Manorama*,
the leading newspaper in Malayalam, the language of the region. Everyone was eager to see Gandhi, or nearly everyone. Missing was a quietly
disillusioned George Joseph, who'd resigned from the Congress and
returned to the practice of law. Also missing were the Brahmans who
controlled the temple and their orthodox supporters. Standing on their
sense of the protocol appropriate to their superior station, the temple's

priests had insisted that it was up to Gandhi to seek an audience with them.

It was the first thing he did. The formal response granted him leave to call at the home of Indanturuttil Nambiatiri, the leader of the orthodox faction, in a section of the temple precincts off-limits to untouchables. Gandhi was there on sufferance himself. As a non-Brahman, the Bania prophet was of insufficient caste status to be invited into the priest's actual house; instead, the meeting had to be held outdoors in a garden pavilion. The Travancore police had a stenographer on hand. Professor Ravindran rescued a transcript of the three-hour conversation from the archive of the old princely state. Today it can be read as an intriguing and comprehensive exposition of Gandhi's views on caste, or as an example of his intellectual nimbleness under pressure. The question it raises is whether Gandhi was searching for the appearance of common ground with the orthodox, not unlike an American politician dancing his way through a meeting with evangelical Christians, or staking out an orthodox position of his own. Sometimes he's Socratic, plying them with questions designed to undermine their certainties. But it's Indanturuttil Nambiatiri who proves to be the more insistent cross-examiner.

"Does Mahatmaji believe in the divinity of the Hindu *shastras* [scriptures]?" he starts out. Gandhi replies, "Yes."

"Does Mahatmaji believe in the Law of *Karma*?" Again the answer is "Yes."

"Does he believe in reincarnation?"

"Yes."

That being the case, Gandhi is presented with the usual, one might even say normative, Hindu deduction: that the miserable lot of outcastes is punishment for bad behavior in past lives. "Let us grant that," he replies, then counters by asking how that gives the high caste a right to do the punishing. The Brahman swats the question away. "We believe it is the ordinance of God," he says.

"True, true," Gandhi replies, still sparring, still seeking to regain the initiative.

Later, pressed on the same point, he continues to sound defensive: "I have granted to you that the differences of birth are due to differences of action. But that does not mean that you can consider one man low and another man high." Gandhi here seems entangled in his own words. If his two propositions—that the untouchable are what they are because of misdeeds in previous lives, still, high and low must be considered equal—were not in total contradiction, they came close. Which, we have to ask, was most compelling for Gandhi, who means to be arguing here for the right of the unapproachables to approach fellow citizens in a public place? The answer should be obvious if his life up to this point is considered to have had any consistency. "No Indian is a coolie by birth," he'd written in his first letter to a Pretoria newspaper when he was not yet twenty-five. He felt more "at home" with the indentured laborers with whom he'd marched in South Africa than with highborn Indians, he'd told a Bombay garden party less than two weeks after his return home. "I am not ashamed of calling myself a scavenger," he would tell Travancore's maharani, or queen, the very next morning, repeating a line he'd first used years before in South Africa. Yet here we find him muttering, "True, true," when faced with a doctrine of predestination presuming evil done in past lives as a fundamental explanation for untouchability and the extremes of inequality it fosters. It's possible that India and deeper reading in its scriptures over time had made him more orthodox. The likelier explanation is that he still could make himself believe in the possibility, as he once put it, of "cleaning Hindu society" and thought of himself here as being now engaged in such an exercise of public hygiene. In any case, it was nothing new for him to present himself as a *sanatani*, or orthodox, Hindu. He'd done so four years earlier in a speech to a conference of the "suppressed classes." There could be no swaraj, he said then, "so long as the Hindus willfully regard untouchability as part of their religion." What was new here was that he'd adjusted his timetable—untouchability's end, as he'd suggested to Charlie Andrews, might have to wait for the departure of the British—so even if he was inclined to theological debate on the ironclad influence of past lives, now was not the time. It would be enough if he could persuade the priests to open the roads.

Perhaps Nehru's summing-up in that 1955 interview has some bearing on Gandhi's surprising dance, his bobbing and weaving, at Vaikom: "His approach was not to go and irritate the masses in their deep convictions . . . Gandhi was always thinking of the masses and of the mind of India and he was trying to lift it in the right direction; to give it gradually more and more things to think about, yet without upsetting it or making it frustrated." Put another way, he believed he could use moral suasion and his own example to build an inclusive sense, common to Brahmans and untouchables alike, of Indian nationhood.

"I am trying myself to be a bridge between blind orthodoxy and those who are victims of that blind orthodoxy," he explains. "I have come here to create peace and friendship between the orthodox and those who are agitating," he's quoted as saying in *Malayala Manorama*. In other words, he presents himself as having come not as a crusader but as a mediator. Self-ordained in this way, he won't stand with one side in opposition to another, even at Vaikom, where it's apparent to him that the orthodox represent no more than a small fraction of the population. To break the impasse, he offers a "sportsman-like" suggestion that the matter of open roads be settled by a referendum limited to caste Hindus. The high priest stolidly stands on principle. "We would not allow this question to be subject to a vote," Indanturuttil Nambiatiri replies.

Immediately after Gandhi exits through his gate, the Brahman holds a purification ceremony in the pavilion where the encounter occurred so as to banish any pollution that may have trailed behind the Mahatma. Today, by the old priest's standards, the place is a veritable sink of pollution, for after his death in 1957, ownership of his residence passed to a trade union affiliated with the Communist Party, the Vaikom Taluk Toddy Tappers Union. A red flag now flies outside, hammers and sickles adorn the facade.

After viewing this distinctly non-Gandhian monument to the vicissitudes of history, I went next door to another mildewed structure where Nambiatiri's aged daughter and son-in-law still reside. The story I heard there was not one of stubborn resistance to change. A decade after Gandhi's first visit, all temples in Travancore were finally thrown open by royal decree to any manner of Hindu, including outcastes. To avoid spiritual pollution, which had become inevitable in their view with the arrival of such unapproachable riffraff, many Namboodiris then stopped praying at the Shiva temple. This was what Indanturuttil Nambiatiri had vowed to do in his encounter with Gandhi if the temples and their approach roads were ever opened by royal decree. "We will forsake those temples and those roads," he'd said. But when the time came, it turns out, the priest wasn't among the boycotters. He continued to supervise the rituals at the Shiva temple; in other words, he clung to his job. "He was prepared to accommodate to change," said the son-in-law, a retired botanist named Krishnan Nambuthiri. "He had a very balanced mind. He was not at all moved by emotions."

I asked how he felt about Gandhi. "He never hated him," the old man said. In that answer, offered eighty-five years after Gandhi's visit next door, sixty-one years after his murder, glowed a last dying ember of the orthodox view he'd encountered that day.

Leaving the meeting with the Brahmans empty-handed, Gandhi went to address a crowd of twenty thousand that had been waiting nearby for word of some kind of outcome. It heard an admission of failure but not defeat. "As you know," he began, "ever since I have set foot on Indian soil after a long exile in South Africa, I have been speaking frankly, fearlessly and freely on the question of untouchability."

It's surprising that the Mahatma feels a need to establish his reformist credentials in this way. Possibly he's aware that he's addressing more than one audience. The first is made up of satyagraha demonstrators and their supporters, another the orthodox; finally, there were those, probably the majority, who are there to bathe in the ennobling mist of darshan. "I claim to be a sanatani Hindu," he goes on, leaning in the other direction. "I have come, therefore, to reason with my orthodox friends. I have come to plead with them . . . I am sorry to confess I was not able to produce the impression I expected to produce on them." The confidence that he would prevail, with which he'd started off his encounter with the Brahmans, is typically Gandhian. It doesn't desert him here. He congratulates those who have been demonstrating for a year on the "gentlemanly battle" they've waged and counsels patience. What he calls a "reasonable solution" may yet be found without the intervention of the government. Essentially, he tells them they must wait until their suffering has moved the hearts of the priestly holdouts he himself had failed to move that afternoon. Reverential as they are, some in his audience shake their heads in dismay and disagreement.

Gandhi runs into more doubts the next day when he meets the satyagrahis at their ashram. One wants to know how long the struggle will last. "A few days or forever," he says offhandedly, setting a standard of selflessness but also placing himself far above the fray. That brings him back, yet again, to South Africa. He thought the first satyagraha campaign would be over in a month there. "It lasted exactly eight years," he says. Someone then asks about fasting unto death. "I shall advise people to let you die," the Mahatma unhelpfully replies.

What exactly is hanging him up? As we follow Gandhi on his first of three Travancore tours, the question keeps arising. In their ambiguity, his own responses were at the time unsatisfying and still are. Outside

Kerala, Gandhi's role in the Vaikom Satyagraha is most often interpreted uncritically as a fulfillment of his values: his unswerving opposition to untouchability, his adherence to nonviolence. Inside Kerala,
where this history is better known, it's usually seen as having shown up a
disguised but unmistakable attachment on his part to the caste system.
Neither view is convincing. What really shows here is the difficulty of
being Gandhi, of balancing his various goals, and, more particularly, the
difficulty of social change in India, of taking down untouchability without cleaving his movement and sowing the "chaos and confusion" he
feared. Not since his stand-down after the Chauri Chaura violence three
years earlier had he been willing to launch a campaign of nonviolent
resistance himself.

Caste, untouchability, and social action are the subjects that come up
for discussion when his tour delivers him to the headquarters of the local
prophet of "one caste, one religion," Narayan Guru. It's the first meeting of the two rishis. They converse for a couple of hours. Gandhi then
emerges to speak to hundreds of Narayan Guru's followers. Presumably,
these are mostly Ezhavas, a group that has virtually hauled itself out of
untouchability. Gandhi addresses them, nevertheless, as members of the
"depressed classes." He speaks of "a wave of impatience going on not
only in Travancore, but throughout the length and breadth of India,
among the depressed classes." He means impatience with the orthodox.
"I assure you it is wrong," he says. He also announces that he has wrung
from Narayan Guru a pledge to take up spinning.

The highly partial version of the encounter handed down over the
generations by Narayan Guru's followers places the guru and not the
Mahatma in the role of tutor. It's on that day, it's said, that Gandhi's
understanding of caste was finally deepened and reformed. "That day he
became a Mahatma," Babu Vijayanath, son of the movement's original
organizer, told me, getting carried away with this guru-centric view. In
reality, the Gandhi who came out of the meeting sounded just like the
Gandhi who went in: as sure of himself and reliant on his own intuitions,
as unlikely to be touched by the arguments of others. Narayan Guru told
him untouchability would not end in a generation. "He thinks I shall
have to appear in another incarnation, before I see the end of this agony,"
Gandhi wryly reported. "I hope to see it in my lifetime, in this age."

There's no evidence that the two men ever discussed a tactical dis-
agreement they may have had. According to a police report discovered in
Travancore's archives, the guru had earlier expressed skepticism about
Gandhi's restrained tactics, wondering why the satyagrahis didn't "assert

their rights and enter the prohibited area forcibly." The aftermath of the Mahatma's visit provides circumstantial backing for this unattributed report. After the Vaikom Satyagraha ended, his direct influence in Travancore waned. Narayan Guru's Ezhava followers, however, continued to press for entry at other temples, using more aggressive tactics, sometimes clashing with caste Hindus. In one such clash, at Thiruvarppu in 1926, the founder of the Vaikom movement, T. K. Madhavan, received a severe beating from which he never fully recovered, according to his son.

Then as now, some of Narayan Guru's followers were inclined to rate the Mahatma lower than their local prophet because of his reluctance to confront the orthodox. A story got about that India's leader had reacted passively after being barred from the Devi temple at Kanyakumari, down south near the tip of the subcontinent, on grounds that his merchant-caste station was too lowly for him to be admitted. He wanted to worship in the temple, so the story in a local newspaper went, but instead meekly bowed to the order to halt and prayed outside, where he stood. Gandhi hardly ever prayed in temples, so the story, which is not well documented, may be viewed skeptically. What's remembered still is the fierce excoriation of a local crusader against untouchability, a Malayalam poet named Sahodaran Ayyappan who'd earlier earned notoriety and risked ostracism by inviting Pulayas and other untouchables to a public feast. Hearing of the Mahatma's supposed retreat, Ayyappan wondered in print about the contrast between the Gandhi who bravely challenged "the British lion" and the Gandhi who still "licks the feet of a Brahman . . . wagging his tail more shamelessly than a dog."

Definitely it was Gandhi who pulled the plug on the original movement by reaching a truce with Travancore's police commissioner, an Englishman named W. H. Pitt, over the heads of local activists, in much the way he'd bargained with Smuts after the 1913 strikes in Natal. The terms of the deal were intentionally ambiguous: The police and their barricades would be withdrawn on condition that the demonstrators continued to stand back from the approach roads. The order barring them would meanwhile be wiped off the books. No rights would be inscribed. But after the orthodox got used to the idea that approachability might now become a practical reality, if not quite a civic right, on most of those roads, all castes and outcastes would be allowed to use them. That's more or less what happened the following November, though entry to the temple was still forbidden to a majority of Hindus, all but the upper castes.

Conspicuous in the whole Vaikom agitation was the absence of any organized effort to recruit Pulayas and other untouchables with less status than the upwardly mobile Ezhavas. Some did take part, but Travancore's one recognized Pulaya leader, a figure with the single name Ayyankali—now memorialized by a large statue in a major traffic circle of the capital, Thiruvananthapuram—kept his distance from Vaikom and the movement to break down barriers to Hindu worship. His cause was the social uplift of his people through their own efforts, not Hindu reform. K. K. Kochu, a Dalit intellectual whom I met near Kottayam, has written that Ayyankali's abstention from Vaikom—his "silence"—is what echoes down over the years for Dalits. That abstention reflects something other than indifference. It points to a rising impulse to act on their own behalf. When Gandhi, on a later trip, finally was introduced to Ayyankali, he hailed him, it's said, as "king of the Pulayas," then invited him to declare his greatest wish. "I only wish that ten from our community would get B.A.'s," the Pulaya king coolly replied.

That wasn't the future Gandhi painted when he met untouchables on his swing through Kerala. Repeating themes in his talk to indentured sugarcane workers in Natal at the end of 1913, he urged them to confront their own bad habits in order to measure up, to earn the equality, which would then be their just due as good Hindus.

"How many among you can read and write?" a chastising Mahatma began one such talk.

"How many are drunkards?"

"How many eat dead flesh?"

"How many eat beef?"

"I know many of you don't take your bath every day. I can see it from the condition of your hair . . . I know you will smell bad." But he also said: "Many Hindus consider it a sin to touch you. I regard it as a sin to say and think that it is a sin to touch you."

This is the Gandhian dialectic, an exercise in fine-tuning a Hindu social order that crushes those at the bottom. In his own way, he's working both sides of the disputed street, trying to tear down unapproachability while hoping to bring the unapproachables into conformity with standards usually deemed to be beyond them. What he's not doing is calling on the "suppressed classes," as he so often termed them, to do anything for themselves beyond bathe and watch what they put in their mouths. Once, in passing, he mentions the possibility that they could attempt passive resistance on their own behalf, but he doesn't encourage it. It was one thing to march against white overlords for limited rights in South Africa, another now to march against Hindu traditionalists.

His last stop in Travancore was at Alwaye, now called Aluva, about forty miles north of Vaikom, where a young Cambridge graduate teaching at a local Christian college witnessed his arrival. "Gandhi was sitting cross-legged in a third-class compartment, his curious gargoyle face showing no special awareness of the crowd and the notables and the cheers of the students." So Malcolm Muggeridge remembered the scene years later.

In his account, thousands of poor villagers pressed forward as usual "to take the dust from his feet." Then Gandhi "caught sight of some untouchables in a sort of roped-off enclosure." Brushing past students shouting political slogans and notables waiting to lay marigold garlands over his head, he went to the untouchables and "started singing with them what sounded like a rather lugubrious hymn, to the obvious consternation of the notables."

In his memoir, written late in life, the English writer doesn't dwell on that moment; his narrative reels off into reflections on the course of the independence movement and the history through which he has lived. But before dismissing Gandhi as an upholder of the system with a deliberately ambiguous message—in other words, as a hypocrite—as some Kerala intellectuals seem inclined to do when they consider Vaikom all these years later, we might pause at that scene in Alwaye. If it was as Muggeridge later described it, what was Gandhi saying and to whom? In the roped-off enclosure, he was raising the subject of common humanity, not only for the sake of the untouchables, but for the students and the notables and the villagers who'd taken the dust from his feet. And, as so often in his unusually well-recorded life, it's the action rather than the always earnest, sometimes contradictory, sometimes moving words that leaps off the page.

8

HAIL, DELIVERER

THOUGH "not a quick despairer," as he once said, Gandhi sometimes flirted with despair. He never gave in to it for long, but the
year before he paid his visit to Vaikom, he'd been close to the
edge. The low point came in the middle of 1924 at the Indian National
Congress meeting in Ahmedabad, the one that watered down his resolution calling for daily spinning as an absolute prerequisite for membership in the movement. If he couldn't persuade his supposed followers
that the charkha, or spinning wheel, was the essential instrument of
Indian self-reliance and freedom, the autocrat in him had been ready to
require that they at least act as if they believed him. Discovering they
were prepared to humor him but not be commanded, he described him
self as "defeated and humbled."

The proof of his sinking spirits lay in the fact that it was Gandhi himself who'd moved the watering down of his own resolution as a way of
avoiding defeat for himself and a possible split. It was, he admitted, a
kind of surrender. In the pointlessness of the debate and the maneuvering that accompanied it, he felt he heard God's voice telling him, or so
he later wrote in imitation King James English, *"Thou fool, knowest not
thou that thou are impossible? Thy time is up."* What he said in the open
meeting was nearly as dark: "I do not know where I stand or what I
should do."

He'd lost not only command of the movement and a sense of direction. He also seems to have lost his firm conviction that he'd internalized
its most accurate compass, that his inner quest would ultimately be synonymous with India's. His reaction to this onset of uncertainty was to
sideline himself from national politics, saying he'd not play an active role

until the six-year prison term to which he'd been sentenced in 1922 finally expired in 1928, even though he'd been released after two years, even though, with perfect inconsistency, he'd immediately offered upon his release to resume his role as the movement's "general." During this self-imposed withdrawal, he'd confine himself, he said, to three topics: untouchability, spinning, and Hindu-Muslim unity. Before long, as a consequence of widespread communal violence, Hindu-Muslim unity had to be struck from the list of his ongoing projects. "What is one to do where one is helpless?" a plaintive Gandhi asked.

Sometimes he almost seemed to sulk. He blamed "educated India" for its tendency to "split into parties." He still could see "only one way" forward himself: his way, to work "from bottom upward." Next he blamed the British, "the third party" in Hindu-Muslim disputes, always casting about for new ways to divide and rule. "The government of India is based on distrust," he said. (His point, on this occasion, was that it sowed distrust by favoring Muslims. Of course, if he'd not favored Muslims himself, the national movement would never have joined the Khilafat agitation.) Venturing into hyperbole, he finally allowed himself to sound as if he were blaming God:

> Hindu-Muslim unity I made a mission of my life. I worked for it in South Africa, I toiled for it here, I did penance for it, but God was not satisfied, God did not want me to take any credit for the work. So I have now washed my hands. I am helpless. I have exhausted all my effort.

Surprisingly, by the time Gandhi speaks in this seemingly abject vein, he has actually started to rebound. He'd interrupted his ceaseless touring of the country to evangelize for the spinning wheel and then spent the whole of 1926 in his ashram outside Ahmedabad, explaining that he needed to rest and reflect. It has been called his "year of silence," but he was hardly silent. Every week there were new articles for *Young India*, including the weekly installments of his autobiography. By January 1927, when he spoke of having "exhausted all my effort," he was ready to get back on the hustings, to resume carrying his message across India. The more he speaks of his helplessness on Hindu-Muslim issues and remoteness from politics—the two, Hindu-Muslim issues and politics, were often synonymous in this period—the clearer it becomes that he views his retreat as a temporary phenomenon. A cross-cultural comparison comes to mind that may seem unhelpful, even wildly inappropriate. The Gandhi who sits at the Sabarmati Ashram in the mid-1920s, holding himself aloof from the politics of the national movement, pursues a strategy that another inner-directed politician would adopt in the waning days of the Third Republic in France several decades later, not in an ashram, but in a village called Colombey-les-Deux-Églises. It's impossible to picture an unbending Charles de Gaulle sitting cross-legged. But Gandhi, as obviously as de Gaulle later, was not just holding himself aloof but biding his time, waiting for his country to summon him back to leadership on his own terms.

He says so in so many words, only sometimes he couches the thought in religious language. Whatever his doubts in 1924, he now seems certain he'll be needed. "I am an optimist because I believe in the efficacy of prayerful thought," he writes to a supporter toward the end of 1926, his year of retreat at the ashram. "When time for action has come, God will give the light and guidance. I therefore watch, wait and pray holding myself in momentary readiness to respond." What "appears to be my inaction," he says in that same period, defending his obsession with the promotion of the spinning wheel, "is really concentrated action."

"I am biding my time," he finally wrote in a letter dated May 1928, "and you will find me leading the country in the field of politics when the country is ready. I have no false modesty about me. I am undoubtedly a politician in my own way, and I have a plan for the country's freedom."

The summons back to leadership came five or so months later, at approximately the same time as what would have been the end of his six-year prison term. By then, the first successful satyagraha campaign in years had wrung a government concession on high land taxes in Gujarat's Bardoli district, the same battleground from which Gandhi had abruptly withdrawn six years earlier in reaction to the Chauri Chaura violence, aborting a painstakingly prepared campaign. Finally, under the leadership of Gandhi's disciple Vallabhbhai Patel, Bardoli Two had restored faith in the tactics of militant nonviolence at a time when a young Bengali firebrand, Subhas Chandra Bose, was just starting to win notice and backing with a call to resistance that promised to be the opposite of passive. "Give me blood and I promise you freedom," Bose said grandiloquently.

The Indian National Congress was deeply divided, not just between Hindus and Muslims, but generationally too, over proposals for constitutional reform designed to be served up as a set of demands to the British: in effect, an ultimatum. The proposals had been drafted by a committee chaired by Motilal Nehru, father of Jawaharlal, the future prime minister. The son, in the forefront of the younger generation, did not support the father's report; neither did the Muslims, represented by Jinnah and Muhammad Ali, now on the verge of his final break with Gandhi. The drama and importance of the moment are probably clearer in the long perspective of history than they were at the time. Gandhi was the one figure in India who had any chance of steering the Nehru Report, as it was known, to formal acceptance by the Congress. That is what he was called upon to do by the senior Nehru in 1928. Being Gandhi, he took the call as the summons back to active leadership for which he'd been waiting for four long years.

So he didn't fasten on the question of how many seats would be reserved for Muslims in the legislative assemblies of states where they were in a minority—that's to say, most states. The Nehru Report had reneged on a promise the Congress had made to the Muslims twelve years earlier, before the rise of Gandhi: that they'd be able to elect their own representatives through separate electorates. Instead, it came up with the idea of reserving for Muslims a minimum number of seats in Hindu-majority provinces, in line with the proportion of Muslims in the population; in the national legislature, it was prepared to concede one-quarter of the seats to Muslims. Jinnah thought Motilal Nehru had set the price for this shift—measured in the number of reserved Muslim seats in the national assembly in particular—too low. Here was a moment for Gandhi to become active again on Hindu-Muslim questions, which had soured him on politics to the point, he said, that he'd "given up reading newspapers." But he had never been much interested in constitutional mechanics; and though usually ready to make concessions in the cause of unity with Muslims, he was focused now on the practical demands of Congress politics and his own restoration, so he let the moment pass.

At a mammoth All Parties Convention held in Calcutta at the end of 1928, Jinnah advanced a series of amendments, the most important of which would guarantee Muslims one-third of the seats in a future central legislature as opposed to the 25 percent Motilal Nehru had contemplated. It wasn't an offer made in the take-it-or-leave-it fashion that would later come to seem characteristic. In Calcutta he could hardly have sounded more accommodating. "We are sons of this land, we have to live together," he said. "I believe there is no progress for India until Muslims and Hindus are united." The Congress, which claimed to represent all Indians, including Muslims, turned a deaf ear. The Jinnah amendments were voted down, and Gandhi kept his distance.

Jinnah took it as a brush-off and walked away, taking with him

Muhammad Ali, the Gandhi ally who'd worn khadi, proselytized for the spinning wheel, given up beef, and even, on the occasion of Gandhi's 1924 fast of "penance" for Hindu-Muslim harmony in Ali's own home, thought to present the Mahatma with a cow saved from the abattoir as a symbol of Muslim respect for Hindu values and sensitivities. Within weeks of this rupture, his brother Shaukat Ali was promising not to attend any meetings with Hindus for a year. "This is the parting of the ways," Jinnah wrote at the time. Disgusted with politics and heartsore over his separation from a younger wife from a non-Muslim background whom he'd loved and by her subsequent early death, Jinnah moved to England for four years. "What is to be done? The Hindus are short-sighted and I think, incorrigible," he'd remark to a friend. Gandhi wasn't happy about the Congress's treatment of Jinnah. But it's doubtful that he ever saw the proud Bombay lawyer in these years as a potential mass leader of Muslims, let alone as a possible ally. Mohammed Ali Jinnah wore no religion on his well-tailored sleeves. How could the Mahatma conceive of speaking to Muslims through such a man?

Inside the Congress, there was still a fight to be waged over the details of the Nehru Report, which called on Britain to grant India dominion status within the British Commonwealth. Jawaharlal Nehru and Bose wanted an immediate declaration in favor of full independence by the Congress, leading the way to immediate confrontation, one that would remain nonviolent only if nonviolence succeeded. Gandhi countered with a temporizing resolution vowing that India would declare independence in two years if Britain failed to grant dominion status by then. Finally it was agreed that Britain would be given just one year—until the end of 1929—to act. That one year, so other resolutions promised, would be dedicated to the discipline of Gandhi's "constructive program," including the removal of untouchability, boycott of foreign cloth, promotion of khadi, prohibition, and the advancement of women. This was all on his insistence, showing he was once again in a position to lay down terms.

But, of course, when the year had passed, India still wasn't a dominion and social reform remained stalled. Swaraj within a year hadn't happened for a second time. So a symbolic independence day now had to be proclaimed for January 26, 1930. It was left entirely up to the Mahatma to decide how the long-threatened campaign of noncooperation would be conducted after that. The movement was larger than it had been at the time of Gandhi's first takeover but harder to lead; by sheer inertia, it pulled in many directions while being herded to the one overriding goal of nationhood. Still, he was effectively back in the position of prime mover that had been formally bestowed on him a decade earlier. As he'd said during his period on the sidelines, "For me there is only one way." That way was inherently confrontational, although it was expressed in a vocabulary of love and nonviolence. It included satyagraha, noncooperation, civil disobedience; the terms, not exactly synonymous, blended into one another, covering a spectrum of meanings that, by now, India and its colonial rulers had come to understand. But the specific tactics for the coming campaign eluded him for weeks.

His inspiration—God given, he'd say—came in two stages. In the first, he took account of his continuing disappointment with the Congress, his sense that it remained an undisciplined, ramshackle coalition of self-regarding interests with little or no serious commitment to social reform. "In the present state of the Congress no civil disobedience can be or should be offered in its name," he wrote in a confidential note to the younger Nehru, whom he'd just designated as its president. The flames of the Chauri Chaura violence, now eight years in the past, still cast lurid shadows in the Mahatma's mind. So his imagination carried him further back, all the way to South Africa, where he claimed to have started the Natal agitation with sixteen chosen ashramites, trained by him at Tolstoy Farm and the Phoenix Settlement. The political stakes were altogether different now. There a small, beleaguered minority sought minimum rights—the repeal of an oppressive tax designed to drive it from the land, an acknowledgment of rudimentary citizenship, permission if not the right to cross internal borders—in exchange for its tacit acknowledgment that political equality was not on the table, could not even be mentioned as a distant goal. Here not just equality but sovereignty—swaraj in the fullest possible meaning of self-determination—was the prize sought in the name of 320 million Indians, including the impoverished "dumb millions," for and of whom the Mahatma habitually spoke.

Gandhi's somewhat rosy version of his heroic personal history on the other subcontinent had merged with his vision of India's destiny; for the moment, at least, they'd be identical. Civil disobedience, he told Nehru, "should be offered by me alone or jointly with a few companions even as I did in South Africa."

The second inspiration—the specifics of what this "self-suffering" vanguard of satyagrahis would actually do, how it would address the common needs of all those millions, how it might be emulated—finally came after the symbolic independence day on January 26, 1930, and many stirring calls by Gandhi on his immediate entourage and the movement at large to steel themselves for struggle. When it came, it had all the beauty and simplicity of a fresh artistic vision realized for the first time, of a discovery in basic science. The self-proclaimed "expert in the satyagraha business" outdid himself this time, symbolically wrapping the nationalist urge for political freedom in the basic values of his "constructive program," intended for the uplift of India's lowliest, its most downcast.

This time the inspiration came in one syllable—salt. Gandhi had periodically experimented with a salt-free diet himself and pressed it on his disciples at Tolstoy Farm. But now he was prepared to campaign on the proposition that "next to water and air, salt is perhaps the greatest necessity of life." It was precious because it was needed by all and heavily taxed by an alien regime, which curtailed its local production. Since the days of the East India Company, the colonial authorities had counted on revenue derived from their salt monopoly and the tax on salt, paid by even the poorest households, Hindu or Muslim. Gandhi's inspiration was that he could march to the shore of the Arabian Sea from the Sabarmati Ashram and there, at a place called Dandi, defy the law— and simultaneously unify India—by simply picking up a chunk of salt.

Sticking to the South African script, he first wrote to Lord Irwin, the viceroy, setting out his intentions and demands as he'd written to Smuts in 1913. "My ambition is no less than to convert the British people through nonviolence," he wrote, "and thus make them see the wrong they have done to India." The viceroy also stuck to the script. Rather than reply directly to the Mahatma, he had his private secretary send a stiff note as Smuts's secretary had done, saying that Lord Irwin was sorry to hear that Gandhi planned to break the law and endanger public peace.

So for the first time since he led indentured strikers across the Transvaal border, sixteen and a half years earlier, Gandhi was ready to march again. In 1927, when he may have suffered a slight stroke, Gandhi's health had broken down. Now, nearly three years later, at sixty-one, he set off on a sun-bathed March morning to tramp more than two hundred miles to the sea, promising never to return to the ashram until India had its freedom. (As events unfolded in the less than half year left to him after India's actual independence in 1947, he never made it back to Ahmedabad.) "The fire of a great resolve is in him, and surpassing love of his miserable countrymen," wrote Jawaharlal Nehru, who watched the launch. In his train followed seventy-eight, or maybe eighty, disciples, including, according to his grandson and biographer

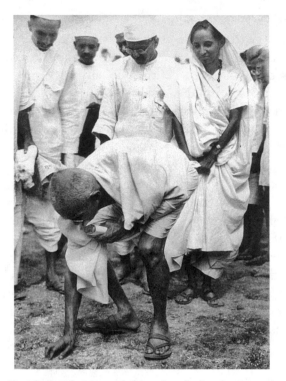

Dandi Beach, 1930, defying law by harvesting salt

Rajmohan Gandhi, two Muslims, one Christian, four untouchables (and therefore, by simple arithmetic, seventy-one, or seventy-three, caste Hindus). Very soon thousands were converging on the dirt roads and paths he traveled to witness this modest, unarmed procession bent on bringing down an empire. Leaning on a bamboo staff and walking ten or twelve miles a day barefoot, passing through scores of villages where blossoms and leaves had been strewn in his path as if for a conquering hero, Gandhi arrived at Dandi twenty-four days later and there, on the morning of April 6, 1930, stooped to harvest his bit of salt, a simple act of defiance swiftly emulated by tens of thousands up and down the subcontinent's two coasts.

"Hail, Deliverer," said the poet Sarojini Naidu, a good friend, standing by his side. Or so legend has it.

Not quite a year later, the Congress movement designated Gandhi as its sole representative, with full negotiating powers, to a conference on the path to Indian self-rule called by the British government. His prestige and authority had never stood higher. It had been an exceedingly crowded and packed twelve months, but Gandhi, whose Salt March had been the catalyst for a vast, largely peaceful upheaval that had shaken the pillars of the Raj, resulting in some ninety thousand arrests across India, had himself spent nearly nine of those months in the relative quiet and seclusion of Yeravda prison near Poona following his arrest on May 5. Just before the arrest, he'd ordered a nonviolent raid on a saltworks belonging to the state monopoly, at a place called Dharasana, 150 miles up the coast from Bombay. Sarojini Naidu, the poet, took the imprisoned leader's place as field marshal, with twenty-five hundred resisters under her command. She ordered them to take the blows of the local police, armed with the long lead-tipped bamboo batons known as lathis, without so much as raising their hands to protect their heads.

There were hundreds of cracked heads and much bloodshed that day as the resisters advanced rank after rank in the greatest example of disciplined nonviolence in the face of officially sanctioned police violence before American civil rights marchers reached the Edmund Pettus Bridge outside Selma, Alabama, thirty-five years later. The spectacle had a momentary impact across the world, a momentous one across India, inspiring illicit salt making on a grand scale up and down the two coasts, leading to scores of further confrontations, with the state now forced to use violence to quell nonviolent resisters in most regions of the subcontinent in its drive to restore its waning authority.

From the prison where he and his father were being held in Allahabad, Jawaharlal Nehru wrote at the end of July to Gandhi in Yeravda prison. "The last four months in India," he said, "have gladdened my heart and have made me prouder of Indian men, women and even children than I have ever been . . . May I congratulate you on the new India you have created by your magic touch! What the future will bring I know not, but the past has made life worth living and our prosaic existence has developed something of epic greatness in it."

Gandhi wasn't freed until January 26, 1931. It was a grace note that the viceroy chose the Congress's wishful, self-proclaimed "independence day," which he might easily have ignored, for his release and that of other movement leaders. It was also a signal that the British hoped to break the impasse that civil disobedience had created, clear the jails by dangling the possibility of a political settlement, and perhaps even achieve the appearance of one by granting a measure of home rule on which the fuzzy word "dominion" might be pinned. Irwin freed Gandhi

the way Smuts had all those years earlier, to enter direct negotiations
with him personally, leading to an ambiguous agreement he'd then have
to interpret and sell to the various parts of the national movement.
Gandhi and the Congress had boycotted the first round of what was
called the Round Table Conference in London that year, which was supposed to chart a path to self-rule for the vast territory of British India,
stretching all the way from the Afghan border to the Burmese, encompassing present-day India, Pakistan, and Bangladesh. It was important to
the viceroy and Whitehall that he show up for the second round.

Britain wasn't bargaining from a position of strength, just out of a
habit of dominance. Deep into a worsening international economic crisis triggered by the bursting of the stock market bubble on Wall Street,
its minority Labor Party government was preoccupied with growing
millions of desperate unemployed in what wasn't yet a welfare state, as
well as questions hovering over the pound sterling, including how long
it could remain tied to the gold standard and thus maintain its position
as the leading reserve currency. From London's perspective it was beginning to be possible to view India as a burden. Labor was the least
imperial-minded of British parties; many of its members, including the
prime minister, Ramsay MacDonald, had voiced sentiments that could
be interpreted as anti-imperialist. It led a weak coalition, and India was
not really high on its agenda. Still, it was possible to imagine circumstances in which it might be inclined to act.

If any such possibility existed, it was essentially snuffed out five days
before Gandhi boarded the SS *Rajputana* in Bombay on August 29,
1931, on his first trip to Europe in sixteen years, which would also prove
to be his last. Splitting his own party, Prime Minister MacDonald
formed a national government in which what remained of his Labor
Party had to share power with the Tories, the party that served in British
politics as the High Church of the empire in general and the Raj in particular. Within ten days of Gandhi's arrival in London, Britain went off
the gold standard, devaluing the pound and rendering the vaunted
Round Table Conference on the future of British India a sideshow
before it had got through the opening round of speeches.

Gandhi made a sly allusion to these developments in his first speech at
the conference, saying he understood that British statesmen were
"wholly engrossed in their domestic affairs, in trying to make two ends
meet." Surrendering control of India, he suggested impishly, could be
one way to balance the budget. Thereafter he paid as little attention to
these shattering events in domestic British politics as his biographers

have since. In shipboard interviews while still at sea, he'd expressed his wish to meet with Winston Churchill, the most strident of the Tory "die-hards" on India issues, but Churchill couldn't find the time. The one previous meeting of the two men, a quarter of a century earlier, would thus remain their only face-to-face encounter. Instead of confronting his biggest antagonist in British public life as he'd hoped, Gandhi had a love-in at Westminster Palace with the small left-wing rump of the Labor Party that had gone into opposition. All along he seemed to understand that the political tides in Britain ensured that the conference would amount to less than an anticlimax, a mere episode, in the slow unraveling of India's ties to the empire.

Gandhi's arrival in London had been front-page news for a few days before, inevitably, his comings and goings and pronouncements were downgraded to briefer and briefer stories on the inside pages. "No living man has, either by precept or example, influenced so vast a number of people in so direct and profound a way," wrote Harold Laski, the well-connected and, more to the point, well-disposed political theorist at the London School of Economics, in the pro-Labor *Daily Herald.* "The history of India in the last fifteen years is largely his history."

But what he'd accomplished was "the easiest part of his task," said Laski, firing off a barrage of rhetorical questions, the ones Gandhi himself regularly posed to his supporters: "Will he be able to bind Hindu and Muslim into a unified outlook? Can he break down the tragic barrier of caste? . . . What is he going to do for social freedom?"

These questions shaped the real agenda of the conference. If Indians today find any significance in the Mahatma's last London visit, it's not because of his encounters with Ramsay MacDonald or, beyond the conference hall, with Charlie Chaplin and George Bernard Shaw. It's because the Round Table Conference, a virtual nonstarter on constitutional issues, became the scene of a political face-off between the national movement, in the person of Gandhi, and aspiring untouchables represented by their first authentic leader to be recognized at the national level, Bhimrao Ramji Ambedkar. The clash of the two Indians may have occurred under the gilded imperial auspices of St. James's Palace decades ago, beyond the memory of any living Indian. One of them may have been comparatively unknown in his own country, the other already canonized there and around the globe as the great spiritual figure of the age. But it resounds in Indian politics to this day, its implications still a matter of controversy. And it shook Gandhi to his core, showing him to be not without the sin of pride when it came to his claim of speaking for the "dumb millions." In the years that followed, he'd redouble the energy he threw into his personal crusade against untouchability, if not into any reexamination of his approach to the issue, in part to justify to himself the large claims he'd made in London.

A wisp of triumphalism had attached to his arrival there. There were instants when Gandhi could be suspected of basking in his own celebrity (swapping platitudes with Chaplin, for instance, of whom he'd never heard until the appointment was set). Anyone who expected him to be overawed by London would have forgotten, or never have known, that he'd trudged its corridors of power on his previous visits there as a petitioner for the Indians of South Africa. The difference this time was more in the attire than the man. Invited with other Round Table delegates to tea at Buckingham Palace with George V, he was subjected to a gruff warning from the king himself against stirring up trouble in what the monarch quaintly took to be his domain. Gandhi knew very well whose domain it was and quietly held his ground. "Your Majesty won't expect me to argue the point with you," he replied evenly. Asked later whether he considered his attire appropriate to the regal surroundings, he was ready with a quip: "The King had on enough for both of us."

Within two months of his visit to the palace, the colonial authorities would lock him up for the third time in what he sometimes called "the King's Hotel"—that's to say, Yeravda prison—in order to quash a campaign he was about to launch. A couple of years after that, he felt so sidelined again that he made a show of resigning from the Indian National Congress. More than ever, then, his pilgrimage was not without its ups and downs as he entered the thirties of the last century and his own sixties. In all of this, the encounter with Ambedkar proved to be pivotal.

By the time Ambedkar returned to India from his second round of studies in the West at the end of 1923, he was already one of the best-credentialed Indians of his era, with a Ph.D. from Columbia University and a second doctorate from the London School of Economics, both in economics, in addition to training in the law at Gray's Inn in London. (In later years, he sometimes succumbed to an Indian tendency to show off degrees, writing on stationery on which his name was followed by a string of initials: "M.A., Ph.D., D.Sc., LL.D., D.Litt.") As an untouchable, he was not just a standout; he was in a class by himself, plainly destined for leadership. Still only thirty-two, he looked for an entry into politics as soon as he could establish a livelihood for himself and the bride, betrothed to him at the age of nine, whom he married when he was just fourteen and who, like Gandhi's Kasturba, then found herself left behind in India when her husband traveled overseas. His academic achievements—financed in part by two reigning monarchs inclined to a reformist position on caste issues, the maharajahs of Baroda and Kolhapur—reflected his own grit and determination, which were not unconnected to the cultural aspirations of the Mahars, an upwardly mobile untouchable subcaste in what's now the state of Maharashtra in western India, as these were transmitted to him by his father, a former army quartermaster.

For an untouchable youth in the early part of the century, he'd had a relatively sheltered boyhood but still had the experience, in his earliest schooling, of being treated as an insidious agent of pollution. His place in the classroom was in the corner, seated on a burlap sack (which he was made to carry to and from school to protect caste Hindus from accidental contact with something he'd touched). When he sought to study Sanskrit, he was steered to Persian instead, on grounds that the language of the Vedas, the earliest sacred texts, did not belong in the mouth or beneath the fingers of an untouchable. So when the time finally came for politics, it was all but inevitable that he'd see himself and be seen as a campaigner for the removal of caste barriers.

But he'd also learned that there could sometimes be a distinction between Brahmanism and Brahmans: that individual members of the high priestly caste could recognize the talents of an untouchable and offer support. His surname, in fact, was a testimonial to that possibility. Originally he'd been named Bhima Sankpal. Because the family name announced its lowly place in the caste system, his father decided to use the name of his native village instead, a common Marathi practice. So the Sankpals were to become the Ambavadekars. The new name had a pronunciation close to that of a Brahman teacher named Ambedkar who'd responded to the young untouchable's promise and provided his lunch on a daily basis. So Bhima took his honored teacher's name. In later life, he would continue to have Brahman supporters, and years after the death of his first wife, by which time he'd become a member of the Indian cabinet, he'd cross caste lines to marry a Brahman woman, an "intermarriage" that would be only a little less rare and shocking to caste sensibilities today than it must have been then.

Ambedkar's earliest petitions and statements reflected his training.

Ambedkar in London

Not unlike Gandhi's first petitions on behalf of Natal's so-called British Indians, they were formal and reasoned in a lawyerly way. Setting out, he didn't have anything like Gandhi's flair for pamphleteering and self-dramatization, but, possibly through imitation, these became learned attributes. Where Gandhi encouraged the burning of government permits and foreign cloth, Ambedkar and his followers burned the *Manusmriti*, a volume of traditional Hindu law bearing on caste. The gesture wasn't as widely noted or imitated, but for Hindus who heard of it, it was undoubtedly more radical and inflammatory.

Much later, in the last year of his life, after resigning from independent India's first cabinet, in which he'd functioned as the prime draftsman of its constitution, he established an enduring role for himself as a religious leader by converting to Buddhism and calling on untouchables to follow his example. Over the next half century millions of Mahars and some others did so. Often this has entailed material sacrifice. With the outlawing of untouchability, independent India established a system of affirmative action, with "reserved" places in schools and government service for Dalits, also known officially as members of the "scheduled castes." But the largely Hindu bureaucracy has been slow to certify that Buddhists could qualify for these benefits. Today the site of Ambedkar's conversion has become a shrine and its anniversary an occasion for pilgrimage. Every October 14, throngs of at least 100,000, perhaps double that, converge on the city of Nagpur at a structure called Deekshabhoomi (which means "place of conversion" in the Marathi language) to celebrate Dhamma Chakra Pravartan Din (Mass Conversion Ceremony Day).

Not dedicated until 2001, the structure now stands as the cathedral of the Ambedkar movement. At first glance, the huge inverted cement bowl looks more like a suburban hockey rink than the Buddhist stupa it's intended to evoke. Underneath the bowl is an open round hall with many pillars decorated with plaster lotus motifs, a seated figure of the Buddha, and a photographic display chronicling the life story of Babasaheb Ambedkar, as his followers now call the movement's founder, using a loving honorific expressing filial feeling and reverence. Buddhism began in India, then all but disappeared for centuries until Ambedkar. It still hasn't found its way home ritualistically. Incense, chanting, and monks are often missing from Deekshabhoomi, which makes the sanctuary seem sterile and almost vacant in comparison to the thronged Buddhist shrines of Colombo, Bangkok, or Phnom Penh. But the religion is obviously putting down roots. At nearby souvenir stands Buddhist tracts sell along with little plaster and wood statuettes of a standing Ambedkar, buttoned up in a double-breasted electric blue suit with a red tie, as prevalent as the seated Buddhas on sale in brass. There are also Ambedkar key rings, medallions, and images. Sometimes he's shown standing beside Lord Buddha, partaking of his nimbus. If not a demigod, he's at least a bodhisattva or saint.

A visitor to Nagpur lands at the sleek new Dr. Babasaheb Ambedkar International Airport, from which there are regular flights to Bangkok and Dubai. A seminary for the training of Buddhist monks has recently opened with an enrollment of thirty-five acolytes under the leadership of a converted Dalit, Vimalkitti Gunasiri, who learned his Pali, the language of the sacred Buddhist texts, in Thailand. In addition, the University of Nagpur grants doctorates to students from what's officially called its Post Graduate Department of Dr. Babasaheb Ambedkar Thought. From the vantage point of the university or the Deekshabhoomi, the answer to the question of which figure, Gandhi or Ambedkar, has had the greatest impact on India's religious life seems nothing less than self-evident.

Such a denouement could not have been imagined in 1930, even by Ambedkar, who, early on, seems to have derived a measure of inspiration from Gandhi and Gandhism. He led satyagraha campaigns to open public water supplies, from reservoirs or wells, to untouchables. One of these campaigns is said to have drawn sixteen thousand untouchables to a Maharashtra town called Mahad, where, an admiring biographer writes, they were "led for the first time in their history by a great leader of their own." Another satyagraha under his command aimed at forcing open the main temple at the holy Hindu city of Nasik, where the young Gandhi had been made to undergo ritual purification. At one of the Mahad demonstrations, Gandhi's picture is said to have been displayed.

It's also reported that the Mahatma's name was chanted at demonstrations Ambedkar inspired or led. But Ambedkar's judgment of the Mahatma was early tinged by noticeable disappointment. "Before Mahatma Gandhi," he acknowledged, "no politician in this country maintained that it is necessary to remove social injustice here in order to do away with tension and conflict." But why, he wondered aloud, had Gandhi not sought to make a vow to eliminate untouchability a prerequisite for Congress membership the way he'd insisted on daily spinning?

His conclusion was balanced and restrained to the point of sounding backhanded. "When one is spurned by everyone," the young Ambedkar said in 1925 after Gandhi had visited Vaikom, "even the sympathy shown by Mahatma Gandhi is of no little importance." By 1927, Ambedkar had been named a member of the provincial assembly of what was then called the Bombay Presidency, but there's no clear indication that Gandhi, who still basically believed in boycotting such appointive positions and who, anyhow, claimed to have given up newspapers, took any notice of him or his campaigns, even those that adopted the method and name of satyagraha. The Mahatma accepted disciples; he did not normally seek them out. Ambedkar had not come to him, nor had he ever aligned himself with the national movement, ever tested its professed opposition to untouchability by offering himself as a potential leader.

So it wasn't until August 1931, two weeks before Gandhi's departure for the London conference, that the two men first met, in Bombay. The owlish Ambedkar was a proud and somewhat moody figure, normally aloof even from his own inner circle of adherents, acutely sensitive to slights. ("I am a difficult man," he would later write, in an attempted self-portrait. "Ordinarily I am as quiet as water and humble as grass. But when I get into a temper I am ungovernable and unmanageable.") This first meeting seems to have occurred at the Mahatma's initiative—he'd even offered to call on the younger man—but according to the account handed down by an Ambedkar biographer, the untouchable leader felt snubbed when Gandhi continued a conversation without even glancing at his visitor when Ambedkar entered the room. Once he had Gandhi's attention, he parried an invitation to set out his views on constitutional matters. "You called me to hear your views," he said, according to the one surviving account. Ambedkar then listened impatiently as the Mahatma summarized his efforts on behalf of untouchables, finally making it clear that he regarded them as ineffectual and halfhearted.

"Gandhiji, I have no homeland," he said. The tone may have been plaintive or angry. The Mahatma may have been taken aback.

"I know you are a patriot of sterling worth," Gandhi said, according to this account, apparently based on notes taken down by one of Ambedkar's supporters.

"How can I call this land my own homeland and this religion my own wherein we are treated worse than cats and dogs, wherein we cannot get water to drink?" Ambedkar persisted, according to this account. (The "wherein's" may be a clue that these remarks were reconstructed or translated by a lawyer, possibly Ambedkar himself.)

Gandhi's one comment on the encounter overlooks the "we" in Ambedkar's outburst as it has been handed down. The comment came a couple of years after the event, by which time he'd taken to using a new name for untouchables, calling them Harijans, or "children of God" (a term rejected by today's Dalits as patronizing). "Till I left for England," he said, speaking of Ambedkar, "I did not know he was a Harijan. I thought he was some Brahman who took a deep interest in Harijans and therefore talked intemperately."

An American scholar, Gail Omvedt, calls that reaction "revelatory of the stereotypes about Dalits that Gandhi held." It's an understandable judgment but probably too easy. The go-betweens who set up the meeting had been caste Hindus friendly to Ambedkar. At Vaikom and elsewhere Gandhi had met Brahmans who campaigned conscientiously on behalf of untouchables. This could have been another such group. He'd also met untouchable leaders like Travancore's Ayyankali. Further back, there was the eminently respectable Vincent Lawrence, the converted untouchable who'd served as his clerk in Durban, briefly lived in his house, and went on to be a community leader there. Gandhi knew untouchables could wear starched collars. But he'd never before met an untouchable intellectual like Ambedkar. No one had.

Their next meeting, in London about a month later, didn't go any better. This time Gandhi summoned Ambedkar, who ended up speaking for three hours "while Gandhi, spinning, listened mutely," according to Omvedt. No version of Ambedkar's long monologue survives. His cause was the social uplift of untouchables, not independence, a subject on which he'd wavered. Did he consider the circumstances under which the two causes could be merged, or was he burning with grievance? Did Gandhi, for his part, say anything to suggest that Ambedkar could make a contribution to the national cause? The answers to these obvious questions are left to our imaginations, along with the question of whether it's really likely that Gandhi would have sat mutely for three hours listening to Ambedkar's harangue. All we know is that this second encounter was decidedly less than a success; the two men, whatever their intentions, continued to speak past each other.

If the Mahatma had nothing to say, why had he invited Ambedkar to call on him? The untouchable leader, already on edge over their impending public engagement at the Round Table Conference, concluded that the cagey older man was hoping to gather ammunition for the debate. That's possible but not the only possibility. Maybe Gandhi had been hoping to find common ground and discovered instead that Ambedkar had stiffened his position. He'd once been opposed to separate electorates for his people on more or less nationalist principles; what he'd wanted, he said at the first Round Table Conference, was universal suffrage and guarantees of adequate representation. The Congress brushed off his moderate proposal, so now he wanted separate electorates, the same as the Muslims were seeking, though Ambedkar had previously spoken against the Muslim demand.

Gandhi's failure to bargain at this point could even have been a token of grudging respect. It had been his position that caste Hindus had to clean up their own practices, not dictate the politics of the dispossessed. He was more than ready to lecture them on diet and sanitation. But he could also ask, "Who are we to uplift Harijans?" The "we" here meant caste Hindus. "We can only atone for our sin against them or discharge the debt we owe them, and this we can do only by adopting them as equal members of society, and not by haranguing them."

In South Africa, Gandhi had the experience of making demands on behalf of a beleaguered minority to a political leader who grasped the justice of his claims but found it politically expedient to adopt a posture of obtuseness. Drawing the parallel himself, Gandhi said Ambedkar's anger at Hindus reminded him of himself "in my early days in South Africa where I was hounded by Europeans wherever I went." Did it ever occur to the Mahatma that in resisting Ambedkar for the sake of harmony in the movement he led, he was casting himself in the role of Smuts? He could be fierce in that resistance but never vituperative, writing of Ambedkar later: "Dr. A. always commands my sympathies in all he says. He needs the gentlest treatment."

And on another occasion: "He has a right even to spit upon me, as every untouchable has, and I would keep on smiling if they did so." This resolutely smiling face was not a mask. It was a measure of the man.

But when he confronted Ambedkar at the Round Table Conference, Gandhi's smile faded.

He may have meant to offer Ambedkar "the gentlest treatment," may not have been thinking of Ambedkar at all, when he led off with a political barb, noting in the politest possible terms that the British had stacked the conference with political lightweights and nonentities as a way of diminishing, of getting around, the national movement. Gandhi, the recognized national leader, was just one of fifty-six delegates, placed by the imperial stage managers on an equal footing with British businessmen, maharajahs, and representatives of various minorities and sects. So Gandhi had a point, but the untouchable spokesman could have once again discerned condescension and taken offense. Then, heedless of overstatement, Gandhi allowed himself to claim, "Above all, the Congress represents, in its essence, the dumb, semi-starved millions scattered over the length and breadth of the land in its 700,000 villages." Now we know this wasn't really his reading of Indian reality. In the setting of St. James's Palace, Gandhi was plainly glossing over his own disappointment in the Congress's failure to do more than pay lip service to his "constructive program" for renewal at the village level. Less than two years earlier, he'd told Nehru that the movement couldn't be trusted to conduct a civil disobedience campaign. But here he was allowing himself rhetorical leeway as the Congress's spokesman and plenipotentiary, staking his claim on what was still not much more than an aspiration.

To Ambedkar's sensitive ears, it was propaganda calculated to belittle him and his struggle for the recognition of untouchables as a distinct and persecuted Indian minority, therefore demanding rebuttal. If the Congress represented the poorest, what role could he have, standing outside the national movement as he did? Three days later Gandhi made a potentially soothing gesture, saying, "Of course, the Congress will share the honor with Dr. Ambedkar of representing the interests of the untouchables." But in the next breath he swept Ambedkar's ideas for untouchable representation off the table. "Special representation" for them, he said, would run counter to their interests.

The clash between Ambedkar and Gandhi became personal in a session of what was named the Minorities Committee, on October 8, 1931, a day after Prime Minister MacDonald called a snap election that would produce a Tory landslide behind the facade of a national unity government, giving the Tories more than three-quarters of the seats in the new

Ambedkar, lower right; Gandhi, center, at Round Table Conference

House of Commons. It was Ambedkar who lit the fuse, ignoring the Mahatma's offer to "share the honor" of representing the untouchables. He may have been nominated by the British, but, nevertheless, Ambedkar said, "I fully represent the claims of my community." Gandhi had no claim, he now seemed to argue, on the support of untouchables: "The Mahatma has always been saying that the Congress stands for the Depressed Classes, and that the Congress represents the Depressed Classes more than I or my colleagues can do. To that claim I can only say that it is one of the many false claims which irresponsible people keep on making."

The untouchable leader didn't stop there. He went on to suggest that the takeover of British India by caste Hindus could be a threat to his people—the bulk of Gandhi's "dumb millions"—fifty or sixty million untouchables by the estimates then in use. "The Depressed Classes are not anxious, they are not clamorous," he said, "they have not started any movement for claiming that there shall be an immediate transfer of power from the British to the Indian people."

Gandhi didn't raise his voice—that was never his way—but he was plainly stung. In his long public life of more than half a century, there's probably no other moment when he spoke as sharply—or as personally—as he now did in picking up the gauntlet Ambedkar had thrown down. This time there was no mention of sharing the honor of representing the untouchables. "I claim myself in my own person to represent the vast mass of the untouchables," he said. "Here I speak not merely on behalf of the Congress, but I speak on my own behalf, and I claim that I would get, if there was a referendum of the untouchables, their vote, and I would top the poll." In that highly charged instant, the Mahatma's ego was as bare as his person.

However it's regarded—as a challenge and response between two political leaders over an issue that was central to each man's sense of mission, or as a description of reality as it then existed in the villages and slums of colonial India, or as a weighty constitutional issue bearing on the best interests of a minority, or as a portent of India's future—the clash was heavily laden with meanings. After eight decades, these require some sorting out.

On the level of mundane Indian reality as it existed in the depths of the Depression era, Gandhi was unquestionably right when he said as he did that morning in the old Tudor palace, "It is not a proper claim which is registered by Dr. Ambedkar when he seeks to speak for the whole of the untouchables of India." Most untouchables in India then would probably not have heard of Ambedkar; he was still little known outside his own region. If most untouchables had heard of any single political leader, it would have been Gandhi. So, yes, he might well have been expected to "top" his imagined poll. This is true even though, in his insistence that the problem of untouchability started with the warped values of caste Hindus and not with the untouchables themselves, he'd done next to nothing to organize and lead untouchables, whose cause, he again insisted, was "as dear to me as life itself."

For all his ambition and maneuvering, Ambedkar would never fare well in electoral politics, and the parties he founded never achieved anything like a national following. Even today in Nagpur, in the heart of Ambedkar country, the last of his parties, the Republican Party, has mutated into no fewer than four distinct versions, each aligned with a particular Dalit leader sitting under a portrait of Ambedkar, claiming to be his true heir. Nevertheless, if a poll were held today in an attempt to measure the relative standing of the Mahatma and the man revered as Babasaheb among the former untouchables, now calling themselves Dalits, there can be little doubt that Ambedkar has finally caught up to Gandhi, that he would "top" it. He stood for the idea that they were the keepers of their own destiny, that they deserved their own movement, their own leaders, like all other Indian communities, castes, and sub-castes, an idea that after four or five generations—despite all the fragmentation and corruption of caste-based electoral politics in the "world's greatest democracy"—most Dalits finally appear to embrace.

On the constitutional issue and the best interests of untouchables, Gandhi had more to say that morning in the palace than his challenger. His essential argument was that any special representation for untouchables—in the form of separate electorates or reserved seats that only untouchables could hold—would work to perpetuate untouchability. "Let the whole world know," he said, "that today there is a body of Hindu reformers who are pledged to remove this blot of untouchability. We do not want on our register and on our census untouchables classified as a separate class . . . Will untouchables remain untouchables in perpetuity? I would far rather that Hinduism died than that untouchability lived."

This was as forceful and pure a statement of principle on the subject as this remarkable advocate ever managed. But he didn't stop there. The encounter had shaken him. The previous week he'd negotiated futilely on constitutional formulas with Jinnah, the Aga Khan, and other Muslim leaders. Now here he was clashing with an untouchable, and even if he had the better of the argument for the moment, he was shrewd enough to understand that the forecast he'd made about the imminent collapse of untouchability remained a far-fetched boast. He'd already declared his sense of helplessness on the question of Hindu-Muslim unity. Did he now glimpse a similar impasse in his fight against untouchability? The achievement of communal unity and the end of caste persecution had been two of his four "pillars" of Indian freedom. At this turning point in London, he could hardly have felt confident about either cause.

How he really felt was implicit in what he had to say about his surprisingly staunch opponent that day. "The great wrong under which he has labored and perhaps the bitter experiences that he has undergone have for the moment warped his judgment," Gandhi said of Ambedkar, after praising his dedication and ability. The Mahatma was again in the grip of the same caution that had led him to predict, during the Vaikom campaign, that "chaos and confusion" could be the result if the cause of temple entry were taken up by the national movement. If the untouchables were fortified with separate political rights, he now said, that would "create a division in Hinduism which I cannot possibly look forward to . . . Those who speak of the political rights of untouchables do not know their India, do not know how Indian society is today constructed." Much lay between the lines here. Though he had not solved the question of untouchability, Gandhi had built a national movement and not just a movement; he'd evoked the sense of nationhood on which it was based. He needed to believe that this could finally be the answer to untouchability. He feared that caste conflict could be its undoing. Implicitly, he was acknowledging that the problem remained to be solved and pledging, once again, to be the one whose passion and example would bring the solution.

"I want to say with all the emphasis I can command," he concluded with a vague but ominous warning, "that if I was the only person to resist this thing I would resist it with my life." Here he was paraphrasing a line from his life-transforming speech in Johannesburg's Empire Theater a quarter of a century earlier. At the turning points of Gandhi's political life, it was always "do or die."

It's not clear that the British or Ambedkar or others at the Round Table Conference grasped the meaning of this warning on hearing it. They may have shrugged it off as rhetoric, failing to understand the importance of vows in the Mahatma's life. But heading off "this thing"— the move not just to give untouchables supposed legal guarantees of equal rights but separate political rights that could be bartered for some measure of political power—had now become a Gandhian vow, complicating and making even more urgent his vow to end untouchability.

Both sides went away with hurt feelings. "This has been the most humiliating day of my life," Gandhi remarked that evening. For his part, Ambedkar would later be quoted as having said of Gandhi that "a more ignorant and more tactless representative could not have been sent" to speak for the Congress at the conference. Gandhi claimed to be a unifying force and a man full of humanity, Ambedkar went on, but he had shown how petty he could be. Ambedkar is not the first person to feel personally offended by Gandhi in this way. If we cast our minds back over two decades to South Africa, we can hear echoes in Ambedkar of the bitter tirades Gandhi evoked from Durban's P. S. Aiyar, the maverick Indian editor who complained that Gandhi presented himself as "a soul of perfection," though he'd produced "no tangible good for anyone."

Gandhi had taken no notice of the editor's attempt to fight the head tax imposed on former indentured laborers, just as he'd later take no notice of Ambedkar's adoption of satyagraha as a tactic to open up Hindu temples and village wells to untouchables. An ocean separated Ambedkar and Aiyar. They probably never heard of each other, but they ended up with the same sense of bitterness over a Gandhi they found elusive and immovable, a Gandhi who seemed to feel that fighting for the indentured or untouchables—causes with which he'd long identified himself—was illegitimate if it was done without his sanction, on time-tables other than his own. Ambedkar eventually revealed a sense of injury he'd nursed for years, so like Aiyar's. "Mr. Gandhi made nonsense of satyagraha," he wrote, referring to the Mahatma's refusal to back one of his temple-entry campaigns. "Why did Mr. Gandhi do this? Only because he did not want to annoy and exasperate the Hindus."

As the London conference was concluding, Jawaharlal Nehru wrote to a supporter of the untouchable leader complaining that Ambedkar's "behavior to Gandhiji had been exceedingly discourteous." More than sharp words was at stake. In the archive of the Nehru Memorial in New Delhi, I came upon a letter Nehru wrote several days later in his official capacity as general secretary of the All India Congress Committee, tossing cold water on an ardent appeal on the subject of untouchability from a rising young congressman in Bombay named S. K. Patil. What the young congressman wanted was a clear stand in support of the Nasik satyagraha, which Ambedkar had launched before heading to London. It was time, he wrote, for Congress to "take sides" on the matter of temple entry; an "authoritative statement" was needed in support of the Nasik satyagraha. Patil, who'd emerge three decades later as a tough political boss in Bombay and a powerful member of the Nehru cabinet, was especially incensed by a Congress leader's statement that the weapon of satyagraha should be reserved for the cause of independence, not be wasted on lesser, more parochial issues like temple entry. If that was the movement's stand, he wrote, then "many of us have not understood Mahatmaji for whom satyagraha is a panacea for all evils."

The rising young politician was unaware that Mahatmaji's stand wasn't nearly as clear-cut as he worshipfully imagined, that seven years earlier, at the time of the Vaikom Satyagraha, Gandhi had actually ruled that the national movement shouldn't get involved in "local" temple-entry campaigns. Nehru didn't go into that history in his reply. He ducked the issue of temple entry for untouchables altogether, saying simply that satyagraha "should not be abused and made a cheap weapon." The issue plainly struck him as a diversion from the main goals of the national struggle. By birth, a Kashmiri pandit, or Brahman, he'd dropped caste from his vocabulary in favor of class. Abolishing untouchability, in his view, was a task for an independent India, something that could be deferred until that long-awaited dawn. Nehru's brush-off of Patil stands as a timely reminder of why Ambedkar was so sore. Congress could not, in fact, be relied on to "share the honor" of representing the untouchables. That was—and would remain—the weak point in Gandhi's otherwise passionate stand.

London had been only round one. Gandhi and Ambedkar would soon clash again, over even higher stakes. Thereafter it wouldn't be long before the rotund future Buddhist would give up on temple-entry campaigns, on Hinduism in general, and on Congress in particular. Gandhi, who'd promised to resist "this thing" with his life, may have been the only one who sensed what was coming.

GANDHI'S GOOD-BYE TODAY, said the headline in London's *Daily Herald* on December 5. In a farewell interview, the Mahatma said that "something indefinable" had changed in the attitude of ordinary Britons toward India. Years later George Orwell, no dewy-eyed admirer, would seem to agree, suggesting that Gandhi's great achievement may have been the creation in Britain of "a large body of opinion sympathetic to Indian independence . . . Gandhi, by keeping up his struggle obstinately and without hatred, disinfected the political air." The best evidence for Orwell's argument may be found in the three months Gandhi spent in England at the height of the Depression.

After stops in Paris and Switzerland, he arrived in Italy on December 11, hoping to meet the pope and Mussolini. The time in London inflated his sense of his stature on the world scene. Now he heard a calling to do what he could to head off another war in Europe. He was hopeful, he confided to the French writer Romain Rolland, that he could make some impression on his Rome stopover. Rolland had written a hagiographic tract hailing Gandhi as India's "Messiah," going so far as to compare him to Buddha and Christ as a "mortal half-god." But he was skeptical about the Mahatma's ability to move Il Duce.

Pope Pius XI sent his regrets but arranged for Gandhi to visit the Sistine Chapel. Unfortunately, there's no image, other than what we can summon to our imaginations, of the slight figure in his loincloth and shawl gazing up contemplatively at a similarly attired, incomparably

At Bombay rally on return from Europe, December 1931

heftier Christ in *The Last Judgment*. More than likely, it was the
Mahatma's first and only real experience of Western painting on religious themes, if we omit the Jesus print he kept over his desk in his
Johannesburg law office. He took it in with some patience, later pronouncing himself deeply moved by a pietà: probably the Michelangelo
in St. Peter's, possibly the Bellini in the Vatican museum. Then at six
o'clock he was ushered into Mussolini's spacious office ("as big as a ball-
room, completely empty except for one big writing table," wrote
Gandhi's English follower Madeleine Slade, the admiral's daughter
whom Gandhi had renamed Mirabehn). The dictator (in what Mirabehn
described as "quite good English") led the conversation, asking his visitor whether he'd "got anything" at the Round Table Conference.

"No indeed," Gandhi replied, "but I had not hoped I would get anything out of it."

What would he do next? Mussolini wanted to know. "It seems I shall
have to start a campaign of civil disobedience," his guest said.

It remained a back-and-forth in this vein between two seasoned politicians until Mussolini solicited Gandhi's thoughts on Europe. "Now you

ask the question that I have been waiting for you to ask," said the Mahatma, launching into what was effectively a summary of arguments about Western decadence he'd set down twenty-two years earlier in *Hind Swaraj* as he traveled back to South Africa from a previous unsuccessful mission to Whitehall. "Europe cannot go on the way it has been going on," he said. "The only alternative is for it to change the whole basis of its economic life, its whole value system."

Gandhi, who hadn't bothered to study up on fascism, may have thought he was speaking against industrialization and colonialism, and therefore, by his lights, for peace. But his actual words could have been spliced seamlessly into one of Il Duce's strident orations. The meeting thus ended on a note of harmony, but it was hardly a meeting of minds, in part because Gandhi had misread his host's.

He sailed from Brindisi for home two days later. From shipboard he wrote to Romain Rolland praising Mussolini for his "service to the poor, his opposition to super-urbanization, his efforts to bring about coordination between capital and labor . . . [and] his passionate love for "his people." Appalled, Rolland wrote an emotional rebuttal, upbraiding his Messiah for passing such casual, ill-informed judgments. Before the letter could be mailed, he learned that Gandhi had been taken out of circulation.

On January 4, 1932, seven days after disembarking in Bombay, the Mahatma awakened at three in the morning to find the commissioner of police, an Englishman in full uniform, standing at the foot of his bed. "Bapu just waking [looked] old, fragile and rather pathetic with the mists of sleep still on his face," a sympathetic British onlooker later wrote.

"Mr. Gandhi," the commissioner said, "it is my duty to arrest you."

"A beautiful smile of welcome broke out on Bapu's face," the onlooker went on, "and now he looked young, strong and confident."

9

FAST UNTO DEATH

T HE CASTE SYSTEM SUPPORTED by Gandhiji is the reason for the plight of Dalits today. Gandhi was not for the Dalits but against them. He insulted Dalits by calling them Harijans." Among India's ex-untouchables, this wasn't a heretical or even an unconventional judgment when voiced in the early 1990s by an aspiring politician named Mayawati who later rose to be chief minister of Uttar Pradesh, a state on the Gangetic plain with a population larger than Russia's by a margin of fifty million; among upwardly mobile Dalits, it was the received wisdom. Mayawati then developed national aspirations that made it necessary for her to soften somewhat her estimate of the Father of the Nation. But the idea that Gandhi was an "enemy" of the most oppressed and deprived of India's poor—the very people to whom he'd professed to have dedicated his life, in whose image he'd deliberately remade his own—lingers in the small galaxy of Dalit Web sites in cyberspace. It's, after all, traceable directly to Babasaheb Ambedkar, who, in one of his less measured pronouncements, branded Gandhi "the number one enemy" of the untouchables. In the heat of controversy, it's usually forgotten that the mercurial Ambedkar also called Gandhi "India's greatest man."

In ongoing debates about Gandhi's attitude to untouchables and caste, it's never difficult to quote the Mahatma against himself. Over half a century he wrote and spoke on the subject with deep conviction, in most instances anyway, but his tactics needed readjusting in different places, at different times. Decades after encouraging intercaste and intercommunal dining at the Phoenix Settlement and Tolstoy Farm in South Africa, or among field workers in his early Indian campaigns such as in the Champaran district of Bihar, he told caste-obsessed audiences in South India, where he was seeking to open minds on the untouchability question, that intercaste dining was a matter of private choice, a personal issue. Before such audiences, he was even more chary about discussing intercaste marriage. Without putting it quite so crassly, he all but assured high-caste Hindus that they could give up the wicked practice of untouchability without ever having to worry about their daughters marrying beneath themselves in the caste system, let alone marrying untouchables. Yet the same Gandhi, in defiance of orthodox Hindus, finally decreed that only intercaste marriages could be performed at his ashram. Eventually he concluded that intercaste marriage wasn't merely permissible but possibly the solution since it would tend to produce "only one caste, known by the beautiful name Bhangi." Considering that a Bhangi, or sweeper, is sometimes despised even by other untouchables, it was a radical thought. (One that remains radical, a lifetime later, in an India in which three fourths of those approached in opinion surveys still voice disapproval of intercaste unions, and where that disapproval not infrequently gets expressed in so-called honor killings of daughters and sisters who stray.)

When Ambedkar unsettled many of his followers by taking a Brahman wife after independence and Gandhi's death, his fellow cabinet member Vallabhbhai Patel wrote him a congratulatory letter noting kindly, or maybe pointedly, that the leader whose sincerity he'd so fiercely questioned would have been pleased. "I agree that Bapu, if he had been alive, would have blessed the marriage," a more mellow Ambedkar wrote back.

To say that Gandhi wasn't absolutely consistent isn't to convict him of hypocrisy; it's to acknowledge that he was a political leader preoccupied with the task of building a nation, or sometimes just holding it together. This is never clearer than in a reply he sent to his soul mate Charlie Andrews, the Anglican priest he first encountered at the end of his stay in South Africa. Andrews, who regularly functioned as Gandhi's personal emissary in England and farther-flung parts of the empire, had urged him to concentrate all his efforts on his fight against untouchability, even if that meant stepping back from the independence movement. "My life is one indivisible whole," Gandhi wrote back. And so were his causes and concerns, listed in the letter to Andrews as "satyagraha, civil resistance, untouchability, Hindu-Muslim unity"—plus, he might have said, assorted add-ons such as diet, prohibition, spinning, hygiene, sanitation, education through vernacular languages, and women's rights, including the right of widows to remarry and the abolition of child marriage—all "indivisible parts of a whole which is truth." And if they were all thought of as one, Gandhi went on in direct reply to the plea from Andrews:

> I can't devote myself entirely to untouchability and say, "Neglect Hindu-Muslim unity or swaraj." All these things run into one another and are interdependent. You will find at one time in my life an emphasis on one thing, at another time on [an]other. But that is just like a pianist, now emphasizing one note and now [an]other.

In this case, the pianist also sees himself as composer and conductor. "Full and final removal of untouchability," he now says, "is utterly impossible without swaraj." This from the man who as early as 1921 had described "the removal of untouchability as an indispensable condition of the attainment of swaraj." It's hard not to view this as a reversal or contradiction. But for the pianist himself, it was just a variation on a theme, a matter of emphasizing now one note and now another. His friend Andrews should have recognized it as such. The man he addressed familiarly as Mohan had long ago warned him, as we've seen, that English domination would probably have to end before India could "become free of the curse of untouchability." That was also back in 1921, so this particular contradiction could hardly be described as newly minted; if anything, it was closer to being a constant feature of his effort to keep India on the path he'd tried to chart. In Gandhi's view, the fact that his best efforts had put an end to neither English domination nor untouchability by 1933 seemed only to strengthen his conviction that these struggles were indivisible parts of a whole. So if he now decided to concentrate on untouchability, he wasn't backing off from the swaraj struggle as Andrews urged and Nehru feared. By his own lights, he was plunging in again.

Still, this time around his agenda had been shaped by others: first Ambedkar, the seemingly irreconcilable untouchable leader, with his demand for separate electorates for the fifty million or so members of the officially designated "depressed classes" he claimed to represent; and then Ramsay MacDonald, the onetime sympathizer with the Indian national struggle now fronting for what was basically a Tory government set on preserving imperial rule. The Round Table Conference had ended with a promise by the British prime minister to devise the compromise formula for elections on the subcontinent—the Communal Award, it was called—that the various Indian communal groups and parties had failed to hammer out among themselves. When finally handed down from Whitehall in August 1932, the award put the royal seal of approval on Ambedkar's demand. In the future, untouchables, like Muslims, would get to elect their own representatives to all Indian legislative bodies; eventually, if the award stood, Gandhi's claim that he and the Congress movement were their real representatives would be put to the severest possible test. Increasingly, the Congress might then be seen not as the national movement but as a loose coalition of Hindus desperate to preserve its majority. This was the outcome—the kind of "special representation" for untouchables—that Gandhi, now sixty-three, had vowed at the conference to "resist with my life" for the high-principled reason that it would tend to institutionalize, and thus perpetuate, untouchability, a status he'd sometimes compared to slavery as he had the indenture system in South Africa.

MacDonald's Communal Award specified that the separate electorate for untouchables would be phased out after twenty years. This might have been intended as a small concession to Gandhi; the arrangement would not be perpetual. In any case, Gandhi was once again sidelined. By the time the award came down, he'd been securely under wraps in Yeravda prison near Poona for seven and a half months, immobilized there, or so the British thought, even though Gandhi had written from prison as early as March to the secretary of state for India, Sir Samuel Hoare, to give fair warning that the vow he'd voiced in London was "not said in the heat of the moment nor by way of rhetoric." If a decision were now taken to create separate electorates for the so-called depressed classes, the letter said, "I must fast unto death." Gandhi assumed but wasn't sure that his warning had been conveyed to MacDonald; after five months, it still hadn't leaked into the public sphere.

India and the world didn't learn of Gandhi's intention to put his life on the line over the narrow issue of untouchable representation until a week before the date he'd set for the start of his fast. The news broke with the release, finally, in London of his letter to Hoare and a subsequent one to MacDonald that set the date for September 20. His jailers soon discovered that, once again, they'd underestimated the Mahatma's ingenuity and determination. His ability to act forcefully and work his will from inside Yeravda's thick walls bears comparison to Harry Houdini's escapes from a padlocked and submerged trunk, only the agility involved here was strictly mental and psychological. Few wondered whether his threat to "fast unto death" unless the award was withdrawn was a trick. *The Times of India,* a Bombay newspaper edited and written by British journalists in that era, headlined Gandhi's "Suicide Threat" and wrote editorially that he'd now shown himself to be "prepared to go to any length that fanaticism may dictate."

The Mahatma had limited privileges as a prisoner: he was allowed to receive visitors and carry on his vast correspondence as long as he steered clear of overt politics; he was capable of dictating fifty letters a day, as if Yeravda were just the latest of his ashrams. Once his fast was accepted by the prison authorities as unavoidable, the restrictions were loosened further so he could take part in political negotiations. So the prisoner, though out of sight, was back onstage as an actor. In no time, he'd provoked a huge crisis for the British, his supporters, and, not least of all, Dr. Ambedkar; a national and international commotion; a storm of anxiety and soul-searching, political maneuvering and forced retreats, all unfolding according to his script. The central issue may have involved nuts-and-bolts politics—the sharing of power with a hopelessly power-less group—but Gandhi found a way to explain his stand in religious terms. Once again he saw himself in a struggle for the souls of Hindus and for an enlightened, egalitarian Hinduism he still hoped to promote as a substitute for a hierarchical, oppressive religious order, which he saw clearly enough even as he sought to infiltrate it from the inside.

To underline what he deemed to be the religious nature of his stand, Gandhi had deliberately responded to only the part of Ramsay Mac-Donald's award dealing with untouchables, saying nothing about the distribution of seats, the voting rights of Muslims, and other controver-sial points on which he opposed the decision. Those points were merely political, he explained to his secretary, Mahadev Desai, who was with him at Yeravda. Mahadev had argued that there was a broader political case that needed to be made before India and the world if the fast were to be understood and accepted, that Gandhi needed to deal with more than untouchables in his letter to the prime minister. Gandhi got the point but was unmoved. "Our own men will be critical. Jawaharlal will not like it at all. He will say that we have had enough of such religion," he acknowledged. "But that does not matter. When I am going to wield a most powerful weapon in my spiritual armory, misinterpretation and the like may never act as a check." A few days later he said, "It is for me a religious question and not a political question."

Retreating into the religious realm is the Mahatma's way of ringing down the curtain on debate, of announcing he has heard the inner voice that vouchsafes the "truth" on which he relies. Months earlier at Yer-avda, after dispatching the first warning to the secretary of state for

India, he'd cut off a discussion of the possible political fallout from a fast by drawing this same line. "What if I am taken for a madman and die? That would be the end of my mahatmaship if it is false and undeserved," he'd said then. "I should be concerned only with my duty as a man of religion."

The principles on which he bases his distinction between the religious and the political when it comes to untouchable voting rights may be inaccessible to a secular Westerner living outside India in the seventh decade of its independence. But for the sake of discussion, it's worth attempting a deeper look. On the surface, the Mahatma's explanation to Mahadev and to his other fellow jailbird, the tough political operative Vallabhbhai Patel, has more to do with his own sense of what he can accomplish as a leader than with any principles on which all Hindus are likely to agree. He says once again that he feels "helpless" on the Muslim question, that, therefore, it will have to be dealt with politically later. With caste Hindus, he believes, he still has the option of resorting to shock therapy on the untouchability question. "Sudden shock is the treatment required," he tells Mahadev and Patel.

If he fails, he foresees "bloodshed" across India between untouchables and caste Hindus. What's surprising in this lurid vision—and perhaps more than a little revealing—is that it's not the downtrodden untouchable whom he sees in this instance as the passive victims of such anarchic conflict. What he imagines, in this one instance anyway, is an uprising from below in which caste Hindus become the victims. "Untouchable hooligans will make common cause with Muslim hooligans and kill caste Hindus," he gloomily predicts. Gandhi was sometimes accused by Jinnah, Ambedkar, and others of siding instinctively with his own. Here, if only in a single uncharacteristic sentence, he convicts himself. The essence of his religious duty, it seems, is saving caste Hindus from themselves and the retribution that awaits them if they don't embrace his prescriptions for reform. Usually, his forebodings are more firmly rooted in the lopsided sociology of Indian villages where the traditional victims would be the probable victims of mob violence. "What does MacDonald know of the 'unapproachables' and the 'invisibles' in the villages of Gujarat?" he asks Mahadev in such a moment. "They would be crushed."

His urgent sense of mission makes it possible for him to brush off his own strictures at the time of the Vaikom Satyagraha, eight years earlier, against fasting as a weapon to soften the hearts of "touchable" caste Hindus on untouchability in general and temple entry in particular. Then he thought temple entry for untouchables should be a local issue; now, suddenly, he's about to make it an urgent national issue; and fasting unto death—a coercive weapon by any measure—is now a religious duty laid on the leader who'd argued, when it served his purposes, that fasting that compels someone to yield "not because he sees the error of his ways but because he cannot bear to see the death of a person who in his opinion perversely chooses to die . . . [was] the worst form of coercion which militates against the fundamental principles of satyagraha." This time he calls it a "penance," meaning that he was undertaking "self-suffering" for the sins of caste Hindus. But Ambedkar—and, to a lesser extent, the British—could only experience the fast as a form of compulsion.

In simplest terms, a method that could be classed as immoral when pursued by others was a religious obligation when undertaken by himself.

William L. Shirer, the youthful correspondent for the *Chicago Tribune* who'd already made a career of interpreting Gandhi, pronounced himself "baffled" by the Mahatma's willingness to die in order to deny the untouchables assured seats in provincial legislatures. "I would have expected Gandhi to support this necessary safeguard for his beloved untouchables," the journalist later wrote. From Vienna, he sent Gandhi a cable asking for an explanation. "You must not be startled by my presuming to know the interests of the depressed classes more than its leaders," Gandhi cabled back in mid-fast. "Though I am not untouchable by birth, for the past fifty years I have been untouchable by choice." (Gandhi's camp, it seems, leaked the exchange to *The Times* of London before Shirer had a chance to file on it, a sign of how far ahead of his time he was in his aptitude for manipulating the press.)

The American journalist's incomprehension was understandable. Even today, it's not easy to sort out Gandhi's motives. Pyarelal, his confidant and eventual biographer, makes it plain that narrow political calculations were not entirely foreign to what he'd soon glorify as "the Epic Fast." In his book of that title, he writes, "With the Hindus and Musalmans struggling to maintain balance of power and the Sikh claim thrown in between, to accommodate the Depressed Class's demand was a mathematical impossibility." There's only one way to understand Pyarelal. "Mathematical" has to do with the number of seats that could conceivably be subtracted from the Congress total under the formula allowing separate electorates for untouchables. It's a point Gandhi never touched on in his letters and public statements except to dismiss it. "Do not believe for one moment that I am interested in the numerical strength of Hindus," he said. But Vallabhbhai Patel regularly speculated on the ways separate electorates could be manipulated by the British to the disadvantage of the Congress. "There is a deep conspiracy in this," he said of the Communal Award. Patel's calculations added up to the political argument Gandhi forswore, but it wasn't an argument for putting his leader's life on the line. In fact, Patel's only reason for supporting the fast was that he knew how hopeless it would be to quarrel with Gandhi's "still small voice." On his own, he couldn't fashion an argument for the fast unto death.

The Mahatma's own thought process isn't easily traced, but clearly it starts with his vow in London to resist Ambedkar's call for separate electorates with his life, even if he was the last opponent remaining. In London he had opposed not just separate electorates but any "special arrangements" for untouchables, even for a period of limited duration. Yet on the eve of the fast, with feverish negotiations in search of a compromise that would save his life already under way, he let it be known that he could accept reserved seats for untouchables as long as the general electorate was allowed to choose among a slate of untouchable candidates in the districts "reserved" for them. The choice of these candidates would be left up to untouchable voters in these districts in a kind of a primary; thus the "separate electorate" would exist for one round, to be replaced by a "joint electorate" in the general election. This was close to Ambedkar's original position, which had once been unacceptable to the Congress. So now, suddenly, the Mahatma was offering his life to block not "special arrangements" for untouchables but merely one particular kind of special arrangement, separate electorates in a general election. With joint electorates—untouchables voting along with everyone else in the "reserved" districts—the Congress would remain in a strong position to elect its own untouchables, even in cases where it failed to secure the support of most untouchable voters. But if Gandhi could now accept an election law that perpetuated the special status of untouchables, in effect recognizing them as an oppressed minority, despite the arguments he'd raised in London, what could be his justification for his fast? What made it a religious penance? Was securing a narrow political advantage by heading off separate electorates a cause worth dying for? Could that plausibly be singled out as the goal?

It wasn't an argument Gandhi could comfortably make to himself, let alone to the country at large. The fight against separate electorates could be justified only if it were part of a larger reformation of Hindu values and society, the one on which Gandhi had been insisting practically since his return from South Africa. Still, the Mahatma waited until the very eve of his fast before springing this huge, additional condition on his supporters. "He would not be satisfied by a mere political agreement between caste Hindus and the Depressed Classes," according to a summary of his remarks made at the time. "He wanted untouchability to go once [and] for all." Very quickly, then, a fast against a special voting advantage for untouchables had to be reinterpreted and promoted as a fast against untouchability itself. This is what made it a religious duty in Gandhi's eyes, a penance.

While negotiations continued and Gandhi's followers geared up a new offensive against caste oppression, the Mahatma himself spent the eve of his fast dictating farewell letters. As always when he prepared himself for a large undertaking, his thoughts drifted back to South Africa and Hermann Kallenbach, whom he'd last seen in London seventeen years earlier. "If God has more work to take from this body it will survive the fiery ordeal," he wrote to Kallenbach in a note that hovered melodramatically between farewell and au revoir. "Then you must try some early day to come and meet. Otherwise good-bye and much love."

The appeal to the country was hardly raised before a reply was heard, one that seemed at first resounding. At temples across India caste Hindus who had hitherto barred untouchables suddenly proclaimed their eagerness to welcome and embrace their previously outcaste brethren— whom Gandhi was trying to re-brand as Harijans—if that's what it would take to keep their Mahatma alive. Temple openings were presented as a kind of security deposit, as proof of a new spirit of generosity and civic-mindedness on the part of caste Hindus. So here we have a double paradox: Gandhi, who'd opposed the use of fasts on temple-entry issues at Vaikom, was now ready to seize on temple openings as proof of the efficacy of his own fast against the Communal Award, which had been transmuted at the hands of this master political alchemist and dramaturge into a fast against untouchability. What's clearer than his deeply intuitive thought process is the instant impact his decision had. Rabindranath Tagore, the Bengali poet who'd stood against his call for bonfires of foreign cloth, instantly seized on the urgency of what he termed Gandhi's "ultimatum" to the Hindu majority.

"If we cheaply dismiss [the fast] with some ceremonials to which we are accustomed and allow the noble life to be wasted with its great meaning missed," the poet declaimed on its first day, "then our people will passively roll down the slope of degradation to the blankness of utter futility." Seventy years old and ailing, Tagore then rushed by train across the subcontinent to be at Gandhi's side in the prison near Poona. "Whole country profoundly stirred by Mahatmaji's penance," he cabled to a friend in London. "Sweeping reforms proceeding apace." How sweeping they were on a village-to-village basis remained to be seen. Decades later it was not unheard of for untouchable women in villages to be assaulted for wearing metal bangles and rings or new saris in bright colors, adornments that could be read as offensively assertive, as denials of their abject status; landlessness, indebtedness, and forced labor remained extreme. There's no sure way of measuring how many caste Hindu minds were profoundly affected and changed to some degree by Gandhi's fast and subsequent crusade against untouchability; many millions might be a reasonable guess, but in India, where a million is a fraction of a percentage point, many millions could fall far short of the wholesale reformation he sought.

Tagore arrived at Gandhi's bedside on the seventh and last day of the fast. Escorted into an isolated courtyard between two prison blocks, he found Gandhi curled up on a simple stringed cot, a *charpoy*, "under the shade of a young mango tree." It was there on the fourth evening of the fast that Dr. Ambedkar had been brought to the bedside of the Mahatma, who appeared to be already much weakened, for the final stage of negotiations on what came to be known as the Poona Pact.

"Mahatmaji, you have been very unfair to us," the untouchable leader began.

"It is always my lot to appear to be unfair. I cannot help it," said Gandhi.

Soon they were into the "mathematical" details as they bore on legislative seats. "I want my compensation," Ambedkar was heard to say. Presumably, he meant payback in seats for giving up the separate electorates. Untouchables, now powerless, needed political power, he said. Gandhi was flexible on seats but a stickler on the timing of a referendum to be held in five or ten years. "Five years or my life," the prostrate but still hard-bargaining Mahatma said, seeming to give way to irritation at their next encounter, much like a Bania haggling over the price of a bolt of cloth. The issue was negotiated away. The final accord provided for joint electorates, reserved seats, and a referendum to be scheduled later, which proved to be never; in fact, Ambedkar had won nearly twice as many reserved seats in his negotiation with Gandhi as he'd been promised in Ramsay MacDonald's proposed award. "You have my fullest sympathy. I am with you in most things you say," the Mahatma had assured the untouchable leader at the outset. Now, it seemed to Ambedkar, he'd delivered.

"I have only one quarrel with you," Ambedkar had replied, according to Mahadev's diary. "That is you work for the so-called national welfare and not for our interests alone. If you devoted yourself entirely to the welfare of the Depressed Classes, you would become our hero." That response may be the closest Ambedkar ever came to seeing Gandhi whole, as the stalwart of the national ideal. The exchange also anticipates the appeal Andrews was about to make in one of his "Dear Mohan" letters that Gandhi focus all his energies on the fight against untouchability. Without giving Ambedkar a direct answer, the fasting Mahatma managed to have the last word. "I am," he said, "an untouchable by adoption, and as such more of an untouchable in mind than you . . . I cannot stand the idea that your community should either in theory or practice be separated from me. We must be one and indivisible."

Whether the contest between Ambedkar and Gandhi is seen as fundamentally a test of principles or wills, the Mahatma's elevation of the fast into what appeared, for the moment at least, to be his final do-or-die campaign had already produced some astonishing results. First there were the telegrams pouring in from all over the subcontinent proclaiming the opening of Hindu temples—some celebrated and revered, many obscure, some that would later turn out to have been nonexistent—to Gandhi's Harijans. Then an emergency conference of caste Hindus hastily assembled in Bombay drafted a manifesto formally calling for equal access for untouchables to all public facilities—not just temples, but also roads, schools, and wells. "No one shall be regarded as an 'untouchable' by reasons of birth," it proclaimed. A parallel gathering of high-caste Bombay women resolved that the barriers faced by untouchables "shall not continue a day longer." Suddenly it became fashionable in various cities, in what proved to be a brief season of grace and loving kindness, for Brahmans to demonstrate their good intentions by dining with untouchables. At Benares Hindu University, a center of orthodoxy, sweepers and cobblers were invited to dinner. Branches of a newly formed Anti-untouchability League—later renamed the Harijan Sevak Sangh, or Harijan Service Society—were springing up all over; funds were collected to launch its programs of uplift. Even Nehru, who acknowledged that he'd initially been put off by Gandhi's "choosing a side issue for his final sacrifice," was bowled over by the result. "What a magician," he wrote, "was this little man sitting in Yeravda Prison, and how well he knew how to pull the strings that move people's hearts!"

These gusts of pious intoxication seemed to douse Ambedkar's habitual skepticism and sweep him along too. "I will never be moved by these methods," he'd said when he first heard of Gandhi's intention to fast. "If Mr. Gandhi wants to fight with his life for the interests of the Hindu community, the Depressed Classes will also be forced to fight with their lives to safeguard their interests." But he'd been moved in spite of himself over the ensuing ten days. The night before Gandhi was expected to break his fast, Ambedkar found himself showered with fervent promises and cheers at the Hindu conference in Bombay, a lovefest unlike anything he'd experienced. He'd been in a fix, he acknowledged when finally he was called on to speak, having to choose between "the life of the greatest man in India" and "the interests of the community." But the fasting Gandhi had eased the way, redeeming himself in Ambedkar's eyes and blessing all untouchables. "I must confess that I was surprised, immensely surprised, when I met him, that there was so much in common between him and me." If the Mahatma had been as forthcoming in London, Ambedkar said with some justice, "it would not have been necessary for him to go through this ordeal." His only worry, he now said, was that caste Hindus might not abide by the accord. "Yes, we will! We will!" roared the crowd.

Gandhi wouldn't take nourishment until he held in his hand the British government's formal acceptance of the compromise, which meant the partial annulment of the Communal Award on which he'd set his sights. Finally, late in the afternoon of September 26, the document was delivered to him by the inspector general of prisons in a "red sealed envelope." Thinking ahead, Gandhi asked the British officer to pass along his request that he be allowed to continue his campaign against untouchability even if he were to be kept in prison. A religious ceremony was then improvised. The prison authorities had thrown open its gates to inmates of the Sabarmati Ashram in Ahmedabad and other Gandhi followers. Restrictions on visitors had been all but abandoned, and about two hundred of them were now in attendance as the time came to end his self-imposed trial. First the courtyard was sprinkled with water, then Tagore was called on to sing a Bengali hymn he himself had set to music. He'd forgotten the melody, he later said, but he sang anyway. ("When the heart is hard and parched up, come upon me with a shower of mercy," the poet's prayer began.) Finally, Kamala Nehru, wife of Jawaharlal who was to die in a Swiss sanatorium four years later, readied a tumbler of orange, or what in India is called sweet lime, juice. (Possibly honey was mixed in, lemon juice with honey being one of Gandhi's favorite cocktails.) Kasturba raised the glass to his lips. More hymns were sung, and heaped-up baskets of fruit, sent to Yeravda by well-wishers, passed from hand to hand. No prison had ever witnessed such a festival, Tagore reflected.

At the end of another overflow public meeting, this one in Poona the next evening, the poet wrote, "The entire audience raising their hands accepted the vow of purifying our social life of grave wrongs that humiliate our humanity." The idea that untouchability was on its way out, that the Mahatma had transformed India and Hinduism with a one-week fast unto death, lingered for a matter of weeks, maybe months. Gandhi at this point seemed to be alone in warning of the danger of backsliding. The night his fast unto death ended, he thought to pledge that it would be resumed if the struggle against untouchability faltered.

Gandhi's fast might conceivably have sown a harvest of enduring social reform had the British not kept the Mahatma and most of the Congress leadership locked away in order to prevent any resumption of civil disobedience on a national scale. Three times in the next eight months Ambedkar dropped by Yeravda prison to consult with Gandhi. For a brief spell, the antagonism between the two receded from view; a kind of convergence now seemed to be faintly possible. In his speeches to untouchable audiences, Ambedkar took to urging his followers to give up meat eating, an appeal Gandhi seldom failed to make to such gatherings in the hope that this would render them more acceptable in the eyes of pious Hindus. The untouchable leader now spoke more of national goals and political rights. Taking up one of the Mahatma's themes, he wrote: "The touchables and untouchables cannot be held together by law, certainly not by any electoral law . . . The only thing that can hold them together is love . . . I want a revolution in the mentality of the caste Hindus."

But the more important the opening of Hindu temples to untouchables became to Gandhi, the less important it seemed to Ambedkar. They could almost be said to be exchanging positions. For Gandhi now temple opening was "the one thing that alone can give new life and new hope to Harijans, as no mere economic uplift can do." For Ambedkar, the key issue was now social equality, not open temples. "To open or not to open temples is a question for you to consider and not for me to agitate," he said, addressing caste Hindus. "If you think it is bad manners not to respect the sacredness of the human personality, open your temples and be a gentleman. If you would rather be a Hindu than a gentle-man, then shut your doors and damn yourself. For I do not care to come." When Gandhi vowed to start a new fast at the beginning of 1933 if the most important South Indian temple dedicated to the god Krishna, the Guruvayur, remained closed to untouchables, Ambedkar urged him not to bother. It's "not necessary for him to stake his life on such a comparatively small issue as temple entry," Ambedkar said.

When from inside Yeravda prison he was about to launch his *Harijan* weekly—a successor to *Indian Opinion* and *Young India*—Gandhi reached out to Ambedkar, asking him for a "message" for the inaugural issue. The gesture evoked a sardonic response that fairly dripped with resentment. "It would be a most unwarranted presumption on my part," Ambedkar wrote, "to suppose that I have sufficient worth in the eyes of the Hindus which would make them treat any message from me with respect." So instead of a "message" he sent a "statement." Apparently, he still did not like the implication that he might be engaged in a common cause with Hindu reformers, including Gandhi. He would simply tell Gandhi and Hindus some home truths. Gandhi made sure that *Harijan* published the tart covering note as well as the statement, which said: "There will be outcastes so long as there are castes. Nothing can eman-cipate the outcaste except the destruction of the caste system." His intention may have been to goad Gandhi rather than to pick a fight, but already they were drawing apart. Eventually, they would both reject the pact they had jointly signed at Yeravda. Gandhi would call the limited use of separate electorates he'd finally agreed to when his life was at stake "a device of Satan, named imperialism." Ambedkar would write: "The Congress sucked the juice out of the Poona Pact and threw the rind in the face of the Untouchables."

The issue on which they soon diverged had hovered between them from the time of their first encounter. It was whether downtrodden untouchables could be effectively mobilized in their own behalf in the dusty exigencies of village India or were doomed to wait for caste Hin-dus to be moved by the religious penance and suffering of "the greatest man in India." In the existing circumstances, each alternative was largely theoretical. The effective mobilization of untouchables and the religious conversion of caste Hindus would each take generations; how many generations, it's still—eight decades later—too soon to tell. Both have advanced, thanks in some measure to Gandhi and Ambedkar, not just in their lives but in what they've been taken to represent in India's dreamy idealization of their struggles. But the pace can reasonably be described as slightly faster than glacial, which is to say, grindingly slow, nowhere near revolutionary.

It took only five weeks after Gandhi ended the "epic fast" for a bill to be introduced in the Madras Legislative Council making it illegal for a temple to remain closed to Harijans if the majority of caste Hindus who used the temple wanted it open. The aim of the bill was to take the decision out of the hands of Brahman priests, such as the Namboodiris at Vaikom, who typically had the final say. The legislative council had little power and needed the viceroy's formal approval even to debate the bill. In the face of rising opposition from orthodox Hindus and the seeming indifference of Harijans, similar legislation introduced in the toothless central assembly stalled. For Gandhi, the legislation took on urgency as a referendum on untouchability. When they met in February 1933, Gandhi implored Ambedkar to support the bills, or at least not oppose them.

"Supposing we are lucky in the case of temple-entry, will they let us fetch water from the wells?" Ambedkar asked.

"Sure," Gandhi replied. "This is bound to follow."

Ambedkar hesitated. What he wanted from Gandhi, the Mahatma wasn't ready to provide—an unambiguous denunciation of the caste system to show he was in earnest about his contention that all Hindus were created equal. Ambedkar had agreed to join the board of the Harijan Sevak Sangh, whose constitution said as much, promising Harijans "absolute equality with the rest of Hindus" and requiring its members to declare: "I do not consider any human being as inferior to me in status and I shall strive my utmost to live by that belief." But within a year he resigned, convinced that this Gandhian organization dedicated to the service of his people was dominated by caste Hindus who were basically uninterested in mobilizing Harijans, as Ambedkar had proposed, in "a campaign all over India to secure to the Depressed Classes the enjoyment of their civic rights."

Finally Ambedkar concluded that the temple-entry legislation had to be read as an insult, another reason to move away from the Mahatma. "Sin and immorality cannot become tolerable because a majority is addicted to them or because the majority chooses to practice them," he said. "If untouchability is a sinful and immoral custom, in the view of the Depressed Classes it must be destroyed without any hesitation even if it was acceptable to the majority."

The same issue—whether Harijan basic rights could be put to a vote by caste Hindus—came up in the conflict over Guruvayur temple. Still locked up at Yeravda but permitted by the authorities to agitate on Harijan issues from behind prison walls, Gandhi kept scheduling and postponing a fast on the opening of the celebrated Krishna temple. A poll was taken in the temple's surroundings, confirming his belief that most caste Hindus were now ready to worship with Harijans. But the temple remained closed to them until after independence in 1947. As late as 1958, ten years after Gandhi's murder, a deflated and dispirited Harijan Sevak Sangh was counting it as a victory that a couple more temples in Benares were at last being opened to Harijans whose equality it had proclaimed a quarter of a century earlier.

In May 1933, when Gandhi finally started his next fast—his second over untouchability in seven months—he was immediately released from jail. Though it lasted twenty-one days—two weeks longer than the so-called epic fast—this second round caused less of a stir. Tagore wrote to say it was a mistake. Nehru, still in jail in Allahabad, threw up his hands. "What can I say about matters I do not understand?" he wrote in a letter to Gandhi.

Ambedkar by this time was looking the other way. Within two years, his movement ended the temple-entry campaigns it had been carrying on in a desultory fashion over the previous decade. The time had come, he proclaimed, for untouchables—now starting to call themselves Dalits, not Harijans—to give up on Hinduism. "I was born a Hindu and have suffered the consequences of untouchability," he said and then immediately vowed: "I will not die a Hindu."

If any admiration, any ambivalence lingered in Ambedkar's feelings about Gandhi after their final falling-out, he labored to repress it. Much of his energy in his late years went into a renewal—and escalation—of bitter polemics against him. "As a Mahatma he may be trying to spiritualize politics," Ambedkar would write. "Whether he has succeeded in it or not, politics have certainly commercialized him. A politician must know that society cannot bear the whole truth, that he must not speak the whole truth if speaking the whole truth is bad for his politics." Gandhi refuses to launch a frontal attack on the caste system, this disillusioned, brainy antagonist finally argues, out of fear that "he will lose his place in politics."

Which is why, he concludes, "The Mahatma appears not to believe in thinking."

The inconsistency was as much Ambedkar's as Gandhi's. The Poona

Pact might have given them a basis for a fruitful division of labor, with Gandhi working to soften up Hindu attachment to the practice of untouchability, leaving room for Ambedkar to mobilize the impoverished and oppressed people Gandhi had named Harijans. More than politics and Ambedkar's ambition got in the way. Gandhi wasn't interested in mobilization outside the Congress. Ambedkar wanted his fair share of power but wasn't prepared to be patronized, which was what would happen, he seemed sure, if he ever surrendered his independence to the Congress. Putting his case against Gandhi in the simplest terms, Ambedkar said: "Obviously, he would like to uplift the Untouchables if he can but not by offending the Hindus." That sentence contains the essence of their conflict. Ambedkar had ceased to think of untouchables as Hindus; Gandhi had not. The basic question was whether they'd be better off in the India of the future as a segregated minority and interest group battling for its rights or as a tolerated adjunct to the majority with recognized rights, an issue, it's fair to say, that remains unresolved after nearly eight decades.

After all his hard bargaining, the untouchable leader eventually discovered that the concessions he'd made to secure an agreement with the fasting Mahatma hadn't elevated him to a national position; he was to get there by another route. As the years wore on, he found himself leader of a series of small cash-starved opposition parties whose influence seldom extended beyond his Mahar base in what became the state of Maharashtra. For this, with mounting asperity, he blamed Gandhi and the Congress. But there's suggestive if somewhat sketchy evidence that, fifteen years after the pact, it may have been Gandhi who advanced Ambedkar's name for a position in independent India's first cabinet. As law minister, he then became the principal author of the 1950 constitution whose Article 17 formally abolished untouchability, a denouement Gandhi did not live to see. So the man now revered as Babasaheb by the ex-untouchables who today call themselves Dalits never reconciled himself with Gandhi, the politician he criticized for being unwilling to tell India "the whole truth," who may, nevertheless, have been responsible for his elevation to the national position he craved.

Ambedkar had a point if he meant to say that Gandhi's status as national leader owed something to a tendency to speak less than "the whole truth." But the Mahatma was more apt to belittle his own mahatmaship than to deny being a politician. So hurling the epithet "Politician!"

against this original, self-created exemplar of leadership—venerated, if imperfectly understood, by most Indians—didn't take much insight or carry much sting. If Ambedkar was saying that the Mahatma's insistence on "truth" as his lodestar was self-serving and therefore delusional, was he also saying he'd have admired the national leader more if he let go of that claim? Gandhi may have been a politician, but there were few, if any, like him in his readiness to summon his followers, or himself, to new and more difficult tests. By the summer of 1933 the man described by Nehru as having "a flair for action" was torn between competing causes, unable to decide whether to focus on a scaled-down campaign of civil disobedience or a full-throated crusade against untouchability. He could argue that the two causes were "indivisible," but his movement and the colonial authorities, in their own ways, pushed him to a choice.

The British still held most of his top Congress colleagues in prison, a practical way of forestalling any new wave of resistance. But Gandhi knew that was precisely what the younger, more educated congressmen wanted. He also knew that the one sure consequence of calling for renewed civil disobedience would be his own reincarceration. First he tried suspending civil disobedience to concentrate on the Harijan cause. This provoked the Bengali firebrand Subhas Chandra Bose to write him off as a failure. Next he attempted to split the difference by calling for individual acts of civil disobedience, as opposed to mass resistance. The new tactic was too much for the British, too little for younger Congressmen like Bose and Nehru. When he announced a small march in defiance of a ban on political demonstrations, he was promptly clapped back into Yeravda. In his previous imprisonment, he'd been allowed to work on his latest weekly newspaper inside the jail so long as it was limited to the discussion of the Harijan cause, which was why he called the paper *Harijan*. This time he was treated as an ordinary convict, with no privileges, no paper. Within two weeks he began yet another fast, his third in eleven months, and came close enough to killing himself that he had to be hospitalized. "Life ceases to interest me if I may not do Harijan work without let or hindrance," he said.

The colonial authorities offered release on condition he abandon civil disobedience, echoing his stilted legalism in a manner that sounded belittling, even faintly mocking. "If Mr. Gandhi now feels," an official statement said, "that life ceases to interest him if he cannot do Harijan work without let or hindrance, the Government are prepared . . . to set him at liberty at once so that he can devote himself wholly and without restriction to the cause of social reform." First he rejected the idea of conditional release; then, released from the hospital unconditionally, he announced he'd not "court imprisonment by offering aggressive civil resistance" for most of the coming year. He'd accept the government's terms as long as he didn't have to acknowledge doing so. He was thus maneuvered into doing what Charles Andrews had urged him to do in the first place, giving way to what he now claimed to be "the breath of life for me, more precious than the daily bread." He was speaking of "Harijan service," which in his mind meant persuading caste Hindus to accept Harijans as their social equals. He couldn't promise to devote himself wholly to that cause until equality was achieved—after all, there was still independence to be won—but he'd do so for the next nine months by touring the country from one end to the other, campaigning for a change of heart by caste Hindus and for funds to be devoted to the cause of "uplift" for his Harijans. Somewhat reluctantly, he thus sentenced himself to becoming a full-time social reformer for that stretch of time.

His commitment was at once a moral obligation and a compromise, an evangelical crusade and a tactical retreat. To many of his followers, it meant he was putting the national movement on hold. To Gandhi himself, it must have seemed the only way forward. His secretary, Mahadev, was in jail. So were Nehru, Patel, Kasturba, even Mirabehn, among thousands of other Congress supporters. His arduous anti-untouchability crusade may have been inadequate in its preparation and follow-up; there may be little proof that it left an enduring impression on the psyches of caste Hindus who turned out by the tens of thousands to hear him (or at least see him).

Ambedkar seldom took note of it; Dalits today don't celebrate it; Gandhi biographers pass over it in a few paragraphs. Yet, hurried and improvised as it undoubtedly was, there's really nothing in Indian annals to which it can be compared. From November 1933 through early August 1934, a period of nine months, Mahatma Gandhi barnstormed strenuously against untouchability from province to province, one dusty town to the next, through the hot season and the rainy season, sometimes on foot from village to village, giving three, four, five speeches a day—six days a week, omitting only Mondays, his "silent day"—mostly to mammoth crowds, drawn by the man rather than his cause. In that time, he traveled more than 12,500 miles by rail, car, and foot, collecting more than 800,000 rupees (equivalent in today's dollars to about $1.7 million) for his new Harijan fund. By comparison, an American presi-

On tour by rail, circa 1934

dential campaign can be viewed as a cushy, leisurely excursion on a luxury liner.

An early conclusion of a British official assigned to keep close tabs on Gandhi's doings was that the frail old man in the loincloth, coming off two prolonged fasts in the previous ten months, was displaying "amazing toughness." Soon it became routine for batteries of orthodox Hindus to intercept him at his rallies or along his route, zealously chanting anti-Gandhi slogans and waving black flags. In Nagpur, where the tour started, eggs were thrown from the balcony of a hall in which he was speaking; in Benares, where it ended, orthodox Hindus, called *sanatanists*, burned his picture. A bomb went off in Poona, and an attempt was made to derail the train on which he traveled from Poona to Bombay. At a place called Jasidih in Bihar, his car was stoned. Scurrilous anti-Gandhi pamphlets appeared at many of these places, targeting him as an enemy of Hindu dharma, a political has-been who promised much and failed to deliver, even calling attention to the massages he received from women in his entourage. Here we come upon the first signs of the viral subculture that would spawn his murder fourteen years later.

More generally, the cleavages among Hindus he had anticipated and feared were now out in the open, but he never turned back. Missionaries travel to lands they deem to be heathen; presenting himself as a Hindu revivalist, Gandhi took his campaign to his own heartland. He didn't have one set piece, what's now called a stump speech, but the same themes reappeared in a more or less impromptu fashion. They all led to the same conclusion. If India were ever to deserve its freedom, he preached, untouchability had to go. Yet at many of the rallies, untouchables were segregated in separate holding pens, either because they were afraid to be seen by caste Hindus as overstepping or because none of the local organizers was alive to the contradiction of putting untouchability on display at an anti-untouchability rally.

Such a tableau confronted Gandhi near the end of the tour when he reached the city of Bhavnagar in his native Gujarat, not far from a college he'd briefly attended. In anticipation of his visit, the civic fathers had thoughtfully set aside money for new, more or less sanitary quarters for the municipality's Bhangis, or sweepers, the untouchables who did its dirtiest work; the plan was to show off Bhavnagar's enlightened spirit by having the dedication of the project coincide with Gandhi's visit. To that end, a large open-sided tent, a patchwork of bright colors called a *shamiana*, had been set up as it would be for any big celebration such as a wedding. "The Bhangis were not allowed to sit in the shamiana put up for the ceremony," a British official reported to his superiors, "but sat outside where Gandhi joined them before proceeding to his seat in the shamiana to lay the foundation stone." Gandhi's mixing with the Bhangis was the only diversion from the script. By stepping into the shamiana, he made things right again. What could he do? Not for the first time, he was up against an India that could be simultaneously worshipful and obdurate.

At a place called Satyabhamapur in the eastern state of Orissa, he was given another reminder of the rocklike durability of the customs he was trying to crack. The Mahatma invited ten members of a local untouchable group called Bauris, along with one Bhangi, to take their meals in his tent. "None of Mr. Gandhi's party, however, dined with these guests," another colonial official reported, laying on the requisite irony, "and the Bauris refused to dine with the sweeper."

The Raj was keeping close tabs. Local officials were commanded to file reports at every stage of the tour. These then traveled up the colonial chain of command to provincial home secretaries, the national home secretary, and, ultimately, the secretary of state for India in Whitehall, each of whom then had an opportunity to add a wry, worldly comment to the file, a "minute," as these notes were known. It was not an abiding

interest in the progress of social reform that engaged the imperial officials at every level. They wanted to make sure Gandhi was abiding by his
pledge to eschew political agitation for the duration of the tour, that he
was not preparing the ground for his next campaign of civil disobedience, for they had long since been convinced that the frail figure in the
loincloth had the power to paralyze their domain and, if allowed to proceed unchecked, shake its foundations; in that sense, he had made them
wary believers in his nonviolent methods of resistance and put them on
guard. The crowds he drew—100,000 in Calcutta, 50,000 in Madras
(now Chennai), 40,000 in Cawnpore (Kanpur), 30,000 in Benares
(Varanasi), up to 25,000 in a dozen other places—could more easily be
attributed to curiosity and the unending quest for a saint's darshan, the
satisfying blankness of an immersion in his glow, than to zeal for his battle against untouchability. But they couldn't be ignored.

Part of making sure that he wasn't preparing the ground for future
campaigns of civil disobedience was keeping track of his avid fund-
raising, ostensibly for the new Harijan Service Society, or Sevak Sangh.
Fearing that the money could be diverted to Congress coffers for political use, the British were intensely interested in knowing how much he
was taking in and where it was going. So the local officials were
instructed to report the exact amount of his "purses," meaning the collections offered up in his honor at practically every stop, even in the
poorest Harijan hovels and slums. Often these sums were reported down
to the last rupee, occasionally down to the *paise*, or small change. An
official in Travancore, for instance, reports that Gandhi auctioned off a
ring that had been donated to his cause for the modest sum of three
rupees and eight paise. Ladies with jewelry were immediate targets: in
Karachi he was reported to have engaged in a tug-of-war with an elderly
woman over a ring she was disinclined to relinquish. "The old lady resolutely refused to part with her ring and resisted Mr. Gandhi's attempt
to remove it forcibly," an official reported. (Writing in the margin of the
report, a higher official drily praised her for her display of Gandhian
resistance.) Everything was subject to auction for the cause of Harijan
uplift, including the gifts, silver boxes, and cups presented to him along
the way—even his time. At some villages, he refused to step out of his
car until he received a purse of sufficient weight; in one place, an additional fifty rupees proved sufficient. "Many women," an official in
Madras noted, "took the precaution of divesting themselves of their jew-
els before coming to his meetings."

Gandhi, the unrelenting Bania turned mendicant, is an object of fascination, sometimes pity, for starchy officials who comment on his "rapacity for money" and "money-grubbing propensities" and then indulge in haughty speculation on whether his mahatmaship has been tarnished. "He was more like a *chetti* [or moneylender] coming around for his interest," one report stated. "One could not but feel sorry for Gandhi," this report said, "a poor old man come down in the world and being hustled about from one function to another, which he seemed only partially able to understand." The officials observe him in different places, with different degrees of bias, at different stages of the tour but agree on several things: that the crowds that turned out to greet him were largely indifferent to his message about Harijans (in fact, could seldom hear it); that he started to soft-pedal and even omit his demands for the opening of temples once he hit the more orthodox Hindu precincts of South India; that it was an open question whether his tour was doing more to strengthen orthodoxy than it was to uproot the hardy weed called untouchability. Their skeptical narrative stands in counterpoint to the pious, heroic accounts of the crusade that appear in installments in Gandhi's weekly *Harijan*, with its agate lists of newly opened temples and wells, newly dedicated separate but equal dormitories and schools for Harijan students, all leaving an impression of a cresting wave of irresistible social reform.

The contrast between the narratives of colonial bystanders and those of enthusiastic domestic adherents is only to be expected. But apart from their renderings of Gandhi's own words, their most precious passages convey particular details more telling than any assessment. "At several places," a British official notes in a part of Orissa where Gandhi's party was denied permission to enter temples, "people were seen carrying away dust that had been touched by his feet." Or there's the description of a sweeper's wife in Nagpur named Abhayanhar who donates her last two bangles. "Tears trickled down Abhayanhar's cheeks," a colonial official wrote. "Gandhi accepted the sacrificial offering and said he had reduced the Abhayanhars to poverty, that they were now true Harijans, the truest Banghis in Nagpur." The official offers no comment; he simply describes what he has seen, leaving a sense that he has seen a communion he doesn't understand but can't get out of his mind.

The Mahatma's own presence of mind, his reliable, low-key magnanimity, show up in these often hostile colonial reports in scattered asides on his disciplined, always calm treatment of orthodox demonstrators who turn out to jeer him and block his way. In Ajmer, in what's now the state of Rajasthan, one of Gandhi's most persistent antagonists, a

Benares Brahman named Lal Nath, thrusts himself forward with a small contingent carrying black flags. He also displays a bleeding head, earned in a confrontation with some Gandhians who'd not gotten the message about nonviolence. Gandhi gives the crowd a stern lecture and invites Lal Nath to the platform to speak his piece against him; the Brahman is soon drowned out by cries of "Shame, shame." In Buxar in Bihar, sanatanists lie down in front of the car carrying Gandhi to a mass meeting, and here too some of them have been beaten. Gandhi visits the injured sanatanists in the hospital and promises to do penance. Told then that the road to the rally is still blocked and that he might be attacked if he insists on going there, Gandhi serenely walks in on foot accompanied by four constables, parting a crowd of five thousand. In the Maharashtrian town of Saonar, where another posse of sanatanists seeks to halt his car, he offers its leader a ride to the rally he's about to address.

A few of the authors of the official reports allow themselves to wonder whether more may be taking place here than has met the eye of their more jaded colleagues. The chief commissioner of Delhi writes that Gandhi, "even in his present role, still has very great influence." He hazards a view that the tides of Indian opinion on untouchability may be slowly shifting. "Although perhaps 60 per cent of Hindus quietly determine not to treat untouchables as equals, they avoid public expression of their views." Sounding optimistic, this high civil servant seems to be suggesting that a substantial minority of caste Hindus have already experienced a kind of conversion on the issue. An official in Bombay takes a similar line. "Though the majority would prefer the movement to fail, most of them," he predicts, "are not likely to actively oppose it. The Sanatanists therefore cannot create a force sufficiently strong to combat and overcome Mr. Gandhi's persistence."

Gandhi himself advanced the idea that after all the orthodox propaganda against him, the passive absorption of his arguments by seemingly inattentive mass audiences added up to an advance. "I am quite sure that the message has appealed to the reason of the masses," he said. "I am also fully aware that all of them are not yet prepared to translate their beliefs into practice. But then I consider it a tremendous gain that the masses have come to believe in the truth of the message." Believe in it grudgingly, he meant. It might not affect their conduct much, he was saying, offering a conclusion not very different from that of the shrewdest colonial officials, but they could no longer justify caste oppression.

It was hard to know then, and it's harder to know now, whether anything like the mental sea change Gandhi hoped for had actually occurred, or to measure the lasting effect. Sometimes he voiced his own doubts. Speaking in private to the tough-minded Vallabhbhai Patel, he was blunter than he allowed himself to be in public. "India is not yet converted to the spinning wheel and certainly not to the removal of untouchability. We can't even say that the whole of the intellectual world is for its removal." In this context, the "intellectuals" to whom he refers are those who were then calling themselves Socialists, talking up the possibilities of "class struggle," and rejecting as "reactionary" and "irrelevant" his focus on untouchability, not granting or even recognizing that it defined the lives of the poorest Indians. The difference was not just one of political idiom. Their identification with the poorest was largely theoretical, resting on the premise that they could be lifted up after independence. Gandhi's was becoming more urgent by the day. If anything, he seems more disposed at the end of the tour, having inspected scores, maybe hundreds of untouchable settlements, to speak in pointed ways about the abject circumstances of his Harijans and the social action that could make a difference. "The only way we can expiate the sin of centuries," he said, "is to befriend the Harijans, by going to their quarters, by hugging their children as you would do your own, by interesting yourselves in their welfare, by finding out whether they have the fresh light and air that you enjoy as of right." Hugging untouchable children might not amount to a social program or advance the cause of swaraj. But in the emerging divide between Gandhi and his movement, which side was really otherworldly and which one down-to-earth?

Near the end of the tour, in a balanced assessment and summing-up of all the accumulated intelligence at his disposal, the chief secretary of the Punjab writes: "People are more critical of his aims and objects and are no longer willing to follow him blindly. But it would be a mistake to regard him as a spent force. Given the occasion, he would still wield very great power and he is still more able than any other Indian to organize a big movement against Government."

Whether Gandhi could organize a big, enduring movement against untouchability remained another question in his own mind, it seems, as much as that of the Raj's agents. It so preoccupied him that when, at the start of 1934, northern Bihar was rocked by a huge earthquake that flattened villages and towns, devastating fields and crops and killing more than seven thousand, he instantly declared the catastrophe to be "divine chastisement" for the persistent sin of untouchability. It's not far-fetched to imagine that Gandhi, at that point just beginning the third month of his anti-untouchability tour, was speaking more out of frustration than conviction. He often appealed to faith as a basis for moral action in society. But he didn't normally go in for the kind of magical thinking that looks for signals of divine wrath in floods and droughts and all the other natural calamities that beset the subcontinent. Perhaps his interpretation of the earthquake, several times repeated as he met hard going on the South Indian portion of his tour, could be taken as a folksy rhetorical trope, as a tool designed to chip away at the resistance he faced. "He has come to realize that the strength of the antagonistic force is more formidable than he at first imagined," reported a British official, attempting to read his mind, several weeks after the disaster.

Nehru and Tagore had managed to support Gandhi's fast unto death. Then, as we've seen, they opposed his second fast against untouchability. Now each was flabbergasted by the readiness of the Mahatma to use superstition to battle superstition. "Anything more opposed to the scientific outlook it would be difficult to imagine," a momentarily disillusioned Nehru wrote in his autobiography, which he was composing in prison. "If the earthquake was a divine punishment for sin, how are we to discover for which sin we are being punished?—for, alas! we have so many." Tagore said Gandhi's logic "far better suits the psychology of his opponents than his own," that the orthodox could just as easily blame the earthquake on his assault on Hindu dharma.

"Our sins and errors, however enormous," wrote the poet, "have not enough force to drag down the structure of creation . . . We, who are immensely grateful to Mahatmaji for inducing his wonder-working inspiration, freedom from fear and feebleness in the minds of his countrymen, feel profoundly hurt, when any words from his mouth may emphasize the elements of unreason in those very minds . . . a fundamental source of all the blind powers that drive us against freedom and self-respect."

In direct response, Gandhi only dug himself in deeper; he wasn't about to deprive himself of a useful argument by conceding that the earthquake and the practice of untouchability in its environs might be unconnected: "I would be untruthful and cowardly if, for the fear of ridicule . . . I did not proclaim my belief from the house-top," he retorted in *Harijan*. "I have the faith that our own sins have more force to ruin that structure [of creation] than any mere physical phenomenon. There is an indissoluble marriage between matter and spirit."

The sanatanists were the largest of the anti-Gandhi groups that turned out with black flags and calls for boycotts of his rallies, but they weren't the only protesters he attracted. In Nagpur, at the start of the tour, untouchables from Ambedkar's own Mahar community were conspicuous by their absence. Two months later, in Travancore, a group called the Self-Respect League appealed to untouchables to boycott Gandhi. In Shiyali, near Coimbatore in what's now Tamil Nadu, two hundred Dalits marched under black flags in opposition to a mahatma ostensibly crusading in their behalf. In Poona, near the end of the tour, there were more boycott appeals by untouchable groups identified with Ambedkar, who, nevertheless, had come himself to call on Gandhi a few days earlier in Bombay. "Dr. Ambedkar complained that the Congress people took interest in the question of the removal of untouchability so long as Mr. Gandhi was present," according to a colonial official's second- or thirdhand intelligence report, "but the moment his back was turned it was forgotten." In his public summing-up, Gandhi pronounced untouchability to be on "its last legs," but his private assessment may have been closer to Ambedkar's. Within a month of the tour's end in August 1934, he let it be known that he was considering "retiring" from the Congress movement on various grounds, including its blatant failure to address "the growing pauperism of the dumb millions."

Six weeks later, he made it official. Fourteen years had passed since he'd first taken over the movement. "I have lost the power to persuade you to my view," he told a Congress meeting. "I have become helpless. It is no use keeping a man like me at the helm of affairs, who has lost his strength." That plaintive "helpless" can be read as a clear, poignant, and, most likely, conscious echo of Gandhi's admissions seven years earlier that he'd lost all hope of being able to sustain the alliance between Muslims and Hindus he'd forged at the time of the Khilafat agitation. It might also be interpreted as another coy bid for a renewed mandate. But this time he seemed to know what the outcome would be.

His tour has just ended. But in saying he felt "helpless," he is speaking not simply of Harijan uplift but also of his whole program of social reform—called the "constructive program"—featuring spinning, prohibition, sanitation, hygiene, education in local languages, an enhanced role for women, along with the struggle against untouchability. The Congress had been paying lip service to it for a decade, but its heart, he now realizes, is elsewhere; it's set on gaining political power, provisionally in the new legislatures, ultimately in an independent India.

He may not have been speaking narrowly or exclusively about untouchability, but it's not much of a stretch to conclude that if Gandhi ended his marathon feeling helpless about the Congress's commitment to his programs of social reform in general, he felt helpless too about its commitment to the specific struggle that had preoccupied him almost entirely for the previous two years, ever since the "epic fast" that had briefly seized the country. He ended the tour at Wardha in central India, his new base of operations, on August 5, 1934, and, two days later, embarked on yet another fast, one of "personal purification" and, he said, prayer for the purification of the Congress. "Purity of this, the greatest national organization," he said, "cannot but help the Harijan movement, since the Congress is also pledged to the removal of the curse." After all the touring and praying, the legislation on opening up Hindu temples to Harijans was allowed to die in the central assembly on August 23. "The sanatanists are now jubilant," Gandhi commented. "We must not mind their joy."

A few weeks later, a noticeably disconsolate Gandhi finally acknowledged that his approach to the issue of untouchability "differed from that of many, if not of most Congressmen" who, he said, "consider that it was a profound error for me to have disturbed the course of the civil resistance struggle by taking up the question in the manner, and at the time I did." Here he was talking again about "the most intellectual Congressmen," now disposed to call themselves Socialists. He was going in the opposite direction from them, he said. He still believed in what he called "the spinning sacrifice" as the "living link" to "the Harijans and the poor"—those he'd been accustomed to describing as "the dumb millions"—but, now he conceded, "a substantial majority of Congressmen have no living faith in it."

In Gandhi's view, the would-be Socialists—however high-minded, however committed—had little or no connection to the India where most Indians resided. "None of them knows the real conditions in Indian villages or perhaps even cares to know them," he observed.

The idea that two Indias could be distilled from the country's myriad versions of itself—the bourgeois one of urban sophisticates and the depressed one of rural misery—would offer a handy framework for speeches and polemics for decades to come. It wasn't the worst distortion. Perhaps there's an omen or at least some perspective in these bits of trivia: the week of Gandhi's "epic fast," Joan Bennett was starring in *Careless Lady* at the Roxy Talkie in Bombay and Eddie Cantor in *Palmy Days* at the Pathé, singing, "There's nothing too good for my baby." It wouldn't have been only British expatriates who filled the movie palace seats or turned out to ooh and aah over the new Chrysler Plymouths on sale at New Era Motors. (What came to be called Bollywood was still a gleam in the eyes of the earliest Indian filmmakers. They'd yet to invade the countryside or hit on the formula of song, dance, and heartache that would become their touchstone. But running alongside mass politics, mass popular culture would soon be in the offing.)

Few congressmen had seen as much of the world beyond India's shores that embraced such fanciful artifacts as Gandhi. He remained convinced that it held no answers for India. In the aftermath of his tour, his penchant for circling back on himself, for reenacting formative stages of his past, again took hold. Just as he withdrew to Tolstoy Farm outside Johannesburg a quarter of a century earlier, just as he retreated from politics during periods of convalescence in 1918 and 1924, Gandhi now proposed to open a new chapter in his life at what he would later name the Satyagraha or Sevagram Ashram outside Wardha, in the boondocks, a small market town in an especially poor, drought-prone, malaria-prone, snake-infested district west of Nagpur in the center of India. There he'd concentrate on showing that his constructive program, with its emphasis on village industries and cleanliness, personal and public, could furnish the 700,000 villages on the as-yet-undivided subcontinent with a replicable model. His retirement from Congress politics would be more symbolic than permanent. Supposedly retired— he never formally rejoined the movement—he'd continue to express views, even attend meetings; and when he did, his will almost always proved to be sovereign. He'd also intervene forcefully as a sort of deus ex machina in Congress leadership fights—for instance, in 1939 when he opposed the election of Subhas Chandra Bose as president and then, after Bose squeaked through, helped undermine him. Pretending to be on the sidelines in Wardha, he was not shy about wielding his authority through his reliable lieutenants in the party's hierarchy. Nevertheless, he never again occupied a formal leadership position and never again claimed, as he had in London, that he was the true leader of the untouchables. In Bombay, a crowd of eighty thousand gave him a standing ovation on what was supposed to be his valedictory day as a congressman, then heard him warn that he'd be "watching from a distance [the] enforcement of principles for which Congress stands."

He meant, of course, his principles. "What I am aiming for," said the man who was supposedly stepping back from the struggle, "is the development of the capacity for civil disobedience." He'd resigned, it soon became clear, but he'd not really retired.

10

VILLAGE OF SERVICE

I F GANDHI'S SHOW IN 1934 of retiring from the Congress movement he'd led and symbolized for nearly a generation had an inner logic, it lay in his acknowledgment that all the Gandhian programs and resolutions it had ratified over the years had made little difference. What the Congress hadn't accomplished under his leadership, he now undertook to do on his own. On one level, he was shaming his supposed followers; on another, he was refusing to give up on his deepest commitments. The new course he set for himself obviously bore some relation to his own submerged doubts about the effectiveness of the anti-untouchability crusade he'd just completed. What he saw on the tour convinced him that his fond promise that cottage industry spinning and weaving could be the salvation for underemployed, landless, debt-enslaved villagers—untouchables and touchables alike—had been overblown and undersold. The spinning wheel had yet to change their grim reality.

"The villagers have a lifeless life," he now said. "Their life is a process of slow starvation." More speeches, he seemed to be saying, could not be the answer. The last part of the anti-untouchability tour, with the ambiguous response of the mammoth crowds he drew, had been for him, he said at its end, "a mechanical performance and a drawn-out agony." Later he allowed himself to disparage the tour as a "circus." He needed now to come to grips with village realities. "We have to work away silently," he said on one occasion. On another he vowed, "We have to become speechless manual laborers living in the villages."

India, of course, would not allow him to go silent; nor, as the main contributor to a weekly newspaper, could he silence himself. Turning sixty-five, he found himself standing restlessly at a crossroads. Here again, we see him reliving an earlier chapter in his life. His urge to get down to constructive work in villages obviously reprised his withdrawal from mass politics in South Africa in 1910, when he and Hermann Kallenbach set up their short-lived Tolstoy Farm. Then he made it his mission to master the basics of farming and the education of children. Now, by working again from the bottom up, he was rededicating himself to turning the tide on what he called, at his tour's end, the downward spiral of poverty he'd seen for himself in villages across the country. After acting out the self-scripted drama of his farewell to the Indian National Congress in Bombay in late October 1934, Gandhi went immediately back to Wardha. A further cross-cultural trivia note: the week he landed there turns out to have been the exact week that—half a world away geographically, and a world away culturally—Cole Porter's *Anything Goes* was having its first performances on the road at Boston's Colonial Theatre; there every evening the romantic lead playing opposite the young Ethel Merman crooned the oxymoronic lyric:

> *You're the top!*
> *You're Mahatma Gandhi.*
> *You're the top!*
> *You're Napoleon brandy.*

Gandhi wouldn't have been amused by this saucy paean to his international celebrity, in the unlikely event he was ever made aware of it. Nothing could have been more alien to his spirit than the Jazz Age cutting loose Porter was ever so lightly satirizing.

For most of the next eight years (a total of 2,588 days "on station," as Indians used to say), sorry, dusty, out-of-the-way Wardha, where temperatures before the monsoon rains soared as high as 118 degrees during his time there, would be his base and main arena of operations. Once he resolved to put down roots, Gandhi was already on the rebound, pronouncing himself "full of plans for village reconstruction." It would be wrong to say he left no mark on the district—dedicated Gandhians can still be found there in small numbers—but the overall result fell far short of the social transformation and healing he initially sought. In recent years, Wardha district has been best known in the proud, supposedly "shining" India of the early twenty-first century as the epicenter for an epidemic of suicides among hopelessly indebted cotton farmers, thousands of whom in the surrounding region are said to have taken their lives over the last two decades after watching commodity prices plummet in the new global marketplace. No one since Gandhi has thought of pointing to it as a model for rural reform.

In the Mahatma's time, his very presence made Wardha a destination. The Working Committee of the Congress Party, its top leadership unit, dutifully trooped to Wardha at least six times to seek his counsel and receive his blessing, though he was now officially a detached alumnus. He'd intended his resignation as a statement that he could neither impose his priorities on the movement nor let go of them. It had been a gesture, an expression of his disappointment. It had also been something of a sham. The party still revolved around him, if not all the time, at least whenever it needed to unravel a tangled issue. "Wardha became the de facto nationalist capital of India," an American scholar writes with pardonable hyperbole.

A motley array of foreign delegations—politicians, pacifists, religious leaders, do-gooders of all complexions—also found its way into this remote hinterland with the expectation that Gandhi could be drawn into a discussion of issues uppermost in their minds, anything from nature cures or nutrition to the fate of the West and the threat of another world war. He was all too easily drawn. Called on to speak as a seer, he seemed determined not to disappoint. By the end of the decade, he was freely doling out advice on how his techniques of nonviolent resistance, if adopted by "a single Jew standing up and refusing to bow to Hitler's decrees," might be enough to "melt Hitler's heart." A Chinese visitor received a similar lecture: nonviolence, Gandhi said, might "shame some Japanese." A representative of the African National Congress of South Africa was told that its leadership had alienated itself from the masses by its adoption of Western dress and manners. "You must not . . . feel ashamed of carrying an assagai, or of going around with only a tiny clout round your loins," said the Mahatma, implicitly offering his own sartorial transformation as a pragmatic political tactic worthy of emulation. His sense that he might have a prophetic role to play only deepened as war clouds darkened. "Who knows," he wrote from Wardha in 1940, "that I will not be an instrument for bringing about peace between Britain and India but also between the warring nations of the earth." Presumably on account of his influence, India was "the last hope of the world."

Only one foreign visitor in these years seemed ready to resist his increasing tendency to translate his experience into dogma. Margaret

Sanger, the founder of the movement that became Planned Parenthood, a proponent of enlightened female sexuality and contraception, stopped by in January 1936 for a conversation in which she stressed the life-enhancing nature of sexual intimacy for women as well as men. As might have been expected, Gandhi took an opposing view, expounding on brahmacharya as a spiritual discipline; his conversation with the American—unlike any he'd previously had with a woman—seems to have sent his worrisomely high blood pressure higher and, by some accounts, left him in a state near nervous collapse.

Physically and emotionally, he was already nearing the edge. A little more than a year after he arrived in the district, Gandhi had decided that it wasn't enough for him to assign his disciples to settle in the most remote villages in a remote district. He needed to understand why they found it such hard going. Typically, he instructed them to begin their missions of service by volunteering as village sanitation officers and scavengers (scooping up human excrement wherever it was to be found, usually beside rural pathways, and then digging proper latrines). The example was not always as effective as he expected. "The people are completely shameless," wrote his faithful secretary and diarist, Mahadev Desai, whose duties included serving as a one-man cleanup detail in an exceptionally unresponsive village called Sindi. "They do not have any feeling at all. It will not be surprising if within a few days they start believing that we are their scavengers."

Gandhi concluded there was only one way for him to understand why villagers were proving so impervious to the selfless example his satyagrahis set before them. What was needed was for him—the man recognized by most of India and most of the world as the country's leader—to settle in a village and live there all by himself, with none of his usual entourage. It made perfect sense to Gandhi but not to his closest associates, who were already nervous about his health and jealous of any change in the Mahatma's life that would limit the time they got to spend in his presence.

The village he selected in Wardha district for this latest of his "experiments with truth" was then called Segaon. It happened to be adjacent to orange and mango orchards owned by an important backer and underwriter of the Mahatma, a wealthy trader named Jamnalal Bajaj who'd been, in the theatrical sense, the angel who produced Gandhi's relocation in Wardha and the host who'd provided lodging for the Mahatma and his entourage. Bajaj also owned the land on which Segaon's untouchables—two-thirds of its population of over six hundred—

huddled; the revenues he collected from the village would subsidize Gandhi's latest experiment.

No road, as yet, connected Segaon to the district's market town, four miles away. India's leader arrived there on foot on April 30, 1936, and, two days later, told the villagers of his intentions. "If you will cooperate with me," he said, "I shall be very happy; if you will not, I shall be content to be absorbed among you as one among the few hundred that live here." As related by Mirabehn, the headman, "a very charming and aristocratic old man, made a graceful and honest speech in which he welcomed the idea of Gandhi coming to live amongst them, but made it quite clear that he personally would not be able to cooperate in Bapu's Harijan program." The hut that he was to occupy, on Segaon's outskirts, had yet to be completed, so that night a makeshift tent was strung up for him under a guava tree. Since there were wild animals in the area— cheetahs, panthers—a trench had to be dug around the patch of ground on which the Mahatma was to sleep. Using the excuse that they were overseeing the completion of his dwelling, several of his entourage slept beside him.

As might have been expected, the Mahatma's ambition to spend a night alone in Segaon would never be fulfilled. Before long, the whole entourage, amounting at times to nearly a hundred persons, was ensconced there. He'd not planned to make his dwelling the center of an ashram, but that's what it became. Thanks largely to Jamnalal Bajaj's generosity, new buildings went up, a road was put through and, eventually, even a phone line so the Mahatma could be reached by the viceroy's offices in New Delhi and the hill station of Simla, to which the top echelons of the Raj retreated in summer when Wardha broiled. Segaon, the village Gandhi briefly intended to make the focus of his energies, inevitably became a sideshow. Fittingly, after March 1940, it would take the name of the ashram that had spontaneously mushroomed alongside it. Ashram and village were both called Sevagram, meaning "Village of Service."

The growth of the ashram was less than a mixed blessing, becoming another distraction from the village work that had drawn him to Segaon in the first place. "Oh God," Gandhi said, "save me from my friends, followers and flatterers."

Today the nearest village houses are around the bend of a dirt road, a couple hundred yards from the ashram, a complex of dark wood structures with long sloping roofs that give an appearance reminiscent of a Buddhist monastery in Kyoto. Sevagram the ashram no longer serves

Ashram grew up around Gandhi as Sevagram

Sevagram the village. With a bookshop, a canteen, and even some modest rooms to rent to pilgrims, it maintains itself as a tourist attraction. The village still looks poor, but some of the houses have TV antennas on their roofs and motorbikes leaning up against their cracked and mildewed cement walls. The houses stand on land that Bajaj signed over to Gandhi and Gandhi signed over to the village's untouchables, who now call themselves Dalits rather than Harijans. When you stroll from the ashram to the one village that received more personal attention from the Mahatma than any other among the 700,000 that existed in his India, a statue comes into view beside a sports field. The figure on the pedestal is not wearing a loincloth. He's wearing a suit painted an electric shade of blue and a painted red tie. It's the figure of Babasaheb Ambedkar. And the former untouchables in what was once Gandhi's chosen village—especially the younger ones—are likelier, when asked, to identify themselves as Buddhists than as Hindus.

For most of Gandhi's first year in Wardha, he'd been less preoccupied with the actual human condition in the surrounding villages than with the task of birthing a new mass organization he'd dreamed up to infuse badly needed energy into his languishing campaign for village self-sufficiency through hand spinning and weaving. He'd invested excessive faith in the spinning wheel, the iconic charkha, as an invincible panacea for village poverty, he now concluded. By itself, it would not be enough to lift rural India out of its misery. Spinning and weaving would retain their place, but they needed to be supplemented by a whole array of traditional crafts that were losing out in competition with processed and manufactured goods being produced more cheaply in city factories and workshops. Villages had once known how to turn out their own handmade pens, ink, and paper; they ground their grains into flour, pressed vegetables for their oils, boiled unrefined sugar, tanned hides into leather, raised bees, harvested honey, ginned cotton by hand. For their own salvation, they needed to do so again, Gandhi taught; and it was a national need to support them not only by wearing homespun khadi but by consciously giving all they produced a preference over manufactured articles, to undo as far as possible the ravages of the Industrial Revolution.

Starting from these premises, the nation's leader suddenly had an urgent need to know whether hand-pounded rice and grain could be shown to be more nutritious than the polished products from the mills. Could hand-husked rice compete in price with mill-husked rice? What use could be made of the husk? Did spinning pay better than husking? Could oil be harvested from orange rinds? Gandhi's letters were full of such questions; in his mind, the answers he received were building blocks of a revised strategy for gaining "the swaraj of our dreams, devoted to the welfare of villages." His new organization needed a constitution, advisers, and a board that would be selfless and nearly full-time; it needed a table of organization reaching down to every district and, ultimately, every village in the vast country. Within a couple of months Gandhi had created all this, on paper at least, and the All India Village Industries Association (AIVIA) came into existence with its national headquarters in previously obscure Wardha, in a building donated, of course, by Gandhi's angel, Bajaj. Gandhi recruited a chartered accountant from Bombay, with postgraduate training in economics from Columbia University, to serve as the organization's director. A Christian, he was known at Columbia as Joseph Cornelius; by the time he got to Wardha, where he stayed until after Gandhi's death, he had become J. C. Kumarappa. Today Kumarappa is occasionally mentioned in India as a pioneer theorist on sustainable farming and appropriate technology; the last Western economist who seems to have been conscious of him or Gandhi as thinkers with something useful to say about the world's poorest was E. F. Schumacher, himself a dissenter from orthodox development doctrines whose book *Small Is Beautiful: Economics as if People Mattered* enjoyed a brief vogue when it appeared in 1973, twenty-five years after Gandhi's death.

The Mahatma denied that his fixation on village industries betokened any dilution of his campaign against untouchability, just as he'd denied a decade earlier that his renewed emphasis on the charkha represented a backing off from his campaign for Hindu-Muslim unity. Many of the spinners were untouchables, he pointed out. There was conspicuous overlap between AIVIA and other organizations he or his followers had launched to advance the Gandhian constructive program in the 700,000 villages: the recently formed Harijan Sevak Sangh, the intended beneficiary of the anti-untouchability tour; the older All India Spinners Association; the Gandhi Seva Sangh, brought into existence by the Congress to further the constructive program to which it paid lip service (not to mention the Goseva Sangh, an association for the protection of cows for which he'd become a patron). For most of these, the lawyer who'd last practiced in Johannesburg drafted constitutions and designed management structures, just as ever since 1920 he had for the Indian National Congress itself. AIVIA's basic document didn't hesitate to articulate a principle that all these organizations implicitly held in common. "The Association," it declared, "shall work under the guidance and advice of Gandhiji." The movement with the largest outreach, the spinners association, boasted that it had penetrated 5,000 villages, but this was a mere fraction of 1 percent of the 700,000.

All the Gandhian organizations shared a common defect: a reliance, in theory, on selfless village interns—in Gandhi's terms, satyagrahis—and the absence of any sure method for discovering, recruiting, training, or sustaining such a vast army of inspired, literate workers uninhibited by inherited constraints of caste. "Full-timers, whole-hoggers, with a live faith in the program and prepared immediately to make the necessary adjustment in their daily life," he said, describing the attributes of the committed workers he sought as if he were placing a classified ad. The "necessary adjustment" would be to lower—drastically—their citified standards of living. They would need to cultivate a life of "rigorous simplicity," he said. What the Maoist leadership in China would seek to do through terror, commands, peer pressure, and relentless ideological drilling when it launched its "down to the countryside" campaign during the Cultural Revolution three decades later, Gandhi hoped to achieve by inspirational example, his own and that of his closest followers. "Workers without character, living far above the ordinary life of villagers, and devoid of the knowledge required of them for their work can produce no impression on the villagers, whether Harijan or other," he said. "If every one of such workers puts on his work a price which village service cannot sustain, ultimately these organizations must be wound up."

Even his closest followers had doubts. "What is the advantage of this work?" Mahadev's son boldly asked the Mahatma. "There is no effect on the villagers. On the contrary they go on giving orders to us to clean various places."

"So! You are already tired!" Gandhi retorted in mock exasperation. He then offered pointers on how the work might be accomplished: "If I am in your place, I will observe carefully. If someone gets up after easing himself, I will immediately go there. If I see any rottenness in the excretia I will tell him gently, 'Your stomach seems to be upset; you should try a particular remedy,' and thus I will try to win him over." After scooping the turds, he went on, he'd then plant flowers on the site and water them. "Cleanliness can be an art," he concluded.

Even at his most visionary, he sometimes lets slip a bleak forecast of what's likely to prove possible, as if steeling himself for disappointment, for a noble failure, as he sets out. "If [the villagers] abuse us," he preaches to his acolytes when only beginning to contemplate the idea of living in a village himself, "let us bear it in silence . . . Let the people defecate wherever they choose. Let us not even ask them to avoid a particular place or go elsewhere. But let us go on cleaning up without a word . . .

"If this does not work, then there is no such thing as non-violence," he concludes.

In which case, he seems to be saying, the work had still to be done as a matter of duty. When one of his workers asked for his formula for solving the problem of untouchability in villages, Gandhi replied: "Silent plodding." On another occasion, he said: "The only way is to sit down in their midst and work away in steadfast faith, as their scavengers, their nurses, their servants, not as their patrons, and to forget all our prejudices, our prepossessions. Let us for a moment forget even swaraj."

This is what his Anglican soul mate Charlie Andrews had urged several years earlier, but of course, as Gandhi said then, he could never forget swaraj.

Gandhi seemed to sense early that the qualifications he declared for what today might be called community organizing had scant potential — really, none at all — for rallying the nonviolent forces he was hoping to send en masse to the villages. "Our ambition is to make at least one member for each of our 700,000 villages," he told a meeting of his village industries association, "but our actual membership is 517!" And many of those were AWOL. It was a conundrum he was hoping to crack during the solitary residence he planned for himself at Segaon. Mirabehn, the English admiral's daughter, had to admit defeat in Sindi, where the villagers came to view her as a source of pollution after she drew water from the well used by the untouchables. Segaon, where she then preceded her teacher, wasn't much better for her. On the verge of a breakdown, having already suffered a bout of typhoid, she was eventually sent off to the Himalayas in 1937 for a rest. After his first ten days at Segaon the previous year, at the height of the hot season, Gandhi himself was strongly urged by his doctors to seek relief in the hills near Bangalore. His rest cure lasted five weeks. It was June 16 before he returned, arriving again on foot in a monsoon downpour that had drenched him to the skin. Soon he came down with malaria.

When the bare narrative of this effort to achieve "oneness" with India's poorest is laid out, it can appear either futile or desperate. It's the effort of the Mahatma to remain true to his vision of swaraj for the dumb millions, despite all that he has learned, or perhaps senses he has yet to learn, about village India. Yet from a distance of more than seven decades, what stands out is the commitment rather than the futility. He could easily have retired to a mansion belonging to one of his millionaire supporters and there directed the national movement from on high; no one would have asked why he wasn't living like a peasant. In his tireless, pertinacious way in the village to which he'd attached himself instead, he was doing more than tilting at windmills. Once again Gandhi was refusing to avert his eyes from a suffering India that seemed largely to have escaped the notice of most educated Indians swept up in the movement he'd been leading.

The degree to which this was true in the 1930s can be gauged by the degree to which it remains true in an India that has hailed itself as free and democratic for several generations. By 2009, after boasting four consecutive years of robust 9 percent growth in economic output, this rising and surprising new India, with its booming market economy at the high end, still had a quarter of its people living in conditions defined by the World Bank as "absolute poverty," meaning that their per capita income was less than a dollar a day; the rate of poverty was declining as a percentage of the total population of nearly 1.2 billion, but in absolute numbers the total of some 300 million was undiminished, accounting for nearly one-third of the globe's poorest people. Almost by definition their children were malnourished and underweight, more than likely to grow up illiterate, if they grew up at all. The number of Indians calculated to be living on less than $1.25 a day was over 400 million, larger than the total population at the time of independence when the poorest represented a bigger proportion of the total; today, as a minority, they can be viewed as a ragged coterie of interest groups and a drag on the rising middle class. Still only 33 percent of all Indians have access, according to the bank's figures, to what it primly calls "improved sanitation." A United Nations survey portrays this reality more bluntly, reporting that 55 percent of the population still defecates out of doors. Given the tripling of population since Gandhi's time, the water supply in villages and towns can still prove vulnerable to disease-bearing organisms; human scavengers still have to be relied upon to carry off much of the subcontinent's night soil, or human waste.

Gandhian economics needs to be viewed in that sobering perspective before being written off as irrelevant or utopian in the era of globalization. His answers to conspicuous issues of rural mass poverty, underemployment, and chronic indebtedness may have been incomplete and untested. Not only did he reject birth control and recommend abstinence as a means of limiting population, but he had no scheme that addressed glaring inequities in land ownership and distribution beyond a wishful, woolly theory of "trusteeship" that basically relied on the benevolence of the wealthy. In his aversion to devices that can be classed as laborsaving, he was stubbornly wrongheaded. But at least he framed basic questions, grappling with the misery at the bottom of the social pyramid. And since that misery has hardly receded, even as living standards have risen for most Indians, it cannot be altogether surprising that Gandhian economics bears a certain resemblance to approaches currently favored by development specialists seeking to confront the same perennial, still urgent problems—for instance, with "microfinance" schemes designed to drive small-scale enterprises, including the traditional handicrafts he promoted, as engines of growth and employment in rural settings. What such latter-day schemes have in common with their unacknowledged Gandhian antecedents is the conviction that solutions must be found where the poorest live, must have some capacity to spark and mobilize their energies.

Gandhi couldn't have forecast and probably wouldn't have admired many aspects of today's globalized India, with its offshore islands of affluent expatriate life in California, New York, the Persian Gulf, and elsewhere, transplanted and now thriving in cultures he'd long ago written off as incorrigibly materialistic: overdeveloped, in his view. Nor would he have been pleased by their repercussions at home, visible in high-rise Florida-style condo developments, largely financed by expatriate cash, spreading across fields where rice and wheat were once cultivated; in no way was this the India of that former expatriate's dreams. Today in the villages and dense, dank shantytowns of the poorest states, mostly in North India, he'd find much that would look familiar. He'd discover that nearly two-thirds of all Indians still live in villages. A Gandhi reborn in these times would probably want to start a campaign somewhere—in Wardha, perhaps.

On May 1, 1936, the day after Gandhi landed at Segaon, he received his first visitor there—none other than Babasaheb Ambedkar, who six months earlier had further estranged himself from the Mahatma by renouncing Hinduism and proclaiming his intention to convert to another religion. Ambedkar had just come from a conference of Sikhs in Amritsar where he'd openly flirted with the possibility of becoming a Sikh, praising the religion for regarding all its adherents as equals. The two leaders sat on the ground, under the guava tree where Gandhi had slept, debating the principles and politics of conversion. Neither one got much satisfaction from the encounter, but they agreed to meet again in Segaon. The inconclusive meeting seems to have been instigated by wealthy supporters of Gandhi who still hoped to keep Ambedkar and his followers in what the Mahatma called "the Hindu fold."

There may be hints here that Gandhi was making a roundabout attempt to woo Ambedkar. According to one of the untouchable leader's biographers, Gandhi's friends "asked Ambedkar why he did not join Gandhi's camp, so that he might have boundless resources at his disposal for the uplift of the Depressed Classes." Ambedkar said they had too many differences. Nehru also had many differences with Gandhi, observed Jamnalal Bajaj, one of the go-betweens. Ambedkar huffily said it was a matter of conscience for him.

The two leaders can be seen as reluctant antagonists, sometimes, in Conrad's sense, as secret sharers—mirror images of each other, with Gandhi finding aspects of his driven, sometimes angry South African self in the younger man, and Ambedkar feeling resentful, even envious, of the sanctity in which the Mahatma wraps himself. "You and I are quite similar," Ambedkar had remarked to Gandhi in the course of their negotiations at Yeravda prison.

The observation had provoked laughter from members of Gandhi's entourage within earshot, but the Mahatma himself had replied, "Yes, that's true." For nearly five years, ever since their first meeting in Bombay in August 1931 before sailing to the Round Table Conference, they'd been circling each other, sizing one another up, jousting at a distance, then putting out tentative feelers. They'd met in London, in Yeravda prison, possibly in Poona after Gandhi's release, and now in Segaon but remained unable to strike an alliance. When Ambedkar was preoccupied with a temple-entry campaign, Gandhi withheld his support. When temple entry became the focus of Gandhi's efforts to combat untouchability, Ambedkar contrarily said that social equality and economic uplift were the real issues. Now that Gandhi had settled on the edge of a village in which his Harijans were a majority in order to engage those very issues, Ambedkar was preoccupied with the need for untouchables to find a way out of Hinduism. If they were ever in sync, it was the way the two hands of a clock come together for an instant every hour. Or, perhaps, the way a chess game ends in stalemate. A couple of years earlier, Ambedkar had said the issue that divided them was Gandhi's refusal to renounce the caste system. Within a few months, seemingly in response, Gandhi had written an article in *Harijan* titled "Caste Has to Go," in which he said, "The present caste system is the very antithesis of Varnashrama," the traditional fourfold ranking of inherited occupations, which he professed to uphold but only on his own terms, with the caveat that true varnashrama was "today nonexistent in practice." In any case, he argued, religious customs derived from Hindu scriptures that were in conflict with "reason" and "universal truths and morals" were unacceptable. Also, Gandhi's article said, there "should be no prohibition of intermarriage or inter-dining." It appeared the same week Ambedkar vowed he wouldn't die a Hindu. By pleading for a varnashrama that, he said, didn't exist, Gandhi left himself some wiggle room, whether out of conviction or political expedience—some cover, that is, with orthodox caste Hindus. Either way, his response wasn't good enough for Ambedkar, who, predictably, dodged whatever opportunity there may have been to strike a religious accord.

Actually, their deepest difference wasn't over doctrine but over sociology, whether untouchables could be, should be, seen as "a separate community" or as an integral part of village India and, by extension, Hindu society as a whole. As interpreted by D. R. Nagaraj, a compelling cultural critic from the South Indian state of Karnataka, Ambedkar regarded the Indian village as "irredeemable" as a social setting for untouchables. Nagaraj, from a lowly subcaste of weavers himself, had endured bonded labor as a child and so had reason to identify himself with Ambedkar's view. But he was simultaneously large-minded enough to champion Gandhi's side of the argument. The high-caste townsman who'd been inspired to recast himself in peasant's garb felt the villages had to be redeemed if there were to be any future for India's poorest.

That tension is what would make the picture of Gandhi and Ambedkar lounging under the guava tree on the outskirts of a broiling Segaon on the Mahatma's first full day there in 1936 so poignant, so emblematic, if such a picture actually existed. Even if he wasn't wearing the starched winged collar that he often favored in this period, the scholarly, corpulent Ambedkar would probably not have looked comfortable in the village setting to which Gandhi, who gave a new definition to spareness, had long since adapted himself. In their face-off, each has a case, neither a workable solution embracing both touchables and untouchables. From the standpoint of today's Dalits, so Nagaraj wrote, "there is a compelling need to achieve a synthesis of the two." Gandhi and Ambedkar, he argued, "are complementary at a fundamental level." What Gandhi offers, this writer said, is the understanding that "the liberation of the untouchable is organically linked to the emancipation of village India." What Ambedkar offers is his insistence that it must include the possibility of liberation from their despised hereditary roles. Trapped in his own paternalism, the man known as the Mahatma wanted everyone to understand that the scavenger's work was honorable and essential. Ambedkar wanted everyone to understand that it was not at all fated, that this same untouchable could ignore the traditional vocation decreed by his caste just as Gandhi the Bania had. ("He has never touched trading which is his ancestral calling," Ambedkar noted in one of his more telling thrusts.) The emphasis of the man revered as Babasaheb was on equal rights. Maybe that's why, decades later, the villagers of Segaon-Sevagram put up his statue, although it was Gandhi and not Ambedkar who gave them their land.

Ambedkar and his followers were not the only untouchables talking conversion in this period. To the south, in the princely state of Travancore, now part of Kerala, there was a distinct restlessness among the upwardly mobile Ezhavas, who had provided the main impetus for the Vaikom Satyagraha. Some Ezhava leaders were reported to have held discussions about the possibility of a mass conversion with the Syrian Christian bishop of Kottayam, near Cochin, the leader of a sect that traced its history in South India back to a legendary visit by Saint Thomas in the second century. The bishop's seat was also near Vaikom, where the Shiva temple still barred Ezhavas and all other untouchables a decade after the satyagraha campaign that Gandhi had tried to control at a distance. The settlement he'd negotiated there with the British police commissioner had, like the one he'd negotiated with Smuts in South Africa, left the fundamental issues unresolved. The impatience of the Ezhavas had risen from year to year, to the point that they were even reported to be putting out feelers too to the London Missionary Society. There was also ferment among Pulayas, a more abject group of Kerala untouchables, some of whom had just become Sikhs.

Talk of conversion brought out a proprietary, even condescending side of Gandhi's attitude to those he interchangeably called "dumb millions" and "Harijans," overlapping but not synonymous terms. In his own religious practice and in abstract discussion, he spoke as a kind of universalist, holding that all religions were different expressions of the same truths. But when it came to outsiders tempting his Harijans away from a Hinduism that systematically rejected them, he could be almost as adamant in opposing that temptation as he was against the rejection. "Would you preach the Gospel to a cow?" he challenged a visiting missionary. "Well, some of the untouchables are worse than cows in their understanding."

In his weekly *Harijan*, he printed a long letter from an American missionary woman objecting to such Gandhian depictions of untouchables, whom she found, so she said, "above, rather than below, the average of mankind." Pushing all his buttons, as might be said these days even about a figure who had no buttons on his person, the American wondered "how you can live among them and hold such a superficial attitude to them? The only explanation that comes to my mind," she said, "is that you either do not know them or you were insincere."

If the American wanted to provoke the Mahatma, she succeeded. Gandhi replied in prideful tones last heard out of his mouth six years earlier at the Round Table Conference in London. Indignant over the foreigner's presumption, he claimed his conclusions were based "on close contact for years with tens of thousands of India's masses, not as a superior being but feeling as one with them." His retort begged the question of what he meant by "close contact." Segaon was supposed to provide the answer.

Preaching through his life was what he'd resolved to do there, but that vow was in constant tension with a long lineup of issues, movements, and gatherings whose proponents and organizers were always trying to reach in and, pleading necessity, pull him out of his village. A half year after Ambedkar's visit in 1936, the religious ferment in Travancore provided one such occasion. Here, for once, there was something to celebrate—a proclamation in the name of the young maharajah, who'd only recently come of age, finally opening all Hindu temples controlled by his state or family to any untouchable inclined to be thought of as a Hindu. "None of our Hindu subjects should by reason of birth, caste or community, be denied the solace of the Hindu faith," the decree declared.

Gandhi's supervision of the Vaikom movement may have had its ambiguous side in the mid-1920s, but he was no longer of two minds about temple entry as a national cause when he carried his anti-untouchability campaign into Travancore in 1934. On that tour, according to the current rajah—younger brother of the one who issued the decree and monarch of a state that no longer exists—Gandhi asked the crown prince, "Will you open the temples?" Today's rajah, who was only twelve then, recalls hearing his brother pledge, "Yes."

A lively old man at the far end of his ninth decade, his tiny frame enveloped in a wraparound lungi, the Travancore maharajah said his sole remaining duty was to go alone to the temple of Vishnu every day when it's closed to all other worshippers for exactly twelve minutes as it had always been down through the generations. There the rajah solemnly reports in private to the deity, as all his forebears had, on what has been happening in his former realm. He didn't know why Dalits still called themselves Dalits, in his view, since untouchability had been abolished, there should be no such group. The decree opening the temples proved to be the dynasty's last hurrah. "People call me a mahatma," Gandhi said when he returned to take his victory lap around the state in 1937, reviving his struggle against untouchability after nearly three years. "They should call you a mahatma." So the old man now recalled the greeting Gandhi bestowed on his brother after the decree.

He hadn't seen such crowds since he bade his supposed farewell to the Indian National Congress. Nor since his 1915 farewell tour in South Africa had he ridden such a wave of celebration and surging hope. Yet as he toured the state for nine days, these crowds were often hushed, seemingly out of reverence for the Mahatma and this moment, theirs as well as his. He was struck by the appearance of the people he called Harijans as he accompanied them into temples from which they'd always been barred. They were "truly captivating," he noted, and "spotlessly clean."

Here in what had been the citadel not only of untouchability but also of unapproachability and unseeability, it was "a dream realized in a manner and in a place where the realization seemed almost unthinkable." Holding prayer meetings in newly opened temples at all his major stops, Gandhi occasionally gave an ecumenical nod to Christians and Muslims, but otherwise, speaking as a Hindu to Hindus, he was hardly secular. He prayed with caste Hindus and Harijans together as if they'd now finally been consecrated as what he'd always held them to be, one people. At nearly every stop he gave them a Sanskrit mantra, saying it was easier to grasp and more trustworthy than scripture. As he interpreted it, his mantra concerned surrender to a God who pervades every atom in the universe; it was about not coveting riches and things. He'd never been more overtly evangelical, more overtly Hindu. It doesn't seem that he ever asked himself whether in this touring of temples and reciting of mantras he might be distancing himself from the large Muslim minority he'd previously championed, making it easier for Jinnah and other Muslim Leaguers to portray him as the leader of the Hindus posing as a national leader.

Only at several stops in Travancore does the social reformer in Gandhi play more than a small supporting role to the evangelist. Still, at one of these, the Mahatma does step forward in his reformer's guise as a truly great soul. Facing a huge congregation of the upwardly mobile formerly untouchable Ezhavas, he asks pointedly why they're celebrating only the opening of the temples to themselves and not untouchables of a lower order such as Pulayas and Pariahs. "I must tell you," he says, "if this vast assembly does not represent these Pulayas, then I am certain that there is no place in your midst for me." The crowd stirs restively; as far as most Ezhavas are concerned, Pulayas are still untouchable, whatever the maharajah has decreed. He has been entering temples, Gandhi goes on, in the spirit of "an untouchable suddenly made touchable." If they would follow in the same spirit, "You will not be satisfied until you have lifted up your brothers and sisters who are supposed to be the least and the lowest to heights which you have attained yourselves. True spiritual regeneration must include economic uplift and the removal of ignorance."

All that was needed was "immediate human contact" and "an army of volunteer workers of the right type."

A memorable moment. But in defining "the right type," the Mahatma again lost touch with the common humanity he meant to serve. Brahmacharya had to be part of his program. He'd now gone a quarter of a century without sex, but lately he'd had trouble banishing thoughts of sex from his mind. Ever since his provocative chat with Margaret Sanger at the end of 1935, the subject kept breaking into the pages of the weekly *Harijan*, partly because of readers writing in to confess to the importance of sex in their marriages, or question his insistent view that marital sex could only be for procreation, not pleasure, or that "sexual science" should be taught but only so long as it was "the science of sex control."

The basic reason sex kept breaking in, it seems clear, was that the Mahatma simply couldn't let the subject drop. In the weeks leading up to his Travancore trip, he'd twice written at length about the misadventures of one Ramnarayan, a social service worker in the Gandhian movement against untouchability in Gandhi's native Porbandar—"an ideal Harijan worker," in Gandhi's view, until he learned that Ramnarayan had been sexually involved with not one but two young women. "What a wide gap between Ramnarayan, the mature servant of Harijans and Ramnarayan the slave of sexual desire!" wrote the Mahatma, naming names with the eagerness of a gossip columnist. Clearly, this hot item offered the movement for social reform he was struggling to build a lesson it couldn't ignore. "No worker who has not overcome lust can hope to render genuine service to the cause of Harijans, communal unity, khadi, cow-protection or village reconstruction," Gandhi decreed, more in anger than in sorrow.

It wasn't only a question of where he could find "an army of volunteer workers of the right type" to advance his many causes in the 700,000 villages. Sometimes he found himself asking whether he was of the right type to be leading it himself. The struggle of the aging Mahatma to achieve what he called "mastery" over his mind and passions after years of dedicated celibacy carries a powerful poignancy—not because it's the antithesis of the scandals on which we normally feed, or because it enables us to view our own life choices as wholesome by comparison to those of this figure who was exemplary in so many other ways. It's poignant, perhaps even tragic, because Gandhi finally convinces himself that there may be a causal relationship—not just an analogy—between his struggle for self-mastery and India's struggle for independence. Just as every village needs a social service worker who has defeated lust, the nation needs a leader who—however pure his conduct—has banished wayward thoughts. If the leader fails in this important way, he may fail in others, causing the nation to suffer.

Bhikhu Parekh, a British scholar of Gujarati background who has written the most careful and sensitive analysis of Gandhi's sexual values and obsessions, provides necessary perspective. "Gandhi's asceticism represented a relatively minor strand within the Hindu cultural tradition," he writes. After all, most Hindu gods are married, and Lord Krishna, beloved for his dalliances, calls the sexual impulse divine. Hindus, says Parekh, celebrate sexual union "as a sacred activity in which time, space and duality are temporarily transcended." That's why so many of the Hindu temples Gandhi wanted to open are covered with erotic sculptures.

The Mahatma's quirky idea that his own self-mastery may be the key to India's doesn't define Gandhi in the last decade of his life but periodically haunts him despite the "rigorous simplicity" of his daily routines, programmed nearly to the minute—from his rising at 4:00 a.m. until he closed his eyes to sleep eighteen hours later—to keep unwelcome thoughts at bay. "I can suppress the enemy but have not been able to expel him altogether," Gandhi wrote, acknowledging his sex urge.

It's in 1936, in the few months between his encounter with Margaret Sanger and his arrival at Segaon village, that he begins to worry about the adequacy of his brahmacharya. In Bombay, recuperating from a collapse brought on by high blood pressure, and from encounters with a dentist who was extracting all his teeth, the Mahatma "experienced a sudden desire for intercourse." Over the years he'd acknowledged wet dreams, but this was different: he was wide awake. With his usual, disarming candor, he tells a female co-worker, whom he has praised as a fellow "votary of brahmacharya," all about it.

"Despite my best efforts," he writes to her several months after the event, "the organ remained aroused. It was an altogether strange and shameful experience."

In less graphic terms, he has already gone public in *Harijan*. "Thank God," he said there, "my much-vaunted Mahatmaship has never fooled me." This is nothing so commonplace or tawdry as a public man admitting to an affair. In its directness and baring of his inner life, it's more like the passage in Saint Augustine's *Confessions* bemoaning "the revolting things I did, and the way my soul was contaminated by my flesh." No one would normally expect to be told what Gandhi has taken it upon himself to reveal. He cannot keep silent, it seems, and go on. What may strike us as an exaggerated response to a normal personal experience of limited interest to others is for Gandhi an introduction to something approaching the dark night of the soul.

Many things are happening at once. He's trying to build an "army" of exemplary village workers who have mastered the urges he himself, in his late sixties, is still struggling to master. He commits himself to becoming one of those workers in his chosen Segaon, where his message is not embraced. He tours Travancore at the tip of the subcontinent one year and visits far-off Frontier Province—a battleground in today's Pakistan—the next. He strategizes with the Congress leadership about whether it should take office on British terms after provincial elections. And, finally, through all this, he tries to find the right degree of closeness or distance that he as an inveterately judgmental father should maintain with his alcoholic eldest son, Harilal, not the least of whose many problems, in Gandhi's view, has been his weakness for prostitutes since the early death of a wife he had loved. Four days before the Mahatma is due to move to Segaon, he meets Harilal in Nagpur. His forty-eight-year-old son asks for money; thinking it would go for drink, Gandhi refuses to give the handout. Then, only two weeks after Gandhi's arrival in his chosen village—bringing with him his high blood pressure and anxiety over his own erotic nightmare—Harilal changes his name to Abdullah and converts to Islam. Five months later, having flung his Oedipal challenge as publicly as possible, taking to public platforms as a Muslim proselytizer, he converts back.

"He remains the same wreck that he was before," Gandhi writes, in an open letter "To My Numerous Muslim Friends," prior to the reconversion. "I do not mind whether he is called Abdullah or Harilal," the letter says, "if, by adopting one name for the other, he becomes a true devotee of God which both the names mean."

But, of course, he does mind. Harilal continues to disappoint, and so, it's beginning to seem, will the village of Segaon, even though he has had the assistance of at least three additional workers there. Still, Gandhi seems to be back in command of his busy life, until April 14, 1938, when, just as he's preparing for a crucial meeting in Bombay with Mohammed Ali Jinnah, who has deflected a couple of invitations to rural Segaon, it all happens again—another erection, another wet dream. Nearing his seventieth year, not only is the Mahatma upset, but, as he later writes to Mirabehn, "That degrading, dirty, torturing experience of 14th April shook me to bits and made me feel as if I was hurled by God from an imaginary paradise where I had no right to be in my uncleanliness."

A week after the ejaculation, he issues a troubled, less explicit statement to the press saying, "For the first time in my public and private life

I seem to have lost self-confidence . . . I find myself for the first time during the past fifty years in a Slough of Despond. I do not consider myself fit for negotiations or any such thing for the moment."

Are we dealing with one history in this relatively compact time frame or several? Even with some unraveling, the answer can never be obvious. Disappointments are piling up. Gandhi, it seems, has found it necessary to shoulder them all. Normally, he's able to keep his disappointments— with himself, with Harilal, with the pace of reconstruction in Segaon, with the rising violence between Muslims and Hindus, with the meager returns on the work for Harijans—in separate compartments. On a daily basis, his demeanor remains cheerful. He's as diligent as ever, writing his articles, keeping up his devotions and correspondence, offering advice to his wide family circle, his most devoted acolytes, and strangers, with all his usual firmness and assurance. He never used the word "sublimation," but he was familiar with the concept. "The man who sits idle cannot control his passionate urge," he said once. "The remedy, therefore, is to keep the body engaged in work." So he fills his days with minutely scheduled tasks. Still, when he admits to feeling let down, a little depressed, it's sometimes hard to tell whether the feeling has a specific source or many, hard to trace the boundaries of the slough of despond he has now entered. Does his flawed brahmacharya really undermine the village strategy? Or could it be the other way round?

"I am after all a sinking ship," he remarks to his faithful Mahadev in September 1938. "Who would want to sail in such a ship?"

Segaon represents his abiding commitment to the "dumb millions." But the story of his involvement there turns out to be a sad one. Here is Gandhi coming to grips with the reality of the Indian village, which he has fervently idealized ever since *Hind Swaraj*, written nearly three decades earlier, before he'd left South Africa, before he'd even thought to test his ideas at Tolstoy Farm. He never breaks his tie to the village, but it takes less than a year before it becomes evident that he's disappointed.

At the end of 1936, before his Travancore trip, he's assailed by a politician there for sounding off on local conditions when he has never even succeeded in getting temples opened up in Ahmedabad, his base for his first sixteen years back in India, where he was on home ground as a Gujarati. Gandhi replies with touching Gandhian directness: "Not only have I not succeeded in having temples opened in Ahmedabad but I have not succeeded in having temples opened even in Wardha after my having established myself there. And what is even more damaging to my reputation is that I have not succeeded in having the only two caste temples in Segaon opened to the Harijans of the little village."

Six months later Gandhi calls a meeting in Segaon to scold the villagers. He has two complaints. One is that they've shirked an obligation they've freely undertaken to supply labor and rocks for a road between his quarters on the outskirts and the village itself, which would connect to a wider road being put through to the town of Wardha. The other involves the old business of sanitation. Gandhi and his co-workers, it seems, are no longer scooping up the village's turds, perhaps because doing so inevitably renders them untouchable in the villagers' eyes and thus makes it harder for them to be accepted. In what appears to be a tactical retreat, therefore, the ashram has actually hired a scavenger for the village. Still the villagers don't cooperate. They continue to defecate along the lanes and refuse to hire out their carts for the removal of human manure.

"I am told that you are indifferent to all that is happening," the Mahatma says. "I cannot make your village neat and clean and sweet-smelling without your cooperation. We have engaged a scavenger here. We pay for his service, but it is for you to keep your streets and lanes clean . . . Nowhere do we come across such apathy."

Gandhi has just returned from an interlude in Gujarat. From there he'd written to a co-worker in Segaon apologizing for his "failure" to spend more time in the village. He has other jobs, he pointed out. By speaking of failure, he said, he didn't "mean that we have not been able to do anything at all. But whatever we have done cannot be said to be of much value." The next day he wrote again, telling one correspondent that his "real work" is still in Segaon and another, "My heart is there." These are reminiscent of letters, long years before, from the Transvaal to the Phoenix Settlement explaining his long absences.

Mahadev Desai sums up the situation in 1940, four years after Gandhi's arrival in Segaon-Sevagram. "There is a hiatus between the villagers and us," he acknowledges. "There is yet no living link between us . . . [We have] not succeeded in coming down to their level and becoming one with them."

By then, various realities have come crashing in on Gandhi. Village reality is one, but also there are the unresolved political issues between Muslims and Hindus and the looming involvement of the colonial power in another world war. Gandhi never loses faith in the central

importance of his "constructive program." In his writings and pronouncements, he campaigns for its principles until the day of his death.
But one by one, he has been forced to recognize that he has been
checked on the causes he'd singled out as "pillars" of swaraj. Mainly
these were Hindu-Muslim unity, the struggle against untouchability,
and village industries as symbolized by the spinning wheel, each an ideal
he brought home to India with him, shaped in large measure by his
experience on another subcontinent.

On Hindu-Muslim unity he'd acknowledged feeling "helpless" as
early as 1926. Eleven years later he repeats the word in a note to Jinnah:
"I am utterly helpless. My faith in unity is as bright as ever; only I see no
daylight out of the impenetrable darkness and, in such distress, I cry out
to God for light."

On untouchability, he writes after the end of his tour in 1934, "Unfortunately the higher castes have failed to identify themselves with their
humbler fellows . . . I have no excuse to offer."

On village work, he's forced to acknowledge his failure to recruit the
corps of self-sacrificing satyagrahis he'd counted on dispatching to the
700,000 villages. He even has doubts about the dozens drawn to his
immediate ambit at Sevagram. Here too he speaks of feeling "helpless."
He cannot prevent the place from becoming a magnet for persons of
uncertain dedication—in Mirabehn's words, "a strange medley of various kinds of cranky people." Sizing them up, the Mahatma himself says,
"Quite a few are only temporary inhabitants and none of them will stay
on after my death." In 1940 he makes one of his service organizations,
the Gandhi Seva Sangh, commit "hari-kari" because it has attracted
unprincipled timeservers and job seekers. Five years later he acknowledges that the All India Village Industries Association, which he had
started with such high hopes in 1934, didn't "show the results it might
have."

"Whatever I do is for the poor," Gandhi finally said with the same
unflinching honesty, "but today I am unable to prove it in Sevagram." As
late as 1945, he's still pondering plans to draw volunteers to Sevagram to
give the village a good cleanup—a clear sign that a decade of Gandhian
ministrations has failed to persuade the villagers to do it for themselves.

It's not difficult to feel sorry for the Gandhi who carries on in his last
decade after having been forced to acknowledge that many of his most
cherished values and programs have not taken root, the Gandhi who
recognizes a decade before it comes to pass that swaraj was now more
likely to come as a result of a war that would exhaust the colonial power

than as a "solid awakening" by a united people who'd achieved self-mastery. "Any extraneous event may put power into our hands," he observed in 1937. "I would not call that swaraj of the people."

It can also be argued that the aging Gandhi, carrying on in the face of such profound disappointments, is as true to himself as he had ever been when he allowed himself to imagine that India could be talked into a social transformation. Seldom does he give in to the politician's usual temptation to blithely sweep away any sense of letdown, to proclaim victory at every juncture. This unsatisfied Gandhi, the one who doesn't know how to pretend, is the one who still makes a claim on Indian social conscience, such as it is.

"We cannot command results," he said. "We can only strive." It's in these years that he had to recognize that the movement that held his image aloft was now marching on without him. "Let no one say that he is a follower of Gandhi," he then said. "It is enough that I should be my own follower."

It's also at this time that he's finally reunited with the dearest of his early followers, Hermann Kallenbach. The Litvak architect from Johannesburg by way of East Prussia, who'd been barred from India and then interned by the British as an enemy alien after the outbreak of World War I, finally lands in Bombay in May 1937. He'd eventually been repatriated to Germany in a prisoner exchange. Adrift there after the armistice, he didn't complete his interrupted journey to Gujarat and Gandhi but found his way back to Joburg instead, where he soon reestablished himself in the comfortable life of a big-time property developer that Gandhi had earlier persuaded him to give up.

Years passed, but the Mahatma never quite let go of his dream of having his old Jewish housemate again at his side, running his Indian ashrams the way he'd run Tolstoy Farm. When they resumed correspondence after the war, they were still Lower House and Upper House. "How I should love to hug you and see you face to face and have you by me during my travels!" Upper House wrote in 1921, when he was already the undisputed leader of the Indian national movement. Twelve years later, writing from South India in the midst of his crusade against untouchability, he still sounds ardent. "You are always before my mind's eye," he tells Lower House. "When are you coming?" These letters offer a glimpse of a loneliness Mahatma Gandhi continued to feel even in the midst of his ashrams, his inner circle of dedicated attendants and followers, and the huge throngs drawn to his public appearances. Maybe that's what Pyarelal is getting at when, later, he's moved to write in his diary, "There is something frightening in Bapu's utter spiritual isolation."

The moment of reunion between the Joburg architect and India's leader was captured by Mahadev Desai in *Harijan*. Kallenbach lingered in Bombay only long enough to pick up an ample khadi wardrobe, then caught a train up the coast that stopped not far from a Gujarati village near the shore where Gandhi was taking a respite from Segaon. He arrived before dawn during morning prayers. "After how many years?" Gandhi asked when prayers were done. Kallenbach bowed at his feet. "Twenty-three," he said as they embraced. "With childish delight," according to Mahadev, Gandhi lifted up a lantern to examine his long-lost friend's features, then pulled at his hair. "So the hair has all turned gray," he said.

Upper House then asked whether Lower House had sailed in first or second class. It was a test to see how far he had lapsed back into his old materialist ways. "Tourist class," the visitor said. "I knew that would be the first question you would ask me."

Kallenbach wore a dhoti, sometimes went bare chested like his host, slept under the stars near Gandhi. It was almost as if twenty-three years had disappeared, he wrote to his brother. He's "just like one of us," said a gratified Gandhi. It doesn't seem, however, that the architect was seriously tempted by the old idea of shutting down his practice and moving to the ashram. What's clear is that his trip had a purpose beyond reconnecting with his old friend; he had a mission. He'd been recruited to make the case for the Zionist cause in Palestine to the Indian leader.

The impetus came from the head of the Political Department of the Jewish Agency in Palestine. Under the British mandate, the agency was the de facto government for the small but growing community of Jewish settlers; the Political Department functioned as its foreign ministry. Its head was Moshe Shertok, who, as Moshe Sharett, would become Israel's second prime minister, succeeding David Ben-Gurion. Shertok, seeking a connection to "the greatest of living Hindus," had learned of Kallenbach's existence from a recent visitor to South Africa. Instantly, it seems, he wrote a long letter to the architect. "There are few people whom circumstances have placed in a position enabling them to render service of an extraordinary character," the letter said. "I am advised and believe that you are at the present moment such a person ... You are in a

Gandhi and Kallenbach reunited, June 1937

unique position to help Zionism in a field where the resources of the Jewish people are so meager as to be practically non-existent."

Kallenbach signed on. Two months before arriving in Bombay, he met Shertok in London and also Chaim Weizmann, the head of the Zionist movement and future first president of Israel. Then he stopped in Palestine, where he was particularly impressed by the early kibbutzim, which reminded him, with their emphasis on hand labor and simple living, of the values Gandhi had inculcated at Tolstoy Farm. (After his death in Johannesburg in 1945, his ashes would be buried at Kibbutz Degania on the Sea of Galilee, Israel's oldest kibbutz, where Tolstoy's influence on the first settlers had been especially marked.) There is no sign that Lower House mentioned his briefings by prominent Zionists to Upper House. But he can hardly be said to have been acting undercover; he'd been openly a Zionist since the days when they lived together in Joburg, when he alternately studied Hebrew and Hindi as he tried to decide whether he'd be moving to Palestine or India.

Now, in the month they had together in 1937, Gandhi eagerly entered into a discussion of the rights and wrongs of Arab-Jewish strife in Palestine. He'd had a firm position on the subject since 1921, at the high tide of the Khilafat movement. Basically, his position was that Indian Hindus ought to support their seventy million Muslim brethren on what was for them an issue of religious principle. His friend urged him to pay sympathetic attention to the Zionist side of the argument. Gandhi promised he would. Kallenbach then had the Jewish Agency furnish the Mahatma with a twenty-five-page essay on the historic, spiritual, and political underpinnings of Zionism, prepared especially for him. "The sender's name is not given," Gandhi noted, but he found the piece "very impressive, deeply interesting." So impressive that he was moved to consider proposing an effort to mediate between Arabs and Jews under his supervision, with Hermann Kallenbach, now back in Johannesburg, as his lead mediator. "I quite clearly see that if you are to play any part in bringing about an honorable settlement," Gandhi writes the architect, "your place is in India." Apparently concerned that his friend might suspect that pressure was being applied for personal reasons, Gandhi adds: "All this I say irrespective of the domestic arrangement between us." Gandhi himself seems as ardent as ever. His wishes are unambiguous, but with what seems an effort, he practices restraint. "I must not force the pace," he writes to his friend in Joburg a half year later. "You must come in your own good time."

After Kallenbach's return to South Africa, Gandhi had turned his hand to distilling his view of the problem in a draft he sends on to his Zionist friend for his approval. "In my opinion the Jews should disclaim any intention of realizing their aspiration under the protection of arms and should rely wholly on the goodwill of Arabs. No exception can possibly be taken to the natural desire of the Jews to found a home in Palestine. But they must wait for its fulfillment till Arab opinion is ripe for it." Gandhi basically wants the Jews to become satyagrahis, the Arabs too. Kallenbach, half won over, sends the draft on to Chaim Weizmann. It's never published.

His offer to mediate in Palestine is just a beginning. At a time when the Mahatma feels increasingly stymied in his efforts to reform India, he becomes increasingly inclined to issue encyclicals on international problems. Obviously, his frustration at home is not the only reason for his readiness to speak out. The world is hurtling toward catastrophe, and as the appointed keeper of the doctrine of nonviolence he feels a responsibility to make himself heard. A series of moral pronouncements flows from his humble quarters near Segaon. In all, they are a mixed bag, full of trenchant moral insights, desperate appeals, and self-deluding simplicities. A subsequent statement on Palestine draws an anguished rebuke from the theologian Martin Buber, a refugee from Hitler who has become prominent in the earliest version of a Jewish peace movement. Buber writes that he "has long known and honored" Gandhi's voice, but what he hears on Palestine he finds "barren of all application to his circumstances." He then goes on to dissect a pronouncement of the Mahatma's on German Jews. Gandhi has prescribed satyagraha as the answer to Nazi barbarism. He has found "an exact parallel" between the plight of the Jews under Hitler and that of the Indians in his time in South Africa. Buber tells Gandhi he lived under Nazi rule before becoming a refugee and saw Jewish attempts at nonviolent resistance. The result was "ineffective, unobserved martyrdom, a martyrdom cast to the winds."

There's reason to believe that Buber's letter, dispatched to Segaon from Jerusalem in March 1939, never reached Gandhi. In any case, by then the Mahatma had already left a distressing trail of futile, well-intentioned missives. He'd written to the Czechs on the uses of satyagraha to combat storm troopers and to the viceroy, offering to mediate between Hitler and his Western prey, including Britain. Within several months, he'd write the first of two letters to the führer himself. "Will you listen to the appeal of one who has deliberately shunned the method of war not without considerable success?" he asked rhetorically, in a desperate, naive mix of humility and ego. The British, who monitored his mail, made sure the letter went nowhere. The letter to Hitler began with the salutation "My friend." Hitler had already indicated what he thought of the Mahatma and his nonviolence. "All you have to do is to shoot Gandhi," he advised a British minister.

Eventually, after the outbreak of war and his own final imprisonment, Gandhi would write to Churchill offering his services in the cause of peace. "I can't imagine anyone with Gandhi's reputation writing so stupid a letter," a new viceroy, Lord Wavell, confides to his diary after intercepting it.

Unrealistic, self-regarding, and dubious in their reasoning as most of these letters were, Gandhi's basic understanding of Churchill's "gathering storm" wasn't always unfocused. "If there ever could be a justifiable war in the name of and for humanity, a war against Germany, to prevent the wanton persecution of a whole race, would be completely justified," he wrote. "But I do not believe in any war."

The onetime sergeant major had volunteered as a noncombatant in the Boer and Zulu wars. He'd offered to serve as the "recruiting agent-in-chief" for the viceroy at the end of the previous world war, even inscribing himself as a candidate for enlistment at the age of fifty. Now, for the first time, he was striking a truly pacifist stance. This can only be understood in the Indian context. The looming issue was whether the national movement could barter its support for the war effort in exchange for a reliable promise of freedom. Put another way—in the way most Indian nationalists at the time understood it—the pivotal issue was whether India could be asked to fight for the freedom of the colonial power when the colonial power's commitment to India's freedom was still uncertain. Gandhi's dogmatic pronouncements on the application of satyagraha to the Jewish-Arab conflict and the menace of Nazi Germany can best be interpreted as trial runs for the penultimate chapter of the Indian struggle. It was as if he sensed that he'd be called back one last time from Segaon to lead his movement, and that this time he might have to put aside whatever lingering loyalty he might still have felt to the British.

However, when Britain finally entered the war, following the Nazi invasion of Poland in September 1939, Gandhi's immediate instinct was to tell the viceroy that he viewed the struggle with "an English heart." This viceroy, Lord Linlithgow, had proclaimed India's entry into the war the previous day without consulting any Indian. Summoned to the Viceregal Lodge in Simla, Gandhi had offered no protest, not even a mild complaint, over this stunning oversight—stemming from habitual presumption and a calculated refusal to negotiate—that would soon ignite a prolonged struggle between the colonial authority and the Indian national movement. Eventually, perhaps inevitably, but only after much wavering, Gandhi would again take on the mantle of leadership to set out the strategy for that confrontation. It would pit him against the British at the height of the war. But in Simla the day after the viceroy's declaration, under the illusion that he had established a warm personal tie to Linlithgow—not unlike what he sentimentally imagined his tie to Smuts to have been a quarter of a century earlier in South Africa— Gandhi by his own testimony "broke down," shedding tears as he pictured the destruction of the houses of Parliament, Westminster Abbey, and the heart of London. "I am in perpetual quarrel with God that he should allow such things to go on," he wrote the next day. "My nonviolence seems almost impotent."

11

MASS MAYHEM

B Y THE END of his seventh decade, Mahatma Gandhi had been forced to recognize that the great majority of his supposed followers hadn't followed him very far when it came to what he'd listed as the four pillars of swaraj. The last and most important of these was supposed to be ahimsa, or nonviolence, which for Gandhi was both a core religious value and his set of patented techniques for militant resistance to injustice. Now, with the eruption of another world war, he was forced to recognize that "Congressmen, barring individual exceptions, do not believe in nonviolence." It would be his lot "to plough a lonely furrow," for it seemed he had "no co-sharer in the out-and-out belief in nonviolence."

Here the Mahatma seems to be deliberately striving for pathos. It's a favorite posture, that of the isolated seeker of truth, and it's not untinged with moral and political pressure, a whiff of emotional blackmail; his closest associates are left to feel guilty over their failure to measure up to his high ideal. Increasingly, this self-portrayal comes to define his sense of his inner reality as well as his political position. He can still draw huge reverential throngs, has a loyal entourage hanging on his every word and wish, but there are intangible, evidently important ways in which he feels himself to be alone. If Gandhi the prophet is to be taken at his word here, the temple of swaraj as he'd conceived it had now collapsed with the crumbling of its last pillar.

But the prophet's declaration of his "out-and-out belief" doesn't remove the political leader from the scene. Gandhi is never more elusive or complex than he is in this final decade of his life and career as he strains to balance his own precepts, values, and self-imposed rules with

Again on tour, 1940

the strategic needs of his movement. It's a strain that only increases as power is seen to be within its grasp. From wrenching questions about the uses of nonviolence in a war against fascism (but not imperialism, as India was quick to catch on) to the just-emerging issue of what he'd term "vivisection"—the carving out and renaming of India's Muslim-majority areas as a state called Pakistan—Gandhi would regularly manage to stand on at least two sides, distinguishing his personal position from that of his movement, before stepping forward at the last hour to offer his loyal support for the position of the movement, and then, almost as regularly, stepping back. As early as 1939, he drew a distinction between himself and his supporters who "want to be true to themselves and to the country which they represent for the time being, even as I want to be true to myself." The idea that country and what he'd long since been used to calling "truth" could pull in opposite directions was a relatively new one, a source of profound inner conflict.

To a bluff British general like Lord Wavell, the penultimate viceroy, it was all an act. Gandhi was a "malevolent old politician, who for all his sanctimonious talk has, I am sure, very little softness in his composition," Wavell wrote after his first encounters with the Mahatma. Had the viceroy's skepticism been anywhere near the mark, the climax of Gandhi's career would amount to little more today than an extended footnote, a kind of tributary to the torrent of onrushing events he tried and largely failed to influence. Instead, Gandhi's last act can be read as a moral saga in its own right, not unworthy of the rubric "tragic" in its fullest, deepest sense. The public issues with which he wrestled retain their importance, but what stands out after all these years is the old man himself as he goes through a series of strenuous self-imposed trials in a time of national crisis, veering at the end of his life between dark despair and irrepressible hope.

If readiness to offer up one's own body and life—what he called "self-suffering"—were the mark of a true votary of Gandhian nonviolence, a true satyagrahi, then the Mahatma's lonely, detached, largely ineffectual last years and months can be invested with grandeur and interpreted as fulfillment. Which was one of the ways that Gandhi, shaping his narrative as always, was inclined to see it. The premonition that he might meet an assassin's bullets became a persistent leitmotif of his private ruminations. More than five years before his actual end in a New Delhi garden on January 30, 1948, he imagined his assailant would be a Muslim, despite all he'd done since the "glorious days" of the Khilafat movement, when, in his recollection, dignity and "nobility of spirit" reigned. "My life is entirely at their disposal," he said. "They are free to put an end to it, whenever they wish to do so." Perhaps he was thinking back to the slaying of his fellow mahatma Swami Shraddhanand at the hands of a Muslim extremist in 1926. His foreboding proved to be partly misplaced. It anticipated the circumstances of his death but not the motive behind the eventual plot or the identity of the plotters. It was Hindu extremists who targeted him. They saw him as pro-Muslim.

At the same time, the tragic narrative can't be easily disentangled from the self-staged, nearly comic subplot of the Mahatma's ins and outs—his repeated exits from leadership of the national movement and his sudden returns. In the months and years following the viceroy's declaration of war on behalf of an India he never bothered to consult, Gandhi's comings and goings get to be like the old stage routine of a performer holding up one end of a very long ladder while exiting stage left, only to reenter stage right an instant later, hoisting the other end.

In September 1939, in the immediate aftermath of the declaration, the Congress rejects a resolution Gandhi drafted. It's the first time in twenty years this has happened; he views it as a "conclusive defeat." The spurned draft promised support of the British war effort by all available nonviolent means. Instead, the Congress sets up a bargaining situation, making its promise of support conditional on a British commitment on independence. Implying the bargain it imagines, it soft-pedals Gandhi's emphasis on nonviolence. Ten months later, in June 1940, it formally votes at Gandhi's request "to absolve him from responsibility for the program and activity which the Congress has to pursue" in order to free him "to pursue his great ideal in his own way." Three months later, after the viceroy has brushed off its demand for a commitment on Indian freedom, it summons Gandhi back to leadership. In December 1941 he's out again, over disagreements about the use of force. A mere two weeks later, he's back on his own terms, only now his terms have started to undergo a subtle shift. Eventually, he makes a reluctant concession: if India is declared independent during the war, he acknowledges, it will probably conclude it needs armed forces; he also agrees that Allied forces could continue to use its territory as a base from which to bomb Japanese positions in Burma and fly arms over the hump to China. These adjustments in his and the Congress's position come painfully, over many months. They've no effect. The British still aren't biting: Winston Churchill, the "die-hard" imperialist, would famously assert that he hadn't become prime minister to preside over the empire's dissolution. Having failed so far to dislodge or even budge the Raj, Gandhi and the Congress prepare for the largest campaign of noncooperation and nonviolent resistance in twelve years, since the Salt March, serving an ultimatum on the British: hand over sovereignty or face the consequences. In 1942, at the height of the Japanese advance across Asia, against the better judgment of Nehru, who took the threat of an invasion seriously, "Quit India!" becomes their cry.

Through all his ins and outs, Gandhi has now moved over three years from unconditional support for the war effort by all available nonviolent means to a threat of nonviolent resistance on a massive scale unless India is freed to make "common cause" with the Allies in ways that wouldn't necessarily be nonviolent. On August 8, 1942, the Congress endorses the "Quit India" resolution, which promises that a free India will "resist aggression with all the armed as well as nonviolent forces at its command." That phrase embodies Gandhi's tacit shift on the question of armed force, his willingness to align himself with Nehru and other Congress leaders. Now he's ready to go full tilt. The coming campaign will be, he promises, "the biggest struggle of my life." Here we've a flash of the fully possessed, "do or die" Gandhi, the fervent commander, who led indentured miners into the Transvaal in 1913, who later promised "swaraj in a year," who subsequently marched to the sea to harvest a handful of salt. But the morning after the vote on the "Quit India" resolution he's arrested again in Bombay and taken as a prisoner to the Aga Khan Palace outside Poona, where he's sidelined for the next twenty-one months until the British, alarmed by his high blood pressure, decide to let him go in order not to have to face an uproar over his dying in detention.

Churchill's cabinet has discussed the idea of deporting Gandhi to Uganda but recognizes finally that its American ally, not to mention the masses of India, might find this hard to swallow. Gandhi's last campaign hadn't achieved anything like his standard of nonviolent discipline. "Mob violence remains rampant over large tracts of the countryside," the viceroy reported to Churchill three weeks after his arrest. By the end of the year, nearly one thousand persons had been killed in clashes with the police; some sixty thousand arrested in the British crackdown on the Congress. Egged on by Churchill, the British searched for evidence that Gandhi, though jailed, had been complicit in this violence, perhaps conspiring with the Japanese. They never found it, but Gandhi's own words before his arrest seemed to hint that he wouldn't be surprised by a surge in rioting. Indian nonviolence had always been imperfect, "limited in both numbers and quality," he coolly told an American correspondent— that is, in the availability of trained satyagrahis who could be relied on to make the requisite self-sacrifice—but "it has infused life into the people which was absent before." He isn't threatening or justifying violence, but assuming for the moment the position of a detached observer, a realist, he seems to be suggesting that this time it couldn't be ruled out. This Gandhi sounds like the pre-Mahatma of 1913 who warned the South African authorities he might lose control of his movement.

Gandhi's moral stubbornness, ascribed by the Mahatma to the dictates of his "inner voice," seems to function in his later years like a suddenly released spring or coil, distancing him from responsibility for far-reaching political decisions. The pattern had been set by the time his last imprisonment ended on May 6, 1944. But Nehru and Patel, the whole Congress Working Committee, remained in jail; the viceroy rebuffed his request to consult them. So, for the next thirteen months, until their release, only he could act on national issues. His most significant venture in that time was an attempt to bridge the widening chasm between the

Indian National Congress and the Muslims—in particular, a resurgent Muslim League under its self-styled Quaid-i-Azam, or "great leader," Mohammed Ali Jinnah.

This was the same Jinnah who'd welcomed him to India nearly three decades earlier with a heartfelt plea for national unity; the nationalist whom Gokhale, Gandhi's sponsor and guru, had earlier hailed as an "ambassador of Hindu-Muslim unity"; who in 1916 lived up to that tribute by cementing an accord between the Congress and the Muslim League that seemed a breakthrough at the time; the same Jinnah, fastidious lawyer that he was, whose belief in constitutional methods had then been so ruffled, so offended, by Gandhi's introduction of mass agitation based on appeals to religious themes (of Muslims as well as Hindus) that he'd walked away from the Congress; the political broker who was, nevertheless, still trying as late as 1928 to find common ground between the two movements on the constitutional shape of an independent India; and who in 1937 offered to enter coalitions with new Congress governments at the provincial level, only to be rebuffed.

He was the same man but no longer the same nationalist. Returning from his four-year exile in England, he paid Gandhi the implicit compliment of imitation. Mass agitation based on religion no longer offended him; it was, he'd learned, the surest path to national leadership. Now he argued that there'd never been and never could be an Indian nation, only Hindu India (Hindustan) and Muslim India (Pakistan)—two equal nations, no matter that one outnumbered the other by better than two to one (roughly three to one if untouchables were counted as Hindus). By Jinnah's reasoning, if Muslims were a nation, they weren't a minority, whatever the population tables showed; any negotiations, he insisted, had to be on that basis. The Quaid's sartorial transformation wasn't as drastic as the Mahatma's, but in place of his smart, custom-tailored double-breasted suits he now sometimes appeared in the long traditional, buttoned-up coat known as a *sherwani* and the rimless cap fashioned from sheep hide that learned Muslims called maulanas favored; henceforth it would sometimes be described as a Jinnah cap, worn in contrast to the white khadi caps donned by congressmen that were everywhere known as Gandhi caps. With skill and considerable cunning, the Quaid had set himself up to be Gandhi's foil.

There'd never been much warmth between these two Gujarati lawyers, but Gandhi, who'd always treated Jinnah with respect and had reached out to him at times when Nehru and most other Congress leaders tended to write him off, now made a point of referring to him as

Quaid-i-Azam. (In 1942, days before the launch of the "Quit India" campaign, he'd even suggested that Jinnah could form a government if the British weren't ready to hand over power to the Congress.) For his part, Jinnah had always made a point of referring to him frostily as "Mr. Gandhi," conspicuously shunning any use of his spiritual honorific. But now the Quaid unbent sufficiently, on one occasion at least, to call him Mahatma. "Give your blessings to me and Mahatma Gandhi so that we might arrive at a settlement," he asked a throng of Muslim Leaguers in Lahore as the day of their summit neared. These small glimmers of regard were enough to make the British worry that the two leaders might form an anticolonial front in the midst of the war. Hindu nationalists worried as well. A mob showed up at Wardha with the intention of physically blocking Gandhi's way when it was time for him to leave for the station to board his train for Bombay to meet Jinnah. Their idea, then as now, was to protest any move to alienate any piece of the "motherland." Prominent in the crowd was a high-strung Brahman editor named Nathuram Godse who several years later, after India's partition, would step forward as the gunman Gandhi had long anticipated.

When the leaders finally faced each other in the study of Jinnah's residence on Mount Pleasant Road in the upscale Malabar Hill section of Bombay on September 9, 1944, in the first of what would be a marathon of fourteen sessions over eighteen days, Jinnah asked for Gandhi's credentials. "I thought you had come here as a Hindu, as a representative of the Hindu Congress," he said archly, according to Gandhi's version of the exchange, fully aware that this formulation would grate on his guest. "No, I have come here neither as a Hindu nor as a representative of the Congress," Gandhi replied. "I have come here as an individual." In that case, his host wanted to know, if they reached an accord, who would "deliver the goods"?

It was a barbed but reasonable question. Setting aside his openly eclectic, nonsectarian approach to religion, not to mention his decades-long quest for "unity," Gandhi had tacitly accepted the idea of a separate Muslim state as a basis for negotiation. Not only had the Congress already voted down the set of proposals he now advanced for discussion; it had done so with his approval. If he was reversing himself, Jinnah wanted to know, who would follow him? Was he even serious? The Pakistan Gandhi was ready to support would enjoy a certain amount of autonomy within an Indian union, which might be a relatively loose federation in which defense and foreign affairs were handled as national concerns. If Pakistan could be kept within India, he allowed himself to

*With Jinnah at the start of Malabar Hill
talks, September 1944*

hope, "heart unity" might yet follow. Putting it in writing at the start of
the third week of talks, Gandhi went a step further, acknowledging a
right of secession for the Muslim-majority areas that could lead to a
"Treaty of Separation" between "two sovereign independent states."

That still wasn't far enough for Jinnah. The Pakistan he had in mind
had to start off as sovereign. It couldn't trust a Hindu-dominated regime
to draw its boundaries or see to the terms of its separation; only by its
own free choice could it find itself inside an independent India. Thus its
destiny and boundaries had to be determined before independence, not
after, as Gandhi kept insisting. Immediately, it was apparent that they
were discussing two different Pakistans, two different ideas, at least, of
the bargaining power Jinnah would wield in any showdown. "I am
amazed at my own patience," Gandhi said after a grueling first session,
which lasted three and a quarter hours.

Godse, the assassin-to-be, and his fellow Hindu chauvinists needn't
have feared that Gandhi would embrace a shrunken Hindustan. His aim,
Gandhi remarked privately, while the talks were still going on, was to
prove to Jinnah "from his own mouth that the whole of the Pakistan
proposition is absurd." His words here convict him of overconfidence.

The Quaid-i-Azam finally became convinced that a wily Gandhi was stringing him along. "I have failed in my task of converting Mr. Gandhi," he said. The "Mr." could be read as a tip-off that the talks had failed.

Jinnah claimed that only the Muslim League could speak for British India's ninety million Muslims and only he could speak for the Muslim League. Gandhi's claim, though couched with infinitely more generosity and tact, was no less sweeping. "Though I represent nobody but myself," he wrote to Jinnah, "I aspire to represent all the inhabitants of India. For I realize in my own person their misery and degradation, which is their common lot, irrespective of class, caste or creed."

Jinnah was so engrossed in the tactics of the moment that he may have outmaneuvered even himself by waiting so long to define his idea of a satisfactory Pakistan, putting it forever beyond reach. (This is so, at least, if, as has sometimes been argued, his actual aim was to secure for Muslims a permanent share of power at the national level within India, rather than a separate state.) Gandhi, a master of the art of compromise, at least by his own estimate, may have been willing now to recognize a right of "self-determination" in Muslim-majority provinces and, therefore, a theoretical right of secession. But he was elusive on the central issue of power. Just as in his bargaining with Ambedkar, he couldn't contemplate any scaling back of his movement's claims—or his own—to represent the whole of India. That was the difficulty with "truth" as a standard for political judgment: it lacked flexibility. Neither the Quaid-i-Azam nor the Mahatma was a completely independent actor. Jinnah had to take care not to shatter the expectations he'd aroused in Muslim-minority provinces that could never be part of any conceivable Pakistan. Gandhi couldn't ignore the rising specter of Hindu militancy. Each needed an act of faith from the other that was next to impossible now that Jinnah had given up on Indian nationalism.

"I could not make any headway with Jinnah because he is a maniac," Gandhi told Louis Fischer. In the next breath he said, "Jinnah is incorruptible and brave." It's a tantalizing statement, seeming almost to imply that Jinnah had been unmoved when Gandhi dangled the possibility of high office.

Having decided he couldn't depend on Gandhi to deliver "the goods," the Quaid-i-Azam continued to be a prideful and elusive negotiator, counting on the British, the waning colonial power, to push a constitutional deal better than any he could hope to wrest from the Congress. Finally, with no words to his followers about such niceties as nonviolence, he gambled on what, with menacing ambiguity, he called "direct action" to force the pace. Direct action, his followers explained, meant mass struggle by nonconstitutional means.

By then, virtually ensuring that some kind of partition, some kind of Pakistan, would be the price to pay for independence, the Congress had reluctantly accepted a British proposal for the creation of an interim government and the start of a constitutional process in which the agreement of the Muslim League was to be treated as a virtual prerequisite. Gandhi, who'd negotiated on a separate Muslim state with Jinnah two years earlier, had swung around to proposing a boycott of the interim government as a way of forestalling Pakistan, keeping it from becoming an inevitability. But his stand was laced with equivocation, as if he knew it stood no chance with the movement he no longer dominated. He said it was based on an "unfounded suspicion," an "intuition," an "instinct." His suspicion was that the division of the country could be cataclysmic.

If he'd pushed his case forcefully and publicly, the Congress might have found it difficult to proceed without him. But he had no appetite for such a test, and couldn't see clearly where it would lead. Instead, on June 23, 1946, the day of decision on the intricate, multistage British plan, he asked permission to be excused. "Is there any reason to detain Bapu further?" asked Maulana Azad, a nationalist Muslim chairing the Working Committee meeting. "Everybody was silent. Everybody understood," writes Narayan Desai, son of Gandhi's devoted secretary, Mahadev, and author of a magisterial Gujarati-language biography of the Mahatma. Pyarelal's version captures the bitterness Gandhi had to swallow. "In that hour of decision they had no use for Bapu," he wrote.

"I know India is not with me," he told Louis Fischer a few days later. "I have not convinced enough Indians of the wisdom of nonviolence."

Jinnah had anticipated a Congress rejection of the British plan. Perhaps he'd hoped that the viceroy would then turn to the Muslim League—meaning him—to form the interim government. "Direct action" can be seen as the consequence of his disappointment. It was an adaptation—calculated, deliberately vague—of the Gandhian tactic of noncooperation, from which he'd recoiled a generation earlier. Jinnah was inevitably asked the day his new campaign was proclaimed, scarcely a month after the fateful Congress decision on the British plan, whether it would be violent. His reply, non-Gandhian in the extreme, was probably meant as psychological mood music rather than as a signal for mob violence. Nevertheless, it was chilling. "I'm not going to discuss ethics," he said.

He'd set Direct Action Day for August 16, 1946. What happened then over four days came to be known as the Great Calcutta Killing. By August 20, some three thousand persons had been beaten, stabbed, hacked, or burned to death in the capital city of Bengal, the only province at the time with a government dominated by the Muslim League. Corpses littered the streets, pulled apart by swarming vultures and dogs. If Muslims were the initial aggressors, the Hindu response was no less organized or brutal. Both sides deployed gangs, armed in advance with swords, knives, the lead-tipped rods called lathis, gasoline and other inflammables. But Calcutta was a Hindu-majority city—Muslims accounting for barely 20 percent of its population—and numbers finally told: more Muslims were killed than Hindus. In New Delhi, Vallabhbhai Patel, one of Gandhi's original disciples, expressed satisfaction over that result. "Sword will be answered by sword," this old Gandhian later warned. But that wasn't the way the story was generally understood or told at the time by caste Hindus who remained convinced that their community had endured the brunt of the attacks. Each side, having suffered grievously, felt thoroughly victimized.

For India's prophet of unity, nonviolence, and peace, these events—the overture for a year and a half of mass mayhem, murder, forced migration, property loss on a vast scale, extensive ethnic cleansing—provided ample reason for despair, enough to bring his whole life into question. Or so he seemed to feel at his lowest ebb. But if he was shaken, he clung ever more fervently to his core value of ahimsa, on which much of India seemed to have given up. And so, after a period of uncertainty over what his role now should be—which "lonely furrow" he should plow—he made his way at the start of his seventy-eighth year to a remote, watery district of Muslim-dominant East Bengal, now Bangladesh, putting himself almost as far in an eastward direction as he could get in what was still India from the center of political decision making in Delhi, a distance of more than a thousand miles. The district, known even then for the extremism of its mullahs, was called Noakhali. It had few phone lines and was actually closer to Mandalay in central Burma than it was to Delhi. As seen from the capital, Gandhi was practically in Southeast Asia.

Noakhali qualified as a destination because it had lately been the scene of another communal mania: gruesome violence, committed mostly by Muslims, in retaliation for the Calcutta bloodletting. Here Hindus had been beheaded, burned alive, raped, forcibly converted to Islam, made to eat beef, and, in the case of at least two and possibly many more women, married off under duress to Muslim men. In an assault on a single household belonging to a Hindu landowner in a village called Karapa, twenty-one men, women, and children were slaughtered. The Calcutta papers soon put the deaths at five thousand, which turned out to be a mighty exaggeration. Two to three hundred proved to be the more likely figure. It was bad enough.

The chief minister of what was still an undivided Bengal, a smooth Muslim politician with an Oxford pedigree named Shaheed Suhrawardy, saw only problems for himself and the Muslim League if Gandhi made it to the troubled area of East Bengal. So he tried to head the Mahatma off, calling on him on October 31 at a small one-story khadi center and ashram at Sodepur, on the outskirts of Calcutta, where the Mahatma often camped. Suhrawardy, who'd reemerge in the 1950s as prime minister of Pakistan, had a reputation among Muslims as well as Hindus for opportunism. Conspiratorial theorists among Hindus could not be convinced that he was anything other than the mastermind behind the Great Calcutta Killing. But he claimed a filial relationship to Gandhi dating back to the Khilafat agitation, and the old man, who had few illusions about Suhrawardy, retained a measure of affection for him from those days. "Shaheed sahib, everyone seems to call you the chief of the goondas," Gandhi began teasingly, using a common term for goons. "Nobody seems to have a good word to say about you!" Lounging on a bolster, the chief minister bantered back, "Mahatmaji, don't people say things about you too?"

Barun Das Gupta, a retired correspondent of *The Hindu* newspaper and son of the founder of the Sodepur ashram, witnessed that exchange as a young man. The impression he retains is that the chief minister was a little tipsy. Suhrawardy did what he could to persuade Gandhi to give up his Noakhali mission, trying out an argument that Gandhi would increasingly hear over the ensuing months: that he could be of more use in Bihar, a predominantly Hindu North Indian province he'd just traversed to get to Calcutta. Six days earlier Hindus there had proclaimed a "Noakhali day," which they'd marked and were still marking by a retaliatory slaughter of their own, including forced conversion of Muslims and razing of Muslim homes. The killing in Noakhali had all but stopped; the killing in Bihar was continuing in a widening swath, far surpassing in numbers of dead the grisly achievement of East Bengal. Before it burned out, it may have resulted in the loss of eight or nine thousand lives.

According to the old *Hindu* correspondent, Gandhi heard Suhrawardy out in silence. The chief minister's argument wasn't lacking in force, but the Mahatma wouldn't be moved; he'd fixed his sights on East Bengal and Noakhali. His instinct and ambition went beyond making a politician's symbolic drop-in to an area in crisis, what now might be discounted as a photo op. He'd settle down and dwell in Noakhali, he'd eventually vow, until the district presented an inspiring example of reconciliation to the rest of the subcontinent. Behind this vow was a peculiarly Gandhian mix of calculation and deep, half-articulated feeling. For his own reasons, he placed a greater emphasis on showing by his presence there that Hindus could live peacefully in the midst of a Muslim majority than on persuading Bihar's Hindus not to massacre Muslims. Noakhali struck him as a greater challenge for himself and his doctrine than Bihar precisely because it was Muslim League territory and thus an area bound to be ceded in any likely partition. Too easily, he persuaded himself that he could calm Bihar's Hindus from afar by going on a partial fast, which involved giving up goat's milk and reducing his meager intake of mashed vegetables; if the killing went on, he warned, he'd take no food at all. With that powerful ultimatum hanging over their collective heads, the new Congress government in Bihar assured him that it could be relied on to restore order. Allowing himself to be detoured away from Muslim-dominated Noakhali would, in his view, be tantamount to ceding the province. He was thus making himself a hostage not only in the cause of peace but that of an undivided India.

Suhrawardy didn't press his point. In a generous gesture, the Muslim League chieftain sportingly laid on a special train to carry the Mahatma and his party to the station nearest his destination, assigning three members of his provincial government to tag along. Gandhi, who now had fifteen months to live, stayed in the vicinity of Noakhali for the next four. He said he'd make himself a Noakhali man, a Bengali, that he might have to stay many years, possibly even be killed there. Noakhali, he said, "may be my last act." With his usual flair for self-dramatization, he raised the stakes from day to day. "If Noakhali is lost," he declared finally, "India is lost." What could he have meant? What was it about this small and obscure, impoverished and virtually submerged patch of delta on the fringe of the subcontinent that so transfixed him?

The answers, though Gandhi provided many, aren't instantly obvious.

In Noakhali, November 1946

It had been the suffering of Hindus—in particular, Pyarelal tells us, "the cry of outraged womanhood"—that had established Noakhali in Gandhi's imagination as a necessary destination: the reports of rapes, forced conversions, followed by the rewarding of Hindu women to Muslim rioters as trophies, sometimes literally at sword's point. Judging from his later preaching, Gandhi's original concept of his mission involved persuading Hindu families to take back wives and daughters who'd been snatched from them rather than reject them as dishonored. He also wanted to persuade them to stay put in their villages where, typically in East Bengal, they were outnumbered four to one, or if they'd already fled to refugee camps, as they had by the tens of thousands, to now open their minds to the idea of returning to rebuild their charred, ruined homes. But as long as communal peace was his overriding objective, he needed a message for the area's Muslim majority as well. For East Bengal's Muslims, avenging Calcutta had been an occasion—it might even be called a pretext—for ousting Hindu landowners and moneylenders, thereby overturning a lopsided agrarian order that oppressed them. The defining social statistic was that the minority Hindus owned 80 percent of the land. In a sense, he'd have to balance "the cry of outraged womanhood" against the cry for a fairer division of the income that could be squeezed from Noakhali's bountiful harvests of fish, rice, jute, coconuts, betel, and papayas.

At his first large prayer meeting, at a place called Chaumuhani on November 7, the elderly Hindu in a loincloth faced an overwhelmingly Muslim crowd of about fifteen thousand. He dwelled on the theme that the Islam he'd studied was a religion of peace. Earlier he'd vowed not to leave East Bengal until "a solitary Hindu girl" could walk safely among Muslims. The Muslim majority needed to tell the women of "the small Hindu minority," he now said, that "while they are there, no one dare cast an evil eye on them." Within a week, he found that two remaining Muslim Leaguers who'd been traveling with him had dropped out after finding themselves criticized in the Muslim press for "dancing attendance on Mr. Gandhi."

Soon he was forced to recognize that Muslims were staying away from his nightly prayer meetings and that the "peace committees" he'd hoped to plant in each village, composed of one respected Muslim and one like-minded Hindu, each vowing to sacrifice his life to prevent new attacks, existed only on paper. Now if he mentioned Pakistan at all, it was only to assert that he was not its enemy. With a rhetorical flourish, the supplicating Mahatma even suggested that if all the Hindus of East Bengal departed, he himself could be the last one remaining in what would then become Pakistan. "If India is destined to be partitioned, I cannot prevent it," he said. "But if every Hindu of East Bengal goes away, I shall still continue to live amongst the Muslims of East Bengal . . . [and] subsist on what they give me." A few nights later he could be found reading out a Jinnah statement warning Muslims that they could forfeit their claim to Pakistan if they indulged in communal violence. Hindus would be safer in Pakistan than Muslims themselves, the Quaid-i-Azam had pledged.

Jinnah's gossamer promise was the obverse of a pious hope that had been slowly forming in Gandhi's mind, which was now not infrequently despairing. By prodding Noakhali Hindus to return to their villages and by living there peacefully himself, he still meant to prove to all the sub-continent's Muslims and Hindus that there was no need for a Pakistan of any size or description. "If the Hindus could live side by side with the Muslims in Noakhali," Pyarelal wrote, putting the Mahatma's utopian vision into his own words, "the two communities could coexist in the rest of India, too, without vivisection of the Motherland. On the answer to the challenge of Noakhali thus hung the fate of India." Having placed himself beyond the very periphery of the subcontinent, he now vowed to make isolated Noakhali central to its destiny.

Consciously or not, Gandhi was following his old impulse to turn inward and go it alone, the one that had caused him a decade earlier to attempt to strike out for the remote village of Segaon by himself in hopes of finding a way through obstructions and caste prohibitions that had blocked and defeated his co-workers: the same impulse that had led, in his South Africa years, to the short-lived experiment in communal living called Tolstoy Farm. In an analogous quest, he now vowed to bury himself in a remote village in Noakhali where he could go without his entourage and take up residence with a Muslim League family. He said that would be his "ideal." If he failed to find willing Muslim hosts there, he'd live by himself. So he headed for an obscure village called Srirampur, not far from the epicenter of the worst Noakhali violence, bringing with him only an interpreter and a stenographer. The interpreter doubled as a Bengali teacher; he'd now be asked to function as well as masseur.

The stenographer normally handled Gandhi's correspondence and whipped up the transcripts of his nightly talks at prayer meetings for the small retinue of journalists that trailed him. A pioneer in the art of press manipulation, Gandhi insisted the journalists file not on the words that had actually come out of his mouth but on versions he "authorized" after his own sometimes heavy editing of the transcripts. The journalists— like the armed police detachment assigned by Suhrawardy to protect him—were also instructed to keep a decent distance so that the Mahatma's sense of his solitary mission would not be compromised.

Gandhi now drafted a statement for the colleagues he was leaving behind. "I find myself in the midst of exaggeration and falsity. I am unable to discover the truth," it said. "Oldest friendships have snapped. Truth and ahimsa by which I swear and which have to my knowledge sustained me for sixty years, seem to fail to show the attributes I ascribed to them." On that unhappy note, he disembarked at Srirampur, where he'd dwell for six weeks in a small wood-frame shelter with walls of corrugated metal and woven palm fronds, making a disciplined effort to push down dark premonitions and thoughts that continued to well up in his mind, waiting for inspiration.

Elderly people still living in the district retain distinct mental images of Gandhi from those days. They picture the public man, animated, soft-spoken, and smiling, his regularly oiled and massaged skin gleaming. A Hindu woman named Moranjibala Nandi, said by her son to be 105, was capable of describing the moment when the Mahatma came into the compound, where she was still living sixty-three years later, to distribute cloth to refugees. She pointed out the spot where he stood, about twenty yards from where, wrapped in a white widow's sari, she now sat crumpled into something like a small ball with only her sunken cheeks and gnarled, expressive fingers showing. "He didn't have a sad face," she said. I heard descriptions of similar encounters from a half-dozen other nonagenarians and octogenarians. But four days after his arrival in Srirampur, his new interpreter and Bengali tutor, a Calcutta intellectual named Nirmal Kumar Bose, heard him muttering to himself in Hindi, "*Kya karun, kya karun?*" "What should I do, what should I do?" the Mahatma was asking.

If Gandhi returned to Srirampur today, he'd easily recognize the place even though the population has tripled over the decades. Where people actually reside and mingle, the bright sunlight is still largely filtered through palm canopies and foliage of other trees that yield their own modest cash crops—betel nut, papaya, mango—planted as densely as possible not for the shade but the cash. The light that seeps through takes on a greenish, seemingly subaqueous quality that's soothing in contrast to the direct rays that then startle the eye when, following the swept dirt paths that are still the main thoroughfares, the visitor emerges on the embankments that frame the rice paddies, long vistas of a stunning electric green in the growing season that turn scrubby and dun colored after the harvests.

When Gandhi took his twice-a-day walks here, the harvest was just beginning; by the time he left, it was in. The men who lounge around the tea stalls at intersections of the paths mostly wrap themselves in lungis, the casual skirts, tied at the waist, seldom seen in North India. When it's hot, as it mostly is in Bangladesh, they don't bother with shirts. Cars don't get to these hubs—even rickshaws are sparse—but buses and trucks can now reach the edge of the village as they couldn't in Gandhi's

In Srirampur

day, when most transport was by canals that have long since been choked by hyacinth plants and blocked by buildings on cement pilings.

"Hardly a wheel turns . . . I saw no motorable road. The bullock cart, one of India's truest symbols, does not exist here," wrote Phillips Talbot, a young American journalist, later a diplomat, who caught up with Gandhi in Noakhali. "The civilization is amphibious."

Viewed superficially, the place today looks timeless, beyond history, becalmed. But mention Gandhi and the short season of slaughter that made Noakhali notorious, more than six decades ago when what's now Bangladesh was still India, and someone who was a child then steps forward to point out landmarks from his time here or, more likely, the sites from which those landmarks have now vanished. The simple cottage that was thrown up for Gandhi is long gone, as is the ruin of a Hindu landowner's large house that was set on fire before the Mahatma came. But any villager with a little gray in his hair knows where they stood. A banyan tree under which a small Hindu shrine was smashed back then is pointed out as a place where the Mahatma once paused to shake his head over the damage. The shrine has since been restored; the village's handful of Hindus pray there for protection against diseases. At a nearby village mosque an elderly attendant named Abdul Rashid Patwari, now ninety, gives a convincing account of Gandhi's visit on one of his morning walks.

The story is known, but in another sense it's prehistoric since history, as it's taught and understood in today's Bangladesh, generally begins with the country's "liberation" from Pakistan in 1971. The short, twenty-four-year existence of East Pakistan, as the country was called before that sundering, is remembered, when it's acknowledged at all, as a time of heavy-handed oppression by Muslims from the Punjab, on the other side of the subcontinent. Jinnah, never a hero among Bengalis, is lost in a deep amnesia. But Gandhi, faintly venerated as a saintly Hindu who came here on a peace mission, retains a presence. Voices become hushed. His name evokes a formal reverence, even among those who have never known the details of his time here.

Such flimsy sentiments are not without value, but the evidence of the failure of the Mahatma's mission here is also on the surface in Srirampur. If the size of the Hindu population was on the order of one-fifth in East Bengal in 1946, it's now closer to one-twentieth in Srirampur; in its vicinity, no more than five hundred souls. Hardly anyone mourns the long-ago partition Gandhi was hoping to ward off by raising up a compelling, shining example of nonviolence that the rest of the subcontinent would have to take into account. That dream is forgotten. What remains is the idea of peace and a lingering impression that it had something to do with good works. There are no memorials for Pakistan in Noakhali, but, amazingly, less than fifteen miles from Srirampur there's a modest Gandhi museum near a town named Joyag, where he once spent a night, part of an underfinanced social service organization called the Gandhi Ashram Trust that traces its inspiration to his time in the district. Its top officers are Hindu, but 80 percent of its beneficiaries are Muslim. There, Bengali women are still taught to spin and weave by hand. The trust hopes it will begin earning a modest profit on its handicrafts sometime soon and thus begin to fulfill the Mahatma's vision. It's enough part of the landscape to maintain good relations with the chairman of the Joyag village council, an orthodox Muslim named Abdue Wahab who has made the pilgrimage to Mecca and ran on the ticket of the Jamaat-i-Islami, a religious party generally classed as militant. "A man like

Gandhi is needed by this society and the world," the Jamaat man told me. Some people in his movement blame him for cooperating with the Gandhi Ashram Trust because Gandhi was a Hindu. "That's due to lack of understanding," Chairman Wahab said, smiling sweetly.

In a nearby village, I sipped the watery, sweet juice of a green coconut with an elderly Hindu and an even more ancient Muslim who remained neighbors as Noakhali became part of Pakistan instead of India, then Bangladesh instead of Pakistan. They now sat side by side. I couldn't be sure whether that was out of long habit or for my benefit. "He brought peace here," the Hindu said piously. "The sad part is no one followed him," the Muslim said. I took that to be a comment on the standard of leadership the country has seen since. History, it seemed in that moment, had simultaneously moved on and stood still. The killings are remembered as a long-ago typhoon, another kind of natural disaster. Gandhi's time here is sanctified or sentimentalized—depending on how the questions are put—as if his mission somehow accomplished its ends, as if the relative absence of communal violence ever since can be attributed to his influence.

That's not how the Mahatma experienced it. Most of Srirampur's Hindus had, in fact, fled by the time he took up residence there. According to Narayan Desai, only three out of two hundred Hindu families remained. In a letter written in his first week there, Gandhi himself boasts, "There is only one Hindu family living in the entire village, the rest are all Muslims." No Muslim League family ever came forward to offer him the refuge he sought, so he remained in his little cabin, venturing out for his walks, which sometimes included calls on ailing children whose Muslim parents were willing to hear his advice about nature cures involving diet and mud poultices. On rare occasions, he left the village for meetings with local Muslim religious or political leaders, who then routinely would dwell on conditions in Bihar, implying not so subtly that it was time for him to move on. Regularly he met with Gandhian workers he'd stationed in nearby villages in the stricken area, drafting new instructions as they reported on the dearth of cooperation from local officials, following these up with appeals to Suhrawardy, who unfailingly responded by pressing him on the pointlessness of his mission in Bengal while Bihar was burning. Assured by Congress leaders in Bihar that peace had been restored, Gandhi resumed his consumption of goat's milk and gradually increased his daily intake of food. (His weight, so

Bose tells us, had dropped to 106½ pounds.) His intelligence on Bihar was more to be trusted than Suhrawardy's, he insisted. But he didn't need reminding that he was making little progress. He just had to look around. Few Hindus were returning to their burned-out homes, despite his assurances or promises of assistance in rebuilding. And Muslims were continuing to distance themselves, boycotting his prayer meetings and the small number of Hindu shopkeepers still in business in the bazaars.

"My unfitness for the task is showing at every step," he declared in the course of his Srirampur sojourn. Once again, it was as if the intractable problem of communal strife in India was somehow internalized within himself, that his failure to work the miracle on which he was bent could be traced to some personal "imperfection" or defect. Ultimately, he'd say exactly that. "I can see there is some grave defect in me somewhere which is the cause of all this. All around me is utter darkness. When will God take me out of this darkness into his light?"

To speed that illumination, a desperate Gandhi took two vows. On December 11, just three weeks after he arrived in Srirampur, he gave up on his pledge to stay in a single place until a glorious refulgence of peace burst forth for all to see. Instead, he said he'd soon extend his mission by venturing on a Noakhali walking tour, staying in a new village every night. As if to prepare for that challenge, he privately vowed to deepen his personal *yajna*, his own course of self-sacrifice. What this phase of his life entailed, he convinced himself, was a further testing of his forty-year commitment to celibacy in order to discover the defect at the root of his "unfitness."

So also on that same day, hours before announcing at his evening prayer meeting his new plan to tour the district walking through its harvested paddy fields and over its rickety bamboo bridges, he sent a telegram to a nephew, Jaisukhlal Gandhi, whose young daughter Manu had nursed the Mahatma's wife nearly three years earlier as she faded from life in detention and finally died of heart failure. Now a shy and unaffected seventeen with an appearance that could not be called striking, the devoted Manu had become a favorite pen pal of Gandhi, who coaxed and cajoled her to rejoin his entourage, all the while insisting he only wanted what was best for her. The telegram to her father was oddly worded. It said: "IF YOU AND MANU SINCERELY ANXIOUS FOR HER TO BE WITH ME AT YOUR RISK, YOU CAN BRING HER."

Gandhi made it sound as if he were giving way to the wishes of father and daughter. In fact, he'd planted the idea himself and cultivated it in an epistolary campaign spanning months. "Manu's place can be nowhere else but here by my side," he'd written. It soon became obvious that the Noakhali Gandhi was now bent on making his young relative his primary personal attendant, the person who'd monitor his daily schedule, see that he was fed exactly what he wanted, measured out precisely in ounces (eight ounces boiled vegetables, eight ounces raw vegetables, two ounces greens, sixteen ounces goat's milk boiled down to four ounces), at exactly the desired time; not only that, the person who'd administer his daily bath and massage, which could take longer than an hour and a half. An ounce of mustard oil and an ounce of lemon juice had to be mixed for the massage, which proceeded "in exactly the same manner every day," according to a memoir Nirmal Bose later wrote: "first one part of the body, then another . . . in invariable succession."

Even that could be considered just the beginning. It turned out that Manu Gandhi would also be expected to play the female lead in the brahmacharya test the Mahatma now saw as essential to his self-purification. Starting in the late 1930s, he'd had female attendants sleep on bedrolls laid out to the side of his; if he experienced tremors or shivers, as sometimes he did, they'd be expected to embrace him until the shaking stopped. Now he planned to have Manu share the same mattress. Perfection would be achieved if the old man and the young woman wore the fewest possible garments, preferably none, and neither one felt the slightest sexual stirring. A perfect brahmachari, he later wrote in a letter, should be "capable of lying naked with naked women, however beautiful they may be, without being in any manner whatsoever sexually aroused." Such a man would be completely free from anger and malice.

Sexlessness was the ideal for which he was striving. His relation to Manu, he told her, would be essentially that of a mother. None of this would go on in secret; other members of his entourage might share the same veranda or room.

What's important here is less Gandhi's belief in the spiritual power to be derived from perfect, serene celibacy than the relation of his striving for self-purification to his lonely mission in Noakhali. Where could the real motivation be located, in his gnawing sense of failure for which a ratcheting up of his brahmacharya might provide healing, or in his need for a human connection, if not the intimacy he'd long since forsworn? There's no obvious answer, except to say the struggle was at the core of his being and that it had never been more anguishing than it was in Srirampur. The two most conspicuous elements of his life there—the mission and the spiritual striving—are usually treated as separate matters. But, here again, they were happening simultaneously, crowding in on each other: in Gandhi's own mind, inextricably connected to the point of being one and the same.

The immediate effect of his summons to Manu was a cascading emotional crisis in his own inner circle, all taking place in the obscurity and shade of mostly Muslim Srirampur but soon seeping into public view. Plainly, the starting point was within Gandhi himself, in his sense that doctrine and mission were failing. "I don't want to return from Bengal defeated," he remarked to a friend a few days after the summons to Manu. "I would rather die, if need be, at the hands of an assassin. But I do not want to court it, much less wish it."

He'd cleared the decks for her arrival by dispatching his closest associates—notably Pyarelal, his secretary, and Pyarelal's sister, Dr. Sushila Nayar—to workstations in other villages. Sushila had previously played the part for which Manu was now being recruited. Back in 1938, Gandhi had tried out a young Jewish woman from Palestine named Hannah Lazar, a niece of Hermann Kallenbach's, who'd trained in massage. "Of course she knows her art," he wrote to her uncle in Johannesburg. "But she can't all of a sudden equal the touch of Sushila who is a competent doctor and who learned massage especially for treating me." Here Gandhi sounds more like a discriminating pasha with a harem than the ascetic he genuinely was.

Now, more than eight years after this letter and just six days after his summons to Manu, Gandhi told Sushila that it would remain her duty to stay in her village—in other words, that she'd not be included on his walking tour, because Manu would be taking care of his most personal needs. Nirmal Bose, who was standing just outside, heard "a deeply anguished cry proceeding from the main room . . . [followed by] two large slaps given on someone's body. The cry then sank down into a heavy sob." When Bose got to the doorway, both Gandhi and Sushila were "bathed in tears." The cries and heavy sob had been the Mahatma's, he realized. Three days later, while bathing Gandhi for what appears to have been the last time, Bose summoned the courage to ask him whether he'd slapped Sushila. "Gandhiji's face wore a sad smile," Bose wrote in his memoir, "and he said, 'No, I did not beat her. I beat my own forehead.' " That same evening, on December 20, 1946, with Manu beside him in his bed for the first time, Gandhi began his supposed yajna, or self-sacrifice, sometimes termed an "experiment" by him.

With Manu, his "walking stick"

"Stick to your word," he wrote in a note to Manu that day. "Don't hide even a single thought from me . . . Have it engraved in your heart that whatever I ask or say will be solely for your good."

Within ten days, Gandhi's stenographer, a young South Indian named Parsuram, quit in protest over his revered leader's nightly cuddle with Manu, which he couldn't fail to have witnessed. Instead of questioning Gandhi's explanation of its spiritual purpose, he registered a political complaint—that the inevitable reports and gossip would alienate public opinion. His argument didn't impress the Mahatma. "I like your frankness and boldness," he wrote to the young man after reading his ten-page letter of resignation. "You are at liberty to publish whatever wrong you have noticed in me and my surroundings." Later he scolded Bose for glossing over in his Bengali interpretation his attempt at one of his prayer meetings to offer a frank public account of the latest test he'd set for himself.

Pyarelal was also drawn into this emotional maelstrom, and not simply because he was partial to his sister. He'd had a crush on Manu himself. Gandhi now promised to keep his secretary at a distance if Manu "does not want even to see him." He could testify to his aide's good character. "Pyarelal's eyes are clean," he wrote to Manu's father a week before she was scheduled to reach Noakhali, "and he is not likely to force himself on anybody." Gandhi then writes to Pyarelal urging him to keep his distance. "I can see that you will not be able to have Manu as a wife," says the revered figure who is now bedding down next to her on a nightly basis. Self-purification, it was already clear, could not be attempted in this world without complications.

Nirmal Bose, the detached Calcutta intellectual serving as Gandhi's Bengali interpreter, wasn't initially judgmental about Gandhi's reliance on Manu. But his allegiance was gradually strained as he observed Gandhi's manipulative way of managing the emotional ripples that ran through his entourage at a moment of national and personal crisis. He felt the Mahatma, in his preoccupation with the feelings of Pyarelal and his sister, was allowing himself to get distracted. "After a life of prolonged brahmacharya," Bose wrote in his diary, "he has become incapable of understanding the problems of love or sex as they exist in the common human plane." So Bose took it upon himself, in conversation and several long letters over the next three months, to acquaint his master with the psychoanalytic concepts of the subconscious, neurosis, and repression. Gandhi jumped on a single passing reference to Freud in one of Bose's letters. He'd read Havelock Ellis and Bertrand Russell on sex but not Freud. It was only the second time, he wrote back, that he'd heard the name. "What is Freudian philosophy?" asked the Mahatma, ever curious. "I have not read any writing of his."

Bose's basic point was made more bluntly in his diary and a letter to a friend than in his correspondence with the Mahatma. It was that Gandhi had allowed himself to use his bedmates as instruments in an experiment undertaken for his own sake and that he thus risked leaving "a mark of injury on personalities of others who are not of the same moral stature . . . and for whom sharing in Gandhiji's experiment is no spiritual necessity." He thought Manu might be an exception but wasn't sure. Despite his restraint, Gandhi got the point. "I do hope you will acquit me of having any lustful designs upon women or girls who have been naked with me," he wrote back. That was the one count on which the Freudian in Bose felt certain of Gandhi's innocence.

Feeling himself to have been distanced by his own frankness, Bose came to doubt he could be of much further use to Gandhi. Finally he asked to be relieved of his duties. In a valedictory letter, he said he saw signs that the Mahatma had, in fact, begun to attain the level of concentrated personal force for which he'd been reaching in these months: "I saw your strength come back in flashes when you rose to heights no one else has reached in our national life."

A week after Gandhi established his grandniece Manu in his household and bed, the urgency and weight of the constitutional crisis in New Delhi descended on the remote village of Srirampur, brought there on a visit of two and a half days by Nehru, now head of an "interim government" still subject to the British viceroy, and Nehru's successor as Congress president, J. B. Kripalani, a follower of Gandhi's for three decades. Given that the Congress president's wife, Sucheta, had shared the Mahatma's bed with him and Manu on one recent night, there was no need for Gandhi to brief his visitors on the yajna he'd just undertaken. According to one account, Nehru himself came to the doorway of the room where Gandhi and Manu slept on his first night in Srirampur; having looked in, he silently stepped away. The sketchy account does not record whether he raised his eyebrows or shook his head.

In the following month, Gandhi would seek to explain his quest to both men in letters. Neither wanted to sit in judgment on the Mahatma. "I can never be disillusioned about you unless I find the marks of insanity and depravity in you," Kripalani replied. "I do not find such marks." Nehru was even more reticent. "I feel a little out of my depth and I hate discussing personal and private matters," he wrote to a mentor he revered but frequently found perplexing, even troublesome.

Gandhi had first singled Nehru out as a Congress leader in 1928 and, while acknowledging conspicuous differences in outlook, had been openly calling him "my heir and successor" since 1934 when he made a show of giving up his own Congress membership. "Jawaharlal is the only man with the drive to take my place," he remarked five years later. For all his doting on Nehru, this was a practical political judgment based on two obvious factors—Nehru's demonstrated mass appeal and tendency in a crisis to bend to the Mahatma's view. He knew his heir would never score high on any checklist of Gandhian values, that the younger man, more a Fabian than a Gandhian, could be expected to promote state planning and nationalized industries over the sort of village-level reconstruction he'd always advocated, that there was little question in his mind about the need for a modern military establishment in a future Indian state. But he waved aside such contradictions, treating them as matters of emphasis. "He says what is uppermost in his mind," Gandhi

With his chosen "successor," 1946

observed in 1938, in a comment as revealing of himself as it was of Nehru, "but he always does what I want. When I am gone he will do what I am doing now. Then he will speak my language."

Later he got closer to the truth, perhaps, when he said of Nehru: "He has made me captive of his love."

But now—with the Noakhali Gandhi out of touch and power shifting rapidly into his hands—Nehru, by inclination as well as necessity, was speaking his own language and listening less. The ostensible point of his journey to Srirampur had been to update Gandhi on a resolution he planned to put before the party the next week, further locking it into a process that could lead to partition and Pakistan; also, Nehru said, it was to urge Gandhi to put Noakhali behind him and return to Delhi so he could be more easily consulted and—this would have gone without saying—privately implored not to stray too far from the emerging party line.

The Mahatma's appetite for grappling with national issues was tickled, but he wasn't tempted to return. He said there was still work to be done in Noakhali; by his own reckoning, his mission there would remain unfinished until the day he died. More compelling was his sense that he'd lost the ability to influence his erstwhile followers, as he'd recently complained in a note to the industrialist G. D. Birla. "My voice," the note said, "carries no weight in the Working Committee . . . I do not like the shape that things are taking and I can't speak out."

Such misgivings, however, didn't stop him from sending Nehru back with "instructions." The document, drafted late on Nehru's last night in Srirampur, pointed in several directions at once. Basically, it said Gandhi had been right in suggesting the Congress reject the British plan; that now that it had failed to heed his advice, it was stuck with the plan; that therefore it needed an accord with Jinnah giving him "a universally acceptable and inoffensive formula for his Pakistan," so long as no territories were compelled to be part of it.

The phrase "acceptable and inoffensive" was telling. It pointed in more or less the same direction as Nehru's unusually dense resolution, which all but smothered its essential acceptance of an unpalatable British formula with a blanket of technicalities, exceptions, and complaints. Between the lines, both Gandhi's "instructions" and Nehru's resolution pointed to the quickest deal for independence, on the best available terms, with the fewest possible concessions to the Muslim League. Obviously, Gandhi meant "acceptable" and "inoffensive" to the Congress and himself, not Jinnah and his followers; he didn't say how that could be accomplished. On one level, he hadn't budged from the position he'd taken when Jinnah broke off talks with him two years earlier. On another, he'd shown that he'd do nothing to delay a handover of power even if it involved two recipients instead of one.

Nehru's resolution was adopted the next week by the All India Congress Committee by something less than acclamation, a vote of 99–52. When a member asked to know Gandhi's advice, Kripalani snapped that it was "irrelevant at this stage," not bothering to cite the woolly "instructions" the Mahatma had written out for Nehru, who'd flown to East Bengal, it seems likely, partly to ensure that Gandhi wouldn't come out on the other side. Gandhi himself had been pleased to paper over his most recent breach with the leadership. "I suggest frequent consultations with an old, tried servant of the nation," he'd written in a fond farewell note to Nehru.

Just two days later, on the second day of the new year, he pulled up stakes in Srirampur and left on his walking tour of Noakhali, with one hand clutching a bamboo staff and the other resting on Manu's shoulder. He was barefoot and would continue without sandals every step of the way for the next two months. In the mornings, the pilgrim's feet were sometimes numbed by cold; on one occasion at least, they bled. Nightly they were pressed and massaged with oil. Srirampur's Muslim villagers lined the path that circled Darikanath pond, a well-stocked fishery, that first morning; a crowd of about a hundred walked in his footsteps, with a detachment of eight armed police and at least as many reporters. The next morning headlines in Calcutta's Indian-owned, pro-Congress, English-language daily, the *Amrita Bazar Patrika*, heralded the launch:

GANDHIJI'S EPIC
TOUR BEGINS

HISTORIC MARCH THROUGH
PADDY FIELDS AND
GREEN GROVES

GANDHIJI LIKELY
TO WORK
MIRACLE

The newspaper kept the tour on its front page every day but one for the next six weeks, conveying the authorized versions of Gandhi's nightly prayer meeting talks. Too early by a matter of decades to have made great television, it faded as a big story elsewhere. So the loneliness and vicissitudes of the trek never really registered beyond Bengal. After the first few days, the crowds dwindled, with Muslims once again conspicuous by their absence. This time there could be little doubt that elements in the Muslim League were promoting a boycott. In the second month, handbills started appearing urging Gandhi to focus on Bihar, amplifying the theme of most Muslim officials he encountered. "Remember Bihar," one said. "We've warned you many times. Go back. Otherwise, you'll be sorry." Obviously meant for his eyes, another said: "Give up your hypocrisy and accept Pakistan."

On some mornings, Gandhi's companions would find that human feces had been deposited, dumped, or spread on paths he could be expected to walk. On his way to a village called Atakora, the old man himself stooped over and started scooping up excrement with dried leaves. A flustered Manu protested that he was putting her to shame. "You don't know the joy it gives me," the Mahatma, now seventy-seven, replied.

In fifty-seven days, he visited forty-seven villages in Noakhali and a neighboring district called Tipperah, trudging 116 miles, barefoot all the way, in order to touch Muslims' hearts through a personal demonstration of his own openheartedness and simplicity. He called it a "pilgrimage." Sometimes he said it was a "penance," for the slaughter Hindus and Muslims had recently inflicted on each other, or his own failure to end it. He greeted every Muslim he passed, even where most of them stolidly refrained from responding. Only three times, in all those days and weeks, all those villages, was he invited to stay in a Muslim home. His followers prefabricated a tidy hut of bamboo panels to be disassembled on a daily basis and, with each new village, reassembled for his comfort. He complained it was "palatial." When he learned it took seven porters to carry his collapsible shelter, he refused to sleep in it, insisting it be converted into a dispensary. If Muslims stayed away from his prayer meetings, he pursued them in their houses and huts. In each new village, Manu was dispatched to call on Muslim women in seclusion. Sometimes she managed to persuade them to meet the Mahatma,

January 1947, bones of Noakhali victims on display for the Mahatma

In his mobile hut, November 1946

sometimes doors were slammed in her face. When young Muslim Leaguers came to his meetings to heckle, he turned back their sharp questions
with calm, reasoned replies.

"How did your ahimsa work in Bihar?" he was pointedly asked in a
village called Paniala.

"It didn't work at all," he replied. "It failed miserably."

"What in your opinion is the cause of the communal riots?" another
asked.

"The idiocy of both communities," said the Mahatma.

Twice in nine weeks, he's brought to exposed human remains left over
from the killings. The first time, on November 11, a stray dog leads him
to the skeletons of the members of a single Hindu household; then, on
January 11, he passes by a *doba*, or pond, that has finally been dragged to
retrieve the bodies of Hindus killed in the earliest and ugliest of these
pogroms at Karpara.

The Mahatma moved on briskly. "It is useless to think about those who are dead," he said. His aim was less to console bereaved Hindus than to stiffen their spines while touching the hearts of Muslims who'd looked away from the carnage, or even approved it. He could only demonstrate his good intentions "by living and moving among those who do not trust me," he said. So every morning, he trudged on, regardless of the reception he encountered. His followers sang religious songs, always including one by Tagore with a Bengali poem called "Walk Alone" as its lyric. Occasionally there was a welcome, occasionally a large crowd. In the fourth week, at a village called Muriam, a warm reception from Muslims was orchestrated by a friendly maulana named Habibullah Batari who, if Pyarelal's account can be accepted, introduced him by saying: "Our community today suffers from the stigma of shedding the blood of our Hindu brothers. Mahatmaji has come to free us of that stain." For Gandhi, this was proof of the possibilities before him and the country. But it was hardly an everyday occurrence. At Panchgaon, four days later, he was urged by the head of the local Muslim League to discontinue his prayer meetings because they offended Muslims and, better yet, end his Noakhali tour altogether.

At the prayer meetings, he'd size up his audiences, then draw familiar themes and messages from the repertoire of a lifetime. If seeking to make the point that he and the village workers he brought with him had come not to sit in judgment but to serve, he'd dwell on all that could be done to improve sanitation and the cleanliness of the district's water. Speaking of lost livelihoods, he'd talk about crafts and what they could do for village uplift. On the fraught, overarching issue of land tenure, he'd say the land belonged to God and those who actually worked it, that reduction in the landlord's share of crops was therefore only just, with the Gandhian proviso that it had to be accomplished without violence.

The value he upheld most insistently was fearlessness. To insure peace, he said, Muslims and Hindus had to be ready to die. It's the message he'd given Czechs and European Jews in the previous decade about how to face the Nazis, the idea that a courageous satyagrahi could "melt the heart" of a tyrant. Repeatedly he asked that the police guards Suhrawardy had sent be withdrawn so as not to weaken the example he was hoping to set through his pilgrimage. (The guards never left. Suhrawardy said it was the government's responsibility to make sure the Mahatma got out of East Bengal alive.) Early on he talked about martyrdom: "The sacrifice of myself and my companions would at least teach [Hindu women] the art of dying with self-respect. It might open the eyes of the oppressors, too." To a refugee who asked how he could expect

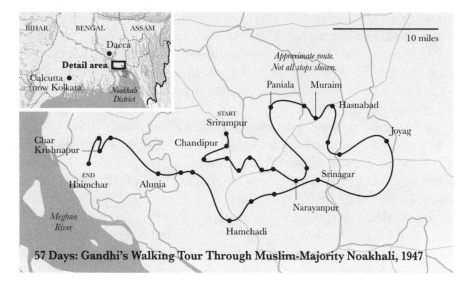

BIHAR   BENGAL   ASSAM
Dacca
Detail area □
Calcutta ●
(now Kolkata)   *Noakhali District*

Approximate route. Not all stops shown.

10 miles

Paniala   Muraim
Hasnabad
START
Srirampur   Joyag
Char Krishnapur   Chandipur
END
Haimchar   Alunia   Srinagar
Meghna River   Narayanpur
Hamchadi

57 Days: Gandhi's Walking Tour Through Muslim-Majority Noakhali, 1947

Hindus to return to villages where they might face attack, he replied: "I do not mind if each and every one of the five hundred families in your area is done to death." Before arriving in Noakhali, he'd struck a similar note speaking to a trio of Gandhian workers who were planning to precede him: "There will be no tears but only joy if tomorrow I get the news that all three of you were killed."

Not infrequently in these months, Gandhi comes across as sounding this extreme, very nearly the fanatic he'd sometimes been accused of being. We may assume it's a figure of speech, not meant to be taken literally. But even Manu isn't immune from his determination to teach that his kind of courage in the cause of peace could be—sometimes had to be—as fierce and selfless as any shown on a battlefield.

On reaching a village called Narayanpur in the third week of the walking tour, Gandhi couldn't find a piece of pumice he used to scrape his feet before soaking them. He'd last used it at a weaver's hut where he'd stopped to warm his chilled feet. Evidently, Manu had left the stone behind. This was a "major error," Gandhi said sternly, ordering her to retrace their steps and find it, which meant following a path through thick jungle in an area where assaults on young women were not unknown. When she asked if she could take a couple of volunteers, Gandhi refused. She had to go alone. The weaver's wife had tossed the stone out, not knowing that the Mahatma counted it as precious. When Manu finally recovered it and returned, Pyarelal tells us, she burst into tears, only to be met by Gandhi's cackle. To him, her afternoon's ordeal was part of their mutual "test."

"If some ruffian had carried you off and you had met your death courageously," he told her, "my heart would have danced with joy. But I would have felt humiliated and unhappy if you had turned back or run away from danger."

Speaking to dispossessed caste Hindus, he was hardly more tender. They needed to understand, he evidently felt, that their privileges and vices had something to do with their present misery. Those who don't labor but live on the toil of others are thieves, he said. It's surprising to discover how often he harps on the evil of untouchability when talking to the Noakhali refugees. He even makes collections there for his Harijan fund. Given that he's speaking to caste Hindus who have recently been burned out of their homesteads in strife with Muslims, it seems, at first, inappropriate, an old man's non sequitur. But untouchability had long since become for Gandhi a metaphor for all forms of social oppression involving "high" and "low." If caste Hindus resist dining and intermarriage with Muslims, he's now prepared to say, they're practicing a form of untouchability; in the back of his mind, he may have harbored the thought that many Muslims descended from untouchables who converted. "He had told us time and again," Pyarelal later wrote, "that the Hindu-Muslim question had its roots in untouchability."

After many years of verbal tiptoeing, it seems, he has ceased to speak in code or measure his words on issues of social equality. It's the end of the long intellectual and political journey that began in Durban when he first had the thought that whites treated Indians the way Indians treated one another, as untouchables. Asked what it would take to heal the rift between Muslims and the mainly Hindu Congress, he replied: "Giving equality to the untouchables." What sounds like a riddle is his way of saying what Ambedkar had been saying all along—that the disease in Hindu society starts with the practices of caste Hindus.

On the second day of his Noakhali walking tour, he addresses a gathering of Hindu women in Chandipur. Just as he once traced an earthquake to God's displeasure over untouchability, he now ascribes the Noakhali calamity to the same transgression. According to the authorized summary of his talk that is more than likely the result of his own rewriting, he said:

> If they still went on disowning the untouchables, more sorrow was in
> store for them. He asked the audience to invite a Harijan every day to

dine with them. If they could not do so, they could call a Harijan before taking a meal and ask him to touch the drinking water or food . . . Unless they did penance for their sins . . . more calamities and more severe ones would overtake them.

The next week he twice urges the Muslim majority of the district not to treat Hindus as untouchables. A month later, still in Noakhali, he's calling for a casteless society. In Kamalapur, he's challenged to say how he feels about intercommunal marriages if he now condones intercaste unions. According to Bose's paraphrase, he responds: "He has not always held this view [but] had long come to the conclusion that an inter-religious marriage was a welcome event whenever it took place." So long, he couldn't refrain from adding, as it wasn't inspired by lust.

As the tour proceeds, Muslims mostly keep a distance. Those who come to the prayer meetings are typically impassive. As described by Phillips Talbot, they "listened quietly to the after-prayer talk, and then went away." The young American wondered if he was witnessing a subtle shift from opposition to "neutral silence." Had he stayed with Gandhi a few weeks more, he'd have had to give up that thin hope. Increasingly, with the tightening of Muslim boycotts—not only of Gandhi's meetings but of Hindu landowners and fishmongers and merchants—the Mahatma finds himself speaking to Hindus on what might be considered Hindu themes. On February 22 he pitches up at a place called Char Krishnapur, a spit of an island in the delta where his audience is predominantly made up of untouchables, called Namasudras in Bengali. As poor as the poorest Muslim peasants, they'd suffered as much as the richest Hindu landlords during the riots. There Gandhi stayed in "a low-roof shelter improvised from charred, corrugated sheets salvaged from a burnt-down homestead." In Haimchar, which turned out to be his last stop, he told Namasudras they needed to lift themselves up by their own efforts; for a start, they could do away with child marriage and promiscuity, so that "the higher castes so-called would be ashamed of their sin against them."

He'd already mapped out the next stage of his village tour, but here, finally, he felt compelled to come to grips with rising criticism on two fronts, one being his own camp and the other Muslim Leaguers. Though little was said in public, Gandhi's own circle was in turmoil over the brahmacharya test: perhaps even more than the nightly cuddle itself, his readiness to defend it openly, as he had in the first three days of February. Muslim Leaguers continued to harp on his stubborn refusal over four months to go to Hindu-dominated Bihar, where Muslims had been the victims. On the surface, the two issues seem unconnected, but it's probably no coincidence that they come to a head in his mind at very nearly the same moment, for in his own mind they'd always been linked.

In Haimchar, Gandhi spends six days with A. V. Thakkar, called Thakkar Bapa, another aging Gujarati, who'd been his closest and most respected co-worker on issues of untouchability. The two old men debate Gandhi's sleeping arrangements, which Thakkar closely observes on a nightly basis. Thakkar is finally persuaded that the yajna has spiritual meaning for the Mahatma but writes what Gandhi later dismisses as "a pathetic letter" to Manu urging her to withdraw from the "experiment," presumably for Gandhi's sake and that of the movement. According to a less than disinterested Pyarelal, Manu then tells Gandhi she sees "no harm in conceding Thakkar Bapa's request for the time being." Angry and unrepentant, Gandhi blames Manu's "lack of perspicacity," we're told by his biographer who is also her disappointed suitor. Conceding nothing, the Mahatma agrees to let her leave his bed. The yajna is suspended, if not over, and so, simultaneously, is the Noakhali walking tour.

Almost at once, he decides to break it off. He'd said he was prepared to spend years in Noakhali and "if necessary, I will die here." But on March 2, 1947, he donned sandals for the first time in two months, since the start of the walking tour, and began the reverse journey toward Bihar.

For four months he'd been fending off appeals from Muslims across India to prove his good faith by confronting the violence Hindus had wrought. His excuses for not going there earlier had come to sound increasingly far-fetched. He'd long since recognized that the Bihar violence had been far worse than that of Bengal. It was now early March, four months after Nehru had been so appalled by the carnage he'd witnessed in Bihar that he'd threatened to order the bombing of Hindu mobs there. Now, all of a sudden, Gandhi finally allowed himself to be moved by a letter from a nationalist Muslim saying that his Congress had done as little to address the violence there as the Muslim League had in East Bengal.

He promised he'd return to keep his commitments in Noakhali. In the months left to him, he kept that trip near the top of his ever-lengthening to-do list. But with partition looming and Hindu-Muslim slaughter spreading like an epidemic across North India—perhaps more like a wildfire, since it burned in some places and skipped over others—

he faced new demands for the balm of his presence. Noakhali kept having to be put off.

At the midpoint of the tour, there'd been a foreshadowing that would later be recalled as fateful. Gandhi had run out of goat's milk and had to take coconut milk instead. Later that evening the stressed-out old man experienced severe diarrhea, started sweating heavily, and finally fainted. That was January 30, 1947. If he died of disease, he told Manu on regaining consciousness, it would prove he'd been a hypocrite. So Manu later wrote in a memoir. She then has him saying: "But if I leave the world with the name of Rama on my lips, only then am I a true brahmachari, a real Mahatma." So it is written in her gospel. Exactly a year later, on January 30, 1948, when he fell at her side, she'd recall these words as a prophecy fulfilled.

By any secular, this-worldly accounting of Gandhi's months in Noakhali district, it would be hard to show a political or social gain. The rupture he hoped to forestall occurred. Pakistan happened. By June 1948, more than one million Hindu refugees had crossed the new international border into the Indian rump state of West Bengal. In the next three years, that number doubled; by 1970, the total of refugees from East Bengal resettled in India exceeded five million. "The makers of the shell bangles that were obligatory ornaments for married Hindu women, the weavers of the fine silks and cottons worn by well-to-do Hindus, the potters who fashioned idols used in Hindu festivals, and the priests and astrologers who presided over Hindu rituals of birth, marriage and death were among the earliest migrants," according to the scholar Joya Chatterji. They'd fled in hot pursuit of the gentry and townsmen who'd employed them. The social order Gandhi had been willing to give his life to reconcile and reform had been—to use his word—"vivisected." Yet partition, as he predicted, had resolved little. It led to a division of land, spoils, and political authority, but majorities on each side of the new Bengal had to coexist with a substantial minority. Though a military government had proclaimed contemporary Bangladesh an Islamic republic, it still contained twelve million Hindus.

And, somehow, Gandhi still seems to register there as a possible source of inspiration. A lifetime after he left Noakhali, I found myself in Dhaka, the capital of this Islamic republic, at a well-attended commemorative gathering of intellectuals and ardent social reformers marking the 140th anniversary of his birth. The minister of law lit a lamp. Verses from the Koran were read, followed by a passage from the Bhagavad Gita, then Buddhist and Christian prayers, making the event as self-consciously inclusive as Gandhi's own prayer meetings. Five Muslims and three Hindus spoke—against religious extremism and for harmony, the rule of law, clean politics, rural development, social equality—dwelling not on the Raj and Gandhi's time but on today's teeming Bangladesh. A half-dozen TV crews recorded their remarks for the evening news, cameras sweeping across the audience, to pick out upturned faces that could be read as inspired. "The fact is that such a man of flesh was born on our subcontinent and we are his descendants," said a woman introduced as a human rights advocate. "I feel his necessity every moment." The gathering ended with one of Gandhi's favorite devotional songs, sweetly sung by a small, evenly balanced group of Hindu and Muslim students, with most of the audience joining in.

As I said, by any secular accounting, it would be difficult to show a political or social gain from Gandhi's four months in Noakhali district, near the end of his life in 1946 and 1947. Yet this happened in 2009.

12

DO OR DIE

EVERYWHERE HE WENT he was urged to go somewhere else. In East Bengal's Noakhali district, where Hindus had been slaughtered, Muslim Leaguers pressed Gandhi to take his pilgrimage off to Bihar and prove there that he was willing to confront a Hindu majority with blood on its hands. Once he finally reached Bihar, Hindu nationalists tried to divert him to the Punjab, where Hindus and Sikhs were being terrorized out of Muslim-majority portions of the province, soon to be sliced off and stitched into a gestating Pakistan. Eventually, with less than two weeks to go to partition and independence, an overstretched and agitated Mahatma popped up in the Punjab and, speaking in Lahore on August 6, 1947, offered perhaps the most surprising of his absolute, flat-out vows. Having said he'd do or die" in Noakhali, then in Bihar, the man who'd ever after be called "Father of the Nation" now promised: "The rest of my life is going to be spent in Pakistan."

He'd been yearning to come to the Punjab, he explained, but now had to rush clear across the subcontinent, all the way back to Noakhali, for he'd committed himself to marking India's independence there on August 15. That's to say, on the day of independent India's birth, he meant to awaken in Pakistan. "I would go there even if I have to die," he said. "But as soon as I am free from Noakhali, I will come to the Punjab."

His head was evidently spinning as, careering bravely from Hindu pillar to Muslim post, he contemplated the impending "vivisection." The only way he could cling to the dream of a united India he'd spun decades earlier on the other side of the Indian Ocean, in Durban and Johannesburg, was to declare that henceforth he'd have two homelands. Perhaps one day they'd be reunited, but for now, obviously, he couldn't be everywhere. This was precisely the point the Congress president, Kripalani, had mournfully made back on June 15, the day Gandhi's movement had put its final seal of approval on the partition plan over his muted objections. He'd followed the Mahatma for thirty years, Kripalani said, but couldn't go any further. He still felt "that he, with his supreme fearlessness, is correct, and my stand [in favor of partition] is defective," but simply didn't see how Gandhi's noble efforts in Bihar could save the Punjab. "Today he himself is groping in the dark . . . Unfortunately for us today though he can enunciate policies, they have in the main to be carried out by others, and these others are not converted to his way of thinking."

That said it all, but Gandhi carried on. His pledge to return to the Punjab and spend the rest of his life in Pakistan had to be diluted two days later in Patna when he promised to return to Bihar after a few weeks in Noakhali. In fact, none of these promises would be kept. Gandhi was now in the final half year of his life. He would never reach Noakhali, never return to Bihar or the Punjab, never set foot in independent Pakistan. In these final months, his view took in the whole subcontinent, but his field of endeavor was limited to two cities. First in Calcutta, then in Delhi, he managed almost single-handedly to roll back tides of violence by embarking on his final fasts "unto death." He was never more heroic, never more a miracle worker, but the Punjab, acting out Kripalani's anxious premonition, still burned with horrendous mass violence: Sikhs and Hindus slaughtering Muslims in the eastern portion of the province, now India; Muslims butchering Hindus and Sikhs, seizing their women, sacking their temples, in West Punjab, now Pakistan. Gandhi's theory that inspired peacemaking in one place could prove contagious, dousing explosions of extreme violence in others, would not be borne out until an exhausted subcontinent had to contemplate the fact of his death. By then, hundreds of thousands had been slain, millions displaced.

"The country was partitioned in order to avoid Hindu-Muslim rioting," Rammanohar Lohia, a Socialist leader, would later write. "Partition produced that which it was intended to avoid in such abundance that one may forever despair of man's intelligence or integrity."

The Mahatma had no elixir other than his presence, his example. Wherever he traveled, his basic strategy was to revive the courage of besieged and vulnerable minorities while shaming and coaxing marauding majorities back to some elementary level of reason, if not compassion. If he'd lived to go to Pakistan, he'd have extended his protection, such as it was, over the Hindu minority. Since his last months came to be spent in what would remain India, it was the Muslim minority that cried out for his moral shield. Circumstances thus cast him as pro-Muslim in the eyes of dispossessed and enraged Hindu and Sikh refugees pouring in from what was becoming Pakistan, in the eyes of Hindu chauvinists generally. Playing the part for which his whole life had prepared him, Gandhi now helped frame the death warrant under which he'd long felt himself to be laboring.

To those charged with the main business of extracting the British and establishing the new states, the Mahatma's successive, overlapping pilgrimages registered mainly as a sideshow. An impatient Nehru said he was "going round with ointment trying to heal one sore spot after another on the body of India." When the partition plan came up for final Congress approval, Nehru was so concerned that Gandhi might break ranks that he had his right-hand man, Krishna Menon, seek the help of Lord Mountbatten, the last viceroy. The Mahatma was in an emotional, unpredictable frame of mind, Menon warned in the first week of June.

The viceroy then made sure to see Gandhi before he next spoke in public at a prayer meeting. A pressing invitation was sent for him to come to the Viceregal Lodge, a 340-room imperial pile in contrasting shades of red sandstone—which the Mahatma had recently proposed turning into a hospital—for what became a virtuoso recital by this great-grandson of Queen Victoria, the first empress of India. The courtly Mountbatten used all the charm and flattery at his command to persuade his guest that the plan was actually a composite of Gandhi's own ideas about non-coercion and self-determination, assuring what he had long sought—the earliest possible departure of the British. Really, the viceroy said, it should be called not the Mountbatten Plan but "the Gandhi Plan." Gandhi must have known this massage was meant for his ego. But it eased the tension he'd been feeling. That evening at his prayer meeting, he said the viceroy was as much opposed to partition as the Congress. Since Hindus and Muslims couldn't agree, the viceroy had "no choice." If this was less than a green light, it was his way of saying proceed with caution.

In using Mountbatten to get to Gandhi in this way on June 4, Nehru might have reflected that Gandhi had regularly dealt with viceroys and other colonial envoys without bothering to consult his own colleagues.

As recently as April 1, Gandhi had "staggered" the newly arrived Mountbatten at their second meeting with the idea of offering Mohammed Ali Jinnah an opportunity to serve as head of the interim government in order to pry him loose from his fixation on Pakistan, long enough, at least, to avoid partition. Jinnah, in this scheme, would be free to include only members of the Muslim League. The corollary that this might have meant sending Congress into the wilderness didn't particularly disturb Gandhi, who'd have considered that a small price to pay for the country's unity, not to mention an opportunity for the movement to renew itself, finally, at its neglected grass roots as he'd been imploring it to do for two decades. It was part of Gandhi's proposal, according to Mountbatten's later reminiscences, that it would be the viceroy, not himself, who'd broach the scheme to Nehru and the other Congress leaders. Mountbatten, understandably, declined to serve as the Mahatma's nuncio. By the time he and Nehru touched on the plan, the viceroy had already been told by his advisers that it was "an old kite" Gandhi had flown before, an idea Jinnah had never taken seriously. Nehru's reaction was openly dismissive. He told the viceroy, with whom he was developing a more confidential relationship than any he had with his colleagues, that Gandhi "had been away for four months and was rapidly getting out of touch."

Gandhi drafted a nine-point summary of his plan. This would be the last of countless petitions and diplomatic notes and aide-mémoire he laid before British colonial authorities on three continents over half a century. Then he had to confess to Mountbatten what Mountbatten already knew: that his idea had attracted next to no support from the Congress high command. "Thus I have to ask you to omit me from your consideration," he wrote abjectly, meaning he now lacked the influence to be considered someone who had to be consulted.

When the viceroy first heard Gandhi's audacious suggestion, he asked what Jinnah would say. "If you tell him I am the author, he will reply, 'Wily Gandhi,' " he predicted. That's close to what Jinnah did say. It's not refuted by what Gandhi himself had to say to the viceroy, if Mountbatten's paraphrase more than two decades after the fact can be accepted as somewhat accurate, rather than written off as a snippet of stray embroidery, a misattributed surmise. "Jinnah won't be able to do very much," Gandhi is supposed to have said, "because in effect you can't coerce a majority by executive acts at the center and he'd have less power than he will think he's going to get." The catch in Gandhi's "wily" scheme had all along been that his imagined Jinnah government would inevitably be responsible to an assembly with a Congress majority that could check it and, eventually, bring it down.

The day after bowing out in his letter to Mountbatten, Gandhi returned to Bihar, where he'd spent scarcely three weeks on his earlier visit. He'd arrived in Bihar late, four months after the worst bloodshed, but found scant signs of remorse among most Hindus, including most congressmen, until he started preaching on themes of repentance, atonement, and unity. Often the killings, he was told, had been accompanied by cries of *"Mahatma Gandhi ki jai!"*—"Glory to Mahatma Gandhi!"

"I hate to hear *Jai* shouts," he said. "They stink in my nostrils when I think that to the shouting of these *Jais*, Hindus massacred innocent men and women, just as Muslims killed Hindus to the shouting of *Allah-o-akbar!* ['God is great!']."

On his second swing through Bihar he managed to stay another two weeks before being summoned back to the capital. His moral authority had perhaps never been higher, but his political isolation couldn't be ignored, leading him to feel, not for the first time, that his career as an active leader might have reached its terminus. The thought still didn't sit easily in his mind. He called himself a "spent bullet" and a "back number." He was now afflicted with a kind of split vision that was becoming chronic. On one level, he was resolute, ready to stand alone; on another, he allowed himself to wonder if the Congress leaders, now going their own way, might have a better grasp on the country's needs. On the train to Bihar, he wrote a letter to his erstwhile disciple Vallabhbhai Patel, now yoked to Nehru in an uneasy duumvirate. "It is just possible," he conceded, "that in administering the affairs of the millions you can see what I cannot. Perhaps I too would act and speak as you do if I were in your place." In context, it sounds like a genuine doubt, not a gesture or courtesy, meant to placate. He's asking whether India can possibly be run on Gandhian lines.

The same sort of split vision shows up in what sounds like a valedictory comment on the efficacy of his campaigns. The nonviolent resistance he'd meant to inspire was muscular, disciplined, brave enough to risk injury, even death; this he called "the nonviolence of the strong." All he'd evoked from the mass of Indians, he now commented, was mere passive resistance, "the nonviolence of the weak." Speaking to an American professor in the first days of independence, he reflects that his career had been all along based on an "illusion." He's not bitter. He even manages to draw a measure of comfort from what he now presents as his disillusion. "He realized that if his vision were not covered by that illusion," according to the summary he authorized of that conversation, "India would never have reached the point it had today." If he'd conned anyone, he seems to be saying, it was himself. With at least a touch of pride, he said he wasn't sorry.

It's monsoon season when he finally embarks on his long-promised return to Noakhali, hoping to arrive in the district in time for the dual independence of Pakistan and India. Going back to Noakhali would be a way of distancing himself from any responsibility for partition without having to denounce the Congress leadership, a way also to express his continued devotion to the cause of Hindu-Muslim "unity," now seemingly down to its last gasp. "I do not like much that is going on here . . . [and] do not want it to be said that I was associated with it," he'd written to Patel before embarking on this latest swing. This time he manages to get no farther than a demoted, deflated Calcutta: capital of the whole subcontinent, the entire Raj, until 1911 when the British announced their intention to shift the seat of government to Delhi; of an undivided Bengal thereafter; now, with partition, about to become the seat of a smallish Hindu-majority Indian rump state to be known as West Bengal.

The Muslim League government had already decamped to Dacca, about to be proclaimed capital of East Pakistan, taking with it the upper tier of Muslims in the civil service and police, which were suddenly, by default, overwhelmingly Hindu again. Anxious Muslims who remained saw the writing on the wall—revenge for the Great Calcutta Killing of the previous year. Just as the Muslim League's chief minister, Suhrawardy, had called on Gandhi then at the Sodepur ashram ten months earlier with the aim of getting him to change his travel plans, another Muslim League delegation waited on him there the day of his arrival, August 9, with an even more urgent plea. They implored him to stay in Calcutta to protect their community now living in terror, according to them, under the shadow of a Congress government.

"We have as much claim on you as the Hindus," the leader of the delegation, a former Calcutta mayor named Mohammad Usman, said on his return the next day. Usman belonged to the same Muslim League that had done much to precipitate the crisis, that only half a year earlier was decrying the Mahatma's mission in East Bengal. But now that Gandhi had actually gone to Bihar and denounced as bestial and barbaric what Hindus had done to their co-religionists there, and now that partition had left them feeling vulnerable in a state where they'd be a minority henceforth and forever, Bengali Muslims left behind in India saw the Mahatma in a new light: as a potential savior. "You yourself have said that you are as much of Muslims as of Hindus," the pleading former mayor said.

Gandhi agreed to delay his return to Noakhali on two conditions. One was that the Muslims guarantee peace and the protection of minority Hindus in Noakhali as he had meant to do; if there were a provocation there, his life would be "forfeit" through fasting, he threatened. The other was that Suhrawardy—who'd rushed to Calcutta from Karachi on hearing of Gandhi's arrival there—join him in a peace committee of two to maintain order in Calcutta as British rule ended.

Suhrawardy was one Muslim League politician whose political fortunes had taken a dive with the advent of Pakistan. The united Bengal he'd governed was about to go out of existence; he would then hold office in neither Pakistan nor India, thanks in part to a quixotic and doomed eleventh-hour push he'd led to keep Bengal united, even if that meant its being partitioned off as a third independent state. The failure of that effort left the chief minister, an Urdu speaker who was not viewed as a true Bengali, as a leader without a following, an isolated, uncommitted actor with what seemed to be dwindling prospects. In the Mahatma's depressed mood, that defined him again as a sympathetic character; it might even be said, as a disappointed fellow sufferer.

The idea of a single Bengal uniting Hindus and Muslims had appealed to Gandhi as a refutation of Jinnah's theory that they were, by definition, two nations—so much so that during the movement's brief spasm in May, this elderly non-Bengali, this beginning student of the Bengali language, had offered to enlist as what amounted to a headquarters warrant officer. "I am quite willing," the aging Mahatma wrote to Suhrawardy then, "to act as your honorary private secretary and live under your roof, till Hindus and Muslims begin to live as the brothers they are."

"What a mad offer!" Suhrawardy was supposed to have responded. "I will have to think ten times before I can fathom its implications." In effect, Gandhi was offering to revive the partnership he'd had a quarter of a century earlier with the Khilafat leader Muhammad Ali.

He wasn't one to waste an inspiration. So taken was he with this latest scheme for reaching across the communal divide that now, three months later, on the eve of independence, he revived it, daring Suhrawardy to move with him into a troubled area of Calcutta whose Muslim residents felt vulnerable, to live with him there under the same roof without military or police protection. The Muslim Leaguer took a night to think it over, then agreed, attaching no conditions. On August 13, with less than two days to go to independence, the two moved into a ramshackle, abandoned mansion in a teeming area called Beliaghata where Muslim *bustee*, or shanty, dwellers lived at close quarters with marginally less impoverished Hindus who lived in houses, into which refugees from East Bengal had lately been crowding. The neighborhood had already been shown to be a tinderbox. Hindu gangs attacked Muslim dwellings with Sten guns and homemade grenades, putting their residents to flight.

On his arrival, Gandhi was greeted with black flags and a chorus of abuse from a crowd of two hundred or so Hindus, some of whom tried to shove their way into the building through the window of the room reserved for the Mahatma. An attempt to close the old shutters was met by a barrage of stones. Once the young Hindu men were more or less calmed down, they demanded to know why Gandhi was so concerned about Muslims.

He faced down the rowdiest in discussions that seem to have gone on for an hour or more. "We don't need your sermons on ahimsa," one of these young Hindus supposedly blurted out to his face. Gandhi told them he wouldn't be bullied, that he'd never give in to force, nor call for help. Then he took up their charge that he was an enemy of Hindus. "Can't you understand that being a Hindu by religion, deed and name, I cannot possibly be an enemy of my own community?" he retorted. To that the young men had no answer. Some finally volunteered to stand guard over him.

A bemused Vallabhbhai Patel was only slightly more understanding. "So you have got detained in Calcutta . . . [in] a notorious den of gangsters and hooligans. And in what company too!" he wrote from New Delhi, where he was running the Home Ministry, making him the Indian official with paramount responsibility for keeping the peace. "It is a terrible risk."

The Hydari Manzil, as the dilapidated one-story villa was known, had only one toilet to accommodate its guests and the hundreds of visitors they attracted daily and only one charpoy, or string cot, which the old man refused to use as a bed, preferring the floor. The strong smell of ammonia, used in a hasty mopping to disinfect the place before the Mahatma moved in, hung in the air that first day. The scale of the villa was the only clue to its former opulence: ceilings about thirty feet high, large casements and doorways, the glass and the doors often smashed. Keeping his distance from the independence celebrations in Delhi, Gandhi made it his headquarters for the first three roller-coaster weeks of Indian independence. Today, with the installation of marble wainscoting, fluorescent lights, and the usual displays of old photographs, it's a museum, yet another Gandhi shrine, only dimly reflective of the fears and passions that surged and then were tamed there in 1947.

He'd been saying that he'd devote himself to fasting and spinning on Independence Day, August 15. When the BBC asked that he record a special independence message, the old man replied: "They must forget that I know English." When All India Radio came with a similar request, he said: "I've run dry." He awoke at 2:00 a.m. that day after only three hours of sleep. Beliaghata was quiet at that early hour, but a small, mostly Muslim crowd was waiting outside to congratulate him on the achievement of freedom. When daylight came, larger crowds began to gather. Strikingly, they were mixed; Hindus and Muslims who'd been taking up offensive and defensive positions days earlier were now celebrating together; according to contemporary reports, they were embracing and calling each other "brothers." The euphoria lasted two weeks. Instead of another Great Calcutta Killing, there was suddenly talk of a Calcutta miracle, which many were quick to attribute to Gandhi's presence and the example he'd set.

With Suhrawardy at the wheel, Gandhi went out for a drive two nights in a row to witness the big civic party, soak up the joy. At first he wouldn't allow himself to be drawn in, even when crowds in a Muslim section surrounded his car crying, *"Jai Hind!"* At his prayer meetings on the fifteenth and sixteenth, he spoke with chagrin about the rampaging celebrants who'd surged through Government House, the former seat of the viceroys (newly turned over to an Indian governor on Independence Day), stealing the silver, defacing pictures more or less in the spirit of the rowdy crowd that celebrated Andrew Jackson's inauguration by ransacking the White House; and as reports came in on rioting in Lahore on the other side of the subcontinent, Gandhi went on mournfully about the bloodshed with which independence was being marked. His doubts about the durability of the Calcutta miracle persisted. "What if this is just a momentary enthusiasm?" he wrote to Patel.

From one moment to the next, he was torn between wariness and hope. As the mixed throngs of Hindus and Muslims that turned out almost daily to hear him and Suhrawardy continued to swell—to half a million or more, it was reported on at least two occasions—he was reminded of the high tide of the Khilafat movement that had swept him into a position of national leadership. "One might almost say that the joy of fraternization is leaping up from hour to hour," he allowed himself to write.

Shaheed Suhrawardy, who'd tried to maneuver him out of Noakhali earlier in the year, now basked in the glow of the Mahatma, paying him tribute for the joy and relief Calcutta was drawing from its astonishing plunge into amity. "All this is due to the infinite mercy of Allah and the good work of our beloved Bapu," this Muslim Leaguer said. Mountbatten, now governor-general of an independent India, noted that a "boundary force" under British officers had been dispatched to the Punjab in hopes of containing the violence there. "In the Punjab," he wrote, "we have 55,000 soldiers and large-scale rioting on our hands. In Bengal our forces consist of one man, and there is no rioting . . . May I be allowed to pay my tribute to the One Man Boundary Force, not forgetting his Second-in-Command, Mr. Suhrawardy."

Mountbatten's letter was delivered to Gandhi on August 30. Gandhi then scheduled his return to Noakhali for September 1. But that day didn't dawn peacefully. On what was to have been his last evening in Calcutta, the Hydari mansion, his Beliaghata command post, was again invaded by surly young Hindus with a score, they said, to settle with Suhrawardy. Luckily, the former chief minister had gone home to pack for the Mahatma's Noakhali trip, for which he'd enlisted. According to Gandhi's account, the invaders were carrying a Hindu man wrapped in bandages who had been stabbed by a Muslim, or so they claimed. On closer examination, it was shown he hadn't been stabbed at all. Gandhi had just retired for the night; at first, he said, he lay still with his eyes shut. Then, hearing shouts and the smashing of more glass, the old man stepped into the adjoining reception room to face the attackers. It was his silent day, the one day a week he refrained from speech, but given the provocation, he made an exception.

"What is all this?" he demanded. "Kill me, kill me, I say. Why don't you kill me?"

He was speaking Hindi. Even after his words were translated into Bengali, they'd no effect. A chunk of brick was thrown at a man mistaken for a Muslim who'd been standing near the Mahatma. "Is this the reality of the peace that was established on August 15th?" a distraught but undaunted Gandhi then asked. "I offer myself for attack."

Again, there had to be a pause for translation. Slowly his words sank in, but as he himself wrote the next day after gathering reports of violent outbreaks around the city, "The Calcutta bubble seems to have burst . . . What was regarded as a miracle has proved a short-lived, nine-day wonder." Within hours, having scrubbed the trip to Noakhali yet again, he'd resolved to stay in place and fast. It was, he'd said, his "fiery weapon," or sometimes, his "infallible weapon." Perhaps this time it would touch hearts in the Punjab as well as Calcutta. "If I lack even the power to pacify the people," he wrote to Patel, "what else is left for me to do?"

The day after the attack on the Hydari mansion, about fifty persons were reported to have been killed and three hundred injured in uncontrolled rioting in Calcutta. Troops were called out, but there weren't nearly enough to handle the situation; the local garrison had been depleted by reassignment of units to crisis areas in North India and the Punjab. The city seemed to be slipping back, heading for a reenactment of the previous year's "great killing," when Gandhi began his fast on September 2.

Two days later it was quiet. Large peace marches, propelled by an urgent sense of necessity, headed for Beliaghata to assure the Mahatma that this time the truce would hold. Militant Hindu groups and known gangsters came and laid at least some of their weapons at his feet. Untold thousands fasted in sympathy, including members of the police. Two Hindus, striving as Gandhian peace workers to protect Muslims under assault, were themselves cut down, thus fulfilling, with the sacrifice of their lives, his most severe definition of satyagraha. All accounts point to one conclusion, that the city was gripped by a sense of how unthinkable, how disgraceful, it would be to let the saintly old man who'd led the independence struggle die within its precincts at what was supposed to be the dawn of India's freedom.

On the evening of the third day, a remarkable gathering, representing virtually the entire religious and political spectrum, crowded into Gandhi's room to urge that he break the fast. There were leaders of the Congress and the Muslim League, of the Sikhs who'd been aroused by reports of the massacres in the Punjab, of the militant Hindu Mahasabha; and there was Shaheed Suhrawardy, the former chief minister, publicly atoning for his failure at the time of the Great Calcutta Killing by orchestrating the proceedings. Living up to the stereotype of his Bania caste, Gandhi bargained before settling.

The delegation would have to meet two conditions to satisfy him. First, they'd have to sign an open-ended pledge that communal violence would never recur in Calcutta; that was the easy part. Second, the pledge would have to include a promise that if it did break out again, each would personally lay down his life to restore peace. The leaders withdrew to another room, then returned with the document he'd demanded. The same Bengali song Tagore had sung at the end of the fast in Yeravda prison fourteen years earlier was sung again as Suhrawardy did the honors, handing Gandhi a small glass of sweet lime juice: "When the heart is hard and parched up, come upon me with a shower of mercy."

Calcutta rejoiced. His old comrade Rajagopalachari, West Bengal's new governor, said nothing Gandhi had achieved, "not even independence," had been "so truly wonderful as his victory over evil in Calcutta." Gandhi's own depiction of his role sounds humble enough but, on a careful reading, reflects his mounting conviction that he'd been chosen to serve as peacemaker. "This sudden upheaval is not the work of one or two men," he wrote on first hearing talk of a Calcutta miracle, before either the renewed violence or the fast that ended it. "We are toys in the hands of God. He makes us dance to His tune."

Three days later, on September 7, he left by train for Delhi, on what would prove to be the final stage in his long life as wanderer and seeker, a perpetual pilgrim, leaving unfulfilled his pledges to return to Noakhali or start a sojourn in Pakistan's portion of the Punjabi killing fields. What kept him in Delhi was the spread of the wildfire of communal violence to the city, which was really in those days two cities that hadn't yet grown together: old Delhi, former Mughal capital, scene of a rebellion against British control nearly a century earlier in which Hindu as well as Muslim troops had fought in the previous century to restore a Muslim dynasty; and New Delhi, proud seat of the foreign imperium, completed as it was losing its grip on the subcontinent, newer in 1947 than such later twentieth-century creations as Brasília or Islamabad are today. Delhi is actually as close to Lahore as Washington is to New York. Suddenly, now, they were worlds apart as traumatized Hindu refugees streamed across the border telling of family members and homes they'd lost, the devastation they'd witnessed. With seeming inevitability, a furious spirit of revenge and sheer human need combined to extend the chain reaction that the Great Calcutta Killing had ignited thirteen months earlier: Hindus driven from their homes in the Punjab now joined forces with local extremists to drive Muslims from their homes in Delhi.

It was still the first month of Indian independence. Soon one in four of the capital's residents would be classed as refugees. By the time Gandhi arrived in Delhi on the morning of September 9, mosques were under attack, mob looting and killing were only beginning to taper off after rolling unchecked for several days, bodies were still being picked up from the streets, and a military curfew had been imposed. Fresh from his "miracle," an understandably shaken but calm Mahatma followed his own drill, doing what he'd done successively over those months in Noakhali, Bihar, and Calcutta: promising to stay in the capital until it was entirely peaceful, to "do or die." This time his favorite shibboleth would burn like a fuse.

So thick were the insecurity and fear gripping the capital that Patel told Gandhi, in no uncertain terms, that he couldn't possibly return to the quarter of the most despised untouchables, the Bhangis, or sweepers, which he'd been pointedly using as his Delhi base for the better part of two years. In his own mind, making Indians and foreigners who wanted to call on him come to the Bhangi colony was simply a logical extension of the struggle against untouchability that he regularly traced to his experiences in South Africa.

Without his knowing it, the Bhangi colony had been partially turned into a stage set before he took up residence there in 1946 by minions of the industrialist G. D. Birla, his chief financial backer. Mr. Gandhi, meet Mr. Potemkin. Margaret Bourke-White, the American photojournalist, has a wonderfully dry description of how they'd razed an authentically miserable shantytown and, banishing half its population, had thrown up, for those allowed to remain, rows of tidy little mud houses with casements and doorways providing decent ventilation, all arrayed on a regular grid of widened paths edged in brick, watered daily to keep down dust. Electricity, electric fans, and phones were part of this new deal, according to her account. There in the somewhat larger but still modest structure that had been put up for Gandhi, near a small freshly whitewashed temple, he conferred with Congress leaders and British cabinet ministers. When he had to leave what was now the most presentable, least malodorous slum in India, for conferences at the palatial Viceregal Lodge, he'd been chauffeured in the industrialist's "milk-white Packard car."

But now the Bhangi colony and its environs had been swamped by refugees, many of them disposed to blame Gandhi for their fate, so it was considered only prudent for him to be reinstalled in Birla House, the industrialist's spacious, high-ceilinged mansion on one of New

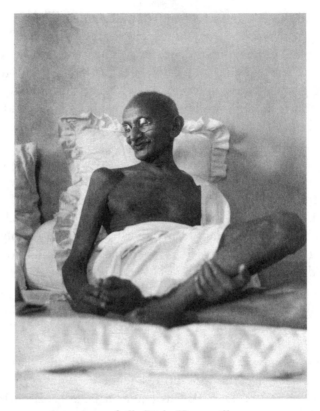

At ease on a frilly Birla House pillow, 1942

Delhi's broad new boulevards, with its deep, carefully tended garden. He
was no stranger to the challenge of maintaining his regime of austerity
in surroundings of luxury. Birla House had been his Delhi base for most
of the two decades before he was inspired to move in with the Bhangis.
On September 16, a week after he arrived in Delhi, he returned to the
neighborhood of the Bhangi colony for a meeting with a right-wing
extremist group that drilled on the banks of the Jamuna nearby. The
Rashtriya Swayamsevak Sangh, or RSS, had been blamed for much of
the violence; it later would be banned in the crackdown on Hindu
extremists following Gandhi's assassination. But instead of condemning
them on this last encounter, the Mahatma tried to find common ground
as one Indian patriot speaking to others in the cause of civil peace. His
session that day with the RSS—which has taken in recent decades to
mentioning his name in its daily roll call of Hindu heroes—was supposed to be followed by a prayer meeting. But rowdy Hindu hecklers
made prayers impossible. *"Gandhi murdabad!"*—"Death to Gandhi!"—

they cried, after an attempt was made to read verses from the Koran, a standard part of his ecumenical ritual. Thereafter, for the next four and a half months, his prayer meetings were held in the presumed security of Mr. Birla's walled garden, where finite crowds could be infiltrated and closely watched by plainclothesmen. Today mansion and garden are preserved as the Gandhi Smriti, the scene of the Mahatma's martyrdom.

The Bhangi colony also has its Gandhi shrine today. Bhangis don't go by that disparaged name anymore. They prefer to call themselves Balmikis (sometimes, in Roman letters, spelled Valmikis) after an ancient saint, Rishi Balmiki (or Valmiki), the mythical author of the *Ramayana*, the Hindu epic, whom they claim as an ancestor and now semideify; or so the figure of the holy man in the small temple hard by the reconstructed Gandhi house seems to suggest. To approach the temple, visitors must remove any footwear. To enter the Gandhi house—or, for that matter, approach the point in the Birla garden where he fell—they must do the same. Perhaps, despite his clearly expressed wishes, his status as something more than a human may still be evolving. Birla House is a major tourist stop. The former Bhangi colony is seldom visited, except at election time when Congress politicians call. But Gandhi's portrait is freshly garlanded there on a regular basis as it is in few other Dalit quarters, if any, across the subcontinent today. Meanwhile, the Balmikis live in four-story cream and maroon concrete apartment houses put up by the state, with cute little balconies attached to each apartment.

When Gandhi stayed there, the quarter was isolated; now its residents have ready access to one of the stations of Delhi's new metro. Mostly, they're still sweepers, drawing something better than starvation wages from the New Delhi Municipal Corporation. But only former Balmikis, the renamed Bhangis, seem to live in these unofficially segregated quarters. The best that can be said is that while their circumstances have obviously improved, their status seems to be evolving in an Indian way with glacial slowness, more than six decades after Gandhi lived among them.

Despite his displacement from the Bhangi colony, Gandhi continued to preach against untouchability in the final four months of his life, a theme second only in his discourse in this time to his harping on the need for Hindus to give up their retaliation against Muslims. "Anger is short madness," he told them, imploring them "to stay their hands." A tour of

Hindu and Muslim refugee camps in which no latrines had been dug and the stench of human excrement was unavoidable instantly reignited the revulsion he'd felt in Calcutta in 1901, in Hardwar in 1915, only this was now 1947 and India was supposed to be free. "Why do [the authorities] tolerate such stink and stench?" he demanded to know. They should insist that the refugees clean up after themselves. "We must tell them that we would give them food and water but not sweepers," he said. "I am a very hard-hearted man."

His prayer meetings, broadcast nightly on the radio for fifteen minutes, became a diurnal part of life in the still-seething capital. A whole lifetime later, it's not easy to gauge the impact of these broadcasts. They didn't attract huge numbers to the prayer meetings in the Birla garden, where the actual crowds, usually in the hundreds, were small compared with the massive throngs of Hindus and Muslims that had turned out to hear him weeks earlier in Calcutta. Jawaharlal Nehru, installed as India's first prime minister, came to sit with him every evening in the relatively small chamber Gandhi occupied on the ground floor, just off a stone patio where he sunned himself after his baths, wearing a broad-brimmed straw peasant's hat that had been given to him in Noakhali. The routine of Nehru's visits left an impression that the old man was being consulted on urgent problems. Left unclear was how much guidance he offered, how likely it was to be heeded.

"They are all mine and also not mine," he said of his old colleagues, now in power, who were sending troops to Kashmir, a measure he couldn't approve but wouldn't deplore. A spinning wheel, a small writing desk, and a thin mattress that folded up during the day were his only possessions of any size in that room. An exhibit case now displays smaller items he kept there, which were notable for their paltriness: wire-frame eyeglasses and their case, a metal fork and spoon, a wood fork and spoon, a knife, a pocket watch, and his walking stick.

He stuck to his causes—discoursing on peace and the desirability of Hindustani as a national language, even the best way to handle compost—and stuck to his daily schedule, rising hours before daybreak for prayers, his walk, meal, bath, enema, and massage. As always, that was the time for him to start in on his correspondence before receiving visitors, Muslim and Hindu, who brought him their sense of Delhi's mood, how near to the surface violence still lurked. What he heard was seldom encouraging. Muslims were still fleeing, and few Hindus were willing to lift a finger, despite his pleas, to make them feel wanted, let alone safe. His own mood reverted to the intermittent uncertainty darkening to despair that had weighed on him in Srirampur. "These days, who listens to me?" he said in his third week back in Delhi. "Mine is a lone voice . . . I have come here and am doing something but I feel I have become useless now."

On October 2, 1947, the last birthday of his life, turning seventy-eight, he said he didn't look forward to another one. "Ever since I came to India," he said, "I have made it my profession to work for communal harmony . . . Today we seem to have become enemies. We assert that there can never be an honest Muslim. A Muslim always remains a worthless fellow. In such a situation, what place do I have in India and what is the point of my being here?" He doesn't know whether to blame himself or the Hindus of Delhi. At one moment he says the citizens of Delhi must have gone mad; at another he wonders aloud, "What sin must I have committed that [God] kept me alive to witness all these horrors?"

As the weeks wear on, his mood, if anything, becomes steadily more lugubrious, even though the level of outright violence, in Delhi at least, falls off. "On the surface things are sufficiently nice," he writes to Rajagopalachari in Calcutta, "but the under-current leaves little hope." Two weeks later he informs a prayer meeting that 137 mosques have been grievously damaged or destroyed in Delhi alone, some of them turned into Hindu temples. This is sheer irreligion, he scolds, not in the least excused by the fact that Hindu temples have been converted into mosques in Pakistan. Three weeks after that, he's still on a tear. "Misdeeds of the Hindus in [India] have to be proclaimed by the Hindus from the roof-tops," he says, "if those of the Muslims in Pakistan are to be arrested or stopped." The dispossessed Hindu refugees and Hindu chauvinists show little sign of being shamed by this fierce Jeremiah in their midst. On the contrary, some of them are easily roused against him, as Gandhi has seen.

India has now been free and independent for about four months. And the leading shaper of that independence remains unsettled and despairing. In the early days of 1948 he broods on the thought that since he'd obviously failed to meet the first half of his injunction to himself to "do or die" in Delhi, it's time for him to test the second. No single catastrophe served as catalyst for his decision to start his seventeenth and final fast on January 13. In the days running up to the fast, he'd been forcefully struck by several indications that matters were on a downward slide. First he received a detailed account of rampant corruption at all levels of the newly empowered Congress movement in the Andhra region of southeastern India. Then some nationalist Muslims asked him to help them emigrate from India to Britain now that it had become clear that they could find no secure place in either India or Pakistan. What a destination for nationalists at the end of their struggle, Gandhi remarks. Finally, Shaheed Suhrawardy, who'd been attempting informal mediation with Jinnah in consultation with Gandhi and who, until that point, had left the Mahatma with the impression that he still considered himself an Indian, now told him that he didn't feel safe moving around Delhi, even by car.

Suhrawardy, who'd been told by Jinnah that he was turning into Gandhi's stooge, returned from Karachi with a request on Pakistan's behalf. He asked Gandhi to intercede to unfreeze Pakistan's share of British India's assets that the new Indian government was bound by treaty to pay, a considerable sum by the standards of the time (500 million rupees, about $145 million at prevailing exchange rates). Gandhi's increasingly disgruntled follower Patel—who was least inclined to follow him on issues touching Muslims—had convinced the cabinet that the money should be withheld pending a settlement on questions such as Kashmir; otherwise, he argued, the assets might be used to buy arms and ammunition. Mountbatten, now the governor-general, had also brought the issue to Gandhi's attention, thereby infuriating Patel, who said the Englishman had no right to lobby against a cabinet decision. Neither the former viceroy nor the former chief minister had any way of imagining that Gandhi's interest in the issue of the assets, which they had stoked, could prove fatal.

Announcing the fast at his prayer meeting on January 12, the Mahatma mentioned the insecurity of Muslims and the Congress's corruption but not the blocked payment to Pakistan. "For some time my helplessness has been eating into my vitals," he said. "It will end as soon as I start a fast . . . I will end the fast when I am convinced that the various communities have resumed their friendly relations, not because of pressure from outside but of their own free will." But on the second day of the fast, the cabinet convened at Birla House, beside a string bed on which the old man was lying, for reconsideration of the frozen assets issue. An aggrieved Patel, momentarily convinced that he was the target of his leader's fast, complained bitterly to Gandhi, then left for Bombay on the fast's third day, though the Mahatma by then had visibly weakened. "Gandhiji is not prepared to listen to me," he's reported to have said. "He seems determined to blacken the names of the Hindus before the whole world."

Confronted with the charge that his fast was on behalf of Muslims and against Hindus, Gandhi readily conceded that it was basically true. "All his life he had stood, as everyone should stand, for minorities and those in need," he said, according to the transcript of his talk that he authorized following the prayer meeting on the first evening of the fast.

The timetable here is vital, for it meshes fatefully and finally locks into the crude cogs of a Hindu extremist plot being pursued with amateurish zeal in the city of Poona, near which the British had imprisoned Gandhi three times for a total of six years. Now with the departure of the British, he could be caricatured there as an enemy of Hindustan. By his assassin's own testimony, it was Gandhi's announcement of his fast on the twelfth that had lit the fuse on the plot he and his main accomplice hatched starting that night; and it was the declaration three days later that the cabinet had reversed itself and decided to transfer the blocked reserves to Pakistan, explaining that it was moved by a desire "to help in every way open to them in the object which Gandhiji has in heart," that had clinched the secret verdict of the conspirators condemning him to death. Patel's absence from Delhi, meanwhile, would ensure that the Home Ministry was without firm leadership. "Every condition given by [Gandhi] for giving up the fast is in favor of Muslims and against the Hindus," Nathuram Godse would later testify at the trial where he was finally sentenced to hang for what he represented as a patriotic imperative. Among Gandhi's conditions had been the return to Muslim custody of the mosques that had been attacked, desecrated, and turned into Hindu temples.

Of the unfreezing of the assets, the assassin would say: "This decision of the people's government was reversed to suit the tune of Gandhiji's fast. It was evident to my mind that the force of public opinion was nothing but a trifle when compared with the leanings of Gandhiji favorable to Pakistan." The victim's sterling virtues were an inherent part of the problem, of the obstacle he represented. "A most severe austerity of life, ceaseless work and lofty character made Gandhiji formidable and irresistible," the assassin said in his ex post facto justification of his deed. Something had to be done if India was ever to pursue its own interests the way other nations pursued theirs. Therefore, said Godse, he "decided to remove Gandhiji from the political stage."

In Delhi there were no large peace processions of Hindus and Muslims as there had been in Calcutta four months earlier until the fifth and next-to-last day of the fast. Then a crowd said to number 100,000 hankerers after peace stretched for about a mile. A few days earlier, a much smaller procession of Sikhs, protesting the slaughter of their people in Pakistan's part of the Punjab, stalked by Birla House chanting, "Blood for blood!" and "Let Gandhi die!"

"What are they shouting?" asked the Mahatma, trying to fall asleep in a darkened room.

"They are shouting, 'Let Gandhi die,' " he was told.

"How many are there?" the seasoned crowd counter asked.

When the answer came, "Not many," he resumed his prayers.

As previously, urgent efforts to appease and satisfy him were pressed by Hindu and Muslim leaders who knew their assigned parts in the play he was staging. Once again they'd have to work together to present a convincing case that conditions for reconciliation had been secured. Telegrams full of brotherly sentiment poured in from Pakistan. A Central Peace Committee, with 130 members, was formed in Delhi. It drafted a declaration promising full compliance with Gandhi's demands. One of these involved the main food market where Hindu merchants and shoppers had been boycotting Muslims. Now the Hindus hastened to lavish food and business on them. And, once again, after the usual haggling and close examination of the signatures on the declaration, making sure there were no holdouts, Gandhi allowed himself to be persuaded, finally ending his last fast on its sixth day, January 18. Surrounded at that moment by the usual broad array of political and religious leaders, including Pakistan's ambassador and Prime Minister Nehru, who quietly let him know he'd been fasting in sympathy for two days, he signaled that he was ready for nourishment.

This time it was the nationalist Muslim Maulana Azad who did the honors, handing the Mahatma the glass of sweet lime juice, fortified with an ounce of glucose. He'd been assured that Delhi was quiet and not just on the surface. No one yet heralded a "Delhi miracle." With events hurtling on, there was hardly time.

On the evening of January 20, as a recovering Gandhi was addressing the prayer meeting in the garden for the first time in nearly a week, the loud bang and fading rumble of an explosion set off a commotion. The bomb had been meant to serve as cover for an attempt on Gandhi's life that evening, but though there were seven conspirators stationed in the garden, including Nathuram Godse, the attempt was never made. Gandhi went on speaking, while the twenty-year-old Hindu refugee who'd been persuaded to ignite the device was finally led away to be submitted to harsh questioning.

"Listen! Listen! Listen everybody!" the Mahatma cried out in a voice fainter than usual on account of his fast. "Nothing has happened." He'd been predicting his own murder for months. His first impression that evening, however, was that the boom must have had something to do with a training exercise by the police or army.

It didn't take long for the investigators to clear away any lingering doubts about the plotters' aim; by the next morning they had information that should have enabled them to trace and round up the bomber's accomplices. They'd found out that one of the plotters was the editor of a militant Marathi-language newspaper in Poona called *Hindu Rashtra* (Hindu Nation), a name that proclaimed its cause. That was Godse. Thus they had ten days to connect what they knew to the man and apprehend him. Why this did not become a matter of urgency has been a subject for speculation and reinvestigation ever since. (A judicial commission of inquiry was still examining the question when I arrived in New Delhi in 1966. It didn't submit its final report until 1969, twenty-one years too late.)

For those ten days in that first January of India's freedom, the clumsiness and confusion of the plotters were pitted against the unbelievable inefficiency and indifference of the police. Gandhi himself fatalistically waved away all congratulations on having survived an attempt on his life. "God will keep me alive so long as he needs me and put an end to my life when he does not need me," he said. "I am only his servant. Why should I worry?"

In that spirit, he objected to a police proposal to search all citizens drawn to the garden for the nightly prayer meetings. His objection helped make the congratulations on his survival premature. For Gandhi it was a matter of principle, a test of his nonviolence. "The rulers of the country have no faith in my non-violence," he said, "They only believe that this police guard will save my life . . . perhaps I am the only believer in nonviolence."

It wasn't that he viewed searches and pat-downs as violent acts in themselves. He instinctively recoiled from the message they'd send about nonviolence as a practical way of relating to the world. How could he preach one set of values while allowing himself to be protected by another? In Noakhali, Calcutta, and Bihar he'd urged simple people, members of besieged minorities, not to flee their homes but to face death bravely, if that's what it took to turn the tide of violence. Now, by applying this code to himself, he left a gaping hole in the security precautions at Birla House. No one recognized Nathuram Godse when he returned to the garden on January 30, though he was well-known to the Poona police as a Hindu extremist, nor noticed that he was packing a big black Beretta pistol.

Gandhi anticipates his impending death so many times in his final days that he almost seems a party to the conspiracy. In the ten days following the bungled bombing in the garden, the subject of his demise crops up in his conversation, correspondence, and prayer meeting talks at least fourteen times. "If somebody fired at me point blank and I faced his bullet with a smile, repeating the name of Rama in my heart, I should indeed be worthy of congratulations," he said on the first day. "I am waiting for such good luck," he said on the second. "I wish I might face the assassin's bullets while lying on your lap and repeating the name of Rama with a smile on my face," he told Manu Gandhi, his grandniece and bedmate, on the third. And so it goes until the evening of January 29, when, with less than twenty-four hours to go in his life's journey, he again tells Manu: "If an explosion took place, as it did last week, or someone shot at me and I received his bullet on my bare chest, without a sigh and with Rama's name on my lips, only then you should say that I was a true mahatma."

So he can't be accused of being blind to the threat. If anything, he imagines it as being just over the horizon, about to come into view at any instant. Meanwhile, his daily spinning goes on, his basic work goes on. He even continues his Bengali lessons, in preparation for the return to Noakhali he still intends to make. And all the old themes continue to run through his talks. At the prayer meeting on January 28, he brings up a renewal of Indian nonviolent resistance in South Africa, having just had some articles on the subject read to him during his bath. The segregation of blacks in the country, he says, is like the segregation of untouchables in India.

"I have seen it with my own eyes," he says. "That is the reason our countrymen there are fighting for their just rights." Hindus and Muslims, in his portrayal, are fighting together against white oppression there. He seems to be offering the Indians of South Africa as exemplars of "unity" to India and Pakistan, just as he did when he returned to India in 1915. "I have lived for twenty years in South Africa," he now says. "Therefore I regard it as my own country like India."

The next evening, in his final prayer meeting talk, he again finds a way back to South Africa. His theme is the self-reliance of South Indians.

He's applying it to a food shortage currently being suffered in Madras, now Tamil Nadu, and that pitches him retrospectively back more than three decades to his march with indentured Tamils into the Transvaal in 1913, his first major exercise in leading a mass movement. They had only a small daily ration of bread and sugar, he recalls, but they managed to forage for food in the wild. So they were an example to the poorest Indians today. "Our salvation and the satisfaction of our needs lies in working honestly," he concludes. Surveying the course of his life from the Transvaal in white-ruled South Africa in 1913 to the capital of independent India in 1948, he settles on that as a core value.

Immediately after that meeting, Gandhi focuses on a memorandum he's drafting on the future of the Indian National Congress, from which he formally resigned nearly fourteen years earlier. Under Nehru, the Congress is effectively now the government of India. "Working honestly" is the memorandum's central theme. Having achieved political independence, Gandhi argues, the Congress "has outlived its use." It needs to give up power and refashion itself as what he names a Lok Sevak Sangh, or a People's Service League, which will subsume all the service organizations for which Gandhi had previously drafted constitutions and rules: the spinners and village industries associations, the cow-protection league, the Harijan Sevak Sangh dedicated to the uplift of the former untouchables.

On the last evening of his life, Mahatma Gandhi dreams again of the revival of the villages. "India has still to attain social, moral and economic independence in terms of its 700,000 villages as distinguished from its cities," he writes.

He dreams on. Each village will have its own village worker, a selfless teetotaler who spins his own yarn, weaves his own khadi, and rejects untouchability "in any shape or form in his own person or in his family."

He finished working on the draft in the morning and handed it to his faithful secretary, Pyarelal, for polishing. Later Pyarelal would publish it as "The Last Will and Testament" of Mahatma Gandhi. Never did it make its way onto the agenda of any meeting of the Indian National Congress as a subject for serious discussion.

In the last hour of his life, however, Gandhi wasn't thinking of disbanding the movement he'd led. Now, as regularly happened throughout his political life, the practical politician takes over from the visionary. Sitting in Birla House with Vallabhbhai Patel, who suspected that he'd lost the confidence of Nehru and even the Mahatma himself, he delves into party politics one last time as a conciliator, soothing a fretful, ailing minister, telling him how important it is for him to stay in the leadership at Nehru's side. This delicate negotiation, between two old comrades, runs ten minutes past the hour at which the compulsively punctual Gandhi always walked into the garden for his prayer meeting. On the way, walking even more briskly than usual, the old man mentions an adjustment he needs to make in his diet, then chides Manu and another grandniece, Abha Gandhi, on both of whom he's lightly leaning—"my walking sticks," he called them—for letting him be late. "I cannot tolerate even one minute's delay at prayer," he grumbles.

Later, when it came time to turn Birla House into a shrine, designers would have 175 cement footprints molded to simulate the vigorous long strides Gandhi took that evening, so different from the slow shuffle choreographed for the stage Gandhi at the end of the opera *Satyagraha*. The footprints run out just beyond four steps he had to mount to reach the prayer ground. They run out at the point at which Nathuram Godse stepped forward, his two hands pressed together in the Indian greeting of *namaste*. According to Godse's own testimony, the black Beretta was concealed between his palms, but Tushar Gandhi, a great-grandson of the Mahatma's who has compiled a sourcebook on the assassination, writes that after handling the weapon, he's convinced it was too large to be hidden in that way. So he has the Beretta concealed under Godse's khaki bush jacket. "There is no way a person could hide the pistol in folded palms," he wrote. "It is too big and too heavy."

Wherever it came from, Manu never saw it. Stepping between Gandhi and the seemingly reverential man with the folded palms, whom she imagines to be reaching out to touch the Mahatma's feet, she's suddenly knocked to the ground. While she's scrambling to retrieve the rosary, notebook, and spittoon she'd been carrying, three shots ring out. Then she hears what for weeks she'd been trained to expect: *"Hei Ra . . . ma! Hei Ra . . . "* She writes, "The sound of bullets had deafened my ears," but also says that she distinctly heard the prayer that Gandhi said would validate his mahatmaship.

The killer Godse and Vishnu Karkare, one of his cohorts stationed nearby, testified that all they heard from their victim was a cry of pain, something like, *"Aaah!"* Pyarelal, after interviewing witnesses, revised Manu's account. He said the last words were *"Rama, Rama."* Gurbachan Singh, a Sikh businessman walking just behind Gandhi, also claimed to have heard the stifled sound of a prayer. Whether a seventy-eight-year-old man who has taken two slugs fired at point-blank range in the abdomen and one in the chest could conceivably have uttered four or five prayerful syllables as he fell is a forensic question not easily answered at a distance of more than six decades. If he could, it might qualify as something of a miracle, of a sort not infrequently ascribed to saints. On that basis, it can be noted that most of Gandhi's many biographers have been content to end the story of his life on this hagiographic note. The belief that he fulfilled his ambition of dying with the name of God on his lips has seldom been challenged, except by Hindu nationalists willing to rationalize, if not defend, the murder of Gandhi. In that sense, the victim succeeded in controlling his narrative until the end by forecasting his assassination as the final test of his mahatmaship.

Some bystanders dug up clumps of bloodstained earth from the garden to keep as holy relics. Manubehn Gandhi saved fingernail clippings. His ashes were scattered at various points across India. The process goes on. Tushar Gandhi recovered some from a vault of the State Bank of India in 1996 and immersed them at the confluence of the Ganges and Jamuna rivers. As recently as 2010, another small cache of this latter-day saint's ashes was strewn off the coast of South Africa, in Durban's harbor, into which Gandhi first sailed more than a century earlier.

Estimates of the crowds that lined the route of his funeral procession ranged from one to two million. The mood was one of remorse as well as grief. Among historians there's general agreement that the murderous hatreds that had lashed the subcontinent for a year and a half finally burned themselves out with the assassination, or at least lapsed into a period of latency. An Indian academic argues that the country was permanently altered for the better by "a certain kind of bodily sacrifice in the public sphere—and a refusal by one outstanding leader to give his consent to the particular conception of the political community that was emerging." That conception—that Muslims had no place in the new India—was rendered illegitimate by the murder of the leading exponent of unity across communal lines. Hindu-Muslim violence continued to flare intermittently and locally thereafter, but there wasn't anything on the scale of the partition-era killing for more than half a century, until 2002, when pogroms against Muslims in Gandhi's home state of Gujarat led to an estimated two thousand deaths in a little more than three months, during which some 200,000 Muslims were driven from their homes. The killings were tacitly sanctioned, even encouraged, by a right-wing Hindu party lineally descended from extremist movements that were banned for a time following Gandhi's assassination on suspicion that they'd been complicit in the murder. That party has held power ever since in the Gujarati state capital named Gandhinagar, after the favorite son who deplored its brand of chauvinism, expressed in a doctrine of national identity called *Hindutva*, usually translated as "Hinduness." As often noted, it's diametrically opposed to the doctrine of Gandhi, who repeated in the last weeks of his struggle against communal violence what he'd started saying a half century earlier in South Africa: that members of the community should see one another neither as Hindus nor as Muslims but as Indians; their religions were a personal—not a public—concern.

"Today we must forget that we are Hindus or Sikhs or Muslims or Parsis," he said on the eve of his final fast. "If we want to conduct the affairs of India properly we must be only Indians. It is of no consequence by what name we call God in our homes. In the work of the nation, all Indians of all faiths are one . . . We are Indians and we must lay down our lives in protecting Hindus, Muslims, Parsis, Sikhs and all others." That view is alive in India, even if it remains partially eclipsed in Gandhinagar.

When it comes to the Father of the Nation, contradictions not surprisingly abound. They start with the decision in the immediate aftermath of the assassination to put the military, still under the command of a British general, in charge of his funeral arrangements. Thus the era's prophet of nonviolence was transported to the cremation ground on an army weapons carrier pulled by two hundred uniformed troops, preceded by armored cars, mounted lancers, and a police regiment. Air force planes dipped their wings and showered rose petals on the mourners. Later a naval vessel would be used for the immersion in the Ganges, near where it flows into the Jamuna, of bones picked from the cremation site. If (as Gandhi had written in his rudimentary Bengali on leaving Calcutta five months earlier) his life was his message, his death was a message that the Indian state now had license to reinterpret its meaning to suit its immediate requirements.

Weeks after his cremation on a tower of sandalwood, his political and spiritual heirs gathered at Sevagram, his last ashram, in a meeting that was supposed to consider how they would now go forward without him. The security forces, fearful of another assassination, insisted that the ashram be ringed with barbed wire to protect Prime Minister Nehru, who was due to attend. Uniformed police stood guard with fixed bayonets. Vinoba Bhave, widely considered Gandhi's spiritual heir, noted that he was meeting Jawaharlal Nehru, his political heir, for the first time. This showed the degree to which the Mahatma had kept the activities of his ashrams and his political initiatives in separate spheres.

Cremation by the Jamuna, January 31, 1948

Nehru acknowledged as much. In a speech that was both touching and revealing, he admitted that he often found it hard to understand Hindustani, the demotic amalgam of Hindi and Urdu that Gandhi promoted as a lingua franca, and that, anyway, he was illiterate in both Hindi and Urdu. He also confessed that he hadn't bothered to keep track of his master's cherished "constructive" programs, didn't "know much about them in any detail," and didn't understand how Gandhi could have proposed to take the Indian National Congress out of politics now that it was responsible for running things. "Congress has now to govern, not to oppose government," the prime minister said firmly. "So it will have to function in a new way, staying within politics."

A little forlornly but without apologies, the prime minister then ticked off other large points of difference between Gandhi's newly empowered political disciples and the man they all called Bapu: on the need for a modern military, for instance, or for rapid industrialization. Yet, he said, these differences were not fundamental. They were all still committed to Gandhi's ideas, meaning presumably his broad goals of binding the nation and tackling poverty. "What we need to consider," he said, "is why the ideas that had so much pull in Bapu's hands do not have that same power in ours."

Gandhi's followers went their various directions, pursued their various programs, some of which continue to this day on their own small islands of Gandhian endeavor scattered around the vastness of India. In Wardha, I met Dr. U. N. Jajoo, a professor of medicine at the Mahatma Gandhi Institute of Medical Science, affiliated with the Kasturba Gandhi Hospital, who starts the training of his students by requiring them to spend fifteen days in nearby villages where the institute has organized health insurance plans and sanitary latrines for each household, along with clean piped water, resulting in a steep drop in infant and childhood mortality rates. The students are expected to survey the health issues in each household, including the poorest, and return at least monthly for the five years of their training. The medicine is modern, the goals Gandhian, and maybe thirty villages have been covered so far. Dr. Jajoo spins the yarn for his own clothes.

In Ahmedabad, I spent a day with the Self Employed Women's Association, known as SEWA, the largest movement in the country that might be called Gandhian, which brings primary health care, midwives, banking services, and training to impoverished, typically illiterate women—many of them Dalits, many Muslims—traditionally condemned to lives of unrelieved menial labor. Ela Bhatt, the movement's founder, told me she's more convinced of Gandhi's relevance than she was when she first started organizing female "headloaders"—women tasked with hauling goods to market on their heads—nearly four decades ago. "He's a measuring rod," she said.

Gandhi lives in Dr. Jajoo, Ela Bhatt, and others, but they've had to find their own ways on the fringe of India's rowdy, often corrupt power politics. No national movement survived him, an outcome he seems, on occasion, to have foreseen. "Let no one say he is a follower of Gandhi," he said. Protean and infinitely quotable, Gandhi bequeathed an example of constant striving, a set of social values, and a method of resistance, one not easily applied to an India ruled by Indians, with a population nearly triple what it was when he perished.

One of the most widely known of his enduring exhortations is for sale as a printed sampler, ready for framing if not embroidering, at the gift shop of his first Indian ashram near Ahmedabad. It's offered to schoolchildren and other tourists there for a few rupees as "Gandhiji's Talisman."

"Whenever you are in doubt, or when the self becomes too much with you, apply the following test," Gandhi urged in this undated note typed out in English just before or after independence, possibly to Pyarelal; possibly to D. G. Tendulkar, an even earlier biographer, the first to publish the note, which the Mahatma signed twice, in Hindi and Bengali; possibly to Manu, or to himself. "Recall the face of the poorest and weakest man whom you may have seen, and ask yourself if the step you contemplate is going to be of any use to him. Will he gain anything by it? Will it restore him to a control over his own life and destiny? In other words, will it lead to swaraj for the hungry and spiritually starving millions? Then you will find your doubt and your self melting away."

Causing doubt and self to melt away is a traditional aim of Indian religious disciplines involving diet, meditation, and prayer. It's causing them to melt away by means of social and political action that stands out as distinctively Gandhian. As leader and model, Gandhi himself mostly passed his "test." But the hungry and spiritually starving millions in large measure remained.

Trying to build a nation, he couldn't easily admit that their interests— those of Hindu and Muslim, of high caste and untouchable—often clashed. He struggled with doubt and self until his last days but made the predicament of the millions his own, whatever the tensions among them, as no other leader of modern times has. And so his flawed efforts as a social visionary and reformer can be more moving in hindsight than his moments of success as a national leader, if only because the independence struggle long ago reached its untidy end.

In India today, the term "Gandhian" is ultimately synonymous with social conscience; his example—of courage, persistence, identification with the poorest, striving for selflessness—still has a power to inspire, more so even than his doctrines of nonviolence and techniques of resistance, certainly more than his assorted dogmas and pronouncements on subjects like spinning, diet, and sex. It may not happen often, but the inspiration is still there to be imbibed; and when it is, the results can still be called Gandhian, even though the man himself, that great soul, never liked or accepted the word.

GLOSSARY

ahimsa: nonviolence.

Allah-o-akbar: "God is great," an Arabic expression heard in Indian mosques.

Arya Samaj: Hindu reform movement.

Balmikis, Valmikis: name taken by untouchable sweepers, after Hindu saint.

Bapu: father, used affectionately for Gandhi.

Bhagavad Gita: portion of Hindu epic *Mahabharata*, embracing teachings of Krishna.

bhai: brother.

Bhangis: sweepers, viewed traditionally as untouchable.

bidi: small cigarette.

brahmacharya, brahmachari: celibacy, a person who vows celibacy.

Brahman: priestly caste.

bustee: shanty, shack.

Chamars: traditionally leather workers, tanners, seen as untouchable.

charkha: spinning wheel.

charpoy: rope bed.

chetti: moneylender.

Dalit: preferred name, nowadays, for untouchables.

darshan: gaining or giving merit by viewing someone or something deemed holy.

dharma: duty, true code or teaching, religion.

dharma yudha: holy struggle, war.

dhoti: wraparound loincloth, usually a single long strip of hand-loomed fabric.

diwan: chief minister, under a rajah, of an Indian princely state.

doba: Bengali word for pond.

Dwarkanath: another name for the god Krishna.

Ezhavas: an upwardly mobile South Indian subcaste, once considered untouchable.

Harijans: name Gandhi attempted to give untouchables, stands for "children of God."

hijrat: exodus by Muslims from a land deemed unholy.

Hind Swaraj: title of 1909 Gandhi tract, meaning Indian self-rule.

Hindu Mahasabha: nationalist movement of orthodox Hindus.

Hindutva: "Hinduness," doctrine of Hindu supremacy.

jati: an endogamous social grouping, not necessarily synonymous with caste.

jihad: Muslim striving for sanctified goals by means nonviolent or otherwise.

kala pani: "the Black Water," standing mainly for the Indian Ocean as a buffer against Western ways.

karma: individual's destiny, shaped by conduct in previous life.

khadi, khaddar: hand-loomed cloth.

Khilafat: caliphate, position in Sunni Islam involving supervision of holy places; Indian movement to preserve Ottoman Caliph.

ki jai!: cry or slogan meaning "glory to," or "Long Live," as in *"Mahatma Gandhi ki jai!"*

Kolis: a loosely defined subcaste in western India with a reputation for lawlessness; possible root of "coolie."

kurta: a loose-fitting tunic.

mahajans: caste elders.

Mahars: an upwardly mobile group in Maharashtra in western India, traditionally deemed untouchable.

mahatma: great soul, a spiritual honorific.

Manusmriti: ancient legal texts governing caste.

maulana: a Muslim religious scholar.

Modh Banias: the merchant subcaste into which Gandhi was born.

Panchama: an outcaste, or untouchable.

Pariah: an untouchable group in South India.

poorna swaraj: complete self-rule; as used by Gandhi, applied to social uplift as well as political independence.

Pulayas: group deemed untouchable in what's now the state of Kerala.

Ramchandra: another name for the god Ram or Rama.

Rashtriya Swayamsevak Sangh (RSS): militant Hindu group banned after Gandhi's assassination, backbone today of right-wing party; name means National Volunteer Association.

rishi: wise man or sage.

ryot: Indian peasant.

sadhu: an ascetic or holy man, often a mendicant.

sanatan, sanatanists: orthodox; orthodox Hindus.

sannyasi: a Hindu who has renounced the world.

satyagraha, satyagrahis: literally, "firmness in truth," the name for Gandhi's doctrine of nonviolent resistance; those who take part in such campaigns.

shamiana: a colorful, sometimes embroidered tent, used in celebrations.

shastras: Hindu scriptures, holy texts.

sherwani: a long coat worn by Muslims.

shuddi: purification ritual used in religious conversions by Hindus; offered by reformist sects to untouchables.

Shudras: lowest order of caste, mostly peasant laborers, traditionally ranks above untouchables.

sjambok: whips made of rhino or hippo hide in South Africa.

swadeshi: self-reliance.

swaraj: self-rule.

tabligh: propagating religious observance by Muslims.

Vande Mataram: "Hail, Mother," a nationalist cry, standing for Mother India.

varna: one of the four main caste orders.

varnashrama dharma: the rules of caste.

yajna: sacrifice of a religious nature.

zamindar: landowner.

GANDHI'S LIFE

A CHRONOLOGY

1869 Born October 2 in the small princely state of Porbandar, in Kathiawad region of present-day Gujarat, on the Arabian Sea.

1876 Family moves to Rajkot, where he attends school.

1883 Marries Kastur Makanji at age thirteen, after betrothal of seven years.

1885 Death of father, Karamchand Gandhi, called Kaba.

1888 Birth of eldest son, Harilal. Sails for England, studies law at Inner Temple.

1891 Completes studies, sails for Bombay.

1892 Birth of second son, Manilal. Admitted to Bombay bar.

1893 Sails to South Africa, arrives Durban.

1894 Becomes secretary of the Natal Indian Congress, opens law office in Durban. Reads Tolstoy's *Kingdom of God Is Within You.*

1896 Returns to India; brings family back to Durban.

1897 Birth of third son, Ramdas.

1899 Leads Indian Ambulance Corps in Anglo-Boer War.

1900 Birth of fourth son, Devadas.

1901 Returns with family to India intending to resettle there. Attends Indian National Congress meeting in Calcutta.

1902 Called back to South Africa to lead fight against discriminatory legislation, brings family.

1903   Opens law office in Johannesburg, launches *Indian Opinion,* a weekly.

1904   Founds rural commune called the Phoenix Settlement north of Durban, inspired by Ruskin's *Unto This Last.*

1906   Assisting in repression of Zulu uprising, raises corps of Indian stretcher bearers. Takes vow of celibacy. Addresses mass meeting of Transvaal Indians in Johannesburg, pledging resistance to Asiatic Registration Bill. Sails for London to seek redress.

1907   Starts first "passive resistance" campaign. Arrested in December, tried, ordered to leave Transvaal.

1908   Replaces term "passive resistance" with "satyagraha." Sentenced to two months, released in three weeks. Assaulted by Pathans for reversing stand on registration boycott. Encourages burning of registration certificates. Arrested at Volksrust, sentenced to two months of hard labor.

1909   As campaign continues, arrested again for failing to produce registration document. Again lobbies in London, writes *Hind Swaraj* on voyage back to South Africa.

1910   Corresponds with Tolstoy, establishes Tolstoy Farm, another commune, with Hermann Kallenbach, a Jewish architect originally from East Prussia.

1911   Suspends campaign against discriminatory legislation on basis of pledge by General Smuts to ease the more onerous provisions.

1913   Abandons Tolstoy Farm, satyagraha resumed. Leads march of indentured miners from mining town of Newcastle in Natal into Transvaal in defiance of law, with 2,221 marchers. Arrested three times in three days, finally sentenced to nine months of hard labor. Strikes of indentured Indian laborers spread to sugar lands and cities. Released after less than six weeks.

1914   Again reaches accord with Smuts, suspends satyagraha. Leaving South Africa, sails to England, arriving as world war breaks out.

1915 Arrives in Bombay January 4, establishes ashram at Ahmedabad.

1916 Tours India, traveling third-class.

1917 Campaigns on behalf of indigo farmers, Champaran region of Bihar.

1918 Leads campaign on behalf of Ahmedabad mill workers. Further satyagraha against taxes on farmers in Gujarat's Kheda district. Seeks unsuccessfully to recruit Indians to join army for service in Europe.

1919 First national satyagraha, in the form of a strike, against repressive legislation. Arrested for defying order on entering Punjab, four days before massacre by British-led troops at Amritsar. Suspends campaign after subsequent outbreaks of violence.

1920 Indian National Congress adopts his program of "noncooperation." Declares its aim to be achievement of swaraj, or self-rule, by nonviolent means. Emerges as Congress leader as well as leader of Khilafat, Muslim movement seeking restoration of Ottoman Caliph.

1921 Launches mass satyagraha over Punjab killings and Khilafat, promising swaraj in a year. Campaigns for charkha, or spinning wheel, and boycott of imported cloth.

1922 Suspends campaign over violence at Chauri Chaura, goes on five-day fast of "penance." Charged with sedition, sentenced to six years in prison.

1924 Released from prison after appendicitis attack, having served two years. Goes on twenty-one-day fast to promote Hindu-Muslim unity.

1926 *Autobiography* is serialized in *Young India* and *Navajivan*, his English and Gujarati weeklies. Stays at ashram, ostensibly withdrawn from politics.

1928 Back in politics, supports call for declaration of independence if self-government is not granted within a year.

1929   Drafts Congress resolution for "complete independence."

1930   Launches nationwide campaign with Salt March, Ahmedabad to Dandi on the Arabian Sea. Jailed without trial as strikes spread nationwide.

1931   Released after eight months, negotiates with viceroy, Lord Irwin. Sails for England, final trip out of India, to attend Round Table Conference to chart India's constitutional future; no accord reached on special voting rights for untouchables, Muslims. Calls on Mussolini in Rome.

1932   Arrested shortly after return to Bombay in response to his call for renewed satyagraha campaign. "Fast unto death" in Yeravda prison forces British and untouchable leader B. R. Ambedkar to relent on plan for separate electorates for untouchable representatives. Simultaneously calls for swift end to discriminatory practices. For a brief time, India seems to heed call.

1933   Still at Yeravda, fasts again for twenty-one days over treatment of untouchables. Released and rearrested, released again after year's second fast.

1934   Barnstorms across India against untouchability, calling on caste Hindus to open all temples. Target of a bomb, first attempt on life, and demonstrations by orthodox Hindus. Resigns from Congress with the express aim of devoting himself to rural development, especially on behalf of untouchables whom he seeks to rename, calling them Harijans (children of God).

1936   Settles at Sevagram, near Wardha, in impoverished area in center of country. New ashram rises there.

1939   Writes letter to Hitler, never delivered.

1942   Launches "Quit India" movement, demanding immediate self-rule in return for support of war effort. Arrested and imprisoned in Aga Khan Palace near Poona.

1944   Wife, Kasturba, dies in detention at Aga Khan Palace. Suffering from high blood pressure, Gandhi is released ten weeks later on health grounds. Begins talks with Mohammed Ali Jinnah, leader of the Muslim League. Talks break down after eighteen days.

1946   Participates in constitutional talks. Attempt made to derail train carrying him to Poona. Responding to eruption of mutual slaughter by Hindus and Muslims in Bengal, rushes to Muslim-majority area called Noakhali to plead for harmony, head off partition. Stays there four months, eventually trekking barefoot from village to village for eight weeks.

1947   Visits riot-torn areas of Bihar where thousands of Muslims have been killed. Speaks against partition but doesn't oppose Congress resolution in its favor. Shuns independence celebration, fasts in Calcutta for end to violence.

1948   Fasts in New Delhi against expulsion and killing of Muslims. Violence ebbs, but two days after he ends fast, a bomb is thrown in the garden of Birla House, where he stays and holds nightly prayer meetings. Ten days later, on January 30, he's shot to death by a Hindu extremist while walking briskly to prayer meeting.

NOTES

EPIGRAPHS

vii   *"I do not know"*: Gandhi to his son Harilal, Oct. 31, 1918, in Mahadev Desai, *Day-to-Day with Gandhi*, vol. 1, p. 260.
vii   *"I deny being a visionary"*: Mahadev Desai, *Day-to-Day with Gandhi*, vol. 2, p. 201.
vii   *"I am not a quick despairer"*: *Collected Works of Mahatma Gandhi* (hereafter *CWMG*), vol. 23, p. 4.
vii   *"For men like me"*: Gandhi to Nirmal Kumar Bose, cited in Parekh, *Colonialism, Tradition, and Reform*, p. 272.

AUTHOR'S NOTE

xiii   *"have been trying all my life"*: Pyarelal, *Epic Fast*, p. 323.
xiv   *"innumerable trunks"*: *CWMG*, vol. 52, p. 399, cited in Brown, *Gandhi and Civil Disobedience*, p. 316.
xiv   *"He increasingly ceased"*: Brown, *Nehru*, p. 106.
xiv   *"the starving toiling millions"*: M. K. Gandhi, *Village Swaraj*, p. 4.
xiv   *"the emancipation"*: Ibid., p. 6.

CHAPTER 1: PROLOGUE: AN UNWELCOME VISITOR

3   *twenty-three-year-old law clerk*: Gandhi had already qualified as a barrister in India, but saying he came to South Africa as a law clerk accurately describes his role in the case for which he was retained, as he himself later acknowledged: "When I went to South Africa I went only as a law clerk," he said in 1937. *CWMG*, vol. 60, p. 101.
4   *"Just as it is a mark"*: Meer, *South African Gandhi*, p. 121.
5   *"eternal negative"*: Erikson, *Gandhi's Truth*, p. 158.
6   *The Gandhi who landed*: Tinker, *Ordeal of Love*, p. 151.
6   *"I believe in walking alone"*: Pyarelal, *Mahatma Gandhi: Last Phase*, vol. 1, p. 495.
7   *transgressing on the pavement*: If this actually happened. T. K. Mahadevan suggests that the Indian who was pushed off the footpath may have been one C. M. Pillay, who wrote a letter to a newspaper describing an incident almost exactly like the one of which Gandhi complained. Mahadevan raises the suspicion that Gandhi read the letter and simply appropriated the experience. See Mahadevan, *Year of the Phoenix*, p. 25.
8   *However, according to the scholar*: Hunt, *Gandhi and the Nonconformists*, p. 40.
8   *"I was tremendously attracted"*: From an archival interview with Millie Polak broadcast by the BBC on May 7, 2004.

8   *It's a theme Gandhi*: Nayar, *Mahatma Gandhi's Last Imprisonment*, p. 298.

9   *"Agent for the Esoteric"*: CWMG, vol. 1, p. 141.

9   *The word "coolie," after all*: Henry Yule and A. C. Burnell, *Hobson-Jobson* (London, reprint, 1985), p. 249. *The Oxford English Dictionary* accepts this derivation, suggesting the term may have been carried to China from Gujarat in the sixteenth century by Portuguese seamen. Another possible derivation is from the Turkish word *quli*, which means laborer or porter and may have found its way into Urdu. In South Africa the term had a racial tinge and was used specifically to refer to Asians, usually Indians, as noted in the *OED Supplement*.

9   *"It is clear that Indian"*: Meer, *South African Gandhi*, pp. 113–14.

11   *"the Magna Charta"*: Ibid., pp. 117–8.

13   *In the many thousands*: CWMG, vol. 8, p. 242.

14   *At first he spoke only*: Swan, *Gandhi: The South African Experience*, p. 51.

14   *a fact of huge and obvious relevance*: Bhikhu Parekh points out that it may have been easier to unite Hindus and Muslims in South Africa, for many of the traders Gandhi initially served there shared a common language and culture. See Parekh, *Gandhi*, p. 9.

14   *When Johannesburg Muslims*: CWMG, vol. 3, p. 366.

15   *"We are not and ought not"*: Ibid., p. 497, cited by Sanghavi, *Agony of Arrival*, p. 81.

15   *"Here in South Africa"*: CWMG, vol. 5, p. 290.

15   *"The Hindu-Mahomedan problem"*: Ibid., vol. 9, p. 507.

15   *By sheer force of personality*: Ibid., vol. 35, p. 385.

16   *"I saw nothing in it"*: M. K. Gandhi, *Satyagraha in South Africa*, p. 99.

16   *Calling on the community*: CWMG, vol. 5, p. 417.

17   *"To give one's life"*: Ibid., vol. 60, p. 38.

17   *Speaking for a second time*: Ibid., vol. 5, p. 421.

18   *close to endorsing that view*: Brown, *Gandhi: Prisoner of Hope*, p. 268.

18   *"A man who deliberately"*: CWMG, vol. 5, p. 420.

18   *Years later, upon learning*: Ibid., vol. 12, p. 264.

18   *"criminal waste of the vital fluid"*: Ibid., vol. 62, p. 279.

18   *A nephew suggested*: M. K. Gandhi, *Satyagraha in South Africa*, p. 109.

19   *"I did not suggest"*: Paxton, *Sonja Schlesin*, p. 36.

19   *"Our ambition"*: Sarid and Bartolf, *Hermann Kallenbach*, p. 15.

19   *It also doesn't demean Doke*: CWMG, vol. 9, p. 415.

20   *"as naked as possible"*: Erikson, *Gandhi's Truth*, p. 153.

21   *"Mr. Gandhi's ephemeral fame"*: *African Chronicle*, April 16, 1913.

23   *"So far as I can judge"*: Nanda, *Three Statesmen*, p. 426.

23   *Reminiscing, many years later*: Nayar, *Mahatma Gandhi's Last Imprisonment*, p. 380; see also Prabhudas Gandhi, *My Childhood with Gandhiji*, p. 142.

23   *The indentured Indians"*: *Indian Opinion*, Oct. 15, 1913.

23   *"It was a bold, dangerous"*: *Indian Opinion*, Oct. 22, 1913.

23   *Later, back in India*: Nirmal Kumar Bose, *Selections from Gandhi* (Ahmedabad, 1957) 2nd ed., pp. 106–7.

23   *"the numberless men"*: Pyarelal, *Epic Fast*, p. 12.

23   *"I know that the only thing"*: M. K. Gandhi, *Young India*, March 2, 1922, cited by Paul F. Power, ed., *The Meanings of Gandhi* (Honolulu, 1971), p. 71.

24   *"The poor have no fears"*: M. K. Gandhi, *Satyagraha in South Africa*, p. 287.

24   *"the Natal underclasses"*: Swan, *Gandhi: The South African Experience*, p. 242.

Swan cites a letter from Gandhi to Kallenbach, dated July 13, 1913, that she located in the Sarvodaya Library at the Phoenix Settlement. The library was destroyed in the factional violence described in the author's note at the beginning of this volume. As far as I have been able to discover, Swan's quotation from this important letter may be all that survives from it.

25 *"I believe implicitly"*: Rudrangshu Mukherjee, ed., *Penguin Gandhi Reader*, p. 207.

25 *"A Scavenger"*: Nayar, *Mahatma Gandhi's Last Imprisonment*, p. 254.

25 *"The idea did occur to me"*: Mahadev Desai, *Diary of Mahadev Desai*, p. 185.

25 *most indentured laborers were low caste*: Bhana, *Indentured Indian Emigrants to Natal*, pp. 71–83.

26 *"realized my vocation"*: Gandhi, *Satyagraha in South Africa*, p. 338.

26 *"a sorry affair"*: Nirmal Kumar Bose, *My Days with Gandhi*, p. 229.

26 *Indians lack a tragic sense*: Naipaul, *Overcrowded Barracoon*, p. 75.

27 *"The saint has left"*: Hancock, *Smuts*, p. 345.

27 *"that they have an instrument"*: Ibid., p. 331.

CHAPTER 2: NO-TOUCHISM

28 *"the least Indian"*: Naipaul, *Area of Darkness*, p. 77 [my italics].

28 *"the quintessence"*: Nehru, *Toward Freedom*, p. 189.

29 *"He looked at India"*: Naipaul, *Area of Darkness*, p. 77.

29 *"I was face to face"*: Gandhi, *Autobiography*, p. 196.

30 *"There were only a few"*: Ibid., pp. 196–97.

30 *Even as a boy*: Andrews, *Mahatma Gandhi*, p. 113.

31 *Just as racial segregation*: Bayly, *Caste, Society, and Politics in India*, chap. 5, especially pp. 196, 210, 226.

32 *"pollution barrier"*: Ibid., pp. 189, 233.

32 *Practices varied*: The following studies have illuminating discussions on these points: Ibid., Dirks, *Castes of Mind*, and Mendelsohn and Vicziany, *Untouchables*.

32 *the coinage "Hinduism"*: See Pennington, *Was Hinduism Invented?* p. 60, also p. 168.

33 *Gandhi was then warned*: Jordens, *Gandhi's Religion*, p. 56.

33 *"It was also a problem"*: Prabhudas Gandhi, *My Childhood with Gandhiji*, p. 59.

34 *Three years later*: Photostat of the certificate is on display at the Sabarmati Ashram Museum.

34 *The Bania in Gandhi*: Doke, *M. K. Gandhi: An Indian Patriot*, p. 52.

34 *The prodigal son*: Pyarelal, *Early Phase*, p. 281.

35 *"I would not so much"*: Gandhi, *Autobiography*, p. 78.

35 *His standing with the Modh Banias*: I am indebted to Narayan Desai, son of Mahadev, Gandhi's secretary, for making this point in an interview in Barodi in April 2008.

36 *"Wherever you see men"*: O'Hanlon, *Caste, Conflict, and Ideology*, p. 71.

37 *"We are all brothers"*: Tolstoy, *Kingdom of God Is Within You*, p. 88. According to Professor Donald Fanger of Harvard, the literal translation would be "carries out my chamber pot."

37 *What Is to Be Done?*: Although the common English title of this Tolstoy volume is the same as that of a more famous tract by Lenin, the Russian titles are differ-

ent. Professor Fanger says the literal translation of the Tolstoy would be "So What Must We Do?"

37 *"when men of our circle"*: Tolstoy, *What Is to Be Done?* p. 272. I've here substituted "latrines" for "sewers" on the advice of Professor Fanger.

37 *"Gandhi," Aurobindo said*: Aurobindo, *India's Rebirth*, p. 173.

38 *But an Indian scholar*: Mahadevan, *Year of the Phoenix*, pp. 70–71.

38 *In any case, by August*: Swan, in *Gandhi: The South African Experience*, pp. 48–50, casts doubt on the assumption that the young Gandhi provided the impetus for the formation of the Natal Indian Congress. She suggests that the traders who subsequently dominated the organization are likely to have employed Gandhi to advance their goals.

38 *"To inquire into the conditions"*: CWMG, vol. 1, p. 132.

38 *"I lived in South Africa"*: Ibid., vol. 33, p. 25.

40 *His wounds have been treated*: Ibid., vol. 2, p. 20.

40 *It takes half a year*: Meer, *Apprenticeship of a Mahatma*, p. 36.

40 *"A regular stream"*: Gandhi, *Autobiography*, p. 135.

40 *"He emerged virtually"*: Sanghavi, *Agony of Arrival*, p. 129.

40 *Gandhi himself doesn't go on*: According to the Durban lawyer Hassim Seedat, who attempted to trace Gandhi's legal papers from this era through the successor firm that inherited them only to be told that they had been thrown out.

41 *"He will cause some trouble"*: Britton, *Gandhi Arrives in South Africa*, p. 300. The location of this document isn't specified in the book. Responding to an e-mail query, its author explained that he did his research "on and off for thirty years," much of it in the archives of colonial Natal, in the branch of the National Archives in Pietermaritzburg, or in British Colonial Office files, now located at the National Archives in Kew.

41 *"have no wish to see"*: CWMG, vol. 1, pp. 273–74, cited by Naidoo, *Tracking Down Historical Myths*, p. 137.

41 *"If that hatred"*: CWMG, vol. 1, p. 143.

41 *In finely honed understatement*: Ibid., pp. 142–63.

42 *"The class of Hindoos"*: *Critic*, Jan. 11, 1895, as quoted in Pyarelal, *Early Phase*, p. 478.

42 *Or, since Pyarelal*: Pyarelal and Nayar, *In Gandhiji's Mirror*, p. 7.

42 *"The barbed shaft penetrated"*: Pyarelal, *Early Phase*, p. 478.

42 *"Has not a just"*: Fischer, *Essential Gandhi*, p. 251. See also M. K. Gandhi, *Selected Political Writings*, p. 118.

42 *"During my campaigns"*: CWMG, vol. 13, p. 278.

43 *"dark and stinking"*: Gandhi, *Autobiography*, p. 149.

43 *He then went into*: Ibid., p. 150.

43 *"But to clean those used*: Ibid., pp. 243–44.

44 *His pique becomes*: CWMG, vol. 67, p. 2.

44 *"close touch with suffering Indians"*: Gandhi, *Autobiography*, p. 177.

45 *"The Indians were not entitled"*: Gandhi, *Satyagraha in South Africa*, p. 76.

45 *So while he has told us*: Gandhi, *Autobiography*, p. 189.

45 *"General Buller had no intention"*: Gandhi, *Satyagraha in South Africa*, p. 77.

46 *"For days they worked"*: Fischer, *Life of Mahatma Gandhi*, p. 63.

46 *"The agony of the General"*: Pyarelal, *Discovery of Satyagraha*, p. 287.

46 *curtained palanquin*: This thought is suggested by the drawing on a French weekly magazine cover on display in the Museum Africa in Johannesburg.

Showing a palanquin used for ferrying wounded officers, the drawing has a legend that describes it as an "ambulance Indienne" in the "guerre au Transvaal." See *Le Petit Journal: Supplément Illustré, Dec. 17, 1899.*

47 *detailed narrative of these events:* Amery, *"Times" History of the War in South Africa,* vol. 1, pp. 245–97.

47 *"Streams of wounded":* Reproduced in *New York Times,* March 3, 1900.

47 *The recruits from the ranks:* Meer, *South African Gandhi,* p. 751.

47 *In the event, no Indians:* Ibid., pp, 749–50.

48 *At the time he finds:* Gandhi, *Satyagraha in South Africa,* p. 78.

48 *"Bapu had found a use":* Mehta, *Mahatma Gandhi and His Apostles,* p. 248.

49 *In a contemporary send-up:* Reprinted in *African Chronicle,* July 4, 1908.

49 *"high-caste men married":* Uma Dhupelia-Mesthrie, *From Cane Fields to Freedom: A Chronicle of Indian South African Life* (Cape Town, 2000), p. 13.

49 *"These two Indians":* Bhana and Pachai, *Documentary History of Indian South Africans,* p. 26.

49 *Except for a rare academic study:* Such as Ebr-Vally, *Kala Pani.*

50 *"without first trying":* Rolland, *Life of Vivekananda and the Universal Gospel,* p. 23.

50 *He condemned India's:* Parekh, *Colonialism, Tradition, and Reform,* p. 235.

51 *Their suppression depresses:* CWMG, vol. 18, pp. 375–76.

51 *"into intimate touch":* Pyarelal, *Discovery of Satyagraha,* p. 396.

51 *"A purer, a nobler":* Mahadevan and Ramachandran, *Quest for Gandhi,* p. 344.

51 *"You will never know":* Shirer, *Gandhi,* p. 37.

51 *"converted the whole carriage":* Gandhi, *Autobiography,* p. 212.

51 *"in retrospect, Gandhi":* Pyarelal, *Discovery of Satyagraha,* p. 396.

CHAPTER 3: AMONG ZULUS

54 *"We were then marched":* CWMG, vol. 8, p. 135.

54 *Similarly, he would later:* Enacted in 1907 by the all-white provincial legislature as soon as self-rule was restored to the former South African Republic. (The 1906 Asiatic Law Amendment Act, passed during the brief period that the Transvaal was counted as a crown colony, had been disallowed by Britain.) The legislation once again barred Indians with no history of previous residence in the Transvaal.

54 *"The spirit of fanaticism":* Huttenback, *Gandhi in South Africa,* p. 198.

54 *It would violate: Natal Mercury,* Jan. 14, 1903. The Orange Free State, one of the four provinces in the original Union of South Africa, barred Indians from taking up residence for nearly ninety years longer, until the dismantling of apartheid.

55 *"for the first time":* Rajmohan Gandhi, *Gandhi,* p. 126.

55 *Brought to Johannesburg:* Doke, *M. K. Gandhi: An Indian Patriot,* p. 151; see also Meer, *South African Gandhi,* pp. 600–601; Itzkin, *Gandhi's Johannesburg,* p. 30.

56 *"a Native lying in bed":* Meer, *South African Gandhi,* p. 601.

56 *"This refined Indian":* Doke, *M. K. Gandhi: Indian Patriot,* p. 152.

56 *"a strong, heavily built":* Meer, *South African Gandhi,* p. 602.

57 *"We may entertain":* Ibid., p. 601.

57 *Is that, as some Indian scholars:* They were speaking speculatively in private conversation.

57 *In strict interpretation of caste:* In the late 1960s, when I was a correspondent in

India, I asked a Hindu religious figure, the Shankaracharya of Puri, whether he could imagine himself sitting and talking to an untouchable. He replied: "I'm talking with you."

57 *"the Indian is being dragged"*: CWMG, vol. 1, p. 150.

57 *"the raw Kaffir"*: Ibid., vol. 2, p. 74.

58 *"About the mixing"*: Ibid., vol. 4, p. 131.

58 *"If there is one thing"*: Ibid., p. 89.

58 *"We believe as much"*: Ibid., vol. 3, p. 453.

58 *"Oh, say have you seen"*: Quoted in Mahadevan, *Year of the Phoenix*, p. 43, clipping in archive of Sabarmati Ashram, Ahmedabad.

58 *"A fair complexion"*: Gandhi, *Satyagraha in South Africa*, pp. 8–9.

59 *"Are Asiatic and Colored races"*: "Mr. Gandhi's Address Before the Y.M.C.A.," *Indian Opinion*, June 6, 1908, in *CWMG*, vol. 8, pp. 242–46.

60 *"If we look into the future"*: CWMG, vol. 8, pp. 232–46.

61 *"these hypocritical distinctions"*: Meer, *South African Gandhi*, pp. 606–7; "My Second Experience in Gaol," *Indian Opinion*, Jan. 30, 1909.

61 *Possibly these are "Native Isaac"*: Diary of Hermann Kallenbach, Sabarmati Ashram archive, Ahmedabad.

62 *"It is understood"*: CWMG, vol. 96, supp. vol. 6, p. 44.

62 *"I regard the Kaffirs"*: CWMG, vol. 10, cited by Green, *Gandhi*, p. 200.

62 *Rajmohan Gandhi, his grandson*: Rajmohan Gandhi, *Gandhi*, p. 149.

62 *And when it comes*: The other two were the Reverend Walter Rubusana, who was elected to the Cape province provincial council, and John Tengo Jabavu, editor of a weekly newspaper printed in English and Xhosa in Cape Town, where Gandhi encountered him. See Uma Dhupelia-Mesthrie, *From Cane Fields to Freedom: A Chronicle of Indian South African Life* (Cape Town, 2000), p. 118. Of course, the absence of other names in Gandhi's writings of the period does not in itself demonstrate that he had no further encounters with African leaders. Recently, in an as-yet-unpublished memoir by a woman named Pauline Padlashuk, an account has come to light of a visit to Tolstoy Farm by Pixley ka Isaka Seme, who, like Dube, was an early officeholder of what became the African National Congress. "Mr. Gandhi told Dr. Seme about his passive resistance movement," this white witness wrote.

62 *A Zulu aristocrat*: Shula Marks, "Ambiguities of Dependence: John L. Dube of Natal," *Journal of South African Studies* 1, no. 2 (1975), p. 163.

63 *"my patron saint"*: Fredrickson, *Black Liberation*, p. 119.

63 *president-general he was called*: Dube himself did not attend the founding session of the new Congress in Bloemfontein. He was elected president in absentia.

63 *"This Mr. Dubey"*: CWMG, vol. 5, p. 55.

63 *"They worked hard"*: Fredrickson, *Black Liberation*, p. 119.

64 *We know that Gopal*: Ilanga lase Natal, Nov. 15, 1912. The entry in Kallenbach's diary for that date, at the archive of the Sabarmati Ashram, doesn't mention the visit to Inanda at all.

65 *"To us at the Phoenix Settlement"*: "A Great Zulu Dead," *Indian Opinion*, Feb. 15, 1946.

65 *"the solidarity between"*: Jacob Zuma, in speech available online at www.info.gov.za/speeches/2000/000/0010161010A1002.htm.>.

66 *The immediate provocation*: The term "poll tax" as it was used in South Africa at that time had nothing to do with elections. See Surendra Bhana, "Gandhi, Indi-

ans, and Africans in South Africa," paper presented at the Kansas African Studies Center, Sept. 12, 2002.

67 *"For the Indian community"*: *CWMG*, vol. 5, p. 366.

68 *Gandhi had the rank*: Ibid., p. 368. Another biographer, D. G. Tendulkar, following the *Autobiography*, makes it twenty-four, including nineteen ex-indentured. Tendulkar, *Mahatma*, vol. 1, p. 76.

68 *In the next few weeks*: This is the surmise of the leading South African scholar on this conflict, Jeff Guy, in his book *Maphumulo Uprising*, p. 101.

69 *"I do not remember"*: Prabhudas Gandhi, *My Childhood with Gandhiji*, p. 42.

69 *But it did say*: See Bhana, "Gandhi, Indians, and Africans in South Africa."

69 *In London, an exile*: Green, *Gandhi*, p. 160.

69 *"Mr. Gandhi speaks with"*: Doke, *M. K. Gandhi: An Indian Patriot*, p. 111.

69 *"It was no trifle"*: Ibid., p. 112.

70 *"My heart was with the Zulus"*: Gandhi, *Autobiography*, p. 279.

70 *As late as 1943*: Nayar, *Mahatma Gandhi's Last Imprisonment*, p. 264.

70 *"These themes"*: Erikson, *Gandhi's Truth*, p. 194.

70 *In part, this may have*: Marks, "Ambiguities of Dependence," p. 54.

71 *"No, I purposely did not"*: *CWMG*, vol. 62, p. 199.

71 *"Yours is a far bigger issue"*: Ibid., vol. 68, p. 273.

71 *"I venture to trust"*: Pietermaritzburg Archives Repository, Government House 1457, Military Affairs, Bhambatha Rebellion Correspondence, Feb. 9, to Dec. 28, 1907. See also M. K. Gandhi to Gov. H. McCallum, Aug. 13, 1907. Thanks to Jeff Guy, at the University of KwaZulu-Natal, who called this passage to my attention.

72 *He had spoken of the need*: Marks, "Ambiguities of Dependence," p. 54.

72 *"decency of wearing clothes"*: Speech at the Natal Missionary Conference, at Durban Town Hall, July 4, 1911. Text in archive of Killie Campbell Library in Durban.

72 *close to the Zulu royal house*: In 1936—twenty-four years after he was elected president of the South African Native National Congress—John Dube was named "Prime Minister" of what was termed the Zulu nation by the reigning Prince Regent.

72 *"Every other question"*: "Sons of the Soil," *Indian Opinion*, Aug. 30, 1913, quoted in Nauriya, *African Element in Gandhi*, p. 48.

73 *"You must know that every one"*: Reprinted in "Sons of the Soil," cited by Nauriya, *African Element in Gandhi*, p. 48.

73 *"About five hundred Indians"*: Document in the Gandhi-Luthuli Documentation Center at the University of KwaZulu-Natal, File 1262/203, 3984, HIST/1893/14.

74 *"people like Indians"*: See Carl Faye, *Zulu References for Interpreters and Students in Documents* (Pietermaritzburg, 1923), which includes "Notes of Proceedings at Meeting with Zulus Held by John L. Dube at Eshowe, Zululand, 30 November 1912."

74 *"anti-Indianism"*: Heather Hughes, "Doubly Elite: Exploring the Life of John Langalibalele Dube," *Journal of Southern African Studies* vol. 27, no. 3 (Sept. 2001): footnote p. 446. The quotation from "The Indian Invasion" came to me in an e-mail from Ms. Hughes.

74 *Later a Zulu newspaper*: Roux, *Time Longer Than Rope*, p. 250.

74 *"Indians cannot make common cause"*: *Harijan*, Feb. 18, 1939.

74 *"Indians and Africans must act"*: A little more than two months before Nazis attacked the Soviet Union, she was delivering what was essentially an antiwar message, but not for Gandhi's reasons.

75 *That night, according to one*: "I Remember," privately circulated memoir by I. C. Meer, edited by E. S. Reddy and Fatima Meer.

75 *"pogrom" against Indians*: Goolam Vahed and Ashwin Desai offer a narrative and analysis of the 1949 riot in *Monty Naiker: Between Reason and Treason* (Pietermaritzburg, 2010), pp. 234–55.

75 *"The inclusion of all"*: CWMG, vol. 87, p. 414.

75 *But few African leaders were ready*: The conspicuous exception was Albert Luthuli who became president of the African National Congress in 1952. Four years later, a few months after Gandhi's murder, Luthuli spoke of "the efficacy of nonviolence as an instrument of struggle in seeking freedom for oppressed people" in a speech at Howard University in Washington that anticipated Martin Luther King, Jr. The first South African to win the Nobel Peace Prize said blacks in the United States as well as Africa should go forward as Gandhi's "undoubted disciples." His notes for the speech are preserved in the archive of the Luthuli Museum in Groutville, KwaZulu-Natal, and cited by Scott Couper in his *Albert Luthuli: Bound by Faith*.

75 *"Many of our grassroots"*: Mandela, *Long Walk to Freedom*, p. 107, cited by Dhupelia-Mesthrie, *Gandhi's Prisoner?* p. 342.

76 *Repeatedly, he courted arrest*: Dhupelia-Mesthrie, *Gandhi's Prisoner?* pp. 353–55.

76 *But Manilal had no organized*: Ibid., p. 355.

76 *At one meeting*: Ibid., pp. 350–51.

76 *"The principle was not"*: Mandela, *Long Walk to Freedom*, p. 111. See also pp. 91, 99.

CHAPTER 4: UPPER HOUSE

80 *"No man or woman living"*: Gandhi to Kallenbach, June 16, 1912, quoted by Hunt and Bhana, "Spiritual Rope-Walkers."

80 *"a grim fight against"*: CWMG, 2nd ed., vol. 58, pp. 118–19.

81 *For five of those years*: Kasturba moved to Tolstoy Farm with two sons in the latter half of 1910 and stayed till September 1912, when she moved back to Phoenix, according to Dhupelia-Mesthrie, *Gandhi's Prisoner?* pp. 96, 104.

81 *Gandhi insists*: Gandhi, *Autobiography*, p. 270.

82 *Colonial Natal was a place*: *Natal Mercury*, June 15, 1903.

82 *"no reason why we should"*: Huttenback, *Gandhi in South Africa*, p. 244. Emphasis mine.

82 *Finally, in 1908*: Ibid., p. 235.

83 *"I use all the money"*: CWMG, vol. 6, p. 433.

83 *"So I kept pouring out"*: Gandhi, *Autobiography*, pp. 252–53.

83 *"One day news came"*: Prabhudas Gandhi, *My Childhood with Gandhiji*, pp. 44–45, 58.

84 *"I could stay there only"*: Gandhi, *Autobiography*, p. 270.

84 *The two centers*: Anand, *Mahatma Gandhi and the Railways*, p. 13.

85 *Physically strong and quick-tempered*: Meer, *South African Gandhi*, p. 1202.
85 *According to Prema Naidoo*: Interview with Prema Naidoo, Johannesburg, Nov. 2007.
85 *"If Thambi Naidoo"*: Gandhi, *Satyagraha in South Africa*, p. 148.
85 *"Mine would be considered"*: Gandhi, *Autobiography*, p. 274.
86 *Gandhi's house still stands*: Itzkin, *Gandhi's Johannesburg*, p. 61.
86 *"His voice was soft"*: Interview with Millie Polak, 1954, from the BBC archive, broadcast on May 7, 2004.
87 *When Harilal was married*: Dalal, *Harilal Gandhi*, p. 10.
87 *In a will drafted in 1909*: CWMG, vol. 96, p. 9.
87 *"He feels that I have"*: Dalal, *Harilal Gandhi*, p. 30.
88 *"almost in the same bed"*: *Harijan*, May 29, 1937. Quoted in an article by Mahadev Desai on Kallenbach's visit to India.
88 *Gandhi early on made a point*: CWMG, vol. 96, p. 9.
88 *One respected Gandhi scholar*: "[James D.] Hunt asserts that their relationship was clearly homoerotic while not homosexual." As related by Weber, *Gandhi as Disciple and Mentor*, p. 74.
88 *Kallenbach, who was raised*: Gandhi, *Satyagraha in South Africa*, p. 301.
89 *He'd thus been in South Africa*: Chapman, *Sandow the Magnificent*, pp. 153–54.
89 *"Your portrait"*: CWMG, vol. 96, pp. 28–29.
89 *The most plausible guesses*: See Joseph S. Alter, *Gandhi's Body: Sex, Diet, and the Politics of Nationalism* (Philadelphia, 2000), p. 36: "Moreover, Gandhi's focused attention on the problems associated with constipation, and his regular use of enemas, can be explained, at least in part, by the need he felt to keep his body immaculately clean."
89 *In the agreement dated*: CWMG, vol. 96, pp. 62–63.
90 *"For the last two years"*: Sarid and Bartolf, *Hermann Kallenbach*, p. 16.
90 *Later it is Kallenbach*: Gandhi, *Autobiography*, p. 294.
90 *"I see death in chocolates"*: CWMG, vol. 96, p. 71.
90 *He sends Kallenbach*: Ibid., p. 129.
90 *a Dutch word*: Jean Branford, *A Dictionary of South African English* (Cape Town, 1980), p. 147.
92 *"Life is very short"*: CWMG, vol. 9, p. 426, citing the original G. K. Chesterton article which appeared in *The Illustrated London News*, Oct. 2, 1909. See also Payne, *Life and Death of Mahatma Gandhi*, p. 213.
92 *"The English have not taken India"*: M. K. Gandhi, *Hind Swaraj*, pp. 39, 114.
92 *"Those in whose name we speak"*: Ibid., p. 70.
93 *"The primary object"*: CWMG, 2nd ed., vol. 11, p. 428.
93 *"I should like to slip out"*: Ibid., p. 428.
93 *"They are more useful"*: M. K. Gandhi, "To the Colonial Born Indian," *Indian Opinion*, July 15, 1911.
93 *"That is my predominant occupation"*: CWMG, 2nd ed., vol. 12, p. 49.
93 *"makes us eat more"*: Ibid., vol. 11, p. 169.
93 *Now, when he eases up*: Ibid., vol. 96, p. 96, where Gandhi informs Kallenbach of the dietary switch. For his earlier insistence on a saltless regime, which he said "purifies the blood to a high degree," see vol. 11, pp. 130, 150, 507–8.
96 *In Gandhi's mind*: Ibid., vol. 11, p. 190.
96 *Upper House is wounded*: Ibid., vol. 96, p. 220.

96   *"Though I love"*: Ibid., p. 166.
97   *"a man of strong feelings"*: Gandhi, *Satyagraha in South Africa*, p. 171, cited in Weber, *Gandhi as Disciple and Mentor*, p. 71.
97   *"morbid sensitiveness"*: CWMG, vol. 96, pp. 118, 183.
97   *The timing of Gandhi's*: Gandhi settled in Johannesburg following his application to the Johannesburg bar on February 16, 1903. Meer, *South African Gandhi*, p. 37.
97   *"whose eyes were always"*: Gandhi, *Autobiography*, p. 222.
98   *"In these conversations"*: Gandhi, *Satyagraha in South Africa*, p. 269.
98   *"I shall be there"*: CWMG, vol. 11, p. 161.
98   *His "inner voice"*: As quoted, for instance, in Nayar, *Mahatma Gandhi's Last Imprisonment*, p. 187.
99   *Threatening renewed resistance*: CWMG, vol. 11, p. 229.
99   *Hundreds of other resisters*: Huttenback, *Gandhi in South Africa*, pp. 264–65.
99   *"a substitute for slavery"*: *Indian Opinion*, March 10, 1908, included in Meer, *South African Gandhi*, p. 964.
100   *"To a starving man"*: *Indian Opinion*, Sept. 17, 1903, included in Meer, *South African Gandhi*, p. 969.
100   *Indian Opinion carried*: *Indian Opinion*, Sept. 16, 1911.
100   *"In spite of your remarks"*: CWMG, vol. 10, p. 465. See also Swan, *Gandhi: The South African Experience*, p. 211.
101   *The most Gandhi had been hoping*: CWMG, vol. 11, p. 130.
101   *"If I felt like being free"*: Ibid., vol. 96, p. 98.
101   *A week later he wrote*: Ibid., p. 99.
101   *For nearly a year*: *African Chronicle*, May 19, 1909, and March 25, 1911. Available on microfilm at the British Library.
101   *"an absolute Hindu"*: *African Chronicle*, June 15 and 8, 1912.
102   *Just ten months later*: *African Chronicle*, April 16, 1913.
102   *"Mr. Gandhi may have been"*: *African Chronicle*, June 10 and Jan. 10, 1914.
103   *Though they'd agreed that*: Rajmohan Gandhi, *Gandhi*, p. 158.
103   *Some days earlier*: *African Chronicle*, Nov. 16, 1912.
103   *Fifteen years after the fact*: Gandhi, *Satyagraha in South Africa*, pp. 270, 242–43.
103   *"Are we not to blame"*: CWMG, vol. 12, p. 207.
104   *"You must return"*: Gandhi, *Satyagraha in South Africa*, p. 268.

CHAPTER 5: LEADING THE INDENTURED

105   *The status of Indians*: Quoted in Millin, *General Smuts*, p. 230.
106   *He wrote a long piece*: CWMG, vol. 12, pp. 132–35.
107   *"Then I am not your wife"*: Ibid., p. 31.
107   *"We congratulate our plucky"*: Ibid., p. 66.
108   *"I have sketched out"*: Ibid., vol. 96, p. 121.
108   *"resolving in my own mind"*: Swan, *Gandhi: The South African Experience*, p. 242.
108   *"When this tax thus fell"*: Gandhi, *Satyagraha in South Africa*, p. 273.
109   *The government was too*: Meer, *South African Gandhi*, p. 47.
109   *On consecutive days*: Kallenbach diary in the archive of the Sabarmati Ashram, Ahmedabad. Naidoo is a Telugu, not a Tamil, name, but Thambi Naidoo was

chairman of the Tamil Benefit Society in Johannesburg, where the term "Tamil" seems to have been used loosely to designate all those of South Indian origin who might also in that era have been called Madrasis.

109 *That evening he and Gandhi*: Kallenbach diary notes, July 3–7, 1913, in the archive of the Sabarmati Ashram, Ahmedabad.

110 *"ringleader"*: *Natal Witness*, Oct. 18, 1913.

110 *Gandhi had used the threat*: CWMG, vol. 12, pp. 214–15.

111 *"But the mere presence"*: Ibid., p. 512.

111 *"It may be difficult"*: Ibid., p. 214.

112 *Natal's attorney general*: Desai and Vahed, *Inside Indenture*, p. 363.

112 *"A peculiar position"*: *Natal Witness*, Oct. 18, 1913.

112 *As the message spread*: Desai and Vahed, *Inside Indenture*, p. 364.

113 *"Any precipitate step"*: *African Chronicle*, Oct. 18, 1913.

114 *"Indians do not fight"*: CWMG, vol. 12, p. 240.

114 *Despite all these signals*: Desai and Vahed, *Inside Indenture*, p. 364.

114 *"We do not believe"*: CWMG, vol. 12, p. 253.

114 *All the women he'd dispatched*: *Star*, Nov. 1, 1913.

115 *The procession*: Bhana and Pachai, *Documentary History of Indian South Africans*, p. 143.

116 *"They struck not"*: Ibid., pp. 142–43.

116 *Here a reporter*: "The Great March: Mr. Gandhi at Work," *Indian Opinion*, Nov. 19, 1913.

116 *Gandhi, in the thick*: "What the British Press Says," *Indian Opinion*, Nov. 19, 1913.

116 *Later he wrote*: Gandhi, *Satyagraha in South Africa*, pp. 296, 299.

116 *"General Smuts will have"*: Ibid., p. 300.

118 *"He gave me strokes"*: Desai and Vahed, *Inside Indenture*, p. 372.

118 *"Any government worth its salt"*: *Transvaal Leader*, Oct. 29, 1913.

119 *The Natal Coal Owners Association*: Desai and Vahed, *Inside Indenture*, p. 369.

119 *Taking their cues*: *The Star*, Nov. 10, 1913.

119 *spread of the strike's seeming flood tide*: Desai and Vahed, *Inside Indenture*, p. 393.

119 *The first walkout*: *Transvaal Leader*, Nov. 5 and 8, 1913.

119 *At the height of the unrest*: Report on Durban Police dated November 17 by Chief Magistrate Percy Binns, National Archives, Pretoria.

120 *Rajmohan Gandhi suggests*: Rajmohan Gandhi, *Gandhi*, p. 167.

120 *"The leaders of the movement"*: "Progress of the Strike: The Durban Conference," *Indian Opinion*, Oct. 29, 1913.

120 *Nevertheless, Vahed and Desai*: Desai and Vahed, *Inside Indenture*, p. 384.

120 *The plantation to which the food*: In the apartheid era, a black township was laid out on lands that had belonged to the old Campbell estate. It was called Kwa-Mashu. Few of its inhabitants were likely to know that "Mashu" was a Zulu rendering of "Marshall," a tribute to the white planter who introduced Gandhi to Dube.

120 *He'd told his supporters*: CWMG, vol. 12, p. 298.

121 *"carnival of violence"*: The full text of Marshall Campbell's letter to Gandhi dated Dec. 30, 1913, can be found at the Killie Campbell Library in Durban in a file that also contains a letter from Colin Campbell to his brother William and a subsequent letter from William to his father. None of these letters shed any light

on the question of what the supposed ballistic examination showed about who fired the bullet that killed the indentured laborer Patchappen, if it was not the planter's son.

121   *"In all our struggles"*: Ibid., pp. 298–99.

121   *By his own testimony*: *Transvaal Leader*, Nov. 28 and 29 and Dec. 19 and 23, 1913.

122   *If he'd not been in jail*: Desai and Vahed, *Inside Indenture*, p. 394.

122   *The Indians had refused*: On November 14, according to Desai and Vahed, *Inside Indenture*, p. 382.

122   *A detachment of police*: Ibid., p. 383.

123   *These themes are regularly*: *Transvaal Leader*, Nov. 19, 1913.

123   *"The Indians were very excited"*: Indian Enquiry Commission Report, presented to Parliament April 1914, p. 8 (available at House of Commons Parliamentary Papers Online, accessible through ProQuest).

123   *"overwhelmed in numbers"*: *Transvaal Leader*, Nov. 28, 1913.

123   *The commission that looked*: Indian Enquiry Commission Report, p. 10.

123   *A witness told Reuters*: Clipping on file in the National Archives, Pretoria.

124   *An indentured laborer*: *Indian Opinion*, Dec. 12, 1913.

124   *The British governor-general*: Lord Gladstone's cable is on file at the National Archives, Pretoria. Contending that Botha and Smuts had reacted to the Indian strikes "with great forbearance," the governor-general declared: "I deprecate official credence being given to outrageous charges telegraphed to India by those who were responsible for the strikes here."

125   *Most of his spare time*: CWMG, vol. 12, p. 270.

125   *He said he'd miss the solitude*: Ibid., p. 272.

126   *Gandhi used it to prepare*: Ibid., p. 276.

126   *"How glorious"*: Ibid., p. 274.

127   *"I saw that it was no matter for grief"*: Ibid., p. 320.

127   *But fresh out of jail*: Ibid., p. 315.

128   *"I explained that they had come out, not as indentured laborers"*: Bhana and Pachai, *Documentary History of Indian South Africans*, p. 142.

128   *In assigning to the strikers*: CWMG, vol. 12, p. 660.

128   *"Mr. Gandhi's performance"*: *African Chronicle*, Dec. 27, 1913, and Jan. 10, 1914. Aiyar was still at his old Durban address in Sept. 1944 when a wartime censorship office intercepted a letter, now on file at the National Archive in Pretoria, that he wrote to the New York office of the Indian National Congress seeking help on the publication of a book on race conflict in South Africa.

129   *"a charter of our freedom"*: CWMG, vol. 12, p. 483.

129   *"a final settlement"*: Ibid., p. 442.

130   *These could be achieved*: Ibid., p. 478.

130   *"We need not fight for votes"*: Ibid., p. 479.

130   *Finally, he had to concede*: Ibid., p. 477.

131   *Between 1914 and 1940*: Uma Dhupelia-Mesthrie, *From Cane Fields to Freedom: A Chronicle of Indian South African Life* (Cape Town, 2000), pp. 16–17.

131   *They had an understanding*: Nanda, *Three Statesmen*, p. 467.

131   *She'd not been consulted*: Interview with Prema Naidoo, Johannesburg, Nov. 2007.

131   *Gandhi thanked*: CWMG, vol. 12, p. 474.

131   *"I am, as ever"*: Ibid., p. 486.

131   *"I am under indenture"*: Ibid., p. 472.

132 *"The Atlantic"*: Rajmohan Gandhi, *Gandhi*, p. 173.

133 *"I have no Kallenbach"*: CWMG, vol. 15, p. 341, cited in Sarid and Bartolf, *Hermann Kallenbach*, p. 64.

CHAPTER 6: WAKING INDIA

139 *He was more "at home"*: CWMG, vol. 13, p. 5.

140 *"teach them why India"*: Ibid., p. 195.

141 *He makes a point*: Hindustani, the spoken language of the North Indian street (and Bollywood), derives its vocabulary from both Sanskrit and Persian, through Hindi and Urdu.

141 *"I should have thought"*: CWMG, vol. 21, p. 14.

141 *"In India, what we want"*: Ibid., p. 73.

141 *"I do not believe"*: Ibid., vol. 16, p. 282.

141 *"the malady of foot-touching"*: Ibid., vol. 20, p. 511.

141 *"In the mere touch"*: Mahadev Desai, *Day-to-Day with Gandhi*, vol. 3, p. 286.

141 *"At night"*: Fischer, *Life of Mahatma Gandhi*, p. 233.

142 *Later, his devoted English follower*: *News Chronicle* (London), Sept. 7, 1930.

142 *Gandhi's first Indian Boswell*: Mahadev Desai, *Day-to-Day with Gandhi*, vol. 3, p. 265.

142 *"We have come for the darshan"*: Ibid., p. 264.

142 *"the people got frightened"*: CWMG, vol. 19, p. 374.

142 *"the four pillars"*: Ibid., vol. 23, p. 53.

143 *The throngs that turned*: See Amin, "Gandhi as Mahatma," pp. 290–340.

144 *"No Indian who aspires"*: CWMG, vol. 14, p. 201.

144 *"morality in action"*: Brown, *Gandhi*, p. 82.

144 *Those Gandhi called*: CWMG, vol. 14, pp. 80, 201.

145 *Fewer than 1 million*: Ibid., vol. 14, p. 203.

145 *Seen that way*: Ibid., vol. 13, p. 200.

145 *Writing to Hermann Kallenbach*: Ibid., vol. 96, p. 212.

146 *"I am an outsider"*: Nanda, *Gandhi*, p. 165.

146 *But Gandhi had large ambitions*: CWMG, vol. 13, p. 33.

146 *At Gokhale's death*: Nanda, *Three Statesmen*, p. 170; also Heimsath, *Indian Nationalism and Hindu Social Reform*, pp. 241–43.

146 *They took seven vows*: CWMG, vol. 13, p. 91.

146 *About half its original intake*: A thumbnail sketch of Imam Abdul Kader Salim Bawazir, originally of Johannesburg's Hamidia Mosque, is provided by Gopalkrishna Gandhi, *A Frank Friendship*, p. 75.

146 *"The object of the Ashram"*: CWMG, vol. 13, p. 91.

146 *"I cannot imagine"*: Ibid., vol. 23, p. 102.

147 *"an instrument for the revival"*: As quoted by Rajmohan Gandhi in *Eight Lives*, p. 150.

148 *"I believe that Hindus"*: Cited in Rajaram, *Gandhi, Khilafat, and the National Movement*, p. 8.

148 *Muhammad Ali, a polished*: Nanda, *Gandhi*, p. 202.

149 *"I came to observe"*: Gandhi, *Autobiography*, p. 349.

149 *Soon he drafted*: Tendulkar, *Mahatma*, vol. 1, p. 162; Pyarelal and Nayar, *In Gandhiji's Mirror*, p. 101.

150   *"A humble and honest"*: Narayan Desai, *My Life Is My Message*, vol. 2, *Satyagraha*, p. 17.

150   *"I have taken in a Pariah"*: CWMG, vol. 96, p. 223.

150   *"I have told Mrs. Gandhi"*: Ibid., vol. 13, pp. 127–28.

150   *"she's making my life hell"*: Ibid., vol. 96, p. 225.

150   *"I had to undertake"*: Ibid., p. 227.

150   *"I have been deserted"*: Ibid., p. 225.

150   *Most will trickle back*: Pyarelal and Nayar, *In Gandhiji's Mirror*, p. 102.

150   *"Your not being with me"*: CWMG, vol. 14, p. 190.

151   *He speaks of moving*: Ibid., vol. 13, p. 128.

151   *"She has beautifully resigned"*: Mahadev Desai, *Day-to-Day with Gandhi*, vol. 1, p. 153.

151   *"She cannot bring herself"*: CWMG, vol. 25, p. 514.

151   *"wall of prejudice"*: Ibid., vol. 26, p. 295.

151   *"This great and indelible crime"*: Ibid., vol. 13, p. 233.

151   *"Not a chest of indigo"*: Pouchepadass, *Champaran and Gandhi*, p. 6.

152   *"We have begun to convince"*: CWMG, vol. 14, p. 538.

152   *"All of us who worked"*: Prasad, *At the Feet of Mahatma Gandhi*, p. 148. In recent years, a Swiss journalist with deep experience of India revisited the Champaran district to see how the initiatives Gandhi and his colleagues began decades earlier had developed. He found virtually no trace of them; instead, a climate of rampant political corruption and oppression. See Imhasly, *Goodbye to Gandhi?* pp. 57–86.

153   *By one estimate*: Shankar Dayal Singh, *Gandhi's First Step*, p. 5.

153   *Later he would call it*: CWMG, vol. 19, p. 88.

153   *Referring back to the Natal strikes*: Ibid., vol. 13, p. 210.

153   *India needed to adopt*: Ibid., p. 232.

153   *"The essence of his teaching"*: Nehru, *Mahatma Gandhi*, p. 23, a passage taken from Nehru's *Discovery of India*.

153   *"This voice was somehow different"*: Nehru, *Mahatma Gandhi*, p. 12, a passage taken from Nehru's *Glimpses of World History*.

154   *Elsewhere he acknowledges*: CWMG, vol. 14, p. 392.

154   *"I have traveled much"*: Ibid., p. 298.

154   *"Without any impertinence"*: Ibid., vol. 19, p. 104.

154   *"did not descend"*: Nehru, *Mahatma Gandhi*, p. 23.

154   *The political bargain*: CWMG, vol. 14, pp. 377–82.

155   *"I love the English nation"*: Ibid., p. 380.

155   *The recruiting agent in chief*: Ibid., p. 443.

155   *What better means*: Ibid., p. 476.

155   *"They will be yours"*: Ibid., p. 454.

155   *Fighting for the empire*: Ibid., p. 440.

155   *"It is clear"*: Ibid., p. 485.

155   *Finally, in August 1918*: Ibid., p. 473.

155   *He would later describe himself*: Ibid., vol. 23, p. 4.

155   *"My failure so far"*: Ibid., vol. 14, p. 480.

156   *Eventually, he goes through*: Rajmohan Gandhi, *Gandhi*, p. 202.

157   *"How can twenty-two crore Hindus"*: CWMG, vol. 16, p. 306.

157   *One of these was a movement*: Kepel, *Jihad*, pp. 44–45.

157   *a complex religious*: A sworn enemy of the Saudi royal family—the last caliph's

eventual successors as keepers of the holy places—bin Laden wasn't fixated on Turks. A Saudi with family roots in Yemen, he held to the ideal of spiritual and temporal authority combined in one potentate and one theocratic state representing all believers. In a videotape made after the 9/11 attacks, bin Laden said what Americans were finally experiencing was what "our Islamic nation has been tasting for more than eighty years of humiliation and disgrace." The eighty years refer to the dismantling of the Ottoman Empire, undermining the caliphate. In other words, he's reviving the Khilafat cause, for which Gandhi campaigned. Faisal Devji has a provocative discussion of these connections in *The Terrorist in Search of Humanity*, in particular on pp. 120–30. "The Mahatma," he writes, "was undoubtedly the most important propagator of the caliphate in modern times."

158 *"Bhai sahib!"*: Jordens, *Swami Shraddhananda*, p. 114.
159 *the month after the first Khilafat*: Gandhi, *Autobiography*, p. 439.
159 *"cheers, tears, embraces"*: Minault, *Khilafat Movement*, p. 82.
159 *In June the Central Khilafat Committee*: CWMG, vol. 17, p. 543.
159 *"It is the duty"*: Ibid., vol. 18, p. 230.
160 *Three months later*: Nanda, *Gandhi*, p. 238.
161 *Mohammed Ali Jinnah*: Rajmohan Gandhi, *Gandhi*, p. 234.
161 *He left the Congress*: Nanda, *Gandhi*, p. 242.
161 *"After the Prophet"*: Rajmohan Gandhi, *Gandhi*, p. 237.
161 *"We laid the foundation"*: Mahadev Desai, *Day-to-Day with Gandhi*, vol. 3, pp. 290–91.
162 *Ultimately, the maulana*: CWMG, vol. 23, p. 567.
162 *By August 1921*: Ibid., vol. 21, p. 10.
162 *That was hardly an excuse*: Minault, *Khilafat Movement*, pp. 145–49; Nanda, *Gandhi*, pp. 311–20.
163 *Gandhi was pointing*: CWMG, vol. 21, pp. 180–81.
163 *"I wish to be in touch"*: Ibid., vol. 24, pp. 456–57.
164 *"It is against our scriptures"*: Nanda, *Gandhi*, p. 289.
164 *"I can wield no influence"*: Rajmohan Gandhi, *Eight Lives*, p. 111.
164 *For him, it was less*: CWMG, vol. 20, p. 90.
164 *It was a cause*: Ibid., vol. 19, p. 92.
164 *While it had nothing*: Ibid., vol. 25, p. 200.
165 *"I am striving"*: Ibid., p. 202.
165 *"the rest of the letter"*: Dhupelia-Mesthrie, *Gandhi's Prisoner?* p. 175.
166 *Shortly after the Mahatma*: Payne, *Life and Death of Mahatma Gandhi*, p. 355.
166 *"Consider the burning"*: Rajmohan Gandhi, *Gandhi*, p. 241. The economist Amartya Sen offers a contemporary view of the debate between the Mahatma and the poet over homespun versus manufactured cloth. "Except for the rather small specialized market for high-quality spun cloth," he writes, "it is hard to make economic sense of hand-spinning, even with wheels less primitive than Gandhi's charkha." But Gandhi's central point had as much to do with social justice, Sen recognizes, as economics. Sen's discussion is in *The Argumentative Indian*, pp. 100–101.
166 *"To a people famishing"*: CWMG, vol. 21, p. 289.
168 *"I got the votes"*: Nanda, *Gandhi*, p. 347.
168 *"Our defeat is in proportion"*: Quoted in ibid., p. 346.
168 *"Gandhi is like a paralytic"*: Quoted in Minault, *Khilafat Movement*, p. 185.

169   *"I personally can never"*: CWMG, vol. 23, pp. 350–51, cited in Nanda, *Gandhi*, p. 344.

CHAPTER 7: UNAPPROACHABILITY

171   *When he intoned*: Jaswant Singh, *Jinnah*, p. 111.
171   *"My heart refuses"*: CWMG, vol. 32, pp. 452, 473–74.
172   The Times of India *spread*: Jaswant Singh, *Jinnah*, p. 113.
172   *His covering letter*: Mahadev Desai, *Day-to-Day with Gandhi*, vol. 9, p. 304.
173   *In his view, Gandhi*: Jordens, *Swami Shraddhananda*, p. 110.
173   *The start of the noncooperation*: Tinker, *Ordeal of Love*, p. 151.
174   *So, in December 1919*: Jordens, *Swami Shraddhananda*, p. 117.
174   *"Is it not true"*: Ibid.
174   *"That was a grave mistake"*: Ibid., p. 119.
174   *"it is a bigger problem"*: CWMG, vol. 19, p. 289.
175   *"While Mahatmaji stood"*: Jordens, *Swami Shraddhananda*, p. 119.
175   *"If all untouchables"*: Ibid., p. 144.
176   *This led to a public exchange*: CWMG, vol. 23, pp. 567–69.
176   *"No propaganda can be allowed"*: Ibid., vol. 24, pp. 145, 148–49.
177   *Bhimrao Ramji Ambedkar*: B. R. Ambedkar, *What Congress and Gandhi Have Done to the Untouchables*, p. 23.
177   *"greatest and most sincere champion"*: Ibid.
177   *Although Gandhi had called*: CWMG, vol. 19, p. 289.
177   *"I am trying to make"*: Ibid., vol. 25, p. 228.
180   *Due to his many years*: Ibid., vol. 26, p. 408.
181   *"To endure or bear hardships"*: Ibid., pp. 264–65.
181   *"One caste, one religion"*: Mendelsohn and Vicziany, *Untouchables*, p. 97.
181   *at first ambivalent*: Interview with M. K. Sanoo, Ernakulam, Jan. 18, 2009.
182   *rename the boy*: Interview with Dr. Babu Vijayanath, Harippad, Jan. 17, 2009. *Malayala Manorama* article of Oct. 15, 1927, describes naming ceremony.
183   *an untouchable leader*: Interview with K. K. Kochu, near Kottayam, Jan. 19, 2009. T. K. Ravindran suggests that this blinding may have been temporary in his book *Eight Furlongs of Freedom*, p. 108.
183   *"I think you should let"*: CWMG, vol. 23, p. 391.
184   *The letter didn't reach*: Joseph, *George Joseph*, pp. 166–69. Gandhi's version of these events can be found in *Removal of Untouchability*, a collection of his writings on that theme, pp. 107–14.
184   *Despite the Congress support*: CWMG, vol. 23, p. 471.
185   *"I personally believe"*: Ibid., p. 519.
185   *The villages were divided*: Rudrangshu Mukherjee, ed., *Penguin Gandhi Reader*, p. 221.
185   *He would also argue*: M. K. Gandhi, *Selected Political Writings*, pp. 124–25.
186   *"I spoke to Gandhi repeatedly"*: Mende, *Conversations with Mr. Nehru*, pp. 27–28.
186   *"The caste system, as it exists"*: CWMG, vol. 59, p. 45.
186   *"If untouchability goes"*: Chandrashanker Shukla, *Conversations of Ganhiji* (Bombay, 1949), p. 59.
186   *harmful both to spiritual and national growth*: Harijan, July 18, 1936, also in Gandhi, *Removal of Untouchability*, p. 36.

186   *"no interest left in life"*: Quoted in Coward, *Indian Critiques of Gandhi*, p. 61.

186   *only remaining varna*: *CWMG*, vol. 80, pp. 222–24, cited by Martin Green in *Gandhi in India: In His Own Words* (Hanover, N.H., 1987), pp. 324–26.

186   *"the deep black ignorance"*: Mahadev Desai, *Day-to-Day with Gandhi*, vol. 6, p. 86.

186   *The meeting took place*: *CWMG*, vol. 24, pp. 90–94. Quotations in these paragraphs are all drawn from a document summarizing conversations with two Vaikom emissaries.

187   *On their return*: Ravindran, *Eight Furlongs of Freedom*, p. 86.

187   *The meeting sent*: Ibid., p. 95.

188   *The freed leaders threw*: Ibid., p. 99.

188   *On his release from jail*: *CWMG*, vol. 24, pp. 268–69.

188   *By the end of the year*: Ibid., vol. 25, p. 349.

188   *Standing on their sense*: Mahadev Desai, *Day-to-Day with Gandhi*, vol. 6, p. 58.

189   *But it's Indanturuttil Nambiatiri*: Ravindran, *Eight Furlongs of Freedom*, pp. 164–91.

190   *"I am not ashamed"*: Mahadev Desai, *Day-to-Day with Gandhi*, vol. 6, p. 84.

190   *The likelier explanation*: *CWMG*, vol. 19, p. 571.

190   *Perhaps Nehru's summing-up*: Mende, *Conversations with Mr. Nehru*, pp. 28–29.

190   *"I am trying myself"*: Mahadev Desai, *Day-to-Day with Gandhi*, vol. 6, p. 83.

191   *"I have come here to create peace"*: *Malayala Manorama*, March 14, 1925.

191   *To break the impasse*: Ravindran, *Eight Furlongs of Freedom*, pp. 187–90.

191   *"We will forsake"*: Raimon, *Selected Documents on the Vaikom Satyagraha*, p. 112.

191   *accommodate to change*: Interview with Krishnan Nambuthiri, Vaikom, Jan. 14, 2009.

192   *a crowd of twenty thousand*: *Malayala Manorama*, March 14, 1925.

192   *"I claim to be a sanatani"*: Mahadev Desai, *Day-to-Day with Gandhi*, vol. 6, pp. 68–70.

192   *"A few days or forever"*: Ibid., pp. 77, 81.

193   *Caste, untouchability, and social action*: Ibid., pp. 84–88.

193   *In reality, the Gandhi*: Interview with Babu Vijayanath, Harippad, Jan. 17, 2009. The visit is also summarized in Mahadev Desai, *Day-to-Day with Gandhi*, vol. 6, pp. 124–25.

193   *"He thinks I shall have to appear"*: Mahadev Desai, *Day-to-Day with Gandhi*, vol. 6, p. 88.

193   *According to a police report*: Ravindran, *Eight Furlongs of Freedom*, p. 340.

194   *In one such clash*: Interview with Dr. Babu Vijayanath, Hariippad, Jan. 17, 2009.

194   *Hearing of the Mahatma's*: This verse was pointed out to me by M. K. Sanoo and subsequently located by journalists at *Malayala Manorama* who translated it.

194   *Definitely it was Gandhi*: Raimon, *Selected Documents on the Vaikom Satyagraha*, p. 203.

195   *K. K. Kochu, a Dalit intellectual*: *Madhyamam*, April 2, 1999.

195   *"I only wish"*: Interview with K. K. Kochu, Kaduthuruthi, Kottayam district, Jan. 18, 2009.

195   *"How many among you"*: Mahadev Desai, *Day-to-Day with Gandhi*, vol. 6, pp. 114–15.

196   *"Gandhi was sitting cross-legged"*: An excellent description, but Mahadev Desai's contemporaneous diary note makes it clear they reached Alwaye by boat and car. Ibid., p. 118.

196   *In his account*: Muggeridge, *Chronicles of Wasted Time*, pp. 109–10.

CHAPTER 8: HAIL, DELIVERER

197 *Discovering they were prepared*: Tendulkar, *Mahatma*, vol. 2, p. 140.
197 *In the pointlessness*: Ibid., p. 142. Emphasis mine.
197 *His reaction to this onset*: Ibid., p. 327.
198 *"What is one to do"*: CWMG, vol. 31, p. 504.
198 *He blamed "educated India"*: Ibid., p. 369.
198 *Next he blamed the British*: Fischer, *Life of Mahatma Gandhi*, pp. 241–42.
198 *"The government of India"*: CWMG, vol. 32, p. 571.
199 *"I am an optimist"*: Ibid., vol. 31, p. 504.
199 *"appears to be my inaction"*: Ibid., p. 368.
199 *"I am biding my time"*: Brown, *Gandhi*, p. 213.
199 *"Give me blood"*: Fischer, *Life of Mahatma Gandhi*, p. 261.
200 *"given up reading newspapers"*: CWMG, vol. 31, p. 554.
200 *At a mammoth All Parties Convention*: Wells, *Ambassador of Hindu-Muslim Unity*, p. 177.
200 *"We are sons of this land"*: Leonard A. Gordon, *Brothers Against the Raj: A Biography of Indian Nationalists*, p. 189.
201 *Within weeks of this rupture*: Tendulkar, *Mahatma*, vol. 2, p. 334. Within two years Muhammad Ali would die in London.
201 *"This is the parting"*: Philips and Wainwright, *Partition of India*, p. 279.
201 *a younger wife*: Ruttie Jinnah was originally a Parsi, a member of a minority composed of Indians of Persian descent who retain their Zoroastrian religion, but converted to Islam before their marriage. On her death, she was buried in a Muslim cemetery with her former husband sobbing at her graveside.
201 *Swaraj within a year*: Brown, *Gandhi*, p. 222, draws the parallel to the 1921 campaign. January 26 is still celebrated in India as Republic Day; August 15, the date on which India actually became independent in 1947, is celebrated as Independence Day.
202 *"For me there is only"*: CWMG, vol. 31, pp. 368–69.
202 *"In the present state"*: Ibid., vol. 42, p. 382.
202 *Civil disobedience, he told Nehru*: Brown, *Gandhi*, p. 235.
203 *"next to water and air"*: Rajmohan Gandhi, *Gandhi*, p. 303.
203 *The viceroy also stuck*: Fischer, *Life of Mahatma Gandhi*, pp. 271–72.
203 *"The fire of a great resolve"*: As quoted in Rajmohan Gandhi, *Gandhi*, p. 309.
204 *"Hail, Deliverer"*: Fischer, *Life of Mahatma Gandhi*, p. 273. Thomas Weber questions whether these words were ever uttered, noting their absence from contemporary accounts and arguing that the quotation first appeared in an article by a British journalist who was actually in Berlin on the day Gandhi reached Dandi. See "Historiography and the Dandi March," in *Gandhi, Gandhism, and the Gandhians*.
205 *"The last four months in India"*: CWMG, vol. 44, p. 468.
206 *Gandhi made a sly allusion*: Ibid., vol. 48, p. 18.
207 *"No living man"*: Harold Laski opinion piece in *Daily Herald* (London), Sept. 11, 1931.
208 *"Your Majesty won't expect"*: Tendulkar, *Mahatma*, vol. 3, p. 127.
208 *By the time Ambedkar returned*: B. R. Ambedkar, *Letters*, p. 220.
209 *betrothed to him at the age of nine*: The marriage apparently took place three

years later, when he would have been seventeen and she twelve, although his biographers cannot agree on their ages. Keer, *Dr. Ambedkar,* p. 20, says he was seventeen; Omvedt, *Ambedkar,* p. 6, says he was fourteen.

209   *For an untouchable youth:* B. R. Ambedkar, *Essential Writings,* p. 52.

209   *When he sought to study:* Keer, *Dr. Ambedkar,* p. 18.

209   *So Bhima took:* Omvedt, *Ambedkar,* p. 4.

211   *One of these campaigns:* Keer, *Dr. Ambedkar,* p. 74.

212   *"When one is spurned":* Zelliot, *From Untouchable to Dalit,* p. 163.

212   *"I am a difficult man":* Omvedt, *Ambedkar,* p. 119.

212   *"You called me to hear":* Keer, *Dr. Ambedkar,* p. 165.

213   *"Gandhiji, I have no homeland":* Ibid., p. 166.

213   *"Till I left for England":* Mahadev Desai, *Diary of Mahadev Desai,* p. 52.

213   *"revelatory of the stereotypes":* Omvedt, *Ambedkar,* p. 43.

213   *The go-betweens who set up:* Zelliot, *From Untouchable to Dalit,* p. 166.

213   *Their next meeting, in London:* Omvedt, *Ambedkar,* p. 43.

214   *Maybe Gandhi had been:* Zelliot, *From Untouchable to Dalit,* p. 166.

214   *"Who are we to uplift Harijans?":* Mahadev Desai, *Diary of Mahadev Desai,* p. 53.

214   *Drawing the parallel himself:* CWMG, vol. 48, p. 224.

214   *"Dr. A. always commands":* Ibid., p. 208.

214   *"He has a right even to spit":* Ibid., pp. 160–61.

215   *"Above all, the Congress represents":* Ibid., p. 16.

215   *Three days later:* Ibid., p. 34.

216   *"I fully represent the claims":* B. R. Ambedkar, *Writings and Speeches,* vol. 3, contains transcripts of the Round Table Conference sessions quoted here. The exchanges between Gandhi and Ambedkar can be found on pp. 661–63 of that volume.

219   *"This has been the most humiliating":* Shirer, *Gandhi,* p. 194, cited in Herman, *Gandhi and Churchill,* p. 372.

219   *"a more ignorant":* Narayan Desai, *My Life Is My Message,* vol. 3, *Satyapath,* p. 169.

219   *Gandhi claimed to be:* B. R. Ambedkar, *Letters,* p. 215.

220   *"Mr. Gandhi made nonsense":* B. R. Ambedkar, *What Congress and Gandhi Have Done to the Untouchables,* p. 275.

220   *As the London conference:* B. R. Ambedkar, *Letters,* p. 215.

220   *Nehru didn't go into that:* Nehru to S. K. Patil, Nov. 31, 1931, Nehru Memorial Museum archive, AICC Papers, G86/3031.

221   *"Gandhi's Good-Bye Today":* *Daily Herald* (London), Dec. 5, 1931.

221   *Years later George Orwell:* George Orwell, "Reflections on Gandhi," in *A Collection of Essays* (Garden City, N.Y., 1954), p. 180.

221   *But he was skeptical:* Rolland, *Mahatma Gandhi,* p. 248.

221   *Pope Pius XI sent his regrets:* Nayar, *Salt Satyagraha,* p. 403; Slade, *Spirit's Pilgrimage,* p. 151.

222   *"No indeed":* Nayar, *Salt Satyagraha,* p. 403. Sushila Nayar completed the biography begun by her brother, who seldom signed himself by his full name, Pyarelal Nayar.

223   *Before the letter could be mailed:* Ibid., p. 405.

223   *On January 4, 1932:* Ibid., p. 414. The Englishman who describes this scene is the ethnologist Verrier Elwin.

CHAPTER 9: FAST UNTO DEATH

224 *"The caste system supported"*: Ajoy Bose, *Behenji*, p. 83.
225 *Eventually he concluded*: Tendulkar, *Mahatma*, vol. 7, p. 154.
225 *honor killings of daughters and sisters*: Jim Yardley, "In India, Caste Honor and Killings Intertwine," *The New York Times*, July 9, 2010, p. 1.
225 *"I agree that Bapu"*: Narayan Desai, *My Life Is My Message*, vol. 3, *Satyapath*, p. 179.
225 *"My life is one indivisible whole"*: CWMG, vol. 55, p. 199.
226 *This from the man*: "The Removal of Untouchability," *Young India*, Oct. 13, 1921.
226 *The man he addressed*: CWMG, vol. 19, p. 289.
227 *a status he'd sometimes compared*: Gandhi, *Removal of Untouchability*, p. 11.
227 *By the time the award*: Tendulkar, *Mahatma*, vol. 3, pp. 159–60.
227 *Gandhi assumed but wasn't sure*: Mahadev Desai, *Diary of Mahadev Desai*, p. 295.
228 *"prepared to go"*: "Suicide Threat," *Times of India*, Sept. 14, 1932.
228 *"Our own men will be critical"*: Mahadev Desai, *Diary of Mahadev Desai*, pp. 293–94, 302. Nehru, who was in jail in this period, admitted in a note in his diary after the conclusion of Gandhi's fast, "I am afraid I am drifting further and further away from him mentally, in spite of my strong emotional attachment to him. His continual references to God irritate me exceedingly. His political actions are often enough guided by an unerring instinct but he does not encourage others to think." Cited in Brown, *Gandhi*, p. 270.
229 *"What if I am taken"*: Mahadev Desai, *Diary of Mahadev Desai*, p. 4.
229 *"Sudden shock is the treatment"*: Ibid., p. 301.
229 *"Untouchable hooligans"*: Ibid.
229 *"What does MacDonald know"*: Verma, *Crusade Against Untouchability*, pp. 38–39.
229 *Then he thought temple entry*: Ravindran, *Eight Furlongs of Freedom*, p. 79.
230 *William L. Shirer*: Shirer, *Gandhi*, pp. 208–10.
230 *"With the Hindus and Musalmans"*: Pyarelal, *Epic Fast*, p. 6.
230 *"Do not believe for one moment"*: Verma, *Crusade Against Untouchability*, p. 27.
231 *Patel regularly speculated*: Narayan Desai, *The Fire and the Rose*, pp. 568–69; Rajmohan Gandhi, *Patel*, pp. 226–28.
232 *"He would not be satisfied"*: Pyarelal, *Epic Fast*, p. 30.
232 *"If God has more work"*: Narayan Desai, *The Fire and the Rose*, p. 569.
232 *"If we cheaply dismiss"*: Tagore, *Mahatmaji and the Depressed Humanity*, pp. 11, 18.
233 *Tagore arrived*: Ibid., p. 22.
233 *"Mahatmaji, you have been"*: Pyarelal, *Epic Fast*, p. 59; Narayan Desai, *The Fire and the Rose*, p. 575; Verma, *Crusade Against Untouchability*, pp. 43–44.
234 *"No one shall be regarded"*: Verma, *Crusade Against Untouchability*, p. 44.
234 *A parallel gathering*: Pyarelal, *Epic Fast*, p. 239.
234 *Even Nehru, who acknowledged*: Nehru, *Toward Freedom*, p. 237.
235 *"I will never be moved"*: *Times of India*, Sept. 14, 1932.
235 *He'd been in a fix*: Pyarelal, *Epic Fast*, pp. 188–89.
236 *Kasturba raised the glass*: Ibid., pp. 79–80.
236 *"The entire audience"*: Tagore, *Mahatmaji and the Depressed Humanity*, p. 29.
236 *The idea that untouchability*: Pyarelal, *Epic Fast*, pp. 79–81.

236 *In his speeches to untouchable*: Keer, *Dr. Ambedkar*, pp. 234, 221.

236 *"the one thing that alone"*: CWMG, vol. 53, p. 131.

236 *"To open or not to open"*: Keer, *Dr. Ambedkar*, p. 229.

237 *"not necessary for him"*: *The Times* (London), Nov. 7, 1932.

237 *Eventually, they would both reject*: Tendulkar, *Mahatma*, vol. 7, p. 151.

237 *"The Congress sucked the juice"*: Mankar, *Denunciation of Poona-Pact*, p. 109.

238 *When they met in February 1933*: Ibid., p. 160.

238 *Ambedkar had agreed to join*: Verma, *Crusade Against Untouchability*, pp. 62–63.

238 *But within a year*: B. R. Ambedkar, *What Congress and Gandhi Have Done to the Untouchables*, p. 135.

238 *"Sin and immorality"*: Keer, *Dr. Ambedkar*, p. 229.

239 *As late as 1958*: Verma, *Crusade Against Untouchability*, p. 196.

239 *In May 1933*: Tendulkar, *Mahatma*, vol. 3, p. 201.

239 *The time had come*: Omvedt, *Ambedkar*, p. 61.

239 *If any admiration*: B. R. Ambedkar, *Annihilation of Caste*, pp. 84–86.

240 *"Obviously, he would like"*: B. R. Ambedkar, *What Congress and Gandhi Have Done to the Untouchables*, p. 277.

240 *But there's suggestive*: Rajmohan Gandhi, *Gandhi*, p. 597.

241 *"a flair for action"*: Nehru, *Toward Freedom*, p. 240.

241 *He also knew that*: This is made clear in a discussion between Nehru and Mahadev Desai, on August 23, 1934, summarized in an as-yet-unpublished English translation of a portion of Mahadev Desai's diary on file at the Gandhi Memorial Library, pp. 121–24.

241 *This provoked the Bengali*: Tendulkar, *Mahatma*, vol. 3, p. 205.

241 *"Life ceases to interest me"*: Ibid., p. 215.

241 *"If Mr. Gandhi now feels"*: Ibid., pp. 215, 217.

242 *He was thus maneuvered*: Ibid., p. 216.

243 *An early conclusion*: The reports by colonial officials on the Gandhi tour are on file in the archive of the Nehru Memorial Museum. Many but not all of these reports have been excerpted in Ray, *Gandhi's Campaign Against Untouchability*.

247 *"I am quite sure"*: Tendulkar, *Mahatma*, vol. 3, p. 281.

248 *"We can't even say"*: Unpublished English translation of a portion of Mahadev Desai's diary, for autumn 1934, on file at the Gandhi Memorial Library. See p. 162.

248 *"The only way we can"*: Tendulkar, *Mahatma*, vol. 3, p. 280.

248 *Near the end of the tour*: Ray, *Gandhi's Campaign Against Untouchability*, p. 220.

248 *It so preoccupied him*: Rajmohan Gandhi, *Gandhi*, p. 362.

249 *"Anything more opposed"*: Nehru, *Toward Freedom*, p. 301.

249 *Tagore said Gandhi's logic*: Rajmohan Gandhi, *Gandhi*, pp. 362–63.

249 *"Our sins and errors"*: Tendulkar, *Mahatma*, vol. 3, p. 250.

249 *"I would be untruthful"*: Ibid., p. 251.

250 *The sanatanists were*: Nayar, *Preparing for Swaraj*, pp. 207–8.

250 *In Poona, near the end*: Ray, *Gandhi's Campaign against Untouchability*, p. 178.

250 *"Dr. Ambedkar complained"*: Ibid., pp. 46–47.

250 *"the growing pauperism"*: CWMG, 2nd ed., vol. 65, pp. 178–79.

250 *"I have lost the power"*: CWMG, vol. 59, p. 218.

251 *He ended the tour at Wardha*: Tendulkar, *Mahatma*, vol. 3, p. 282.

251 *"The sanatanists are now"*: Ibid., p. 283.

251 *"a profound error for me"*: Ibid., p. 297.

251 *He was going in the opposite*: Ibid., pp. 280, 296.
251 *"None of them knows"*: CWMG, vol. 61, p. 403, cited in Brown, *Gandhi*, p. 292.
253 *"What I am aiming for"*: Tendulkar, *Mahatma*, vol. 4, p. 304.

CHAPTER 10: VILLAGE OF SERVICE

254 *"The villagers have a lifeless life"*: Nayar, *Preparing for Swaraj*, p. 301.
254 *"a mechanical performance"*: *Harijan*, Aug. 17, 1934.
254 *Later he allowed himself*: CWMG, vol. 60, p. 58.
254 *"We have to work away"*: Tendulkar, *Mahatma*, vol. 5, p. 245.
254 *"We have to become speechless"*: CWMG, 2nd ed., vol. 65, p. 432.
255 *Now, by working again*: CWMG, vol. 59, p. 179.
255 *Once he resolved*: Ibid, p. 312.
256 *"Wardha became the de facto"*: Weber, *Gandhi as Disciple and Mentor*, p. 104.
256 *By the end of the decade*: Tendulkar, *Mahatma*, vol. 5, pp. 17–18.
256 *"shame some Japanese"*: Ibid., p. 14.
256 *"You must not"*: Ibid., p. 15. It's not clear whether a translator, editor, or Gandhi himself was responsible for this odd misuse of the word "clout" for what might have been termed a codpiece, breechcloth, cup, or even "jewel case." In one of its more obscure definitions, "clout" can refer to a leather or iron patch.
256 *"Who knows"*: Ibid., p. 347.
257 *As might have been expected*: Payne, *Life and Death of Mahatma Gandhi*, pp. 464–65. Also see Rajmohan Gandhi, *Gandhi*, pp. 406–7.
257 *"The people are completely shameless"*: Narayan Desai, *The Fire and the Rose*, pp. 601–2.
258 *No road, as yet*: Slade, *Spirit's Pilgrimage*, pp. 202–3.
258 *"If you will cooperate"*: CWMG, vol. 62, p. 332.
258 *"a very charming"*: Slade, *Spirit's Pilgrimage*, p. 203.
258 *The hut that he was to occupy*: Nayar, *Preparing for Swaraj*, p. 366.
258 *Ashram and village*: Rajmohan Gandhi, *Gandhi*, pp. 380–81.
258 *"Oh God"*: CWMG, vol. 59, p. 402.
260 *Gandhi's letters were full*: CWMG, 2nd ed., vol. 65, p. 371.
260 *A Christian, he was known*: Kumarappa had studied economics at Columbia University with Edwin Seligman, who also taught Ambedkar.
260 *the last Western economist*: See reference in E. F. Schumacher, who quotes Kumarappa briefly. *Small Is Beautiful: Economics as if People Mattered* (Point Roberts, Wash., reprint, 1999), p. 39.
261 *"The Association"*: CWMG, vol. 59, p. 452.
261 *"Full-timers, whole-hoggers"*: Ibid., p. 411.
261 *"necessary adjustment"*: Ibid., vol. 62, p. 319.
262 *"So! You are already tired!"*: Narayan Desai, *The Fire and the Rose*, pp. 602–3.
262 *"If this does not work"*: CWMG, vol. 62, p. 239.
262 *When one of his workers*: Tendulkar, *Mahatma*, vol. 4, p. 96.
262 *"The only way is to sit"*: CWMG, vol. 62, p. 379.
262 *"Our ambition is to make"*: Ibid., p. 378.
263 *Soon he came down*: Slade, *Spirit's Pilgrimage*, p. 207.
264 *A United Nations survey*: Malise Ruthven, "Excremental India," *New York Review of Books*, May 13, 2010.

264   *What such latter-day*: Muhammad Yunus, the Nobel Peace Prize laureate who
      leads the Grameen Bank in neighboring Bangladesh, is aware of similarities
      between his approach to rural poverty and Gandhi's, but does not cite the
      Mahatma as an influence on the development of his thinking in his book *Banker
      to the Poor* (New Delhi, 2007). The same is true of Fazle Hasan Abed, the leader
      of the even larger BRAC Bank, also in Bangladesh, another pioneer in what is
      called "social entrepreneurship." See Ian Smillie, *Freedom from Want* (Sterling,
      Va., 2009).

265   *According to one of the untouchable*: Keer, *Dr. Ambedkar*, p. 268.

266   *The observation had provoked*: Narayan Desai, *My Life Is My Message*, vol. 3,
      Satyapath, p. 172.

266   *Within a few months*: "Caste Has to Go," *Harijan*, Nov. 16, 1935; *CWMG*,
      vol. 62, pp. 121–22.

266   *Actually, their deepest difference*: *CWMG*, vol. 67, p. 359.

266   *As interpreted by D. R. Nagaraj*: Nagaraj, *Flaming Feet*, p. 39.

267   *From the standpoint*: Ibid., pp. 24–25.

268   *The impatience of the Ezhavas*: Tendulkar, *Mahatma*, vol. 4, p. 97.

268   *"Would you preach the Gospel"*: Ibid., p. 101.

268   *In his weekly*: *CWMG*, vol. 65, p. 296.

268   *Indignant over the foreigner's*: *Harijan*, June 12, 1937.

269   *"None of our Hindu subjects"*: Mahadev Desai, *Epic of Travancore*, p. 40.

269   *So the old man now recalled*: Interview with the maharajah of Travancore, Jan. 15,
      2009.

269   *"truly captivating"*: *CWMG*, vol. 64, p. 255.

270   *At nearly every stop*: Mahadev Desai, *Epic of Travancore*, pp. 218–19.

270   *"I must tell you"*: *CWMG*, vol. 64, p. 248.

271   *Ever since his provocative*: Ibid., p. 62.

271   *"What a wide gap"*: Ibid., p. 132.

271   *"No worker who has not"*: Ibid., p. 61.

272   *"Gandhi's asceticism"*: Parekh, *Colonialism, Tradition, and Reform*, pp. 205–6.

272   *"I can suppress the enemy"*: Ibid., p. 207.

272   *In Bombay, recuperating*: *CWMG*, vol. 62, pp. 428–30.

272   *In less graphic terms*: Ibid., p. 212.

272   *"the revolting things"*: Saint Augustine, *Confessions*, translated by Garry Wills
      (New York, 2006), p. 27.

273   *"He remains the same wreck"*: Dalal, *Harilal Gandhi*, p. 105.

273   *"That degrading, dirty"*: *CWMG*, vol. 67, p. 61.

273   *"For the first time"*: Ibid., p. 37.

274   *"I am after all"*: Cited by Thomson, *Gandhi and His Ashramas*, p. 228.

274   *"Not only have I not"*: *CWMG*, vol. 64, p. 175.

275   *"I am told that you are indifferent"*: Ibid., vol. 65, p. 301.

275   *By speaking of failure*: Ibid., p. 240.

275   *"There is a hiatus"*: Thomson, *Gandhi and His Ashramas*, p. 219.

276   *an ideal he brought home*: Gandhi started advocating spinning before he'd ever
      touched a spinning wheel. The idea, he later said, came to him during his 1909
      trip to London "as in a flash." He didn't even know the difference between a
      spinning wheel and a handloom. In *Hind Swaraj*, written on his 1909 voyage
      back to South Africa, he writes of "ancient and sacred handlooms" when, so it
      seems, he's thinking of the charkha. See an extended footnote on this point by

Anthony J. Parel in his edition of *Hind Swaraj*, p. 230. Narayan Desai makes the same point in the first volume of *My Life Is My Message*, p. 459.

276 *"I am utterly helpless"*: CWMG, vol. 65, p. 231.

276 *"Unfortunately the higher castes"*: CWMG, 2nd ed., vol. 70, p. 461.

276 *"a strange medley"*: Slade, *Spirit's Pilgrimage*, p. 191.

276 *"Quite a few are only temporary"*: CWMG, vol. 67, p. 327.

276 *"show the results"*: Mark Lindley, *J. C. Kumarappa: Mahatma Gandhi's Economist* (Mumbai, 2007), p. 144.

276 *"Whatever I do"*: CWMG, vol. 73, cited in Thomson, *Gandhi and His Ashramas*, p. 209.

276 *As late as 1945*: Pyarelal, *Mahatma Gandhi: Last Phase*, vol. 1, p. 48.

276 *It's not difficult to feel*: Thomson, *Gandhi and His Ashramas*, p. 227.

277 *"We cannot command"*: Tendulkar, *Mahatma*, vol. 5, p. 79.

277 *"Let no one say"*: Ibid., p. 245.

277 *"How I should love"*: CWMG, vol. 96, pp. 277, 284.

278 *"There is something frightening"*: Pyarelal, *Mahatma Gandhi: Last Phase*, vol. 1, pp. 104–5.

278 *The moment of reunion*: *Harijan*, May 29, 1937.

278 *Kallenbach wore a dhoti*: Sarid and Bartolf, *Hermann Kallenbach*, p. 73.

278 *"There are few people"*: Shimoni, *Gandhi, Satyagraha, and the Jews*, pp. 28–29.

280 *firm position on the subject*: See CWMG, vol. 19, p. 472, where Gandhi, on March 23, 1921, disputes the British right to make a commitment on Palestine to the Jews.

280 *"The sender's name"*: Shimoni, *Gandhi, Satyagraha, and the Jews*, p. 35.

280 *"I quite clearly see"*: CWMG, vol. 96, pp. 290, 292.

280 *"In my opinion the Jews"*: Sarid and Bartolf, *Hermann Kallenbach*, pp. 75–76.

281 *Buber writes*: Shimoni, *Gandhi, Satyagraha, and the Jews*, pp. 40–47.

281 *"Will you listen"*: Tendulkar, *Mahatma*, vol. 5, p. 160.

281 *The letter to Hitler began*: Rajmohan Gandhi, *Gandhi*, p. 400.

281 *"I can't imagine anyone"*: Mansergh and Lumby, *Transfer of Power*, vol. 5, p. 41.

281 *"If there ever could be"*: Rajmohan Gandhi, *Gandhi*, p. 400.

282 *However, when Britain finally*: Ibid., p. 425.

282 *"I am in perpetual quarrel"*: CWMG, vol. 70, p. 162.

CHAPTER 11: MASS MAYHEM

283 *"Congressmen, barring individual"*: CWMG, vol. 70, pp. 113–14.

284 *As early as 1939*: Ibid., p. 114.

284 *To a bluff British general*: Wavell, *Viceroy's Journal*, p. 236.

285 *"My life is entirely"*: Tendulkar, *Mahatma*, vol. 6, p. 156.

285 *It's the first time*: CWMG, vol. 70, p. 113.

286 *Ten months later*: Rajmohan Gandhi, *Gandhi*, p. 436.

286 *Through all his ins and outs*: Tendulkar, *Mahatma*, vol. 6, p. 125.

286 *On August 8, 1942*: Mansergh and Lumby, *Transfer of Power*, vol. 2, p. 622.

286 *"the biggest struggle"*: Tendulkar, *Mahatma*, vol. 6, p. 153.

287 *"Mob violence remains"*: Mansergh and Lumby, *Transfer of Power*, vol. 2, p. 853.

287 *Indian nonviolence had always been*: Tendulkar, *Mahatma*, vol. 6, p. 129.

289 *In 1942, days before*: Jaswant Singh, *Jinnah*, p. 308.

289   *"Give your blessings"*: Tendulkar, *Mahatma*, vol. 6, p. 271.

289   *"I thought you had come"*: Pyarelal, *Mahatma Gandhi: Last Phase*, vol. 1, p. 88.

289   *Not only had the Congress*: Jaswant Singh, *Jinnah*, p. 540.

290   *Putting it in writing*: Ibid., p. 541.

290   *"I am amazed"*: Pyarelal, *Mahatma Gandhi: Last Phase*, vol. 1, p. 88.

290   *His aim, Gandhi remarked*: Ibid., p. 91.

291   *"I have failed"*: Tendulkar, *Mahatma*, vol. 6, p. 276.

291   *"Though I represent nobody"*: Ibid., p. 279.

291   *This is so, at least*: See, for instance, Jalal, *Sole Spokesman*.

291   *"I could not make any"*: Fischer, *Life of Mahatma Gandhi*, p. 437.

292   *"Is there any reason"*: Narayan Desai, *My Life Is My Message*, vol. 4, *Svarpan*, pp. 225–26.

292   *"In that hour of decision"*: Pyarelal, *Mahatma Gandhi: Last Phase*, vol. 1, p. 239.

292   *"India is not with me"*: Fischer, *Life of Mahatma Gandhi*, p. 424.

293   *"I'm not going to discuss"*: Pyarelal, *Mahatma Gandhi: Last Phase*, vol. 1, p. 252.

293   *"Sword will be answered"*: Ibid., p. 464.

293   *The district, known even then*: Gandhi's first involvement in the affairs of Noakhali district came in 1940 when he was approached by Hindus there who represented themselves as being threatened by Muslim violence. He urged them to defend themselves by nonviolent means but then added what was for him an unusual but not unprecedented piece of advice: "If the capacity for nonviolent self-defense is lacking, then there need be no hesitation in using violent means." Tendulkar, *Mahatma*, vol. 5, p. 249.

294   *Hindus had been beheaded*: Scores of Hindu women were said to have been forced into marriage with Muslim men, but when Phillips Talbot caught up with Gandhi there, so he reported, just two cases of abduction and marriage had been proved. Talbot, *American Witness to India's Partition*, p. 203.

294   *"Shaheed sahib, everyone"*: Pyarelal, *Mahatma Gandhi: Last Phase*, vol. 1, p. 358.

294   *The impression he retains*: Interview with Barun Das Gupta, Kolkata, Oct. 2009.

295   *Before it burned out*: The Muslim League claimed that fifty thousand Muslims had been slaughtered in Bihar. The official figure put the toll at under five thousand. The American Friends Service Committee estimated ten thousand, a tally Gandhi accepted on at least one occasion.

295   *Suhrawardy didn't press*: Pyarelal, *Mahatma Gandhi: Last Phase*, vol. 1, pp. 387, 397.

295   *"If Noakhali is lost"*: Ibid., p. 405.

295   *The answers, though Gandhi*: Ibid., p. 356.

297   *At his first large prayer*: Ibid., pp. 370, 373.

297   *Within a week, he found*: Ibid., p. 378.

297   *"If India is destined"*: Ibid., pp. 379, 383.

298   *"If the Hindus could live"*: Ibid., p. 381.

298   *In an analogous quest*: Nirmal Kumar Bose, *My Days with Gandhi*, p. 47.

298   *"I find myself in the midst"*: Ibid., pp. 46–47.

299   *But four days after*: Ibid., p. 63.

300   *"Hardly a wheel turns"*: Talbot, *American Witness to India's Partition*, p. 202.

301   *If the size of the Hindu population*: The figure generally given for the number of Hindus remaining in Bangladesh as a whole is on the order of 12 million, which would be about 10 percent of the country's total population. In Pakistan, a country with a population nearly half again larger—about 170 million—only about

3 million Hindus remain. India's Muslim population of 140 million—out of a total of 1.2 billion—is exceeded by those of only Indonesia and Pakistan.

302 *"That's due to lack"*: Interview with Abdue Wahab, Joyag, Bangladesh, Oct. 2009. The chairman of the local Jamaat was not necessarily expressing a heretical view in speaking well of Gandhi. Faisal Devji notes that the movement's founder, Abul Ala Mawdudi, "sang the Mahatma's praises." Devji, *Terrorist in Search of Humanity*, p. 133.

302 *According to Narayan Desai*: Narayan Desai, *My Life Is My Message*, vol. 4, *Svarpan*, p. 271; CWMG, vol. 86, p. 162.

303 *"My unfitness for the task"*: Pyarelal, *Mahatma Gandhi: Last Phase*, vol. 1, p. 431.

303 *"I can see there is some"*: Ibid., p. 470.

303 *The telegram to her father*: CWMG, vol. 86, p. 215.

304 *"Manu's place can be nowhere"*: Narayan Desai, *My Life Is My Message*, vol. 4, *Svarpan*, p. 303.

304 *It soon became obvious*: Nirmal Kumar Bose, *My Days with Gandhi*, pp. 73–75.

304 *A perfect brahmachari*: Pyarelal, *Mahatma Gandhi: Last Phase*, vol. 1, p. 591.

304 *None of this would go on*: Gandhi's yajna with Manubehn has been discussed in varying degrees of detail in Nirmal Kumar Bose, *My Days with Gandhi*; Narayan Desai, *My Life Is My Message*, vol. 4, *Svarpan*; Pyarelal, *Mahatma Gandhi: Last Phase*, vol. 2; Mehta, *Mahatma Gandhi and His Apostles*. It can also be followed in the correspondence in Gandhi's *Collected Works*, especially vol. 86.

305 *"I don't want to return"*: CWMG, vol. 86, p. 224.

305 *"Of course she knows her art"*: Ibid., vol. 96, p. 295.

305 *"a deeply anguished"*: Nirmal Kumar Bose, *My Days with Gandhi*, pp. 95, 101.

306 *"Stick to your word"*: Narayan Desai, *My Life Is My Message*, vol. 4, *Svarpan*, p. 304.

306 *"I like your frankness"*: Nirmal Kumar Bose, *My Days with Gandhi*, p. 118.

306 *Pyarelal was also drawn*: CWMG, vol. 85, p. 221.

307 *"I can see that you will not"*: Ibid., vol. 94, p. 337.

307 *"After a life of prolonged"*: Nirmal Kumar Bose, *My Days with Gandhi*, p. 135.

307 *He'd read Havelock Ellis*: Pyarelal, *Mahatma Gandhi: Last Phase*, vol. 1, p. 588.

307 *"What is Freudian philosophy?"*: Nirmal Kumar Bose, *My Days with Gandhi*, p. 158.

307 *Bose's basic point*: Ibid., pp. 150–51.

307 *"I do hope you will acquit me"*: Ibid., p. 153.

308 *"I saw your strength come back"*: Ibid., p. 161.

308 *Given that the Congress*: Rajmohan Gandhi, *Gandhi*, p. 551.

308 *According to one account*: Maksud, *Gandhi, Nehru, and Noakhali*, p. 41.

308 *"I can never be disillusioned"*: Rajmohan Gandhi, *Gandhi*, p. 554.

308 *"I feel a little out of my depth"*: Brown, *Nehru*, p. 169.

308 *"Jawaharlal is the only man"*: Hingorani, *Gandhi on Nehru*, pp. 12–13.

308 *his heir would never score high*: Gandhi and Nehru had exchanged letters laying out their differences in October and November 1945. See Nehru, *Bunch of Old Letters*, pp. 509–16. Also see Tendulkar, *Mahatma*, vol. 8, pp. 302–6.

308 *"He says what is uppermost"*: Hingorani, *Gandhi on Nehru*, p. 12.

309 *"He has made me captive"*: Pyarelal, *Mahatma Gandhi: Last Phase*, vol. 2, p. 251.

310 *"My voice"*: CWMG, vol. 86, p. 295.

310 *Basically, it said Gandhi*: Pyarelal, *Mahatma Gandhi: Last Phase*, vol. 2, p. 483.

310 *When a member asked*: See *Amrita Bazar Patrika*, Jan. 6, 1946.

310 *"I suggest frequent consultations"*: Pyarelal, *Mahatma Gandhi: Last Phase*, vol. 2, p. 482; *CWMG*, vol. 86, p. 286.

311 *"Remember Bihar"*: Pyarelal, *Mahatma Gandhi: Last Phase*, vol. 1, p. 557.

311 *"You don't know the joy"*: Ibid., p. 509.

313 *"It failed miserably"*: From the diary of Nirmal Kumar Bose, p. 991, archive of the Asiatic Society, Kolkata.

313 *"What in your opinion"*: Fischer, *Life of Mahatma Gandhi*, p. 451.

313 *Twice in nine weeks*: Pyarelal, *Mahatma Gandhi: Last Phase*, vol. 1, p. 380.

314 *He could only demonstrate*: From the diary of Nirmal Kumar Bose, p. 887, archive of the Asiatic Society, Kolkata.

314 *"Our community today suffers"*: Pyarelal, *Mahatma Gandhi: Last Phase*, vol. 1, pp. 518, 520.

314 *Early on he talked*: Ibid., pp. 386, 372.

315 *"There will be no tears"*: Ibid., p. 321.

316 *"If some ruffian"*: Ibid., p. 505.

316 *Speaking to dispossessed*: *CWMG*, vol. 86, p. 305.

316 *"He had told us"*: Pyarelal, *Mahatma Gandhi: Last Phase*, vol. 1, p. 417.

316 *"Giving equality"*: Fischer, *Life of Mahatma Gandhi*, p. 436.

316 *"If they still went on"*: *CWMG*, vol. 86, p. 305.

317 *The next week he twice urges*: Ibid., pp. 348–50, 459.

317 *"He has not always held"*: From the diary of Nirmal Kumar Bose, p. 1251, archive of the Asiatic Society, Kolkata.

317 *"listened quietly"*: Talbot, *American Witness to India's Partition*, p. 202.

317 *There Gandhi stayed*: Pyarelal, *Mahatma Gandhi: Last Phase*, vol. 1, p. 559.

317 *In Haimchar, which turned out*: *CWMG*, vol. 87, p. 17.

317 *Though little was said in public*: Tidrick, *Gandhi*, p. 315.

318 *Thakkar is finally persuaded*: *CWMG*, vol. 87, p. 63.

318 *According to a less*: Pyarelal, *Mahatma Gandhi: Last Phase*, vol. 1, p. 587.

318 *He'd said he was prepared*: Ibid., p. 356.

318 *Nehru had been so appalled*: Fischer, *Life of Mahatma Gandhi*, p. 445.

319 *"But if I leave"*: Manubehn Gandhi, *Lonely Pilgrim*, p. 157, cited by Narayan Desai, *My Life Is My Message*, vol. 4, *Svarpan*, p. 287. Rama is an incarnation of Vishnu, and the hero of the *Ramayana*, the Hindu epic. Gandhi takes his name as a synonym for "God."

319 *By June 1948*: Chatterji, *Spoils of Partition*, pp. 112–19.

320 *The gathering ended*: The song they sang was a variation on an old devotional hymn, "Raghupati Raghav Raja Ram," often described as Gandhi's favorite hymn. Routinely, he would attach a line that proclaimed: "God or Allah is your name / Lord, bless everyone with this wisdom." The words continue to recite many names for God, ending in a call for unity. On this occasion the improvised lyric included references to Buddhists and Christians.

CHAPTER 12: DO OR DIE

321 *"The rest of my life"*: *CWMG*, vol. 89, pp. 10–11.

321 *The only way he could cling*: Ibid., p. 21.

322 *"Today he himself"*: Narayan Desai, *My Life Is My Message*, vol. 4, *Svarpan*, p. 393.

322   *By then, hundreds of thousands*: The influx of refugees is well described by Guha in *India After Gandhi*, pp. 97–108.

322   *"The country was partitioned"*: Lohia, *Guilty Men of India's Partition*, p. 44.

323   *An impatient Nehru said*: Tunzelmann, *Indian Summer*, p. 388.

323   *A pressing invitation*: Tendulkar, *Mahatma*, vol. 7, p. 162. He had also proposed giving the Viceregal Lodge to the Harijans.

323   *Since Hindus and Muslims*: Campbell-Johnson, *Mission with Mountbatten*, p. 110.

324   *It was part of Gandhi's proposal*: Collins and Lapierre, *Mountbatten and the Partition of India*, pp. 34–35.

324   *Mountbatten, understandably, declined*: Campbell-Johnson, *Mission with Mountbatten*, p. 55.

324   *"Thus I have to ask you"*: Pyarelal, *Mahatma Gandhi: Last Phase*, vol. 2, p. 85.

324   *When the viceroy first heard*: Campbell-Johnson, *Mission with Mountbatten*, p. 52.

324   *"Jinnah won't be able"*: Collins and Lapierre, *Mountbatten and the Partition of India*, p. 33.

325   *Often the killings*: CWMG, vol. 87, p. 52.

325   *"I hate to hear"*: Pyarelal, *Mahatma Gandhi: Last Phase*, vol. 2, p. 52.

325   *"spent bullet"*: Ibid., p. 309; Nirmal Kumar Bose, *My Days with Gandhi*, p. 208; see also M. K. Gandhi, *Delhi Diary*, p. 147.

325   *"It is just possible"*: Pyarelal, *Mahatma Gandhi: Last Phase*, vol. 2, p. 85.

326   *"He realized that if his vision"*: CWMG, vol. 89, p. 62.

326   *"I do not like much"*: Pyarelal, *Mahatma Gandhi: Last Phase*, vol. 2, p. 329.

326   *"We have as much claim"*: Ibid., p. 363.

327   *"I am quite willing"*: Ibid., p. 183.

328   *"We don't need your sermons"*: Ibid., p. 367.

328   *"Can't you understand"*: Ibid., p. 365.

329   *When the BBC asked*: Nirmal Kumar Bose, *My Days with Gandhi*, p. 224.

329   *"I've run dry"*: Tendulkar, vol. 8, *Mahatma*, p. 80.

329   *"What if this is just"*: CWMG, vol. 89, p. 55.

330   *"One might almost say"*: Ibid., p. 49.

330   *"All this is due"*: Gopalkrishna Gandhi, *A Frank Friendship*, p. 501.

330   *"In the Punjab"*: Ibid., p. 517.

330   *"What is all this?"*: Narayan Desai, *My Life Is My Message*, vol. 4, *Svarpan*, pp. 422–23.

331   *"The Calcutta bubble"*: CWMG, vol. 89, p. 131.

331   *"fiery weapon"*: Ibid., p. 134.

331   *The day after the attack*: Dalton, *Mahatma Gandhi*, p. 154.

332   *"When the heart is hard"*: Narayan Desai, *My Life Is My Message*, vol. 4, *Svarpan*, p. 434.

332   *His old comrade*: Dalton, *Mahatma Gandhi*, p. 158.

332   *"This sudden upheaval"*: CWMG, vol. 89, p. 49.

333   *wonderfully dry description*: Bourke-White, *Halfway to Freedom*, pp. 81–82.

333   *When he had to leave*: Ibid., p. 90.

334   *But rowdy Hindu hecklers*: CWMG, vol. 89, p. 195.

335   *"Anger is short madness"*: Ibid., p. 167.

336   *"Why do [the authorities] tolerate"*: Ibid., p. 184.

336   *"They are all mine"*: Ibid., p. 480.

337 *"These days, who listens to me?"*: Ibid., p. 237.

337 *"Ever since I came to India"*: Ibid., p. 275. See also p. 524.

337 *"What sin must I"*: Ibid., p. 525.

337 *"On the surface things"*: Ibid., p. 483.

337 *"Misdeeds of the Hindus"*: Ibid., vol. 90, p. 228.

337 No single catastrophe: Some say it was his fifteenth or sixteenth fast. Narayan Desai makes it thirty. Narayan Desai, *My Life Is My Message*, vol. 4, *Svarpan*, pp. 472–73.

338 *Mountbatten, now the governor-general*: Rajmohan Gandhi, *Gandhi*, p. 612; Suhrawardy, *Memoirs*, p. 34; Ziegler, *Mountbatten*, p. 462; CWMG, vol. 96, p. 568.

338 *"For some time my helplessness"*: Manubehn Gandhi, *Last Glimpses of Bapu*, p. 108.

338 *"Gandhiji is not prepared"*: Azad, *India Wins Freedom*, p. 236.

339 *"All his life he had stood"*: M. K. Gandhi, *Delhi Diary*, p. 336.

339 *By his assassin's own testimony*: Malgonkar, *Men Who Killed Gandhi*, p. 344; Tushar A. Gandhi, *"Let's Kill Gandhi!"* p. 58.

339 *Patel's absence from Delhi*: The home minister left Delhi to travel to Gandhi's native Kathiawad region to bring the holdout princely states there into the Indian Union, a mission in which Gandhi had a personal interest. But he was also stung by the decision of the cabinet, under the pressure of Gandhi's fast, to release the reserves he had only just frozen. Before leaving Delhi, he wrote to Gandhi asking that he be allowed to resign. Rajmohan Gandhi, *Patel*, pp. 462–63.

339 *Of the unfreezing of the assets*: Malgonkar, *Men Who Killed Gandhi*, p. 341, reproduction of paragraph 126 of Godse's statement.

340 *A few days earlier*: Pyarelal, *Mahatma Gandhi: Last Phase*, vol. 2, p. 711.

341 *"Listen! Listen!"*: Tendulkar, *Mahatma*, vol. 8, p. 273.

341 *"God will keep me alive"*: Manubehn Gandhi, *Last Glimpses of Bapu*, p. 224.

341 *"The rulers of the country"*: Ibid., p. 225

342 *"If somebody fired"*: Ibid., pp. 222, 228, 234, 298.

342 *"I have seen it"*: Ibid., p. 279.

343 *"Our salvation"*: Ibid., p. 293.

343 *Immediately after that meeting*: Ibid., pp. 293–97.

343 *Later Pyarelal would publish*: Pyarelal, *Mahatma Gandhi: Last Phase*, vol. 2, p. 819.

343 *Never did it make its way*: Narayan Desai, *My Life Is My Message*, vol. 4, *Svarpan*, p. 479.

344 *On the way, walking*: Manubehn Gandhi, *Last Glimpses of Bapu*, p. 308.

344 *"There is no way"*: Tushar A. Gandhi, *"Let's Kill Gandhi!"* p. 780.

344 *"The sound of bullets"*: Manubehn Gandhi, *Last Glimpses of Bapu*, p. 309.

344 *The killer Godse*: Malgonkar, *Men Who Killed Gandhi*, pp. 250–51.

344 *He said the last words*: Pyarelal, *Mahatma Gandhi: Last Phase*, vol. 2, p. 861.

345 *The belief that he fulfilled*: See Nandy, "Final Encounter," pp. 470–93.

345 *"a certain kind of bodily sacrifice"*: Gyanendra Pandey quoted in Hardiman, *Gandhi in His Time and Ours*, pp. 190–91.

346 *"Today we must forget that we are Hindus"*: CWMG, vol. 90, pp. 403–4.

346 *When it comes to the Father of the Nation*: Payne, *Life and Death of Mahatma Gandhi*, pp. 598–99.

347　*"Congress has now to govern"*: Gopalkrishna Gandhi, *Gandhi Is Gone*, p. 61.

347　*"What we need to consider"*: Ibid., p. 60.

348　*"Let no one say"*: Tendulkar, *Mahatma*, vol. 5, p. 245.

348　*"Whenever you are in doubt"*: Pyarelal, *Mahatma Gandhi: Last Phase*, vol. 2, p. 65. The note seems never to have been published in Gandhi's lifetime. It is reproduced in an inset following p. 288 in the final volume of Tendulkar's eight-volume biography, first published in 1954 by the Government of India.

SOURCES

I. GANDHI WRITINGS

Autobiography: The Story of My Experiments with Truth. Translated by Mahadev Desai. New York, 1983.

The Collected Works of Mahatma Gandhi. 97 vols. Ahmedabad, 1958–94.

Delhi Diary: Prayer Speeches from 10-9-47 to 3-1-48. Ahmedabad, 1948.

Gandhi on Nehru. Edited by Anand T. Hingorani. New Delhi, 1993.

Hind Swaraj and Other Writings. Edited by Anthony J. Parel. Cambridge, U.K., 1997.

The Moral and Political Writings of Mahatma Gandhi. Vol. 3. Edited by Raghavan Iyer. Oxford, 1985–87.

The Penguin Gandhi Reader. Edited by Rudrangshu Mukherjee. New Delhi, 1996.

The Removal of Untouchability. Ahmedabad, 1954.

Satyagraha in South Africa. Ahmedabad, 1950.

Selected Political Writings. Edited by Dennis Dalton. Indianapolis, 1996.

The South African Gandhi: Speeches and Writings of M. K. Gandhi, 1893–1914. Edited by Fatima Meer. Durban, 1994.

Village Swaraj. Ahmedabad, 1962.

GANDHI'S NEWSPAPERS

Indian Opinion. Originally published at the Phoenix Settlement in South Africa, reproduced on three CD-ROMs by the National Gandhi Museum, New Delhi.

Harijan (1933–55). Reprinted in 19 volumes with an introduction by Joan Bondurant. New York, 1973.

II. OTHER SOURCES AND STUDIES

Ahir, D. C. *The Legacy of Dr. Ambedkar.* New Delhi, 1990.

Aiyar, P. Subramaniam. *Conflict of Races in South Africa.* Durban, 1946.

———*The Indian Problem in South Africa.* Durban, 1975.

Ambedkar, B. R. *Annihilation of Caste.* Reprint, New Delhi, 2008.

———. *Essential Writings.* Edited by Valerian Rodrigues. New Delhi, 2002.

———. *Letters.* Edited by Surendra Ajnat. Jalandhar, 1993.

———. *What Congress and Gandhi Have Done to the Untouchables.* 2nd ed. Bombay, 1946.

———. *Writings and Speeches.* Edited by Vasant Moon. 17 vols. Nagpur, 1989.

Ambedkar, Mahesh, *Dr. Bhimrao Ambedkar: The Architect of Modern India.* New Delhi, 2005.

Amery, L. S., ed. *The "Times" History of the War in South Africa, 1899–1900.* Vol. 1. London, 1900.

Amin, Shahid. "Gandhi as Mahatma: Gorakhpur District, Eastern U.P., 1921–22." In *Selected Subaltern Studies*, edited by Ranajit Guha and Gayatri Chakravorty Spivak. New York, 1988.

Anand, Y. P. *Mahatma Gandhi and the Railways*. Ahmedabad, 2002.

Andrews, Charles F. *Mahatma Gandhi: His Life and Ideas*. Woodstock, Vt., 2003.

Arnold, David. *Gandhi*. London, 2001.

Ashe, Geoffrey. *Gandhi*. New York, 1968.

Aurobindo, Sri. *India's Rebirth: A Selection from Sri Aurobindo's Writings, Talks, and Speeches*. Mysore, 2000.

Azad, Maulana Abul Kalam. *India Wins Freedom*. Rev. ed. New Delhi, 1988.

Bakshi, S. R. *Gandhi and Hindu-Muslim Unity*. New Delhi, 1987.

Bayly, Susan. *Caste, Society, and Politics in India from the Eighteenth Century to the Modern Age*. Cambridge, U.K., 2001.

Bhana, Surendra. *Gandhi's Legacy: The Natal Indian Congress, 1894–1994*. Pietermaritzburg, 1997.

———. *Indentured Indian Emigrants to Natal, 1860–1902*. New Delhi, 1991.

Bhana, Surendra, and Bridglal Pachai, eds. *A Documentary History of Indian South Africans*. Cape Town, 1984.

Bhana, Surendra, and Goolam Vahed. *The Making of a Political Reformer: Gandhi in South Africa, 1893–1914*. New Delhi, 2005.

Bose, Ajoy. *Behenji: A Political Biography of Mayawati*. New Delhi, 2008.

Bose, Nirmal Kumar. *My Days with Gandhi*. New Delhi, 1974.

———. *Studies in Gandhism*. Calcutta, 1962.

Bourke-White, Margaret. *Halfway to Freedom: A Report on the New India*. New York, 1949.

Britton, Burnett. *Gandhi Arrives in South Africa*. Canton, Maine, 1999.

Brown, Judith M. *Gandhi and Civil Disobedience: The Mahatma in Indian Politics, 1928–1934*. Cambridge, U.K., 1977.

———. *Gandhi: Prisoner of Hope*. New Haven, Conn., 1991.

———. *Gandhi's Rise to Power, 1915–1922*. Cambridge, U.K., 1972.

———. *Nehru: A Political Life*. New Haven, Conn., 2003.

———, ed. *Gandhi and South Africa: Principles and Politics*. Pietermaritzburg, 1996.

Campbell-Johnson, Alan. *Mission with Mountbatten*. New York, 1985.

Carstairs, G. Morris. *The Twice-Born: A Study of a Community of High-Caste Hindus*. Bloomington, Ind., 1967.

Chapman, David L. *Sandow the Magnificent: Eugen Sandow and the Beginnings of Bodybuilding*. Urbana, Ill., 1994.

Chatterjee, Margaret. *Gandhi and His Jewish Friends*. London, 1992.

———. *Gandhi's Religious Thought*. Notre Dame, Ind., 1983.

Chatterjee, Partha. "Nationalist Thought and the Colonial World." In *The Partha Chatterjee Omnibus*. New Delhi, 2005.

Chatterji, Joya. *Bengal Divided: Hindu Communalism and Partition, 1932–1947*. Cambridge, U.K., 1994.

———. *The Spoils of Partition: Bengal and India*. Cambridge, U.K., 2007.

Collins, Larry, and Dominique Lapierre. *Mountbatten and the Partition of India*. New Delhi, 1982.

Couper, Scott. *Albert Luthuli: Bound by Faith*. Pietermaritzburg, 2010.

Coward, Harold, ed. *Indian Critiques of Gandhi*. Albany, N.Y., 2003.

Dalal, Chandulal Bhagubhai. *Harilal Gandhi: A Life.* Translated by Tridip Suhrud. New Delhi, 2007.

Dalton, Dennis. *Mahatma Gandhi: Nonviolent Power in Action.* New York, 2000.

Das, Suranjan. *Communal Riots in Bengal, 1905–1947.* Delhi, 1991.

Dasgupta, Ajit K. *Gandhi's Economic Thought.* London, 1996.

Desai, Ashwin, and Goolam Vahed. *Inside Indenture: A South African Story, 1860–1914.* Durban, 2007.

Desai, Mahadev. *Day-to-Day with Gandhi, Diaries, 1917–1927.* 9 vols. Varanasi, 1968–74.

———. *The Diary of Mahadev Desai: Yeravda-Pact Eve, 1932.* Ahmedabad, 1953.

———. *The Epic of Travancore.* Ahmedabad, 1937.

Desai, Narayan. *The Fire and the Rose: A Biography of Mahadevbhai.* Ahmedabad, 1995.

———. *My Gandhi.* Ahmedabad, 1999.

———. *My Life Is My Message.* 4 vols. Translated by Tridip Suhrud. New Delhi, 2009.

Devanesen, Chandran D. S. *The Making of the Mahatma.* New Delhi, 1969.

Devji, Faisal, *The Terrorist in Search of Humanity: Militant Islam and Global Politics.* New York, 2008.

Dhupelia-Mesthrie, Uma. *Gandhi's Prisoner? The Life of Gandhi's Son Manilal.* Cape Town, 2004.

Dirks, Nicholas B. *Castes of Mind: Colonialism and the Making of Modern India.* Princeton, N.J., 2001.

Doke, Joseph J. *M. K. Gandhi: An Indian Patriot in South Africa.* Wardha, 1956.

Ebr-Vally, Rehana. *Kala Pani: Caste and Colour in South Africa.* Cape Town, 2001.

Erikson, Erik H. *Gandhi's Truth: On the Origins of Militant Nonviolence.* New York, 1970.

Fischer, Louis. *The Life of Mahatma Gandhi.* New York, 1962.

———, ed. *The Essential Gandhi: His Life, Work, and Ideas: An Anthology.* New York, 1963.

Fredrickson, George M. *Black Liberation: A Comparative History of Black Ideologies in the United States and South Africa.* New York, 1996.

Gandhi, Gopalkrishna. *A Frank Friendship: Gandhi and Bengal: A Descriptive Chronology.* Calcutta, 2007.

———, ed. *Gandhi Is Gone: Who Will Guide Us Now?* Ranikhet, 2009.

Gandhi, Manubehn. *Bapu—My Mother.* Ahmedabad, 1949.

———. *The End of an Epoch.* Ahmedabad, 1962.

———. *Last Glimpses of Bapu.* Agra, 1962.

———. *The Lonely Pilgrim: Gandhi's Noakhali Pilgrimage.* Ahmedabad, 1964.

———. *The Miracle of Calcutta.* Ahmedabad, 1959.

Gandhi, Prabhudas. *My Childhood with Gandhiji.* Ahmedabad, 1957.

Gandhi, Rajmohan. *Eight Lives: A Study of the Hindu-Muslim Encounter.* Albany, N.Y., 1986.

———. *Gandhi: The Man, His People, and the Empire.* London, 2007.

———. *Patel: A Life.* Ahmedabad, 1991.

Gandhi, Tushar A. *"Let's Kill Gandhi!" A Chronicle of His Last Days, the Conspiracy, Murder, Investigation, and Trial.* New Delhi, 2007.

Geertz, Clifford. "Gandhi: Non-violence as Therapy." *New York Review of Books,* Nov. 20, 1962.

Gordon, Leonard A. *Bengal: The Nationalist Movement, 1876–1940.* New York, 1974.
———. *Brothers Against the Raj: Sarat and Subhas Chandra Bose.* New Delhi, 2000.
Goswami, K. P. *Mahatma Gandhi: A Chronology.* New Delhi, 1994.
Green, Martin. *Gandhi: Voice of a New Age Revolution.* New York, 1993.
Grenier, Richard. "The Gandhi Nobody Knows." *Commentary,* March 1983.
Guha, Ramachandra. *India After Gandhi.* New York, 2007.
Guy, Jeff. *The Maphumulo Uprising: War, Law, and Ritual in the Zulu Rebellion.* Scottsville, South Africa, 2005.
———. *Remembering the Rebellion: The Zulu Uprising of 1906.* Scottsville, South Africa, 2005.
Hancock, W. K., *Smuts: The Sanguine Years, 1870–1919.* Cambridge, U.K., 1962.
Hardiman, David. *Gandhi in His Time and Ours: The Global Legacy of His Ideas.* New York, 2003.
Heimsath, Charles H. *Indian Nationalism and Hindu Social Reform.* Princeton, N.J., 1964.
Herman, Arthur. *Gandhi and Churchill: The Epic Rivalry That Destroyed an Empire and Forged Our Age.* New York, 2008.
Hughes, Heather. "Doubly Elite: Exploring the Life of John Langalibalele Dube." *Journal of Southern Africa Studies* 27, no. 3 (Sept. 2001).
Hunt, James D. *An American Looks at Gandhi.* New Delhi, 2005.
———. *Gandhi and the Nonconformists: Encounters in South Africa.* New Delhi, 1986.
———. *Gandhi in London.* New Delhi, 1978.
Hunt, James D. and Surendra Bhana. "Spiritual Rope-Walkers: Gandhi, Kallenbach, and the Tolstoy Farm, 1910–13." *South African Historical Journal* 58, no. 1 (2007), pp. 174–202.
Huttenback, Robert A. *Gandhi in South Africa: British Imperialism and the Indian Question, 1860–1914.* Ithaca, N.Y., 1971.
Hyslop, Jonathan. *Gandhi, Mandela, and the African Problem* (in draft).
Imhasly, Bernard. *Goodbye to Gandhi? Travels in the New India.* New Delhi, 2007.
Itzkin, Eric. *Gandhi's Johannesburg: Birthplace of Satyagraha.* Johannesburg, 2000.
Iyer, Raghavan. *The Moral and Political Thought of Mahatma Gandhi.* New Delhi, 2000.
———. *The Moral and Political Writings of Mahatma Gandhi.* Vol. 3. Oxford, 1987.
Jaffrelot, Cristophe. *Dr. Ambedkar and Untouchability.* New York, 2005.
Jalal, Ayesha, *The Sole Spokesman: Jinnah, the Muslim League, and the Demand for Pakistan.* Lahore, 1999.
Jones, Kenneth W. *Socio-Religious Reform Movements in British India.* Cambridge, U.K., 1989.
Jordens, J. T. F. *Gandhi's Religion: A Homespun Shawl.* London, 1998.
———. *Swami Shraddhananda: His Life and Causes.* Oxford, 1981.
Joseph, George Gheverghese. *George Joseph: The Life and Times of a Kerala Christian Nationalist.* New Delhi, 2003.
Juergensmeyer, Mark. *Religion as Social Vision: The Movement Against Untouchability in 20th-Century Punjab.* Berkeley, Calif., 1982.
———. "Saint Gandhi." In *Saints and Virtues,* edited by John Stratton Hawley. Berkeley, Calif., 1987.
Kasturi, Bhashyam, *Walking Alone: Gandhi and India's Partition.* New Delhi, 1999.
Keer, Dhananjay. *Dr. Ambedkar: Life and Mission.* Mumbai, 1990.
Kepel, Gilles. *Jihad: The Trail of Political Islam.* London, 2003.

Kochu, K. K. "Vaikom Satyagraha: Lessons of a Re-reading." *Madhyamam*, April 2, 1999.

Kuber, W. N. *Ambedkar: A Critical Study*. New Delhi, 2001.

Limaye, Madhu. *Manu, Gandhi, and Ambedkar*. New Delhi, 1995.

Lohia, Rammanohar. *Guilty Men of India's Partition*. New Delhi, 1960.

Mahadevan, T. K., *Gandhi, My Refrain: Controversial Essays*. Bombay, 1973.

———. *The Year of the Phoenix: Gandhi's Pivotal Year, 1893–94*. Chicago, 1982.

Mahadevan, T. K. and G. Ramachandran, eds. *Quest for Gandhi*. New Delhi, 1970.

Maksud, Syed Abul. *Gandhi, Nehru, and Noakhali*. Dhaka, 2008.

———. *Pyarelal's Unpublished Correspondence: The Noakhali Peace Mission*. Dhaka, 2006.

Malgonkar, Manohar. *The Men Who Killed Gandhi*. New Delhi, 2008.

Mandela, Nelson. *Long Walk to Freedom: The Autobiography of Nelson Mandela*. Boston, 1994.

Mankar, Vijay. *Denunciation of Poona Pact: 75 Years of Political Stooging and Religious Slavery*. Nagpur, 2007.

Mansergh, Nicholas, and E. W. R. Lumby, eds. *The Transfer of Power, 1942–47*. 12 vols. London, 1970–83.

Markovits, Claude. *The Un-Gandhian Gandhi: The Life and Afterlife of the Mahatma*. London, 2004.

Marks, Shula. *Reluctant Rebellion: The 1906–8 Disturbances in Natal*. Oxford, 1970.

Meer, Fatima. *Apprenticeship of a Mahatma: A Biography of M. K. Gandhi, 1869–1914*. Moka, Mauritius, 1994.

Mehta, Ved. *Mahatma Gandhi and His Apostles*. New Haven, Conn., 1976.

Mende, Tibor. *Conversations with Mr. Nehru*. London, 1956.

Mendelsohn, Oliver, and Marika Vicziany. *The Untouchables: Subordination, Poverty, and the State in Modern India*. Cambridge, U.K., 1998.

Millin, Sarah Gertrude. *General Smuts*. Boston, 1936.

Minault, Gail. *The Khilafat Movement: Religious Symbolism and Political Mobilization in India*. New York, 1982.

Muggeridge, Malcolm. *Chronicles of Wasted Time*. Vol. 1. New York, 1973.

Nagaraj, D. R. *The Flaming Feet: A Study of the Dalit Movement in India*. Bangalore, 1993.

Naidoo, Jay. "Was Gandhi's South African Struggle Inspired by Race, Class, or Nation?" In *Tracking Down Historical Myths*. Johannesburg, 1989.

Naipaul, V. S. *An Area of Darkness*. London, 1964.

———. *The Overcrowded Barracoon*. London, 1972.

———. *A Writer's People*. London, 2007.

Nanda, B. R. *Gandhi and His Critics*. New Delhi, 1993.

———. *Gandhi: Pan-Islamism, Imperialism, and Nationalism in India*. New Delhi, 2002.

———. *Mahatma Gandhi: A Biography*. Delhi, 1996.

———. *Three Statesmen: Gokhale, Gandhi, and Nehru*. New Delhi, 1995.

Nandy, Ashis. "Final Encounter: The Politics of the Assassination of Gandhi." In *Exiled at Home*. New Delhi, 2005.

Nauriya, Anil. *The African Element in Gandhi*. New Delhi, 2006.

Nayar, Sushila. *Mahatma Gandhi's Last Imprisonment: The Inside Story*. New Delhi, 1996.

———. *Preparing for Swaraj*. Vol. 7 of *Mahatma Gandhi*. Ahmedabad, 1996.

———. *Salt Satyagraha: The Watershed*. Vol. 6 of *Mahatma Gandhi*. Ahmedabad, 1995.

Nehru, Jawaharlal. *A Bunch of Old Letters*. New Delhi, 2005.

———. *Mahatma Gandhi*. New Delhi, 1977.

———. *Toward Freedom*. Boston, 1958.

Nussbaum, Martha C. *The Clash Within: Democracy, Religious Violence, and India's Future*. Cambridge, Mass., 2007.

O'Hanlon, Rosalind. *Caste, Conflict, and Ideology: Mahatma Jotirao Phule and Low Caste Protest in Nineteenth-Century Western India*. Cambridge, U.K., 1985.

Omvedt, Gail. *Ambedkar: Towards an Enlightened India*. New Delhi, 2004.

Pakenham, Thomas. *The Boer War*. New York, 1979.

Parekh, Bhikhu. *Colonialism, Tradition, and Reform: An Analysis of Gandhi's Political Discourse*. Rev. ed. New Delhi, 1999.

———. *Gandhi: A Very Short Introduction*. Oxford, 1997.

———. *Gandhi's Political Philosophy: A Critical Examination*. Notre Dame, Ind., 1989.

Parikh, Nilam. *Gandhiji's Lost Jewel: Harilal Gandhi*. New Delhi, 2001.

Paxton, George. *Sonja Schlesin: Gandhi's South African Secretary*. Glasgow, 2006.

Payne, Robert. *The Life and Death of Mahatma Gandhi*. New York, 1969.

Pennington, Brian K. *Was Hinduism Invented? Britons, Indians, and the Colonial Construction of Religion*. New York, 2005.

Philips, C. H., and Mary Wainwright, eds. *The Partition of India: Policies and Perspectives, 1935–1947*. Cambridge, Mass., 1970.

Pouchepadass, Jacques. *Champaran and Gandhi: Planters, Peasants, and Gandhian Politics*. New Delhi, 1999.

Prasad, Rajendra. *At the Feet of Mahatma Gandhi*. Bombay, 1961.

Pyarelal. *The Discovery of Satyagraha—on the Threshold*. Vol. 2 of *Mahatma Gandhi*. Ahmedabad, 1980.

———. *The Early Phase*. Vol. 1 of *Mahatma Gandhi*. Ahmedabad, 1965.

———. *The Epic Fast*. Ahmedabad, 1932.

———. *Mahatma Gandhi: The Last Phase*. 2 vols. Ahmedabad, 1956, 1958.

Pyarelal, and Sushila Nayar. *In Gandhiji's Mirror*. New Delhi, 2004.

Raimon, S. ed. *Selected Documents on the Vaikom Satyagraha*. Thiruvananthapuram, 2006.

Rajaram, N. S. *Gandhi, Khilafat, and the National Movement*. Bangalore, 1999.

Ramamurthy, V. *From the Pages of "The Hindu": Mahatma Gandhi: The Last 200 Days*. Chennai, 2005.

Rattu, Nanak Chand. *Last Few Years of Dr. Ambedkar*. New Delhi, 1997.

Ravindran, T. K. *Eight Furlongs of Freedom*. New Delhi, 1980.

Ray, Baren, ed. *Gandhi's Campaign Against Untouchability, 1933–34: An Account from the Raj's Secret Official Reports*. New Delhi, 1996.

Rolland, Romain. *The Life of Vivekananda and the Universal Gospel*. Reprint, Kolkata, 2003.

———. *Mahatma Gandhi: The Man Who Became One with the Universal Being*. New York, 1924.

Roux, Edward. *Time Longer Than Rope: The Black Man's Struggle for Freedom in South Africa*. 2nd ed. Madison, Wis., 1964.

Ruskin, John. *Unto This Last and Other Writings*. Edited by Clive Wilmer. London, 1997.

Sanghavi, Nagindas. *The Agony of Arrival: Gandhi, the South Africa Years.* New Delhi, 2006.

Sarid, Isa, and Christian Bartolf. *Hermann Kallenbach: Mahatma Gandhi's Friend in South Africa.* Berlin, 1997.

Sen, Amartya. *The Argumentative Indian: Writings on Indian History, Culture, and Identity.* New York, 2005.

Shimoni, Gideon. *Gandhi, Satyagraha, and the Jews: A Formative Factor in India's Policy Towards Israel.* Jerusalem, 1977.

Shirer, William L. *Gandhi: A Memoir.* New York, 1982.

———. *Twentieth Century Journey: The Start, 1904–1930.* New York, 1976.

Shourie, Arun. *Worshipping False Gods: Ambedkar and the Facts Which Have Been Erased.* New Delhi, 1997.

Shukla, Chandrashanker. *Conversations of Gandhiji.* Bombay, 1949.

Singh, Jaswant. *Jinnah: India, Partition, Independence.* New Delhi, 2009.

Singh, Shankar Dayal. *Gandhi's First Step: Champaran Movement.* New Delhi, 1994.

Slade, Madeleine. *The Spirit's Pilgrimage.* New York, 1960.

Sontakke, Y. D., ed. *Thoughts of Dr. Babasaheb Ambedkar.* New Delhi, 2004.

Soske, Jon. "'Wash Me Black Again': African Nationalism, the Indian Diaspora, and KwaZulu-Natal, 1944–60." Ph.D. diss., University of Toronto, 2009.

Suhrawardy, Huseyn Shaheed. *Memoirs.* Edited by Mohammad H. R. Talukdar. Dhaka, 1987.

Swan, Maureen. *Gandhi: The South African Experience.* Johannesburg, 1985.

———. "The 1913 Natal Indian Strike." *Journal of Southern African Studies* 10, no. 2 (April 1984).

Tagore, Rabindranath, *Mahatmaji and the Depressed Humanity.* New Delhi, 2002.

Talbot, Phillips. *An American Witness to India's Partition.* New Delhi, 2007.

Tendulkar, D. G. *Mahatma: Life of Mohandas Karamchand Gandhi.* 8 vols. New Delhi, 1960–63.

Thomson, Mark, *Gandhi and His Ashramas.* Bombay, 1993

Tidrick, Kathryn. *Gandhi: A Political and Spiritual Life.* New York, 2006.

Tinker, Hugh. *A New System of Slavery: The Export of Indian Labour Overseas, 1830–1920.* London, 1974.

———. *The Ordeal of Love: C. F. Andrews and India.* Delhi, 1998.

Tolstoy, Leo. *The Kingdom of God Is Within You.* New York, 2005.

———. *What Is to Be Done?* Reprint of 1899 ed., n.d.

Tuker, Francis. *While Memory Serves.* London, 1950.

Tunzelmann, Alex von. *Indian Summer: The Secret History of the End of an Empire.* New York, 2007.

Verma, Mukut Behari, ed. *Crusade Against Untouchability: History of the Harijan Sevak Sangh.* Delhi, 1971.

Virasai, Banphot. "The Emergence and Making of a Mass Movement Leader: Portrait of Mahatma Gandhi in South Africa, 1893–1914." Ph.D. diss., University of California, Berkeley, 1968.

Wavell, Archibald Percival. *The Viceroy's Journal.* Edited by Penderel Moon. London, 1973.

Weber, Thomas. *Gandhi as Disciple and Mentor.* New Delhi, 2007.

———. *Gandhi, Gandhism, and the Gandhians.* New Delhi, 2006.

Wells, Ian Bryant. *Ambassador of Hindu-Muslim Unity: Jinnah's Early Politics.* New Delhi, 2006.

Wolpert, Stanley. *Gandhi's Passion: The Life and Legacy of Mahatma Gandhi.* New York, 2001.

Zelliot, Eleanor. *From Untouchable to Dalit: Essays on the Ambedkar Movement.* 3rd ed. New Delhi, 2001.

Ziegler, Philip. *Mountbatten: A Biography.* New York, 1985.

ACKNOWLEDGMENTS

As part of my attempt to find a fresh way of looking at the ever-evolving Gandhi who traveled home to India after two decades in South Africa, I found it necessary to visit most of the places that were important in his long life, from his birthplace in Porbandar to the site of his assassination in a New Delhi garden. In all, I logged three trips to India and two to South Africa in three years. Even now I find it hard to offer a simple explanation of what these journeys were about. It's true they gave me a chance to delve into archives in Durban, Pretoria, Ahmedabad, Kolkata, and New Delhi—London too—but that was never their primary purpose. I could go through the motions of scholarship, sometimes experience the excitement of a small discovery, but I'm not a scholar. There was also the chance to chat with old men and women who had come into contact with the Mahatma as children or, more often, with descendants of Gandhi and people who mattered in his life. Such conversations were more in my line as a reporter, but, given the passage of generations, they could seldom be more than suggestive. Still, the reporter in me felt a compulsion to journey to places to which Gandhi had trekked, from Volksrust on the border of what was once the Transvaal to Noakhali district in what became Bangladesh, in order to view his past as it was refracted through our present. I felt I needed to set foot in such places if I was to come to any real understanding of the flow of his life, the contours of his struggle.

Whatever I was seeking, these excursions spun off an added dividend. They brought me into contact, however fleeting, with an international community of scholars on four continents who have pondered Gandhi's life, times, and contradictions, the influences he imbibed and the values he embraced, more deeply and systematically than I ever could. The exchange of information and insight in these encounters was mostly one way, especially at the outset. Essentially, these were tutorials in which one meeting and reference, personal or scholarly, or both, led to another. It should be obvious that none of my tutors bear any responsibility for my readings of basic Gandhi texts or the direction my inquiry took. What they provided were useful insights, references, and cautions.

As he traveled from place to place, the tutee piled up debts that now need to be declared.

The Gandhi descendants I met, three grandchildren and two great-grandchildren, have been active keepers of his legacy. These were the biographer Rajmohan Gandhi; his brother Gopalkrishna Gandhi who, among his other posts as a civil servant, became India's first ambassador to post-apartheid South Africa; their South African cousin Ela Gandhi of Durban, a member of the first democratically chosen South African parliament; and her nieces, Kirti Menon of Johannesburg and the scholar Uma Dhupelia-Mesthrie of Cape Town, each of whom dealt patiently with my queries. Others in South Africa who offered guidance or constructively challenged my thinking included Keith Breckenridge and Isabel Hofmeyr, who participated in a seminar at Witwatersrand University that gently critiqued my chapter on Gandhi's sparse relations with Africans. I received invaluable assistance from Mwele Cele of the Killie Campbell Africana Library in Durban, who scanned the pages of the Zulu-language newspaper *Ilanga lase Natal* for mentions of Gandhi and also introduced me to the Reverend Scott Couper, an American missionary-scholar who was my guide to Inanda, where he lives. Jeff Guy and Goolam Vahed of the University of KwaZulu-Natal put me in touch with references I'd never have found on my own. At the start of my plunge into the literature on Indian indentured labor in South Africa, Surendra Bhana of the University of Kansas, a pioneering researcher on that subject, was generous with scholarly citations and guidance. The writers Aziz Hassim and Ronnie Govender had stimulating thoughts on the popular memory of Gandhi as it has been handed down over the generations of South African Indians. Eric Itzkin spent an afternoon showing me Johannesburg's Gandhi sites. Firoz Cachalia and Jonathan Hyslop each had thought deeply about Gandhi's place in the South Africa of his times and its history as it has since been told. Heather Hughes, author of a forthcoming biography of John Dube, proved a generous and spirited interlocutor on e-mail. Professor Donald Fanger of Harvard kindly checked the translations of a couple of Tolstoy passages against the original Russian.

Before the first of my excursions to India, I had dinner in Westminster at the House of Lords with Bhikhu Parekh, one of its members and an eminent interpreter of Gandhi's thought. In Gujarat, I had the privilege of meeting Narayan Desai, son of Gandhi's longtime secretary and diarist, and Tridip Suhrud, a Gandhi scholar and translator of Narayan Desai's four-volume biography of the Mahatma; also, Achyut Yagnik, a political scientist, and Sudarshan Iyenger, vice chancellor of the Gujarat Vidyapith, a university founded by the Mahatma with the aim of training generations of committed field-workers in his methods and values. I gained valuable suggestions and impressions from contemporary social activists in Gujarat, notably Mirai Chatterjee of the Self Employed Women's Association (known as SEWA) and Martin Macwan, a Dalit organizer and educator, founder of the Dalit Shakti Kendra (or Dalit Empowerment Center). In Nagpur, I met Pradip Algrave, an Ambedkar scholar; Shreenivas Khadewale, a Gandhian economist; and Jogendra Kawade, leader of an Ambedkerite political faction. In New Delhi, I was helped by Varsha Das of the National Gandhi Museum and Uttam Sinha, its librarian, who made available a translation of portions of Mahadev Desai's Gujarati-language diary that have yet to be published in English.

My trip through Kerala was facilitated at every turn by the boundless generosity of my friends Mammen and Prema Matthew. The Matthew family's newspaper, *Malayala Manorama*, served as my magic carpet, meeting all my transportation, scheduling, and research needs, to the point of presenting me with a custom-bound volume of all the paper's coverage of Gandhi's four tours through the old kingdoms of Travancore and Cochin, later merged into the modern state, all skillfully translated into English for my sake. *Malayala Manorama*—in the person of one its editors, A. V. Harisankar, who became my traveling companion and friend—also arranged meetings for me with Kerala writers and scholars including N. K. Joshi, a popular historian and crusader for Dalit rights; P. J. Cherian of the Kerala Council for Historical Research; Rajan Gurukkal, vice chancellor of Mahatma Gandhi University at Kottayam; M. K. Sanu, a biographer of Narayan Guru; T. K. Ravindran, author of a history of the Vaikom satyagraha; and the Dalit intellectual K. K. Kochu.

Two distinguished Bengali thinkers, Amartya Sen of Harvard and Cambridge universities, and Partha Chatterjee, of Columbia and the Center for Studies in Social Sciences in Kolkata, graciously endured my recitation of plans for a visit to the two fragments of what was once a united Bengal, then made useful suggestions. In Dhaka, the Bangladeshi capital, I encountered a range of strong viewpoints from scholars and public intellectuals including Debapriya Bhattacharya, Badruddin Umar, Syed Abul Maksud, A. K. Roy, Imtiaz Ahmed, Anisuzzaman (a professor emeritus at the University of Dhaka who uses only one name), and Sharirar Kabir. I also had an opportunity to talk about Gandhi with

Fazle Hasan Abed, founder and chairman of BRAC, a welfare organization that evolved into a huge bank, becoming a reliable source of credit for the rural craftsmen the Mahatma struggled to uplift. Raha Naba Kumar, director of the Gandhi Ashram Trust in the village of Joyag, was my host and guide during a visit to Noakhali district. Among those I met in Kolkata were Rudrangshu Mukherjee, Ranabir Samaddar, the historian Amalendu De and economist Amlan Datta; Pushpakanjan Chatterjee, a centenarian Gandhi follower; and Supriya Munshi, longtime director of the Gandhi Memorial Museum at Barrackpore. I'm especially grateful to resourceful journalistic colleagues who smoothed the way for me in these places: Chandra Sekhar Bhattacharjee in Kolkata, Julfikar Ali Manik in Dhaka, and Pradip Kumar Maitra in Nagpur. And while I'm rolling the credits, I should mention the bed, board, and warm friendship provided by old pals—Bim Bissell in Delhi, Lily and David Goldblatt in Joburg, and Lindy and Francis Wilson in Cape Town.

The tutor on whom I leaned most shamelessly was David Lelyveld, a scholar in Indian Muslim history who never once accused me of trespassing on his turf. That could be because long exposure to Indian cultural values has left him with undue regard for the status of elder brother, but I don't really think so. Nor, at this late stage, can it be explained by the fact that I got there first (given that my affair with India, intermittent though it has been, started a couple of years before his own). The only explanation is the obvious one: that my brother truly is a generous person. I hope he won't be embarrassed by this effort and thank him with a full heart for his painstaking reading of my manuscript, on account of which there are certainly fewer errors and examples of weak reasoning in this book than otherwise would have been the case. The same can be said for the thoughtful backstopping I received from two other readers: E. S. Reddy, a retired United Nations official living in New York who has devoted years to assembling—and sharing—an archive of Gandhi materials, with particular attention to the South Africa period; and Jon Soske, a young Oklahoman I first met in Toronto whose doctoral dissertation takes a searching look at relations between Indians and Zulus in Natal in the last century.

I was helped to the finish line by Catherine Talese, who gathered nearly all the photographs that appear in these pages and efficiently secured the rights for me to use them. Hassim Seedat of Durban allowed me to browse in his extensive library and copy a rare photo of Gandhi in 1913 on which he claims copyright. Archie Tse, a colleague from *The New York Times*, provided the maps. Jai Anand Kasturi and Lee Hadbavny, graduate students in South Asian studies at Columbia University, labored long hours to assemble my endnotes and check sources. Steven Rattazzi answered technology alarms, ensuring that my pages remained backed up in spite of my innate obliviousness. Andrew Wylie and Scott Moyers of the Wylie Agency provided unwavering support from the moment I first proposed to tackle this exhaustively written about but seemingly inexhaustible figure. One reads a lot about the state of book publishing these days, but this experience has left me with a starry-eyed feeling that it could never have been better. Sonny Mehta was persuaded that I might have something original to say, and Jon Segal, my editor, gave me every opportunity to say it, letting me know when I was straining his attention by repeating myself or digressing from a digression. It has been particularly satisfying to be reunited with Jon, who (if he'll allow the word) midwifed my book on apartheid a quarter of a century ago. I'm glad too that Peter Andersen oversaw the book's design.

Finally, a word about Janny Scott, who happened into my life at its darkest hour. If it hadn't been for her, I might never have summoned the concentration or energy to pursue this project. Which is the least I can say about what she means to me.

INDEX

Page numbers in *italics* refer to illustrations.

A NOTE ABOUT THE AUTHOR

Joseph Lelyveld's interest in Gandhi dates back to tours in India and South Africa as a foreign correspondent for *The New York Times*, where he worked for nearly four decades, ending up as executive editor from 1994 to 2001. His book on apartheid, *Move Your Shadow: South Africa, Black and White*, won the Pulitzer Prize for General Nonfiction. He is also the author of *Omaha Blues: A Memory Loop*. He lives in New York.

A NOTE ON THE TYPE

This book was set in Janson, a typeface long thought to have been made by the Dutchman Anton Janson, who was a practicing typefounder in Leipzig during the years 1668–1687. However, it has been conclusively demonstrated that these types are actually the work on Nicholas Kis (1650–1702), a Hungarian, who most probably learned his trade from the master Dutch typefounder Dirk Voskens.

Composed by North Market Street Graphics,
Lancaster, Pennsylvania
Printed and bound by Berryville Graphics,
Berryville, Virginia
Maps by Archie Tse
Designed by Peter A. Andersen